PELICAN BOOKS

KING: A Critical Biography

David L. Lewis was born in Arkansas and spent
part of his boyhood in Georgia, attending
Booker T. Washington High School, where
Martin Luther King, Jr., was once a pupil. He
was graduated from Fisk University in 1956,
and went on to Columbia and the London School
of Economics for advanced degrees in history,
receiving his Ph.D. in 1962. Married and the
father of a son, he is now Associate Professor
of History at Morgan State College.

Lewis began King's biography as an exercise in
contemporary history, but it became "a passion
for comprehension of the true significance of
Martin Luther King and through him something
of the nitty-gritty reality of blackness—
collective and personal—in America."

KING

A Critical Biography

DAVID L. LEWIS

PENGUIN BOOKS INC
BALTIMORE, MARYLAND

Penguin Books Inc
7110 Ambassador Road
Baltimore, Maryland 21207

First published by Praeger Publishers, Inc. 1970 by
arrangement with Penguin Books Inc
Published in Pelican Books 1971

ISBN 0 14 021307 4

Printed in the United States of America

Acknowledgments: All the photographs are used by
arrangement with Wide World Photos, Inc.
"If You Miss Me at the Back of the Bus"—
words by Carver Neblett, music traditional.
© Copyright 1963 by Sanga Music, Inc.
All rights reserved. Used by permission.

Contents

Preface		ix
1	Doctor, Lawyer—Preacher?	3
2	The Philosopher King	27
3	Stride Toward Freedom	46
4	Satyagraha, Home-grown	85
5	Skirmishing in Atlanta	112
6	Albany, Georgia—Nonviolence in Black and White	140
7	Birmingham—Nonviolence in Black, Violence in White	171
8	The Strength of a Dream	210
9	Crisis and Compromise—The Walk to Selma Bridge	264
10	The Fire Next Time	297
11	The Pied Piper of Hamlin Avenue—Chicago and Mississippi	313
12	Killers of the Dream	354
Epilogue: Free at Last		390
Notes		399
Selected Bibliography		417
Index		439

A section of photographs follows page 148

Preface

IN THE THIRD CHAPTER of this book, I describe the visit of
Martin Luther King, Jr., to Fisk University in February, 1956.
Until I began the research for his biography, I had forgotten
that I had been one of the students who had listened to him
then in the quiet and comfortable International Student
Center. In 1961, I came home, briefly, to Atlanta, Georgia,
from England, where I was a graduate student. While I was
in Atlanta, Attorney Donald Hollowell, who was representing
Martin King in the infamous De Kalb County case, invited
me to accompany him, his client, Coretta King, and the Reverend Mr. King, Sr., on a drive to Judge Oscar Mitchell's court
for a final judgment. I was then twenty-four, slightly arrogant,
pre-emptively talkative, and eager to return to London to
finish the remaining chapters of my doctoral dissertation.
Until I began writing this biography, I had forgotten this
incident. Then I recalled the drive, the conversation, and
something of the personalities of the people in the car. It had
seemed to me at the time that the three Kings, although indi-
vidually quite different, shared the characteristics of being
neither socially smooth nor intellectually impressive. The
third and last time I met Martin King, sometime in 1962, he
and his father were present at a politically significant social
gathering in the home of a prominent black Atlanta family.
The senior King shook hands with me and pleasantly surprised me by his knowledge of my career since the time I had
left Atlanta. I soon forgot this encounter also, because I went
literally from this conversation to Army basic training at Fort
Jackson, South Carolina.

Martin King won a victory in Birmingham, Alabama, revealed his dream from the steps of the Lincoln Memorial, and

visited Oslo and Stockholm to receive the Nobel Peace Prize, while I was an enlisted man on duty in Germany and, later, a member of the faculty of the University of Ghana. Like any American black indignant about the denial of his basic rights, I was stirred by these events. I had never been stirred by the personality or nonviolent doctrine of Martin King, however. He remained for me essentially a Baptist preacher whose extraordinary rhetorical abilities were not quite matched by practical intelligence and political radicalism. If I had generally avoided acceptance of my parents' prejudices, their deep antipathy to the ideas of Booker T. Washington had, nonetheless, become part of my intellectual and emotional baggage. Martin King was a humble man who called on his people to suffer terrible indignities in order to redeem their oppressors. Booker Washington had praised the use of the toothbrush as the symbol of black self-improvement; I believed that the self-effacement of nonviolent passive resistance was an equally silly and demeaning prescription for black progress. The great reservoir of religious fervor housed by the black church, from which Martin King drew his main strength, was for me a retrograde force, a brake on the dignity and political intelligence of the race.

The day Martin King was assassinated, I had reached a decision that I had never imagined would be mine to make. I had been asked to consider writing this biography just two weeks earlier. As I was drafting the letter of acceptance to the publisher, the news of the Lorraine Motel tragedy was announced. Suddenly, what had begun as primarily a fascination with an exercise in professional craft—a competent work unrelated to my own specialty—became a passion for comprehension of the true significance of Martin King and, through him, something of the nitty-gritty reality of blackness, collective and personal, in America. In my months of traveling, researching, and writing, I tried to reconstruct the civil rights movement and the spiritual odyssey of Martin King, from its beginnings on Atlanta's Auburn Avenue to the finish on the balcony of the Memphis motel. When I wrote the last page of the book, it was April 4, 1969, the first anniversary of his death, and I cannot now say that I have not been stirred by the man and his philosophy. I think I understand why, on three occasions, my reactions to Martin King were unenthusiastic and why those reactions were self-indicting and much too harsh but not entirely wrong.

I know, better than most of its readers will, the extent to which this biography fails. I have tried to be thorough and objective but also empathetic, without once bothering, however, to consider the racial or ideological advantages or disadvantages of the facts or thoughts that this work contains. There are people, black and white, who will argue that objectivity is a pose, a defense, that some middle-class blacks just naturally strike up. For them, this book's only value will be like that of an enemy's captured munitions depot. Such people were the first to attack Martin King for his objectivity, and that is pretty good company for one of his biographers. Criticisms of a nonpartisan nature are a much more serious matter. There will be a fair number of these, I suspect. It is a comfort to me, if not an adequate defense against them, that my convictions about the serious limitations of instant history have not dissipated with the writing of this biography.

The number of people who could be compromised by an expression of appreciation for making this book possible would run on for pages. Most of them will probably be relieved to be thanked in person or by letter. There are, nevertheless, several whose encouragement, criticism, and hours of research or proofreading must not remain anonymous. There is Wendell Holbrook, my research assistant, who had no idea that he was going to work so hard; I had none that he was going to work so superlatively well. There is Howard Silverman, who taught the bulk of one of my courses. Then there are Henry S. Robinson, Annette Pinckney, Tiff Carroll, and Gail Tucker, who suffered a bit with prose and spelling; Andrew Keller, who was an invaluable source for the oral tradition of Morehouse College; Stephen Banker, who passed on a number of useful tips from his nest in the National Press Building; Caroline "Dash" Davis, whose good parties and good liquor cabinet suffered, I fear, some abuse at my hands during the last few months of writing; Julian Bond, Chevene King, and Professor Benjamin Quarles, who read portions of the manuscript and warned me away from many of my worst mistakes; and Preston King and William Weatherby, who conspired to have me write this book. An expression of appreciation is owed, as well, to Dr. Howard Gottlieb, director of the Martin Luther King, Jr., Collection at Boston University. Finally, I must thank the Faculty Research Committee of Morgan State College for a generous stipend to help defray my expenses. Of course, they, no more than the captive editor and typist who is my wife, can be blamed for my shortcomings. Unfortunately, I cannot thank Martin King's widow and parents and the officials of the Southern Christian Leadership Conference, as they refused to be interviewed until after the publication of Coretta King's book. However, Mrs. King's book appeared before the final revisions of this manuscript were made.

D. L. L.

Washington, D. C.
October, 1969

King

1

Doctor, Lawyer — Preacher?

> No other offense has ever been visited with such
> severe penalties as seeking to help the oppressed.
>
> CLARENCE DARROW

LOCAL BLACKS IN MONTGOMERY now point out with awe the
place where Rosa Parks was put off the bus and into custody,
often remarking, "That's where it all began." By "all" they
mean not only the Montgomery bus boycott but the story of
Dr. Martin Luther King, Jr., who was born "a Negro" in Atlanta on January 15, 1929. Hindsight now suggests that his
emergence as a civil rights leader, locally and then nationally,
was inevitable in that place at that time. Yet Dr. King himself, when he passed that bus stop years later, marveled at
what a different course the whole Rosa Parks incident might
have taken and also, therefore, his own life. Part of him, the
private man, was impressed by the pattern of coincidences
and accidental good timing common to the lives of all famous
men, and the other part of him was full of wonderment at
what he saw as the Lord's work.

The decision to become a minister like his father had required years of deliberation. The ministry itself he had once
dismissed as too unintellectual, even too archaic, to speak
effectively on contemporary problems. Medicine and certainly
the law had been more congenial and meaningful pursuits.
And yet, finally, he had come round to deciding that it should

3

be the ministry after all, and eventually he was even reasonably confident that he wanted a Southern pastorate. And so he had come to Montgomery.

In retrospect, these doubts seem unlikely, as if he must have been blind to the inevitable course of his life. The most casual acquaintance of the King family's would probably have predicted that "Mike" King (he would become "Martin Luther" and "Dr. King" later) was destined from birth for the cloth. His maternal grandfather, the Reverend Alfred Daniel Williams, had founded Ebenezer Baptist Church, and Mike's father, Martin, Sr., had made it one of the largest and most prestigious Baptist churches in Atlanta. Mike's upbringing was pious and deeply influenced by the immensely varied activities arising out of his father's pastoral responsibilities. His precocious vocabulary and uncanny appreciation for the rhythms of language were clearly the patrimony of two generations of fundamentalist ministry. Mike knew by instinct the code that unlocked the powerful emotions of black worshipers. When he was only four, his mother regularly took him to smaller churches in the Atlanta area, where the people "rocked with joy"" to his rendering of religious songs.

The King family belonged to what is known as the school of hard preaching, of which cult of personality, an occasional pinch of exploitation, and sulfurous evangelism are indispensable ingredients. In this tradition, it is not enough to be called to preach. To be a success, you have to be a strong, attractive personality—a man's man but not unattractive to the good sisters of the congregation. Mike's maternal grandfather was such a personality. The Reverend Alfred Daniel Williams had a few credits in theology at Morehouse College's department of religion, but he spoke the broken English of the people he served, as much out of pride in his rough origins as from inability to master sinuous rules of grammar in adult life. The family still recalls Reverend Williams' mischievous putdown of one of his parishioners, a paragon of proper English, who made a nuisance of himself with his grammatical corrections. Reverend Williams once observed, after the tally of the Sunday collection plate, "I done give a hundred dollars but the gentleman who corrected me *has* given nothing."

As one of the rare people in the black community who was financially secure and independent of the whites, Mike's maternal grandfather was able to play an important role in race relations. He bore lasting psychological scars from the 1906 Atlanta race riot, and, when the city's blacks, spurred by the riot, organized a strong local chapter of the recently founded National Association for the Advancement of Colored People, he was one of its charter members. With other prominent citizens, he led a successful movement to defeat a city bond issue that made no provisions for the construction of black public high schools. As a result, Booker T. Washington High School, the city's first school for black secondary education, was built in the mid-1920's. The local Hearst newspaper, *The Georgian*, paid a high price for its editorial denunciation of the opponents of the bond issue as "dirty and ignorant" protestors. Reverend Williams and his colleagues called for a boycott of the newspaper, and this contributed to its eventual demise.

Memories of this boycott must have been very strong in Mike's childhood, and inevitably it recalls the more famous bus boycott that he was to lead in Montgomery several decades later. A less inquisitive young mind, secure in such a family tradition, would easily have been persuaded by the example his grandfather and father had made of the potential of the ministry for civic contribution. Mike's father had carried on very much in Reverend Williams' footsteps. He was one of the charter members of the Atlanta Voters' League, an active Republican, and a sponsor of programs for Atlanta youth. Educated at his own expense at Morehouse College, he was later elected to the college's board of trustees. He gave Mike as strong an example as his maternal grandfather had, and yet, in spite of them both, Mike's doubts about his own future persisted.

The source of these doubts lay partly in his relations with his indomitable father. Michael Luther King, Sr. (his father said the boy's name was Martin, but his mother called him Michael) retained, under a black Puritan crust, the pugnacity of his Stockbridge, Georgia, youth. Until he was fifteen, he had never had more than three months of schooling in any year, and to win a Morehouse degree was, therefore, a remarkable achievement. Despite the crippling disadvantages of rural poverty, Mike, Sr., had determined to make good his angry response to the few youngsters in his community who were better off. "I may smell like a mule," he would say, "but I don't think like one." Powerfully built, he was an alert and self-reliant youngster. He once fought and defeated James Albert, his father, for drunkenly abusing his mother. He also succeeded in outwitting the white farmer-landlord to whom his father had become, as was the inexorable pattern of the time and region, deeply indebted. It was at the end of the planting season, when accounts were squared, and for the first time James Albert King was told that the value of his cotton crop exactly balanced his debts. The son, after waiting a suitable interval for both men to solemnize this unprecedented event, stupified them by announcing that some $1,000 worth of cotton seed, omitted from the tally, could be kept by his father.

Years later, in rigidly segregated Atlanta, whites were still periodically surprised by Reverend King's forthright opposition to racial effrontery. The arrogant traffic policeman, drawling through a lecture begun with the traditional salutation "Boy," was instantly reprimanded with Reverend King's impatient correction, "That's a boy," pointing to Mike sitting beside him, "I'm a man." One of Mike's most vivid memories of Southern prejudice occurred when a shoe clerk declined to serve him unless he and his father moved to the rear of the store. "We'll either buy shoes sitting here or we won't buy any shoes at all," his father growled, and he marched Mike toward the door.

The iron constitution of King, Sr., had been proof against the economic and psychological acids of Southern debasement. In the 1930's, when 65 per cent of Atlanta's able-bodied black male population was unemployed, he had nearly fulfilled his vow, made in the kitchen of his mother's white employers, that some day he would have "a brick house, and my brick house is going to be as fine as any brick house." If the twelve-room dwelling near the intersection of Auburn and Boulevard was of wood, the spaciousness of its rooms and garden and the sedateness of the neighborhood made it then, as now, a thoroughly desirable, almost princely, place. The brick house would come later.

"If he had one weakness," President Benjamin Mays of Morehouse observes of King, Sr., "it was those children," Christine, Mike, and A. D. A beneficiary of that lavish love, Mike at times found it too enveloping, too omnipresent. It would not have been wholesome for his ego if Mike, Jr., had not squirmed somewhat, had not resisted the strong leads set by his father. Unasked and unrequired, King, Sr., was always on hand to advise, cajole, and protect. Papa wished to play the grand impressario for all his children, but, with M. L., as the family called Mike, Jr., the boy's special promise made this role more thrilling. For one who desired only the readily available success and neighborhood acclaim of a successful minister's son, such a relationship would have appealed as the fitting filial symmetry in a father's grand design. The many Atlantans who frequently remarked that the elder King was "a character" would have looked upon the son in much the same way, as a character and a chip off the old block. It is possible that Mike even resented, subconsciously, this patriarchal presumptuousness and that his early determina-

tion to have nothing to do with the ministry was motivated
by a desire to escape the professional prison that his well-
meaning curator was constructing.

Equally to the point, however, was the influence of black
bourgeois Atlanta. The Kings were certainly materially successful. The head of the house was undeniably a figure in the
politics of the community. But Atlanta was socially a complex city. Elsewhere in the South, in Charleston or Savannah,
say, the dubious honor of being descended from "free Negroes" or house slaves and possessing a complexion light
enough to make one's race a matter of conjecture were a
considerable advantage. And, if mulatto status was reinforced
by wealth, actual or a generation removed, and a shadowy
ancestral contribution during Reconstruction, then social status could be maintained for a time by adherence to quaint
antebellum protocol and haughty refusal to socialize with
parvenus. In the border states and in the North, social status
tended to accord more nearly with wealth, however acquired.

Atlanta, however, struck a balance between the extremes.
Skin color and putative family tradition were not sufficient
of themselves to maintain a family's social prominence. On
the other hand, recent wealth, and certainly illicit wealth
(such as from gambling or contraband), offered only the possibility of achieving social respectability one or two generations later. Fortuitous marriage into the mulatto "aristocracy," appropriate membership of one's wife in one of three
exclusive distaff clubs, the possession of an Atlanta University or, later, a Morehouse, a Spelman, or a Northern college
degree, and a pew in one of a select number of dignified
churches, as well as affluence, constituted the prerequisites for
belonging to the black upper class in Atlanta. Moreover,
while the class of black professionals was elsewhere limited
to a small number of ministers, lawyers, teachers, a physician,
a mortician or two, and frugal postal employees, in Atlanta
there was a large and varied professional class. The black com-

munity comprised a sizable number of college professors, contractors, real estate agents, several insurance executives and bankers, many marginal businessmen, and a number of physicians, dentists, and morticians. By 1945, its businesses could boast of a total book value approaching $30 million.

The spine of this remarkable affluence had its base almost at the doorstep of the King place on Auburn Avenue. On either side of the street were homes sheltering Atlanta's black elite, whose robust businesses lined upper Auburn, "Sweet Auburn," as its unofficial historian, the black newspaperman I. P Reynolds, called it. Much of the vitality of Atlanta's black enterprise was the result of the unusual leadership of Hemon E. Perry, an unlettered black immigrant from the Southwest. In 1913, Perry founded the Standard Life Insurance Company, whose paper assets totaled more than $10 million before its collapse in 1924. With generous loans to himself from Standard Life, Perry established a variety of "service" enterprises (black businesses servicing the black market) such as dry-cleaning businesses, a drugstore, a mortgage association, a construction concern, and a Tennessee coal-mining operation. His attempt to develop Atlanta's then remote west side as a preserve for exclusive homes owned by blacks resulted in the fatal overextension of his financial resources, and his empire soon completely folded. Perry became a legend and an inspiration to the adventurous young men who flocked to Atlanta to salvage what fragments of it remained. The west side soon became the park for the black affluent that he had intended. As Standard Life foundered, other enterprises were already rising to sustain the black business community. Atlanta Life Insurance Company, founded by barber Alonzo F. Herndon in 1905, had assets in excess of $19 million by 1948. Atlanta Mutual Building Loan and Savings Association, established in 1920 and reorganized by John P. Whittaker seventeen years later, grew lustily, as did Citizens Trust Bank, founded early in the

1920's. The latter became America's third largest black financial institution, with assets of more than $4 million by 1949, and the sole black member of the Federal Reserve system. There was also Southwestern Fidelity and Fire Insurance Company, organized by Charles E. Maxey, Mutual Federal Savings and Loan Association, and Aiken Construction Corporation, which played a dominant role in west-side housing construction after World War II. Atlanta also boasted the nation's only black news daily, the *Atlanta World*, established by William A. Scott, Jr., in 1928 and published daily after 1932, as well as the only black radio station, WERD.

All these enterprises rose on Auburn Avenue and were complemented by several religious institutions, such as Big Bethel African Methodist Episcopal Church, a tremendous granite and pseudo-Romanesque structure, and Ebenezer Baptist Church, slightly more than two blocks away. High up Auburn and off to the side, in the very center of the burgeoning white business district, was the pinnacle of black religious respectability, the First Congregational Church.

On the other side of town, the major artery was Hunter Street. Here, Atlanta University, called "old Atlanta U." to distinguish it from the later center for graduate studies bearing its name, was situated. Later, Morehouse and Spelman colleges were to relocate in the Chestnut Street area, behind Atlanta University. Much later, Morris Brown College, Clark College, and the new Atlanta University would complete the development of the black university center. The famous scholar W. E. B. DuBois was a faculty member at Atlanta University shortly after the turn of the century, and James Weldon Johnson and Walter White were two of its renowned graduates. Next to the residence of the president of Atlanta University, Alonzo Herndon erected a colonnaded mansion of Italian brick, still one of the more splendid in the South, that provided the black aristocracy with a setting for its somewhat stilted levees and receptions. Farther down

Hunter Street, the Pitts family built a commodious brick home in the wild territory that Hemon Perry had begun to explore. Hunter Street became a muddy red clay trail, disappearing into the luxuriant brush just beyond the Pitts' driveway. But other houses were raised shortly thereafter—this was early in the 1930's—and, soon after the war, it was no longer fashionable to reside on the Auburn Avenue side of town.

The Atlanta of Mike King's teens was professionally diverse and socially sophisticated. To be the son of a successful Baptist minister was an estimable birthright, certainly, but there were many other standards, supplementary and competing, by which to gauge community status. Within the local Baptist community, he became aware that the congregations at the Wheat Street and Friendship churches were more refined in their Sunday worship, the ministers more rigorously intellectual than at his own Ebenezer. Thus, his experiences in his father's church and his growing awareness of the polished standards within the black community persuaded Mike that the ministry that he knew was neither intellectually nor socially high-toned. Meanwhile, there was an adolescent's world of time in which to select a career. For the present, he was absorbed by the normal adventure of growing up.

Insulated against the most brutal aspects of Southern bigotry, Mike continued, nevertheless, to encounter its puzzling and bitter manifestations. The incident in the shoe store rankled deeply. More disappointing, however, was the defection of two cherished white playmates whose parents owned a small store in the neighborhood. When Mike was old enough to attend elementary school, he discovered that his playmates' parents had forbidden them to associate with him and his brother. "Don't let this thing impress you. Don't let it make you feel you're not as good as white people. You're as good as anyone else, and don't you forget it," his mother told him. He had good reason to believe her, but the experi-

ence left its small cicatrice. Five years later, at eleven, he
experienced a bewilderingly gratuitous indignity. A white
woman he had never seen before walked up to him in a
department store and slapped his face. "The little nigger
stepped on my foot," she explained. This experience also
left its mark. "As far back as I could remember, I had resented segregation," Mike said many years afterward. He was
fortunate that his encounters with racism did not turn his
resentment into blind anger or despair.

The loss of the two white companions was more than compensated by new friendships. At Yonge Street Elementary
School and then at David T. Howard Elementary School, to
which he transferred in his third year, Mike met William
Murphy and Emmett Proctor, alert youngsters whose parents
were civic leaders. Emmett's grandmother Carrie (the widow
of C. L. Harper, head of the Atlanta NAACP and principal
of the sole Negro public high school, Booker T. Washington), has never yet adjusted to the phenomenon of Martin
Luther King, Jr., the charismatic international figure. She
recalls only a boisterous and mischievous boy tussling incessantly with her nephew, scampering under the back porch,
and howling about a bruised knee. The humorless, Buddha-
like figure portrayed by journalists years later was by all accounts a coltishly rugged youngster possessed of a considerable degree of street savvy. He could take care of himself in a
fight, but his preferred mode of self-defense was verbal rather
than physical. One Sunday, after listening to a spellbindingly
eloquent visiting preacher, Mike promised his mother, "Someday, I'm going to have me some big words like that." He
worked on that promise regularly, and he was usually able to
cow a would-be opponent with first-class words, but not always. His brother, A. D., could sometimes be downright
contemptuous of Mike's verbal defense. Mike was compelled
to resort to more forceful expedients, in one memorable
instance a crushing smash on the head with a telephone
receiver.

One of his biographers has examined Mike's adolescent propensity for nonviolence. It is, he concludes, largely myth. "Gandhis are not born; they invent themselves," Lerone Bennett observes. This is not altogether correct, either, though. They are born, but they develop their traits over a period of years. And, during the incubatory period of sanctity, Mike could demonstrate a robust capacity to assert his physical prowess. A difference of opinion or a question of property rights was not infrequently resolved by the challenge "Let's go to the grass." He was an excellent wrestler; moreover, he remained throughout his adult life immensely fond of professional boxing. But there is some basis for retrospectively depicting Mike as an adolescent exponent of nonviolence. His father observes that, when the rod was applied, Mike exhibited an almost philosophical stoicism, not a whimper, not a murmur of protest. "There was always something special about M. L.," he recalls, reflecting upon the early years. "Even before he could read, he kept books around him, he just liked the idea of having them." A further indication of pubescent nonviolence was Mike's passive acceptance of a drubbing from "Black Billy," the bully of David T. Howard Elementary School, and from an unknown youngster who roughly contested right of way through a drugstore turnstile. At least one of his high school teachers remembers being impressed by his moodiness.

Two early attempts at suicide are also evidence of a warp of personality that may have cradled a brooding disinclination to compete. It would appear that his abhorrence of violence and sympathy for tragedy occasionally reached pathological proportions. The first attempt at suicide followed his brother's accidental injury of his beloved maternal grandmother (it appeared that A. D. had killed her). Mike hurled himself from the upstairs window of the house. A second attempt came in 1941, when he was twelve. Mrs. Williams died of a heart attack after he had stolen away to sin by watching a parade on Sunday. Mike leapt again from the same window. One might read into his morbid conduct the desire to assume the suffering of others and to expiate it by subjecting himself to immolation and even death. How significant, after all, was his preference in church for the song, "I Want to Be More and More Like Jesus"?

But suicide leaps from haystack heights do not take the lives of healthy, nimble boys. Silent submission to parental discipline and unresisting defeat at the hands of neighborhood toughs are sometimes the wisest courses when confronting more powerful and determined adversaries. Moreover, in the case of the neighborhood toughs, a sense of bourgeois superiority may have motivated Mike to suffer the lesser indignity of not fighting a social inferior. There were some youngsters with whom one did not "go to the grass." And, if he was occasionally aloof in school, there is ample evidence that more often he was a combative participant. He was an active swimmer and tennis player and a prized member of the neighborhood baseball and football teams. William Murphy, Real "Rooster" Cash, Oliver "Sack" Jones, Howard "Mole" Everett, and other close friends saw Mike as an uncomplicated companion, a good mimic, and an excellent amateur athlete. He could surely use big words like nobody else they knew. But they did not hold that against him, because he was, after all, a preacher's son. They would surely have grinned if it had been put to them that Mike would grow up to become America's leading exponent of the doctrine of passive nonviolent resistance to social injustice. Still, he was subject to violent swings in mood and he did prefer to talk rather than fight; perhaps, on reflection, they might not have found such a prediction too bizarre.

Like his buddies, Mike shouldered the responsibility of a paper route, delivering the black daily when he was eight years old and later, at thirteen, the white daily, the *Atlanta Journal.* The paper routes were regarded as exercises in manly self-reliance and mastery of money, indispensable aptitudes

for the sons of privileged black families. When he reached
his teens, Mike spent a large portion, considerably more than
his peers, of his newspaper profits on clothes. Apparently he
spent well, for he was given the sobriquet "Tweed" because
of his penchant for stylish and exquisitely woven suits. He
gave equal attention to his foot wear, always luminously
buffed patent leather shoes whose costliness increased with
the years.

In 1941, the family moved from the old homestead to that
brick house the senior King had prophesied he would one day
own. This was a larger structure, three blocks away at 193
Boulevard. The move coincided with the completion of the
new Ebenezer church at its present site on Auburn Avenue;
the family's affairs were prospering. In a few years, the question of dynastic succession would become crucial. Mike's
younger brother, A. D., had made it unequivocally clear that
he would not accept the mantle of his father. Furthermore,
A. D. wholly lacked the commanding presence of his father
as well as Mike's keen intelligence and verbal polish. But
Mike, too, remained adamant in his disinclination to enter
the ministry. He was content, for the present, to roam about
the city with Mole, Sack, and Rooster, practicing at courtship, and applying himself rather desultorily to his studies.
At the end of his second year at the Atlanta University
laboratory high school, the board of trustees decided, for reasons of economy, to discontinue its experiment in secondary
education. The following year, he followed his privileged classmates to the mammoth public secondary institution, Booker
T. Washington. Under the principalship of C. L. Harper,
Washington High School afforded strict, conventional, and
generally competent instruction.

Memories are now dim as to Mike's adjustment at Washington High. It was probably relatively successful, although
several of the youngsters from the laboratory school found
the democracy of the place somewhat abrasive and missed

the individual attention they had been accustomed to. Having already received indifferent piano lessons, Mike was able to take up the violin in the music department. The results must not have been felicitous, for the violin lessons have never been mentioned by King's earlier biographers. Mrs. India Amos remembers his violin case invariably and stubbornly obstructing the aisle between the booths in her husband's drugstore and soda fountain at the corner of Ashby and Hunter streets. The new school may also have provided a challenging arena in which to measure himself against the cruder forensic talents and more direct protocol of courtship of public-school peers. The fact that, in transferring to Washington High, he was allowed to skip the ninth grade no doubt provided an extra incentive to strive to create a mature impression. His chief extracurricular passion was rewarded by the Elks, who bestowed upon him their annual oratorical prize for his presentation that year of a topic dealing with the Negro and the Constitution. But one of his experiences with oratory was as cruel as any of the racial contretemps by which he had been previously beleaguered. Years later, his smothered anger at being compelled with his fellow high school debaters to surrender his seat to white passengers boarding the bus returning from Valdosta, Georgia, was eloquently communicated to a correspondent from *Time* magazine. Cursed by the driver, they had had to stand in the aisle for 90 miles. "It was a night I'll never forget. I don't think I have ever been so deeply angry in my life."

There were, fortunately, occasional antidotes to such outrages. In the summer of his junior year in high school, Mike traveled north with A. D. for the first time, to work as a laborer on a Connecticut tobacco farm. Several high school seniors and college students were in the group, most of whom, like Mike, had accepted harvesting contracts far less from economic necessity than in a spirit of adolescent wanderlust and Puritan desire to inure themselves to the rigors of phy-

sical hardship. The freedom of movement, the casual soci-
ability of Northern whites, and the cultural offerings of Hartford were exhilarating. The veil of mystery and peril that
cloaked the relations between the races in the South appeared
to be totally absent in the North. One might go freely where
personal inclination led and pocket money permitted. Mike
does not appear to have noticed, however, that Hartford
blacks made little display either of affluence or of cultural
inclinations. Indeed, it would be late in his career before he
perceived clearly the different but no less stultifying forces of
discrimination in the North. For him, the experience was
uniquely pleasurable and enlightening, until, that is, he returned to Atlanta. Compelled to sit behind a curtain when
he entered the dining car on the train home, Mike felt "as if
the curtain had been dropped on my selfhood." He referred
to the "bitter pill" of returning to the omnipresent, routine
inhumanity of Southern segregation. He nearly hated whites
at that period, an emotion that he normally rejected as the
most unworthy and toxic affliction of the spirit of American
blacks. For a time, he believed he "could envision myself
playing a part in breaking down the legal barriers to Negro
rights." The emotion was commendable, but it was premature. He was not an activist yet, and, with the end of the
summer approaching, there was little time left for grave racial
preoccupations.

Wishing to enter Morehouse College, he studied hard. But
there was no good reason for a bright young man to spend
the required years at Washington High. Almost a decade
later, the Ford Foundation, reaching the same conclusion,
was to provide Fisk and Morehouse colleges with funds to
establish an early-entrants program for second- and third-
year black high school students, enabling them to enter college without diplomas, in order to pursue specially enriched
curricula. President Mays of Morehouse, who was concerned
about the mangling of black talent by segregated high schools

and was worried that wartime conscription would seriously deplete his enrollment, pioneered a special program for gifted high school students at Morehouse. After successfully completing a battery of Morehouse-designed tests, Mike entered the college in September, 1944, again skipping a high school grade. He was fifteen. His father was delighted, as was his mother, for matriculation at Morehouse represented a continuum in family tradition. Articulate and precocious, Mike would add luster to the family. Moreover, although his father was careful not to make the point, Mike would remain at home for those four college years, time enough to prevail upon him to enter the ministry and accept the co-pastorship of Ebenezer.

Morehouse in the 1940's was not very different from the institution it is today. Shaded by magnolias, it shared a spacious, walled campus with the new Atlanta University administration building and library. The architectural candor of its three box-like classroom buildings and the dormitory, with its anemic steeple, formed a horseshoe around President Mays' residence that gave the school a village-like neatness and an almost inconsequential air that totally belied its excellence. It was, despite its size, a consciously arrogant place. The incessant exhortation to conduct oneself as a Morehouse man was almost fanatically absorbed by the school's four hundred students. And the requirements of manhood were enhanced by the nearby presence of Rockefeller-supported Spelman College, cloistered and female.

The Morehouse faculty, whose salaries were almost risible, sublimated this inadequacy through exemplary dedication. Claude "Pop" Dansby in mathematics was exclusively devoted to his subject and his charges. George D. Kelsey in theology was a paragon of pedagogical clarity. Samuel Williams in philosophy was tireless in discharging his mandate to excite and perplex the gifted but often fettered young minds entrusted to him. Gladstone L. Chandler, professor of

English, was ingenious in devising shortcuts to passable grammar and smoother prose. Walter Chivers, who was to supervise Mike in his major, sociology, was a relentless analyst of social systems. And the personality of the statuesque and white-maned Dr. Mays permeated the milieu of the college with firm but unobtrusive moral guidance. But the most significant aspect of Morehouse was its pervasive confidence that, by remaining an oasis for the unrestrained pursuit of knowledge, neither modest means nor racial discrimination could prevent talented young men from overcoming the apparently hopeless limitations imposed by a hostile and exclusive white world. As with his predecessor, President Archer, Dr. Mays' favorite poem was Henley's "Invictus," and Morehouse men catechized themselves with its lines.

Mike entered Morehouse determined to study medicine, a respectable, independent, and socially beneficent profession. No one, it appears, had bothered to inform him that he was both temperamentally and intellectually unsuited for this profession. He made the discovery unaided during his freshman and sophomore years. For one who accepted so much on faith in later life, Mike's chief difficulty with the sciences was precisely his inability to embrace principles without question. Behind the theorem and the fundamental law, he sought to grasp the fallible and human process by which they were devised. John Y. Moreland, an intimate classmate, recalls Mike's unorthodox encounter with statistics. It was impossible, says Moreland, for Mike to accept the reduction of social forces and animate entities to mere numbers. He was appalled by what he took to be the apathetic fallacy of statistics. This skepticism was part of a larger dialectical gestalt. Moreland observes that Mike was never satisfied when he was bested in a discussion. But he evinced little more satisfaction when an argument of his own overwhelmed an opponent by force of sheer data. The issue for Mike was always to persuade as much by sincerity as by fact and logic.

His classmates were often surprised to hear him revive a several-days-old discussion, equipped with additional reasons and renewed passion.

It is curious that his proclivity for dogged enquiry and his resolve to penetrate to the source of problems fell short of translating themselves into superior marks in philosophy. Every Morehouse freshman was required to take Professor Williams' two-semester introductory course, Philosophy 361 and 362. Mike earned a grade of only C. "He came to Morehouse rather young," Professor Williams remarks, "and it is not always the case that a student comes to full flower so young. So I would not say that he was the most outstanding student we had, for he was not." Although introductory, the course was thorough in analysis and vast in scope, and Mike was simply too immature, at fifteen, to demonstrate the philosophical aptitude that distinguished his record later at Crozer Theological Seminary. As Professor Williams pushed his charges through the works of Moses to those of Marx, Mike earmarked their writings for future and more leisurely review. In the margins of his mind he registered quick reactions to Socrates, Plato, and Aristotle. He retained also an impressionistic evaluation of Macchiavelli, Descartes, and Kant. They pressed on from Hegel before Mike was properly introduced, but he succumbed to an almost uncritical fascination with the Hegelian dialectic. He was simultaneously drawn to and repelled by Marx, and it would require a season of hard study at Crozer before he could come to terms with philosophical communism. One of the works Professor Williams had Mike read, Thoreau's essay *On Civil Disobedience*, stirred him more deeply and permanently than any other classroom encounter of the period.

The reasons for Mike's decision to pursue a major in sociology have never been adequately explained. Perhaps his unsuitability for the premedical sciences and his demonstrated talent in the humanities commended the discipline to him as the ideal compromise between the firm methodology of the sciences and the exciting imprecision of the arts. Sociology purported to be an exact discipline requiring mastery of disagreeable statistics, but its data were derived from the vibrant stuff of human interaction. Moreover, a major in sociology was thoroughly acceptable to law schools, and his aptitudes pointed to a brilliant career in the legal profession. Although Professor Chivers was a thorough realist, much of Mike's instruction in sociology came through the direct medium of summer employment in white Atlanta firms. Chivers had stressed to his students that, as far as they were concerned, the primary evil was racism, of which the economic system was the root.

Two of Mike's vacation jobs indelibly impressed upon his mind the veracity of his professor's remark. The hapless blacks who toiled for Railway Express and the Southern Spring Bed Mattress Company were subjected to conditions of appalling degradation. They were abused daily by people whose only protection against similar treatment was their white skin. Blacks were fired capriciously, even after years of faithful service. And, of course, their wages were ridiculously inadequate. Mike perceived that, even if the whites received better pay, relatively, both races earned less than was their due, because of the racism contrived and sustained by their invisible employers. When the Railway Express foreman persisted in calling him "nigger," Mike had the means to quit his job and still dress in a manner befitting the nickname "Tweed." But he appreciated then as never before the degree of his good fortune. During school terms, he was able to discuss these anomalies candidly with his friends and the professors. "I realized that nobody there was afraid," he had remarked soon after entering Morehouse, and the fearlessness of the institution braced him for the trials ahead.

Morehouse men not only learned to be fearless in the College's bracing environment. They also mastered the art of chivalrous courtship. Mike developed early the aggressiveness typical of the short male. When he left Morehouse, he would be five feet seven inches tall and weigh slightly less than 170 pounds. He was healthy, agile, and solidly built. The young ladies he courted remember his short height only as an afterthought. His sartorial fastidiousness and his confident charm and eloquence are the primary legacies of his enterprise among Atlanta's belles. Mike's selection of pretty girls was as careful as the choice of his wardrobe. Among them was Rose Martin, daughter of the vice-president of Atlanta Life Insurance Company; Betty Milton, daughter of the president of Citizens Trust; Juanita Sellers, whose father was one of the community's most prosperous morticians, and Mattawilda Dobbs, the future operatic soprano, whose father held the venerable Masonic title Worshipful Master. Lacking aquiline features and long straight hair—near-white attributes upon which black mothers placed a pathetically dogmatic value—Mike charmed with his mellifluent baritone. The genteel damsels of the black aristocracy were told of the Rubicons they caused to be crossed, of the calamitous Waterloos their mere existence created, of the Troys of whose destruction they were the source:

On desperate seas, long wont to roam,
Thy hyacinth hair, thy classic face,
Thy Naiad airs have brought me home
To the glory that was Greece and the grandeur that was Rome.

One catches distinctly the cadences of that earnest, deep voice, the vowels distended three times their normal length. And one pictures the pleasure mirrored in the lovely face of a feminine listener. Mike King played hard, dressed well, and attempted to be a great lover.

Mike's junior year at Morehouse was momentous. In retrospect, it was actually the point in time at which the intrinsic strains of his nature and the exemplary influence of two grand personalities conjoined and culminated. Had he persisted in his aversion to the ministry, he would have become an incompetent physician whose bedside manner might nevertheless have spared him the wrath of the community. With far less effort, he would have become a trial lawyer in the mold of a William Jennings Bryan. He might even have become an inspiring sociology chairman in a segregated college. But he was subtly impressed by George Kelsey and Benjamin Mays. Kelsey demonstrated the old biblical literalism and almost carnival pulpit dramaturgy that had disturbed Mike in his formative years as being entirely irrelevant to the contemporary minister's mission of spiritual salvation and social amelioration. The good pastor, Kelsey maintained, is also a good philosopher.

Mike observed the embodiment of Kelsean principles each Tuesday morning when President Mays addressed the student body in chapel. Chapel was compulsory throughout the week, but Dr. Mays endeavored to make Tuesday mornings a special occasion. Some men are special because of what they say, others because of what they do. Dr. Mays was special in both senses. His Bates College Phi Beta Kappa key gleaming from the podium, he had the uncanny ability to interest a restive student body, to invest commonplace observations with an intensity and intimacy of experience that enthralled young men who were, on other mornings, usually sleepy or indifferent. "There are some faces one notices," Dr. Mays observes. "You can tell when a student is interested in what one has to say." He noticed that Martin King, Jr., was interested. Several times, Mike approached Dr. Mays to pursue some point he had raised in his inspirational talks.

It was about the same time that President Mays became better acquainted with the King family. Reverend King was one of his trustees and so it was natural that the President of Morehouse began to visit the King homestead. Before the end of the year, Mike announced to his mother that he had decided to enter the ministry. The senior King could not have been more pleased but, knowing his son's independence, he required that Mike undertake a trial sermon. Its success was such that, before the young novitiate had finished, he was compelled to repair to the main auditorium of Ebenezer in order to accommodate the swelling crowd.

He had found his metier. The senior year at Morehouse merely served to reinforce his commitment. Because he resided off campus, Mike did not participate in the Morehouse men's strike against the dining hall and their complementary sympathy demonstration in support of Spelman girls, who were also distressed by their own living conditions. Nor was he active in student government. His area of competence remained the oratorical forum, where he had won first prize in the Webb Oratorical Contest in his sophomore year. The fact that he did not belong to the college debating team is explained by his failure to join a fraternity while he was an undergraduate. During his era, the debating team was jealously restricted to members of one of the Greek letter societies. He did belong to the college chapter of the NAACP and to the Intercollegiate Council, an interracial body comprised of students from the Atlanta University Center and the several white schools in Atlanta. The latter experience somewhat reassured him about the fundamental decency of whites. "The wholesome relations we had in this group convinced me that we have many white persons as allies, particularly among the younger generation. I had been ready to resent the whole white race, but, as I got to see more of white people, my resentment was softened and a spirit of cooperation took its place." And, as usual, there were the steadying friendships Mike was always so adroit at achieving to crest him over the personal anxieties and larger social dilemmas that continued to tug at him. Walter McCall, Robert Williams, Charles Evans Morton, and Philip Lenud formed the nucleus of his group of friends. In his dealings with them and

others, the pattern of behavior that he was to designate as
"ambivert" (outgoing but a bit withdrawn) fully emerged.
Faithful and ingenuous, Mike also gave the distinct impression
of unusual self-control and almost moody introspection.

Equipped with the prestigious Morehouse bachelor's degree
and ordained a minister in the Baptist faith, Martin Luther
King, Jr., closed one of the most significant chapters in his life
in June, 1948. From the point of view of his father, Mike
might have ended his formal education at this stage. His sociology marks had been outstanding. His maturity at nineteen
was cause for general community comment. The co-pastorship
of Ebenezer awaited him. But Mike, inspired by the examples
of Kelsey and Mays, was determined to crown his preparation
for the ministry with advanced degrees. His special convictions
about the purpose of education were published in the Morehouse student journal, *The Maroon Tiger*, during his final
year. "The Purpose of Education" is a manifesto of Kingian
values. The author lamented that "as I engage in the so-called
bull-sessions around and about the school, I too often find that
most college men have a misconception of the purpose of
education." The majority of students was seeking, from the
college experience, the tools with which to exploit the trusting masses for its own material security. Others expected the
bachelor's degree to transplant them to heights of privilege
and leadership without the intermediate apprenticeship of
hard work and civic commitment. Too many of his Morehouse peers had lost sight of the nonutilitarian values of
education. They had emphasized utility at the expense of
morality. It was worth noting, Mike concluded, that the
former governor of Georgia, Eugene Talmadge, was a Phi
Beta Kappa. He concluded, "The function of education,
therefore, is to teach one to think intensively and to think
critically. But education which stops with efficiency may prove
the greatest menace to society. The most dangerous criminal
may be the man gifted with reason, but with no morals."

Obviously, a graduating senior who thought as keenly and

felt as deeply about the society he was preparing to enter would demand more time to ponder his existential and professional roles. President Mays and Professor Kelsey energetically defended Mike's desire to pursue his studies. In fact, Mike's father needed only the appearance of pressure to be persuaded. He knew that his son would not lose his gift of turning on the "rousements" because of an advanced degree in theology. A special ally at this time was the venerable J. Pius Barbour, a Morehouse graduate who had attended Crozer Theological Seminary in Chester, Pennsylvania, early in the 1930's, had graduated with distinction, and was now one of the most respected members of the National Baptist Convention. Reverend Barbour had known the King family intimately for many years. It was he who suggested that Mike matriculate for the bachelor of divinity degree at Crozer, the logical next step, it seemed, in grooming himself for what lay ahead.

2

The Philosopher King

> The championship of social justice is almost the
> only way left open to a Christian nowadays to
> gain the crown of martyrdom.
>
> WALTER RAUSCHENBUSCH

CHESTER, PENNSYLVANIA, the site of Crozer Theological Seminary, is an ugly industrial city with a population of about
66,000. It was here that William Penn and his followers first
set foot on the real estate that a debt-ridden British sovereign
had granted to his worrisome Quaker subjects. Little of the
original spirit of brotherly love remained at the time that
Mike King was a student there. A highly conservative pluto-
cracy ruled the city, through bosses.

Large parts of Chester, the better parts, were off limits to
the black population, which subsisted in unpicturesque squalor in the western section of town. For the most part, the
black students at Crozer confined their social activity to Edwards Street, where there was a combination drugstore and
soda fountain run by a friendly and industrious black family.
This street was further endeared to Mike, because a classmate had an aunt who lived there and prepared the collard
greens that both of them relished. Around the corner, on
Sixteenth Street, was the imposing brick church and parsonage of J. Pius Barbour. The menu of the Barbour household
reflected the affluence of its master's profession. Mike especially enjoyed Mrs. Barbour's steak bathed in spicy sauce.

"He could eat more than any little man you ever saw in your life," his former host comments. This must have been true, for Mike once confessed that "eating is my great sin." The diversions of Edwards Street and the Southern warmth of the Barbour home did much to compensate for the general coldness and subtle bigotry of Chester and Crozer.

L. Harold DeWolf, his dissertation supervisor at Boston University, contends that Mike exhibited no symptoms of racial malaise during their close relationship. When they happened to discuss his apparent racial equableness several years later, Mike remarked that his parents' lectures on this subject had equipped him with a sturdy armor against prejudice. In the fall of 1948, however, he had not yet achieved this state of imperturbability. Racial stereotypes beset him on all sides. He resolved not to be too friendly, not to smile when greeting classmates. He must not be thought to be a "happy-go-lucky darky." Seriousness, personal neatness, and punctuality were the desiderata of the moment:

> I was well aware of the typical white stereotype of the Negro, that he is always late, that he's loud and always laughing, that he's dirty and messy, and for a while I was terribly conscious of trying to avoid identification with it. If I were a minute late to class, I was almost morbidly conscious of it and sure that everyone else noticed it. Rather than be thought of as always laughing, I'm afraid I was grimly serious for a time.

He dressed impeccably, brushed his short hair mercilessly, and studied unrelentingly. He was, of course, too intelligent, too sensitive and superior, to spend his youth fighting vulgar stereotypes. Moreover, he possessed a proud family heritage and a most adequate monthly allowance, which made such dour conduct abnormal. Nonetheless, the initial behavioral pattern adopted at Crozer never entirely vanished in later years when he was in the presence of whites. One of his Crozer professors, Kenneth Lee Smith, who knew him well, always believed Mike to be reserved and humorless.

Reverend Hal Carter of Montgomery, whom Mike encouraged to enroll at Crozer, states that Mike thought of the three years in Chester as even more rewarding than his stay at Boston University. Dr. Sankey L. Blanton, president of Crozer, frequently invited Mike to his home and, while Mrs. Blanton endeavored to satiate a boundless appetite, Dr. Blanton and his student discoursed animatedly about the theologians and philosophers whose views at that time excited Mike. In his New Testament course, Professor Morton Scott Enslin also provided salutary direction through the morass of problems beleaguring Mike. But it was Professors George W. Davis and Kenneth Lee Smith who were of greatest assistance to him. In Professor Davis' course on the psychology of religious personalities, Mike first encountered a detailed analysis of Gandhi's philosophy of nonviolence. Under the guidance of Professor Smith, he renewed his acquaintance with the works of Walter Rauschenbusch, Reinhold Niebuhr, and Paul Tillich. Through both professors, he was introduced to the writings of Edgar S. Brightman and Nelson Wieman. Classroom work was felicitously augmented by innumerable nocturnal discussions with Professor Smith who, then a bachelor with a recent Ph.D. from Duke University, lived a few doors down the hall from Mike. In those dormitory debates, as well as in the classroom, Professor Smith observed his student's growing fascination with Rauschenbusch's philosophy of the Social Gospel. "It has been my conviction ever since reading Rauschenbusch," Mike wrote later, "that any religion which professes to be concerned about the souls of men and is not concerned about the social and economic conditions that scar the soul is a spiritually moribund religion."

The origins of the Social Gospel movement were neither primarily American nor exclusively Protestant. The social ideals expressed by Pope Leo XIII in the encyclical *Rerum Novarum* also contributed to its development. In reaction to excessive laissez-faire capitalism, the German philosophers

Adolf von Harnack and Albrecht Ritschl had formulated the basic ideas several decades before they were evangelized by Washington Gladden and expositorily presented by Rauschenbusch and George D. Herron. The naked exploitation of American capitalism, the shameless perversion of the science of evolution at the hands of Herbert Spencer, William Graham Sumner, and Andrew Carnegie, and the collusion of the federal government provoked a violent reaction from a number of religious leaders and scholars at the beginning of the twentieth century. If Andrew Carnegie spoke for the industrial establishment when he wrote, in *Gospel of Wealth*, that brutal competition is salutary because, by destroying the poor, "it insures the survival of the fittest in every department," Gladden spoke for the outraged humanitarians in demanding that workers be granted "belligerent rights" against their employers. Rauschenbusch issued the call to revolutionary social reform when he proclaimed, in *A Theology for the Social Gospel*, that "when once the common land of a nation, and its mines and waters, have become the private property of a privileged band, nothing short of a social earthquake can pry them from their right of collecting private taxes."

In Reverend Barbour's living room, Mike turned over these problems with his learned and sympathetic host. Barbour, like Professor Smith, was no sentimental exponent of the Social Gospel but a hardheaded Niebuhrian. He did not believe that the significance of Jesus' life confirmed the optimistic argument of the Social Gospellers. Rather, the appropriate lesson to be learned was that of man's limited capacity for self-improvement, despite the coming of the Redeemer, and of his total inability to save himself without divine intercession. Speaking of the Social Gospellers, Niebuhr wrote that "they do not believe that man remains a tragic creature who needs the divine mercy as much at the end as at the beginning of his moral endeavors." Barbour had no such illusions. Aside from the Rauschenbusch-Niebuhr dispute, Mike and Barbour discussed the peculiarly unsettling ideas in the theological behaviorism of the philosopher, Nelson Wieman, perhaps more than they did any other subject. Mike was negatively fascinated by Wieman, by the fundamental questions that his philosophy posed but the conventional theologians utterly failed to answer. At Boston University, his perplexity over Wieman would drive him to devote his doctoral dissertation to a comparison of Wieman's and Tillich's ideas of God.

Meanwhile, at Crozer, he pursued the ramifications of the Social Gospel. Its reading of the New Testament accorded with Mike's progressive view of society and sanguine view of human nature. The philosophy maintained that the eschatology of Christianity is in the historical triumph of political democracy. The witness of Christ and message of the prophets, Rauschenbusch argued, point to precisely such a secular culmination. The historical Jesus was merely an exemplary figure whose model conduct, if collectively emulated, would produce the millennial peace promised by the Gospels. Consequently, the doctrine of original sin was radically minimized by the Social Gospellers. Evil was construed as the result of an insufficiency of education and the egoisms of class or caste.

It was logical that this school would view the limitations on man resulting from the fall as thoroughly eradicable through the agency of universal education. Its confidence in social salvation was so complete that it permitted the question of personal immortality to be resolved according to individual preference. Furthermore, the Social Gospel held that the economic complement of democracy is socialism. Although not subscribing to Marxism, Rauschenbusch observed that the theory of surplus value, the concept of class struggle, and the process of dialectical materialism are far more exact and empirically convincing explanations of the systemic instability of capitalism than any offered by its defenders.

These years at Crozer were also eventful outside the class-rooms and library. There was still in Mike much of the sporting and amorous character of the "Tweed" of high school and Morehouse days. Reverend Barbour noticed an interesting and amusing dichotomy in his conduct. During the day, Mike was the Faustian student. His spare moments were given over to visits to the Barbour household and delivering an occasional sermon in one of the local churches. He had no time for frivolity. The evenings were quite different. There were many unattached young ladies in the Chester community, many of whom had thrilled to his splendid metaphors and rich baritone, sounding from the Sunday pulpit. During the evenings, along Edwards Street, he and Walter McCall, a Morehouse man who had entered the seminary in Mike's second semester, displayed a healthy, nonacademic interest in these young ladies. They were not usually very attractive. Mike was prone to refer to most of them as "light" sisters, his adjective for female acquaintances who were triumphs of matter over mind. Apparently, though, he must have made parlously definite commitments to a few of them. On the morning of his graduation from Crozer, Reverend Barbour received a plaintive telephone call. It appeared that several young ladies, each unbeknownst to the others, intended to be present at the ceremonies to represent themselves as Mike's fiancées. Reverend Barbour was asked to seek them out, take them in hand, and sit with them as though they were members of his congregation. It must be assumed that, after the graduation ceremonies, Mike availed himself to the fullest of his oratorical powers to assuage the injured dignity of this potential seraglio.

Although sticky and embarrassing, this incident was primarily humorous. There was, however, a deeply tragic romantic encounter for Mike while at Crozer. Elected president of the student body in his third year, he was more involved in the social life of the campus than he had previously been. His contacts with the families of the faculty and staff became necessarily more frequent and casual. He had scarcely noticed the attractive daughter of the white superintendent of buildings and grounds, but before the end of the first semester, their relationship had deepened into serious mutual attraction. Although he was obviously popular with his white classmates, his position carried no immunity from the campus racism that always lay just below the surface. His good friends Dupree Jordan and Francis Steward, both white Georgians, might have stood by him, but public knowledge of a white sweetheart, notwithstanding the Christian training of its student body, would have created a *cause célèbre* at Crozer.

Fortunately, interested members of the black community intervened. When Mike was seen with the young lady in one of the black cafés, Reverend Barbour was informed. He was told by Mike that they were in love and wished Barbour to marry them. A long fatherly lecture ensued, ending with a plea that the couple weigh the horrendous complications that usually accompanied intermarriage. Mike did so. And so did the young lady's family. She left Chester before the end of the academic year. Mike's disappointment was profound, although he was probably subsequently grateful for the advice of his mentor. The experience was repressed, but in later years Mike permitted it to surface, on occasion, when he felt able to lay aside his public mask and reflect candidly in the company of one or two intimates upon the *Weltschmerz* of prejudice.

Sometime before this romance, Mike and Walter McCall had been subjected to the vagaries of Northern prejudice in the small New Jersey village of Maple Shade, near Camden. With two dates, they had sought service in a restaurant whose staff politely ignored their repeated requests for a menu. When they insisted, the proprietor suggested that "the best thing would be for you to leave." They refused, were threatened by the owner's pistol, and finally left only because of the

danger to the girls. Returning half an hour later with a policeman, Mike and McCall obtained the promises of three students from the University of Pennsylvania to testify to the
proprietor's violation of the state civil rights code. The matter
was duly turned over to the Camden branch of the NAACP,
which filed suit. The two students were to be cruelly deceived,
however, for their witnesses, now embarrassed by their initial
temerity, professed not to recall the circumstances of the case
and declined to testify. It is remarkable that Mike could
nevertheless maintain his faith in the inevitability of racial
progress.

While he wrestled with the romantic distractions of his
final year at Crozer, he was also deeply absorbed by a number
of intellectual problems. In *Stride Toward Freedom*, he wrote
"Not until I entered Crozer Theological Seminary in 1948,
however, did I begin a serious intellectual quest for a method
to eliminate social evil." An important aspect of this quest
was his auditing of courses in philosophy and theology at the
University of Pennsylvania. During one of his trips to Philadelphia, Mike learned that Dr. Mordecai Johnson, president
of Howard University, was to offer a lecture at Fellowship
House about his recent trip to India. Several Sundays later,
he was at Fellowship House to hear Dr. Johnson's report on
his Indian travels. Professor Davis had lectured on Gandhi's
concept of *Satyagraha* and his students had questioned him
spiritedly about the Mahatma's beliefs. But in Dr. Johnson's
presentation, Gandhi's spiritual leadership and pacifist techniques attained an immediate and luminescent dimension
that Mike might otherwise never have apprehended. "His
message was so profound and electrifying that I left the meeting and bought a half-dozen books on Gandhi's life and
works." It would be erroneous, however, to suppose that Mike
left Fellowship House converted to Gandhism. The relevance
of the Indian experience to his search for a method to eradicate evil would occur to him only later, in the crucible of the

Montgomery boycott, and then only after a felicitous cue from an unexpected source.

Pacifism remained very much in the air during his final year, however. Shortly before Dr. Johnson's lecture, the noted pacifist A. J. Muste had visited Crozer. Muste was executive secretary of the Fellowship of Reconciliation from 1940 to 1953, to which Niebuhr, Bayard Rustin, and James Farmer at one time belonged. Several of the members of the Fellowship of Reconciliation had been instrumental in founding the Congress of Racial Equality (CORE) in 1942. Muste's pacifism impressed Mike as unrealistic, partly because of his awareness of Niebuhr's salient criticisms. Nevertheless, he reserved final judgment. "A. J.'s sincerity and his hardheaded ability to defend his position stayed with me through the years," he said.

"Martin King began as an uncritical disciple of Rauschenbusch and I started from a position as an uncritical Niebuhrian," says Professor Smith. By his third year, Mike had in fact come to appreciate the naïveté of much of the Social Gospel position. Its "superficial optimism" and tendency to identify "the Kingdom of God with a particular social and economic system" no longer appealed. He might have added that the distress he felt over the works of Nietzsche, Marx, and Niebuhr had reached a chronic state. *Genealogy of Morals* and *Will to Power* temporarily derailed Mike. He read that the supposed power of love is really the impotence engendered by a slave morality. He was troubled but not as profoundly as he may have supposed. Nietzsche was too shrilly atheistic and egocentric to maim him in his philosophic growth. Marx was far more threatening. During his Christmas holidays in 1949, Mike devoted himself exclusively to a study of his works. It was not the positive contentions of communism that disturbed him. He was pained by Marxism because, as he saw it, it was the most compromising of Christian heresies, arising out of the failure of the Christian church to resist the social

exploitation and moral indifference rampant with the growth
of industrial capitalism. "With all its false assumptions and
evil methods, communism grew as a protest against the hard-
ships of the underprivileged," Mike wrote. He could never
accept without reservation a philosophy that was atheistic and
deterministic, but his conviction that Marx had constructed a
valid schema for assaying the defects of capitalism was so
intense that Reverend Barbour thinks that Mike was "economically a Marxist."

The problem of Niebuhr was to agitate Mike for a number
of years. Niebuhr's arguments against the Panglossism of the
Social Gospel awoke in him the sense of realism firmly im-
planted by racial discrimination and the counsels of his practical parents. "I became so enamored of [Niebuhr's] social
ethics that I almost fell into the trap of accepting uncritically
everything that he wrote," Mike admitted. The pacifism of
Gandhi and Muste, Niebuhr contended, could succeed only if
the oppressors shared the morality of the oppressed. The
British in India were wise, fundamentally decent, and tired.
Gandhi's campaign made sense there. But gentlemanly oppressors are a luxury, Niebuhr contended: "If we believe that
if Britain had only been fortunate enough to produce 30 per
cent of conscientious objectors to military society, Hitler's
heart would have been softened and he would not have dared
to attack Poland, we hold a faith which no historic reality
justifies." The best defense against tyranny is a responsible
and positive opposition to evil. Niebuhr deprecated the
sanguine pacifist confidence that ethical rectitude would
gradually triumph merely because of its normative desirability.
This species of moral naïveté is tantamount to collusion with
evil.

To deal with Niebuhr, Mike reviewed the writings of
Gandhi, Muste, and Richard Gregg (*The Power of Nonviolence*). This enabled him to grasp what he took to be the
essential flaw in Niebuhr's antipacifism. "True pacifism," he

reasoned, "is not unrealistic submission to evil power, as Niebuhr contends. It is rather a courageous confrontation of evil
by the power of love, in the faith that it is better to be the
recipient of violence that the inflicter of it." But Niebuhr's
admonitions were instructive in that they commended a form
of Christian pragmatism in assessing social systems that radically qualified the reassuring teleology of the Social Gospel.
Christ was not invariably on the side of the proponents of
democratic government, mixed economy, and world government, the philosopher reminded. His great contribution to
contemporary theology, Mike concluded, was that Niebuhr
"refuted the false optimism characteristic of a great segment
of Protestant liberalism."

The problems raised by Reinhold Niebuhr worried Mike
into an insight whose implications he was to pursue doggedly
during the next three years. He perceived that the philosophical affirmations of Niebuhr (and of Nietzsche and Marx, as
well, for that matter) were determined by a particular view
of man's spiritual nature. And man's intrinsic nature, Mike
concluded, could be discerned only in conjunction with a
consideration of the nature of evil and of God. For Niebuhr,
the drama of the cross and what he termed the "permanent
myths" in Christianity made inescapable the truth that evil
is objective and ineradicable. It resides in human fallibility
and is exacerbated by the refusal of mankind to accept its
finite endowments. Thus, if evil (original sin) is real, then
man's ultimate concern must be personal salvation. "All of us
continue to be," Niebuhr affirmed, "even in our highest moral
achievements, in contradiction to God and therefore require
His mercy." "While I still believed in man's potential for
good," Mike explained, "Niebuhr made me realize his potential for evil as well." He did not become a Niebuhrian, but
he went more than half way in his direction and took Rauschenbusch along with him.

In June, 1951, Mike graduated from Crozer with the highest grade average in his class. He delivered the valedictory address and was awarded the Pearl M. Plafker citation for the most outstanding student and the J. Lewis Crozer fellowship of $1,300 for graduate study. From his parents he received a green Chevrolet. Again, the following September, the cycle began that would end in another degree. At Boston University, he enrolled as a doctoral candidate in the faculty of philosophy under Professor Edgar S. Brightman. His adjustment to the impersonality of the city and newness of the University was made easier by the companionship of Philip Lenud from Morehouse, who was enrolled in the divinity school at neighboring Tufts University. Aggressive and sociable, Philip had assembled a variegated coterie of friends and acquainted himself with some of the more interesting spots in the black section of Boston. For entertainment, Mike and Philip frequented the Totem Pole, a lively nightclub, and, to satisfy Mike's craving for Southern cuisine, they regularly patronized Mrs. Jackson's Western Lunch Box. He and Philip decided to pool their resources and, at the end of Mike's first semester, they took rooms on Massachusetts Avenue across from the Savoy Ballroom. A comment on the incompleteness of Northern racial comity is revealed by the fact that they never attended the almost nightly college dances at the Savoy, fearing the glacial reception their presence might elicit. They were sufficiently absorbed, in any case, by the universe of searching discourse and debate pivoting around the Philosophical Club, a loosely knit forum they had organized that met each Friday or Saturday night at their apartment. Initially, the members of the Philosophical Club were black male university students. Not long after its inception, however, it became interracial and, more pleasantly, sexually integrated.

To broaden his intellectual base, Mike took for two years courses in Harvard's department of philosophy parallel to his own at Boston University. There his critical appreciation of the philosophers of existentialism (Kierkegaard, Heidegger, Sartre) was supplemented. His appreciation of Hegel had also been greatly enriched by Professor Brightman (who died at the end of Mike's first year). Mike was never to alter his belief in the materialization of spirit through the medium of the dialectic. His Rauschenbuschian leanings were to persuade him, further, that the course of world history, seen in its most complete dimensions, moves toward the universal justice anticipated in Hegel's *Philosophy of Right*. Professor Allan Knight Chalmers and Walter Meulder, dean of the School of Theology at Boston University, sustained his interest in the practical applications of nonviolent philosophies. He began to realize that "the method is passive physically, but strongly active spiritually."

His examination books during this period reveal a vast program of reading whose dividends were reflected in a knowledge that ranged from superficial or highly derivative to not so superficial and bordering on original. He had prepared for his qualifying examination in the history of philosophy by reviewing introductory works in philosophy. His treatment of the Milesian, Pythagorean, Eleatic, and Atomist philosophers of Greece is correct and competent though largely confined to the scrapings of key terms and summary generalizations from standard texts. It is, nonetheless, an impressive examination booklet, and Professor L. Harold DeWolf's mark of "excellent" is probably not overly generous. Mike's two treatments of personalism are models of clarity and mature analysis, particularly the portions dealing with Renouvier, Hermann Lotze, and Borden P. Bowne. He perceived the epistemological and ethical relativism of Renouvier and appreciated its slight advance over the solipsism inherent in Berkeley's radical idealism but put it firmly aside as too "relativistic and finitistic." With Bowne, Knudson, and Brightman, Mike continued the search for a synthesis reconciling ethical and epistemological subjectivity and idealism. Brightman greatly im-

proved upon the ideas of Bowne by grafting a definite methodology onto the latter's personalism. By the time he was
ready to write his dissertation, Mike had succeeded in reconciling, to his own satisfaction, the antipodal interpretations
of the human condition that so bitterly divided the philosophers and theologians he had determined to master: the
dilemma of relativism versus idealism. "Personalism's insistence that only personality—finite and infinite—is ultimately
real strengthened me in two convictions: it gave me metaphysical basis and philosophical grounding for the idea of a
personal God, and it gave me a metaphysical basis for the
dignity and worth of all human personality," Mike wrote.

The consolations of philosophy sustained and challenged
Mike King, but he needed more than the stimulation of
dedicated professors and provocative philosophical tomes to
round out his life. As he told Mrs. Powell, an Atlantan residing in Boston, "Mary, I wish I knew a few girls from down
home to go out with. I tell you, these Boston girls are something else. The ones I've been seeing are so reserved." And
Mrs. Powell could tell by the way Mike drawled out his plea in
the Western Lunch Box that day that he really did need the
familiar and empathetic companionship of a Southern girl.
She suggested that it might be possible for him to arrange a
meeting with Coretta Scott, a graduate of Antioch College,
presently studying voice at the New England Conservatory of
Music.

Miss Scott was the daughter of a prosperous storekeeper
from Marion, Alabama. She was attractive and endowed with
charm and intelligence. Mike was almost tactless in importun-
ing Mrs. Powell for the address. He also wanted her to convey
to Miss Scott a description of himself that was scarcely in
keeping with the love of truth he displayed in the classroom.
Mrs. Powell, although willing, warned him that Coretta was
exceedingly reserved in her dealings with unknown young men
and inclined to be contemptuous of ministers of the gospel.

Nevertheless, a telephone number was given, and Mike phoned Coretta a few days later. Martin King, Jr., was certainly not inexperienced in his dealings with women. Indeed, he fancied himself something of a Don Juan. And, had Coretta been the ordinary female, ready to be dazzled by the ordinary suitor, Mike's clichéd introduction, delivered in his most liquid baritone, might have been overwhelming. "I am like Napoleon at Waterloo before your charms," he oozed into the telephone receiver. Coretta's rejoinder to his fulsome salutation was devastating: "Why, that's absurd. You haven't seen me yet."

The future Mrs. King was a remarkable young woman. Like Reverend Alfred Daniel Williams, her father had bravely stood against the hopeless statistics of black triumph over white tyranny and won. For generations the blacks in Perry County, Alabama, had been the victims of brutality, overt and subtle, that reduced the overwhelming majority to a level of such placid and almost grateful servitude as to appear to justify the Southern white's stereotypes about its dependency and idiocy. Somehow, though, the Scott family had managed to cling to the few acres of land it had obtained at the end of the Civil War. Obadiah Scott held to the quaintly courageous view that "If you look a white man in the eyes, he won't harm you." The family had avoided personal harm but not the destruction by fire of its dearly bought mill. The Depression years were exceedingly bitter. The Scotts struggled on, and, by the end of World War II, they owned a combination filling station and grocery store, a trucking firm, and a chicken farm. The right combination of money and personal application afforded Coretta the opportunity to attend Antioch College. She had earned outstanding marks at the interracially staffed Lincoln Missionary School in Marion, Alabama. At Antioch, she maintained an adequate grade average and also experienced, like Martin at Crozer, a memorable lecture. The young pacifist Bayard Rustin delivered several talks at the

college, and Coretta was profoundly impressed. She was an
activist by upbringing. Years later, in the King's Montgomery
kitchen, Coretta confided to Professor DeWolf that, as a
student, she had made up her mind that she would never
marry a man who was not highly intelligent and not a civil
rights activist. At the time of their meeting, the philosophical
Martin King supplied only the first half of her matrimonial
imperative.

Despite Mary Powell's sincere representations of Mike's
estimable qualities, Coretta inclined to view him as "an older
man, pious, narrow-minded, and not too well-trained, like
most of the preachers I had known around my Marion, Alabama, home." Mike's inauspicious telephone call had not
helped matters. Their first meeting was memorable. The
philosophy student had the good sense to drop the "jivey"
superlatives that had served him so well in the past. Instead,
he discussed politics and philosophy and was so impressed by
his date's conversational competence that he blurted out, "Oh,
I see you know about some other things besides music." As
the evening wore on, Coretta thought a great deal about this
short, confident, and eloquent preacher. Decidedly, he was not
a garden variety Baptist minister. She was impressed. She was
scarcely prepared, however, for a proposal of marriage at the
end of this first date. "The more I saw of him, the more I
liked him," Coretta admitted. After seeing more of him, she
decided to accede to his repeated offers of marriage. Martin's
father, "Daddy" King to Coretta, interposed strong objections, however. "I wanted Martin to marry another girl," he
admits, "and I wanted him to get married soon." The other
girl belong to a properly bourgeois Atlanta family. Coretta
lacked her poise and social connections. Martin and his sister
finally overcame Reverend King's objections, and, on June
18, 1953, the couple was married, in the garden of Coretta's
Marion, Alabama, home, by Mike's father. She gained by this
union a man who would fulfill her criteria for a mate more
completely than any other American male born in her gen-

eration could have. But it was only human that, in the midst
of her happiness, she reflected that she had sacrificed her years
of preparation as a singer, that her artistic talents and careerist
drives would have to be subordinated to the requirements of
connubial companionship and homemaking.

They returned to Boston in the green Chevrolet in the fall
of 1953. Mike had to discuss the general outlines and goals
of his dissertation. For two years, he had been under the
direction of L. Harold DeWolf, professor of systematic theology, a stimulating teacher and, like Brightman, a personal-
ist. Mike had been principally concerned to resolve aspects of
the problem of the nature of God as conceived by man. To
sharpen his own position, he elected to investigate the divergent theisms of Henry Wieman and Paul Tillich. At a ten-
day religious retreat in 1935, held at Fletcher Farm in Proc-
torsville, Vermont, Tillich and Wieman had monopolized
the discussions to argue strongly divergent concepts of God.
Tillich proclaimed that, while he accepted the need for
pluralism in human affairs, he was a transcendental monist.
Wieman, on the other hand, was the leading exponent of behaviorism in theology. He defined God as "that something
upon which human life is most dependent for its security, welfare, and increasing abundance . . . that something of supreme value which constitutes the most important condition."
For Tillich, God was beyond definition and description. Indeed, his intellectual humility before what he called the
"Abyss" was such that Tillich denied the possibility of a
Christian philosophy.

Mike prepared his dissertation, "A Comparison of the Conceptions of God in the Thinking of Paul Tillich and Henry
Nelson Wieman," with more than his usual meticulous discipline. He sought the advice of Reinhold Niebuhr. And,
from Ascona, Switzerland, Paul Tillich wrote, in response to a
letter late in 1953, to encourage him in the selection of his
topic and to confirm that, to his knowledge, it had not been
formally explored. In a second letter, written more than a

year later, Tillich proposed a meeting upon his return to Harvard after a year in Scotland. If the meeting actually occurred, there appears to be no record of it.

Although his dissertation was completed in Montgomery and not submitted for approval until late in 1955, Mike reached his central conclusion well before that time. "All the conclusions of Tillich and Wieman," he wrote, "seem to point to an impersonal God." These conclusions were erroneous, he believed. God is much more to the human experience than the "creative event" of Wieman or the *esse ipsum* of Tillich. He is more than the historic process of Hegel or the energy upon which Rauschenbusch's evolution toward the secular kingdom depended. In the end, Mike most nearly approached the Niebuhrian emphasis upon a personal, orthodox God offering personal salvation. Human nature requires far more than theological abstractions to guide it. "Reason is darkened by sin," he wrote sometime later. "Reason, devoid of the purifying power of faith, can never free itself from distortions and rationalizations."

Martin Luther King, Jr., was not an original philosopher, although, after Morehouse, it was perhaps the thing he most desired to be. There are legions of audiences that spent Sunday mornings, convocation periods, and evenings in auditoriums listening to him rhapsodically enumerate the principal ideas in Western philosophy from Thales of Miletus to Camus. And there are few who followed his career who have not heard his favorite discourse on the meaning and significance of *eros*, *philia*, and *agape*. Such displays of encyclopedic knowledge sprang partly from a Baptist preacher's love of showmanship, and Mike was a superb actor. Partly, too, this was the venial intellectual arrogance of a young man who held a doctorate from one of the nation's better universities. But there was, undeniably, also an element of self-deception and self-mystification as to his philosophical acumen.

A candid assessment of his abilities must hold that, despite his broad reading and rigorous application, Mike lacked the comprehensive critical apparatus and the inspired vision that bless good philosophers. Although he was of a tolerant cast of mind, his intellectual range was, in fact, narrow. "Being raised in a rather strict fundamentalist tradition," he wrote, "I was occasionally shocked as my intellectual journey carried me through new and sometimes complex doctrinal lands." Much of his philosophical intelligence was partial and impressionistic. There is no indication that he was familiar with European logical positivism. Nor was he abreast of the literary ferment around Proust, Joyce, Kafka, Hemingway, Dos Passos, and Faulkner that agitated his generation of students. Neither Crozer nor Boston University entirely wrenched him from the cast set by his parochial, if advantaged, Atlanta upbringing. Highly sensitive and intelligent, highly competent scholastically, capable of occasional insights bordering on genius, his intelligence was essentially derivative.

3

Stride Toward Freedom

> Lift every voice and sing till earth and heaven
> ring, ring with the harmony of liberty.
>
> JAMES WELDON JOHNSON

ONE SATURDAY AFTERNOON in January, 1954, as he drove to
Montgomery, Alabama, listening to the strains of a favorite
Donizetti aria on his radio, Mike King was positive that he
had made the correct choice in Dexter Avenue Baptist
Church. Dexter's standards, he knew, were formidably high.
His predecessor there, Reverend Vernon Johns, immensely
respected if not loved, was emotional only in the domain of
civil rights and given to sparse, iconoclastic eloquence. For his
first test, therefore, Mike had burnished his finest sermon,
edited out its more purple phrases, tightened its concepts. But
he retained a judicious combination of grand images, resonant
polysyllables, and reasonably obscure references. Oratorical
restraint and intellectual clarity were important, but Dexter's
congregation was not so sophisticated as to relish the bland
and slumberous variety of homiletics typical of more sedate
white Protestant services. King's "The Three Dimensions of a
Complete Life" was carefully composed to satisfy his parishioners. Reverend Hal Carter, then an assistant pastor of Dexter,
remembers this sermon as splendidly composed and masterfully delivered. The congregation was highly impressed. Mike

returned to Atlanta for the remainder of the Christmas holidays, and then went on to Boston University, reasonably confident that the church's trustees would invite him to be its pastor. He had been pastor of Dexter for a little more than a year when the incident of Rosa Parks occurred.

Had Rosa Parks been less primly composed, had her diction betrayed the mangled speech of the ordinary black passenger, the outcome of Thursday, December 1, 1955, could have been different. The infraction of the Montgomery City Bus Lines' seating regulations might not have been handled with what was, by Southern etiquette, uncustomary circumspection. Even unprotesting compliance with the command to move toward the rear was not infrequently accompanied by threats, blows, and, in one recent instance, death. Driver J. F. Blake did not know Mrs. Rosa Parks. But it was apparent to him that his quietly adamant passenger was not drunk, was not deranged, and certainly was not ordinary. Moreover, he was not generally given to violence, and to use expletives before the amazed and slightly embarrassed white passengers (several of whom were female) struck him as unprofessional. Court Square, in the heart of town, was exceedingly busy that evening, because of Christmas shopping. Traffic was hectic and thickening. Blake's decision to summon the police appeared to offer the most expedient solution to this extraordinary dilemma. Officers Day and Mixon arrived almost immediately, to place Mrs. Parks in custody.

As Blake drove to the next stop, black passengers shook their heads commiseratively and muttered the "Lawd, Lawds" that had been reserved for generations for acts of futile resistance to white injustice. It is probable that some of them deplored Mrs. Parks' behavior. More than a year before, a black witness had lectured Reverend Johns, who had refused to surrender his seat to a white: "You ought to knowed better." What Mrs. Parks had done defied a canon that white Montgomery had enforced with such ruthless vigor through

the decades that it was now obeyed with alacrity and almost
without reflection by the majority of the city's black citizens.
By her dignified bearing during her arrest and arraignment
and because of her impeccable reputation in the black community, Mrs. Parks' defiance compelled the city to charge
her explicitly with the violation of the municipal ordinance
governing racial accommodation on publicly owned vehicles,
and not, as was usually the case, with the elastic offense of
disorderly conduct. The cursory mention of this event deep
between the pages of the *Montgomery Advertiser* could not
belie its portent. Mrs. Parks' action was highly unusual, but,
despite the city's tyrannizing racism, there was evidence that
it was neither unprecedented nor unlikely to be repeated. Indeed, it was the fourth in a series of similar acts of defiance
that year. Three ladies, Miss Colvin, Mrs. Smith, and Mrs.
Browder, had refused on different occasions to evacuate their
seats upon the command of a bus driver.

A change in race relations, subterranean, cautious, and only
tentatively directed, was under way in Montgomery. The community had recently been stirred by the outrageous interroga-
tion and trial of young Jeremiah Reeves, a black musician
convicted of raping a white woman. The local and state chapters of the NAACP were still battling for his life in the courts.
The nullification by the U.S. Supreme Court of the doctrine
of separate equality in education had provided a massive antidote to black despair throughout the South in 1954. And,
within Montgomery's black community, there was the irascible
and eccentric militancy of Reverend Johns, the stolid and
fearless generalship of pullman porter E. D. Nixon, and the
sound instruction in regional politics of Alabama State College's Professor Rufus Lewis. Martin Luther King, Jr., had
not been there long and, therefore, even though he was highly
esteemed for his oratory and academic achievements, he was
not yet an influential leader.

The news of Mrs. Parks' arrest spread rapidly by telephone
to the leaders of the black community. She had contacted

Mrs. Nixon immediately, and, by late that evening, Thursday, December 1, a plan for the unprecedented mobilization of Montgomery blacks was imminent. Nixon, who had been on the move most of the day, learned of the arrest when he returned briefly to his NAACP office and read his secretary's note to phone his wife. Mrs. Nixon's details were spotty, and so he rang the police department. His name meant nothing to the young desk clerk, and he was told that the matter was none of his "God-damned business"—standard police etiquette when dealing with assertive "niggers." Undaunted, Nixon went directly to the police station to arrange Mrs. Parks' release. When he phoned Mrs. Jo Ann Robinson, president of the Women's Political Council and an assistant professor of English at black Alabama State College, he found that Attorney Fred Gray had already apprised her of the situation.

Mrs. Robinson's organization, created in 1951 in response to the refusal of the local white League of Women Voters to integrate, had a membership of nearly two hundred. Benefiting from the slight differential in forbearance shown by Southern whites in their dealings with black women as opposed to black men, and exceedingly fortunate in the caliber of its leadership, the Women's Political Council had taken the initiative in demanding fairer treatment for the city's black citizens. A handful of courageous men, such as Attorney Gray, Mr. Nixon, and Professor James Pierce, had collaborated with the Council. It had succeeded, in 1955, in pressuring the white merchants to negotiate out of existence the separation of drinking fountains and the custom of not supplying titles of Mrs. and Miss when billing female customers. In September, a delegation from the Council, joined by Attorney Gray and Professor Pierce, met with the Montgomery Parks and Recreation Board to demand equal recreational facilities for blacks. Mrs. Robinson and her colleagues had even begun to lay the strategy for a boycott of the city's buses. Only the discovery that a defendant who had been arrested some months before, for refusing to yield her seat to a white, was also an unwed mother prevented the plan from being put into action.

"This is what we've been waiting for," Nixon boomed into the telephone receiver. Mrs. Robinson agreed, stated that Fred Gray thought likewise, and enthusiastically pleaded with him to take the lead in organizing a community boycott. An hour or so earlier, when he was driving Mrs. Parks home from the police station, Nixon had praised her courage and speculated about the reaction of the community to her trial the following Monday. He asked if she were willing to be the symbol that would galvanize the black citizenry. He scarcely needed to remind her of the risks. Her previous service as secretary for the local NAACP chapter was a potent weapon in the hands of the opposition. She would certainly not be able to keep her job as seamstress in one of the city's large department stores. Mrs. Parks agreed to cooperate in any plan he devised. Although her action that Thursday evening had been wholly unprompted, she may have realized subconsciously that, behind her demur to Driver Blake, an entire community was ready to assert its rights at long last. "She was anchored to that seat," Mike King wrote, "by the accumulated indignities of days gone by and the boundless aspirations of generations yet unborn." In her gracious humility, Mrs. Parks simply stated that she had not moved because she was "tired."

Confirmed in his initial reaction by the Women's Political Council and pressed by it to persuade the community, Nixon awakened his wife late that night to tell her that he had decided to spearhead a boycott of the buses. Shortly after 5 A.M. Friday morning, Nixon phoned Reverend Martin Luther King, Jr., the third person on his list of Montgomery leaders who still did not have news of the arrest. He told him about Mrs. Parks' trouble and asked him to join a committee to organize a boycott. Although he was in sympathy with the proposal, Martin asked for time to reflect: "Brother Nixon, let me think it out a while. Call me back." Nixon continued down his list. Martin had only recently declined the presidency of the local NAACP because of his pastoral responsibilities. Yolanda Denise, his first child, was only two weeks old. Moreover, on several occasions he had watched jealousies, opportunism, and apathy corrode noble undertakings in the black community. He had doubts about the dependability of many of his fellow ministers. With the exception of the quixotic Reverend Johns, they had not been notably active in civil rights. "The apparent apathy of Negro ministers," Martin confessed, "presented a special problem." Mrs. Robinson less charitably charged that they were busy "preaching God and raising their salaries." When Nixon telephoned the second time, however, Martin immediately offered his cooperation. In the interim, Martin had conferred with Reverend Ralph David Abernathy, Mrs. Parks' pastor and the first name on Nixon's list.

Ralph Abernathy was an exception to the ministerial torpor of Montgomery. Short and corpulent, deliberate of movement, slow and confidential in speech, he and Martin were already inseparable friends. "He looked older than his years" (he was then twenty-nine years old), Ralph's friend said, "but a boyish smile always lurked beneath the surface of his face." He was a practical man and a rousing speaker. Although he possessed a bachelor's degree from the segregated local state college, where he had once taught sociology, Ralph's intellectual pretentions were modest. Dexter Avenue Baptist Church was the place to go if one wished to experience the messages of Socrates, Aquinas, and Hegel in their full contemporary relevance. For straightforward preaching, one went to Ralph's church, Montgomery First Baptist. The atmosphere lent itself to shouts of "amen," shrieks of joy, and general getting to the nitty gritty of things. He knew the people better than Martin did because he came from Marengo County, Alabama, the heart of the Black Belt. But unlike the

typical product of that region, Ralph was combative. His
father owned a 500-acre plantation, and the son could boast
that he had "never worked a day for a white man." Nixon was
not surprised that Ralph was prepared to help organize a
boycott.

Now the three, Nixon, Ralph, and Martin, worked in concert to alert the other leaders and to propose decisive action.
The ladies of the Council were even busier. The boycott was,
after all, their idea; and Mrs. Mary Fair Burks and Jo Ann
Robinson were determined to maneuver the men, especially
the ministers, into a firm position from which retreat would
be difficult and embarrassing. By early afternoon, Friday,
December 2, Mrs. Robinson had prepared ten stencils, each
containing this statement in duplicate:

> Don't ride the bus to work, to town, to school, or any place
> Monday, December 5.
>
> Another Negro woman has been arrested and put in jail because
> she refused to give up her bus seat.
>
> Don't ride the bus to work, to town, to school, or anywhere
> on Monday. If you work, take a cab, or share a ride, or walk.
>
> Come to a mass meeting, Monday at 7:00 P.M., at the Holt
> Street Baptist Church for further instruction.

Then she drove to Alabama State College, where she cor-
ralled two loyal students. They entered the administration
building, unauthorized, and reproduced 40,000 copies of the
statement. Before 5 P.M., the bulk of the copies had been
distributed to the community by students and members of
the Council. Meanwhile, Nixon, Abernathy, and King had
obtained the sanction of the president of the Baptist Ministerial Alliance, Reverend H. H. Hubbard, to use that organization's name in their summons to the clergy to meet that
evening at 7 P.M. in the Dexter Avenue Baptist Church.
Reverend Abernathy acted as emissary to the Methodist
ministers, most of whom were attending a meeting in a local
church. A number of key figures were contacted, at Mr.

Nixon's request, by the widow of a prominent dentist, Mrs. A. A. West.

Before the Dexter meeting was convened, two developments occurred that were to give decisive shape to the course of events in Montgomery. Mr. Nixon left the city late in the morning to make his scheduled railroad run; had he been present, Reverend King believed, "he would probably have been automatically selected to preside." Nixon, the unquestioned senior leader of the community, was a key figure in A. Philip Randolph's Brotherhood of Sleeping Car Porters and perhaps unsurpassed in his intimate knowledge of the workings of the local white establishment. Had he been able to serve, it is highly unlikely that Martin's talents would have been fully utilized. In all probability, Nixon would have fulfilled the 1948 prediction of an enthusiastic French writer that he would set the South on fire. As Professor Lawrence D. Reddick observes, a number of impressionable journalists were to leave Montgomery convinced that Nixon was the *primum mobile* of the boycott.

The second development was the acquisition by the *Montgomery Advertiser* of the text of Mrs. Robinson's leaflet. Martin King believed that an illiterate servant had given her leaflet to her white employer to be read to her. The employer contacted the newspaper. Nixon, however, dismisses this explanation, for he relates that, before departing on Friday, he had contacted Joe Azbell of the *Advertiser*. "I knew this reporter very well," he says. "I talked to him, and I told him, I said, here, you got a chance to do something for Negroes. If you promise you'll play it up strong in your paper Sunday, I'll give you a hot tip." The character of Azbell and the relative objectivity of his subsequent reporting dispose one to accept the Nixon explanation.

The meeting at Dexter was half an hour late in starting. In the absence of Nixon, the group elected Reverend L. Roy Bennett, president of the Interdenominational Ministerial

Alliance, as its chairman. To the impatient Jo Ann Robinson, it seemed that the wrangle over the selection of a chairman and procedural matters was interminable, the ministers doing almost all the talking. Reverend Bennett was not an altogether felicitous choice. Accustomed to playing a prominent role, he opened the meeting on a highly peremptory note, forbidding all discussion of the agenda he proposed and refusing to entertain questions or points of order. Forty-five minutes of pandemonium ensued before Reverend Bennett acceded to the will of the majority that a period of discussion precede the formation of committees and the issuing of directives to the community. Then, falteringly, contentiously, the meeting assumed direction and corporate purpose.

Surprisingly, there was not one cautious suggestion that the proposed boycott might be unwise or untimely. All the participants had been inspired by the example of the gentle Mrs. Parks. The ministers, never a predictable lot, endorsed the plan unanimously. They agreed to take the issue to their congregations that Sunday. They also decided to distribute additional leaflets, amending Jo Ann Robinson's text slightly, to ensure maximal community knowledge. Martin offered to have them run off on his church's mimeograph machine. A final matter of great importance concerned the cooperation of the city's eighteen black taxi companies; Reverend W. J. Powell of the African Methodist Episcopal Zion denomination was vouchsafed this responsibility. The meeting adjourned shortly before midnight. The preliminary strategy had been completed for one of America's most epochal developments.

The following day, Saturday, was a day of community preparation. The ladies of the Women's Political Council pre-empted innumerable telephone circuits in fulfillment of their leaders' mandate to spread the word. Barbershops became forums for expostulation and debate. In the bars and pool halls, idle teenagers and community toughs reverentially re-enacted the saga of Rosa Parks and solemnized their respect for the lady by vowing to "beat hell out of a few bus drivers." Ministers, after double-checking the resolve of their colleagues, prepared to deliver uncompromising homilies to their congregations to defy the devilish bus company. And the taxi committee went about its business with heartening success. By day's end, nearly all the black sections of Montgomery had received a quota of leaflets.

Contrary to Martin King's recollection, the *Montgomery Advertiser* had nothing to say about these activities that day. Sunday morning, however, was momentous. As the ministers exhorted their folds, Joe Azbell's front-page article in the *Advertiser* alerted the entire population of Montgomery, black and white, to the impending boycott. After church, the leaders continued to organize the community. Black solidarity was, unbelievably, almost total. Late that night, Martin received a telephone call from a member of the taxi committee. The taxi companies had unanimously agreed to transport boycotters for the same fare charged by the bus company.

Before December 1, the number of blacks who had challenged the city's public transportation ordinance numbered, in living memory, less than a dozen. On the morning of December 5, less than a dozen boarded the city buses. Before going to Mrs. Parks' trial, Martin roamed the city by car to gauge the success of the boycott. He observed that each bus passing through black neighborhoods was escorted by two motorcycle policemen, purportedly to protect passengers from "goon squads" assigned to dissuade blacks from flouting the boycott. The arrest of Fred Daniels on such a charge only amused the black citizens, for he was immediately released after his alleged victim revised her testimony to the effect that this young man had only been helping her cross the street. The buses were empty. By 9 A.M., as he drove to the courthouse, Martin knew with absolute certainty that the boycott was a success.

Mrs. Parks' trial was brief, the verdict predetermined. She was fined $10 for her crime and charged to pay the court costs. Her attorney, Fred Gray, immediately filed an appeal. Afterward, on the courthouse steps, Abernathy, Nixon, and Reverend E. N. French, another member of the African Methodist Episcopal Zion faith, discussed with Martin the desirability of forming a permanent organization to superintend the boycott. Martin readily agreed, and they separated with the understanding that the matter would be aired at a 3 P.M. meeting to be convoked by Reverend Bennett.

The Montgomery Improvement Association (MIA) was the brainchild of Ralph Abernathy. Its leader was to be chosen by Ed Nixon. A dynamic speaker was required, one with intelligence and character. Martin possessed these qualities abundantly. But there were additional prerequisites of a less innocent nature. Whoever headed the MIA, to be effective, must not have resided in Montgomery's querulous black community long enough to have acquired a great many enemies. Such a person would ideally be able to pack up for another job elsewhere, in the likely event of failure of the movement and retribution from the white community. He should also be sufficiently naïve, or brave, to accept designation as the exclusive leader of the boycott. Ed Nixon knew the weak spots in the community's stamina. The men who had attended the Dexter meeting did not lack courage on the whole, but they were practical men, burdened by family responsibilities and uniformly circumscribed in their professional options. Nixon informally polled the reactions to Martin Luther King of several key persons who were to attend the 3 P.M. meeting. They were favorable. At the meeting, as Martin settled into his chair, he heard Professor Rufus Lewis nominate him to the presidency of the MIA. Instantly, the motion was seconded and carried. "The action caught me unawares," he confessed. "It happened so quickly that I did not even have time to think it through."

A Sunday sermon required from Martin an average of fifteen hours of preparation. In less than three, he would address the largest gathering he had ever confronted on an issue more portentous in its practical ramifications than any he had ever contemplated. Moreover, Ed Nixon had seen to it that the responsibilities of his role were unambiguous. Before Reverend Bennett's meeting adjourned, several participants had recommended that, in the interests of secrecy, the evening mass meeting be restricted to song and prayer, that no public announcement be made of the names of MIA officers, and that unsigned mimeographed instructions be carefully distributed to the audience. One participant even suggested that the total success of a one-day boycott was sufficient proof of the power of the black community. Nixon, thoroughly disgusted, informed them that they were "acting like little boys." The opposition would learn, sooner or later, that Martin was president of the MIA, Reverend Bennett its vice-president, Reverend E. N. French its corresponding secretary, Mrs. Erna A. Dungee its financial secretary, and Nixon, himself, its treasurer. Candor now was assurance of courage later, Nixon declared. With considerable trepidation, the force of this argument was conceded.

As Martin left for his South Jackson Street parsonage, he anxiously pondered the implications of his instantaneous and unsought promotion. Less than one hour now remained before his appearance at the Holt Street Baptist Church. Upon learning of his election to the presidency of the new organization, Coretta reassured him that "whatever you do, you have my backing." This was more than the vote of confidence of a dutiful wife. She and Martin had discussed the philosophical aspects of the boycott late Sunday night, and he had told her of his emotions upon first reading Thoreau's essay "Civil Disobedience." Passive acceptance of evil, he told Coretta, is tantamount to its perpetration. The two Niebuhrians Kenneth Smith and J. Pius Barbour would have been pleased if

they had heard him say his. Martin now went into his study.
Twenty minutes remained. Written preparation was impossible. He had no alternative but to address the meeting without notes. At 6:50 P.M., he left for the church.

Nearly four thousand people were standing outside Holt
Street Church when Martin arrived. The unseasonable
warmth of the December evening had encouraged people to
attend. A prayer, a scripture reading, and then Reverend
Bennett presented Martin Luther King. It is a safe prediction
that no black minister will ever again affect his listeners in
quite the same manner as Martin Luther King did that
evening. It was the beginning of an era. Cadence of voice,
rhetoric, and sincerity combined to fill the church with
exaltation, music, threnody, and common sense. First he told
of Mrs. Parks' abuse; then he catalogued the injustices of the
bus company. Then he spoke directly to the audience, and
over the crescendos of "amen" he proclaimed,

> But there comes a time when people get tired. We are here
> this evening to say to those who have mistreated us so long that
> we are tired—tired of being segregated and humiliated, tired of
> being kicked about by the brutal feet of oppression. We have
> no alternative but to protest. For many years, we have shown
> amazing patience. We have sometimes given our white brothers
> the feeling that we liked the way we were being treated. But we
> come here tonight to be saved from that patience that makes
> us patient with anything less than freedom and justice.

Ed Nixon and Jo Ann Robinson exchanged thankful glances.
They were deeply moved too but not beyond the ability to
ponder the difficult way ahead. After Mrs. Parks diffidently acknowledged the ovation of the audience, Ralph Abernathy presented the three-point demands of the boycott: (1) courteous
treatment by bus drivers; (2) a first-come first-served seating
arrangement, with blacks filling the rear and whites the front;
and (3) the employment of black drivers on predominantly
black routes.

People, even the most apathetic and brutalized people, do tire of injustice, as Martin Luther King had said. And the discontent of Montgomery blacks was the first chapter in a book of racial unrest the conclusion of which it is still not possible to write. What began in Montgomery, Alabama, was to be repeated throughout the South, mainly for the same reasons. In that city, 50,000 blacks feared the arbitrary power of 70,000 whites. If he was not a member of the minuscule black upper class, the black denizen of Montgomery had a median annual income of $970, as opposed to the $1,730 of a white laborer. His housing conditions were atrocious. Only 31 per cent of his neighbors possessed indoor flush toilets, while 94 per cent of the whites were able to perform their necessary functions aseptically with no need to leave their houses. The black man's schools and public recreation facilities were patently inferior, and, if some youngsters received a decent education, it was due mainly to fortunate parental endowment and, infrequently, superhuman pedagogy. He knew the police force to be invariably disrespectful and usually brutal. He had never exercised the right of ballot. Only two thousand Negroes in Montgomery County were registered, and almost all of them were white-collar workers. And, irrespective of the level to which his education and income rose, there were only three points of interracial social contact in Montgomery: the two Air Force bases, on which a large number of blacks worked, and the Alabama Human Relations Council, which, by virtue of its size, afforded only a quite small number of black civic leaders and ministers the opportunity to meet their white counterparts.

News of the 1954 Supreme Court decision outlawing segregated education reached the Montgomery black citizen, and buoyed him up for a time. Late in the summer of the following year, he learned of the brutal lynching of fourteen-year-old Emmett Till in Mississippi, and he was cast down by this news. It put him in mind of the almost certain fate in store

for young Jeremiah Reeves. Six days before Mrs. Parks' bus
ride, good news came again from the outside world. The Interstate Commerce Commission banned racial segregation on
all vehicles and in all facilities engaged in travel between the
states. Segregation in Montgomery remained, nonetheless,
as much the law of life, and death, as ever. And its most egregious manifestation was the bus company. Cursed and often
assaulted by armed drivers who periodically had killed without
provocation, compelled to board from the rear door after
depositing the fare in the driver's box, strictly forbidden from
ever seating himself in the first four rows, reserved for whites,
the average black citizen seethed inwardly and obeyed the
law.

When young Claudette Colvin was yanked off a bus, hand-
cuffed, and jailed for not surrendering her seat early in 1954,
he wished good luck to the citizens' committee that was
formed to remonstrate with the bus company, but he remained skeptical and redoubled his caution. In March, 1955,
the committee—Martin served on it—finally met with the disarmingly cordial but unyielding officials, and conditions remained as before. Now, almost nine months later, the black
citizen learned that there had been another incident, widespread community anger, and another citizens' committee.
But, on the evening of December 5, despite the failures of the
past and an extreme caution that had become second nature,
this ordinary black citizen jumped to his feet at Holt Street
Baptist Church to applaud the defiant words of Martin Luther
King, Jr.

Martin's morning-after observation that "after ascending
the mountain on Monday night, I woke up Tuesday morning
urgently aware that I had to leave the heights and come back
to earth," aptly reflects the alternately dominant strains in
his personality—grandiosity and common sense. On Wednesday morning, at about 10 A.M., the community leadership
met with him at the Alabama Negro Baptist Center to or-

ganize the permanent committee of the MIA. At this and
another meeting shortly thereafter, the personnel of the
finance, transportation, program, and strategy committees
was selected. Reverend R. J. Glasco, director of the Baptist
Center, accepted the chairmanship of the first, Rufus Lewis
that of the second; Ralph took charge of the third, and
Martin headed the strategy, or negotiating, committee, ably
assisted by Ralph Abernathy, Ed Nixon, Jo Ann Robinson,
Rufus Lewis, Mrs. West, and six others. The membership of
these four committees, with that of the executive board, over-
lapped because of the diverse talents of the Association's
members and because of its limited numbers. Its total initial
membership was thirty-seven, more than half of which
(twenty) belonged to the clergy. There were six women, two
of whom were wives of a dentist and a physician. The pro-
fessions were represented by one physician, three college professors, and two lawyers. Later, Martin invited Reverend
Robert Graetz, pastor of the black Lutheran Trinity Church
and president of the Alabama Human Relations Council, to
join the executive board. Martin had been active in the
Council, having served as its vice-president. Reverend Graetz
was to be the sole white participant in the deliberations of
the MIA.

The immediate reaction of white Montgomery to the boycott was mixed with incredulity and pragmatic forbearance. If
it was astonished by the solidarity of the black citizens, it
was certainly not ignorant of the reasons for it. The formalis-
tic verdict that race relations in Montgomery were ideal was
not truly believed by all whites. A little patience, a few
diplomatic feints, if required, and a measure of intimidation,
and, they believed, the boycott would collapse ignominiously
of black inconstancy, fractiousness, and cowardice. Ed Nixon
had sensed this attitude in the Chief of Police, who had
patronizingly ordered one of Montgomery's two black policemen to escort Nixon home with the $700 collected at the

Monday-night meeting. Reporter Azbell had given objective and dramatic front-page coverage of the meeting. Local radio and television had even transmitted its proceedings. On Wednesday, the city and the bus company, prodded by the Alabama Human Relations Council, agreed to confer with the leaders of the boycott at 11 A.M. the next day. Two days of nearly total withdrawal of black patronage, representing 75 per cent of its revenue, had already caused acute financial embarrassment for the Montgomery City Line.

Martin confessed that he approached the Thursday-morning meeting with "unwarranted optimism." His conviction that ordinarily reasonable men could be reasonable in matters involving race was to be cruelly betrayed. Mayor W. A. "Tackie" Gayle and his two commissioners, Clyde Sellers and Frank A. Parks, struck a pose of attentive accessibility to argument. The attorneys for the bus company, J. E. Bagley and Jack Crenshaw, however, were spiritedly hostile, especially Crenshaw. Concluding his review of the long history of abuse by the company, Martin presented the three-point proposal drawn up by the MIA. For a brief moment, compromise seemed possible. Commissioner Parks languidly offered that the proposed seating arrangement could be harmonized with the city's cherished segregation ordinances. But Crenshaw strenuously demurred. What the MIA proposed was illegal, he contended. Furthermore, and this was the gravamen of the case, one black victory would set in motion a concatenation of others. The blacks "would go about boasting of a victory that they had won over the white people; and this we will not stand for." Martin and the others swore solemnly that they would effectively contain the enthusiasm of their followers if the seating plan were accepted. But their cause was lost now. Crenshaw had successfully transmuted the issues into the eternal antinomies of black and white. Further discussion was useless. The opposition promised the MIA leaders that the courtesy of the company's drivers would improve, but nothing more. As the meeting dissolved, Commissioner Sellers ominously referred to a municipal law that prescribed a minimum fare for taxis. Martin knew then that the community's reliance upon this form of transportation was doomed.

The creation of a car pool and its maintenance at peak efficiency over a twelve-month period was the great technical achievement of the boycott. Details for its organization were passed to Martin by phone from his friend Reverend Theodore Jemison, who had mounted a successful bus boycott in Baton Rouge, Louisiana, during the summer of 1953. At the MIA mass rally that evening, one hundred and fifty people volunteered their automobiles. In less than a week, the system had been fully perfected. There were forty-eight dispatch and forty-two collection stations, and traffic between them flowed with what the local White Citizens Council lamented as "military precision." A most significant lateral effect of the car pool was that it constituted a psychological *levée en masse*. The more affluent blacks had never ridden the buses. Many of the "Big Negroes" in Martin's congregation had only casual dealings with the stratum of society that formed the bulk of the bus company's clientele. The car pool permitted the more fortunate to involve themselves materially in the struggle, to derive from it a sense of sacrifice and service; and the example of their fidelity alimented the epidemic of courage and resolution afflicting thousands of humble maids and handymen. Out of the mythopoeism of the car pool were to come tales of patrician black women who drove their Cadillacs long hours, of physicians and morticians who curtailed their professional schedules to make runs and who made their office phones and secretaries available, of pharmacists who filled prescriptions by one phone and simultaneously gave dispatch instructions over another, of whites who offered rides (three even joined the pool) or walked to signal their approval of events. For many a dowager and a dentist, this was the finest hour of civism. Their services were inestimable. Still, a large number of people preferred to walk in order to manifest their commitment. "Jump in, Grandmother," a driver invited, "You don't need to walk." "I'm not walking for myself," the old woman said, barely slowing her weary shuffle, "I'm walking for my children and my grandchildren."

While the black community rapidly united and mobilized its resources, white Montgomery continued to tack back and forth between inflexibility, incipient if limited sympathy, and refusal to admit the seriousness of the boycott. City hall and the bus company remained adamant. Yet the letters published in the *Advertiser* during this period were generally conciliatory. One week after its commencement, the paper printed Miss Juliette Morgan's remarkable comment on the boycott. "Not since the first battle of the Marne has the taxi been put to as good use as it has this last week in Montgomery. However, the spirit animating our Negro citizens as they ride these taxis or walk from the heart of Cloverdale to Mobile Road has been more like that of Gandhi than of the 'taxicab army' that saved Paris." In her conclusion, Miss Morgan cited the ideals of Thoreau as justifications of the boycott and the Mahatma's "salt march" as an archetypal example of its tactics. These were the first public words on the relevance of Gandhi and Thoreau to the boycott. Three days later, two more letters of support were published. One of them, from Mrs. Helen R. Goss clearly exposed the sentiment of the enlightened whites whose utterances would wane, then cease altogether, as the battle dragged on. Mrs. Goss had heard of unseemly behavior by transit personnel to black passengers: "I find it hard to believe that any fair-minded person can under those circumstances derive any more pleasure than I do from the comfort of having a seat while others who have paid the same fare are not allowed to occupy vacant seats merely because they happen to belong to a different race."

It is significant that, while it continued to publish sym-

pathetic letters, the *Advertiser* banished news of the boycott
from its front page on the day that Miss Morgan's letter appeared. Then, on December 17, headlines announced that
the second meeting of city, bus, and MIA officials would take
place that day. Martin and his colleagues noted this article
with interest, because it confirmed recent information that
an emissary of the Chicago parent company, National City
Lines, Inc., had been in Montgomery for two days to confer
with local officials. It had been the MIA, however, that had
wired the National City Lines president to dispatch a representative to moderate the intractable position of its subsidiary
company.

Thus, the second meeting with the city transpired in two
phases, the first of which was a preliminary, cordial, and
wholly inconclusive exchange on the morning of December
17. The mayor's Citizens Committee members were the soul
of affability. Reverend Henry E. Russell, brother of the Georgia
senator, was especially cordial. Mayor Gayle and his two commissioners were polite. Two mysterious black guests of the
mayor were ignored by both parties. Bagley and Crenshaw
appeared with the Northern emissary, C. K. Totten. Martin
again presented the demands of the boycotters. By prior accord, Totten rose to reject the demands of the MIA, repro-
ducing in every particular but that of the Southern drawl the
earlier presentation of Crenshaw. Martin reproached Totten,
with some acerbity, for his deliberate failure to confer with
the black leadership. In turn, he was gravely and eloquently
reproved by one of the white ministers of the Citizens Committee for dereliction of ministerial duties. Salvation, not
public transportation, he said, was the province of the pastor.
More moralizing occurred, and the meeting was adjourned
until Monday at 10 A.M., December 19.

The second round was far less cordial and a conclusive
failure. Martin objected to the presence of Luther Ingalls,
secretary of the Montgomery White Citizens Council. He

was set upon by the whites, who deplored in chorus his intolerance and obduracy as chief negotiator for the black community. They argued that with King out of the way, real progress could be made. Ralph Abernathy instantly defended Martin, reiterating the faith of his colleagues in the latter's character and abilities. Further discussion was pointless, and the last meeting between the foes ended with a tentative agreement to deliberate at an unspecified future date.

The next climactic point in the bus boycott would occur on the night of January 30, when Martin's home was dynamited. Between these dates, relations between the races steadily deteriorated. The worsening straits of the bus company, the unity and unanticipated negotiating savvy of the blacks, the surfacing of extremist white elements, and the growing national interest in Montgomery created an environment of deepening frustration and hatred. It was during this period that the stream of vitriolic telephone calls to MIA personnel began. Mrs. Elmer H. Reynolds, the Association's first secretary, was its first casualty. Overwrought, on the verge of total nervous collapse, she reluctantly tendered her resignation, and Mrs. Maude Ballou replaced her.

A graver peril was the crippling inconvenience that the MIA experienced by having to move its headquarters four times. The directors of the Alabama Negro Baptist Center, the first hosts of the Association, were informed of the condign disapproval of their white Southern Baptist benefactors. Rufus Lewis's Citizens Club was then placed at the disposal of the MIA. Lewis was immediately threatened with cancellation of his license. Temporary arrangements were made at the First Baptist Church while the search continued for a safe permanent seat. Ultimately, this was provided by the Bricklayers Union, a black organization that had constructed its own office building.

Pressure worked both ways, however. By the third month of the boycott, the restricted travel of blacks had resulted in the loss to local merchants of more than $1 million. The loss of revenue caused the business community to mobilize. Its representatives, Men of Montgomery, actively sought a compromise solution. When this failed, the group resorted to innuendo and character assassination. In its one or two meetings with MIA leaders, the business leadership complained of Martin's conduct and intimated that an equitable solution would emerge if he were replaced by an established community leader. Martin confessed that he wavered under this divisive pressure, but then, at a boycott rally, a massive vote of confidence lifted his doubts. Meanwhile, the woes of the Montgomery City Lines mounted. The *Advertiser* noted, as inconspicuously as front-page citation allowed, the company's request to the city for permission to increase its fares. "We just can't live," it quoted a despairing official as saying. The following morning, January 5, Montgomery was informed of its new bus rates, five cents more for adult, three cents more for student fares. The price of transfer tickets was also increased. But the lethal effect of the boycott could be offset in this manner only temporarily.

More than two weeks were to pass before the city fathers formulated a plan as unprincipled as it was clever. Around 8 p.m. on Saturday, January 21, Coretta summoned Martin to the telephone. Carl T. Rowan, editorial writer of the *Minneapolis Tribune*, gave him the shocking news that the teletypes of the Associated Press wire service carried the news that the boycott had been settled. The terms of the alleged agreement were disappointing to Rowan, who had been one of the first outside reporters to cover the Montgomery crisis. Charity and a natural desire to conceal the possibility that unmitigated idiocy was displayed have conspired to shroud the role that three black ministers played in this supposititious compact. When Martin questioned them subsequently, they protested that they had been unscrupulously misrepresented by the city. In any case, the *Advertiser*'s press was, at that moment, preparing a headline account of the settlement: "City Commission States Position on Bus Services." The agreement called for uniform courtesy to all passengers, reservation of ten seats fore and ten seats aft to whites and black respectively; additional buses would be assigned to black routes during rush hours; the hiring of black drivers, the city decreed, was not a matter it could adjudicate.

Rowan's message probably saved the boycott from collapse. Throughout the night and the next morning, MIA leaders methodically crisscrossed the black community to denounce the forthcoming pseudo-agreement. By 1 A.M., most bars and nightspots had been canvassed, and preachers completed the task Sunday morning from their pulpits. The timing of the city's announcement was also fortunate for the boycott: Few people needed to ride buses on Sunday.

Anger was fed by chagrin in city hall as a result of this latest misfire. Tuesday's headlines proclaimed "Mayor Stops Boycott Talks." "It is time to be frank about this matter," Mayor Gayle announced, "The white people are firm in their convictions that they do not care whether the Negroes ever ride a city bus again if it means that the social fabric of our community is to be destroyed so that Negroes will start riding the buses again."

Within the next few days, the city escalated its intimidation of blacks. Indiscriminate arrests for patently fabricated violations began to occur. Clusters of blacks awaiting the dispatch of car-pool vehicles were threatened with vagrancy and illegal-hitchhiking charges. It was widely rumored that drivers' licenses and insurance policies were to be arbitrarily canceled. The car pool lost a number of volunteers as a result. The city's policy of attacking ordinary citizens instead of risking further outmaneuvering by their leaders appeared to be succeeding. Whites threatened their domestics with dismissal if they supported the boycott; few of them were clever enough to reply, as one did, "Yes, Ma'am. I just told all my young 'uns that this kind of thing is white folks' business and we just stay off the buses till they get this whole thing settled." If the whites had been able to surmount the psychological indignity of admitting the magnitude of the boycott threat, they would undoubtedly have grasped the advisability of enjoining the car pool at this moment. Fred Gray continued to marvel gratefully at the providential sluggishness of his opponents' legal advisors.

On the verge of possible success, Montgomery compelled its black citizens—as so many other Southern cities were to do subsequently—to revive their courage almost in spite of themselves. Four days after virtual declaration of open war, two policemen arrested Martin for speeding. The news spread quickly, bringing a large number of excited people to the jail. At first, the officials refused to allow his release, but, as the crowds grew larger, Ralph Abernathy's entreaty to be allowed to arrange for the posting of a cash bond was granted. Martin's arrest was therapeutic; once again, the entire black community experienced that sense of desperate unity and mission by which it had been enveloped in the first hours of the struggle. "From that night on," Martin told Coretta, "my commitment to the struggle for freedom was stronger than ever before." He spoke for the people he was leading, as well.

"Let us keep moving with the faith that what we are doing is right, and with the even greater faith that God is with us in the struggle." Martin King uttered these words before an MIA assembly moments after learning that his home had been dynamited and without certain knowledge of the welfare of his family. During the preceding week, the communication of a possible plot to assassinate him, the anonymous distemper of white extremists unleashed by telephone, and his arrest had nearly wrecked him. If he had indulged himself a moment's outrage against whites, few students of nonviolence would have reproached him. His conduct on the porch of his demolished home was remarkable.

At about 9:15 P.M., January 30, Coretta and a friend had been chatting in the living room of the South Jackson Street parsonage when they heard the thump of an object tossed on the front porch. The Kings' baby was sleeping in the rear of the house, so, believing themselves safer there, the two ladies were just retreating to the bedroom when the front of the house shook, rattled, and coughed a barrage of glass into the room they had just vacated. As the din subsided, Coretta, in admirable control of herself, answered the telephone. "Yes, I did it," said a woman's nasal voice, "And I'm just sorry I didn't kill all you bastards."

Martin pushed and pleaded his way to his house through a crowd of more than three hundred furious blacks, a few of them armed. As he did, he overheard alarming threats being exchanged. One man, told to move on by the police, turned angrily and shouted, "You white folks is always pushin' us around. Now you got your .38 and I got mine so let's battle it out." Finally, Martin reached the front door. Minutes later, having been assured by Coretta that they were all unharmed, Martin returned to the porch at the urgent request of Mayor Gayle and the police commissioner. There was no danger of a race riot, but the volatility of the crisis made it imperative to prevent trigger-happy and nervous policemen from being provoked by the uncustomary belligerence of a small number of irate bystanders. Martin asked for quiet: "We believe in law and order. Don't get panicky. Don't do anything at all. Don't get your weapons. He who lives by the sword will perish by the sword. Remember, that is what God said. We are not advocating violence. We want to love our enemies. We must love our white brothers no matter what they do to us." The crowd dispersed and the crisis passed.

On February 10, twelve thousand whites flocked to hear Senator James O. Eastland fulminate, at the invitation of the White Citizens Council. Some of the senator's listeners had probably been among those who had tossed several sticks of dynamite on Ed Nixon's lawn nine days before and later bombed the residence of Reverend Robert Graetz. Whites were mobilizing throughout the state. Seventy miles from Montgomery, at Anniston, Miss Autherine Lucy had been admitted, under federal court order, to the University of Alabama and forthwith suspended by its trustees on spurious grounds. Miss Lucy was black. But, even as whites listened to the reassuring harangue of Senator Eastland, five Montgomery women had filed suit in the U.S. District Court, on February 1, to have the state's transportation laws invalidated. Two days later, Mrs. Jeanette Reese, one of the plaintiffs, withdrew from the suit. She alleged that she had not understood Attorney Gray's explanation of its purpose. "You know I don't want nothing to do with that mess," she was reported to have told Mayor Gayle. The other ladies remained steadfast, and a hearing before a three-judge panel was set for May 11, 1956.

The Montgomery boycott struggle gained support from a number of outside sources. Although monthly operating expenses were in excess of $5,000 (fifteen station wagons were acquired in January for the car pool), adequate donations flowed to the Association from literally every corner of the world. Ed Nixon, who was then treasurer, estimates that by March, the MIA had received nearly $64,000. The NAACP donated generously through its numerous local chapters. Religious and civic organizations contributed a significant amount of money. The United Auto Workers sent a check for $35,000. And, from Singapore, Tokyo, New Delhi, London, and Paris, and hundreds of other cities came the donations of concerned, private citizens, many of whose emotions must have been expressed by the poignant letter of the Swiss donor who explained in quaint English, "Since I have no possibility to help you in an efficacious manner (this is such a bad feeling, believe me) and I burningly would like to do just something, I send you these 500 dollars. . . . You would make me a very great pleasure, if you accepted, because what else could I do?"

The financial support was invaluable, but other forms of support were equally helpful. There was Ralph Bunche's telegram praising Martin for the splendid work he was accomplishing in the "vineyards of democracy." Toward the end of February, Bayard Rustin, a persuasive pacifist and redoubtable organizer, and Reverend Glenn E. Smiley, a white Methodist minister from Texas and field secretary for A. J. Muste's Fellowship of Reconciliation, arrived in Montgomery. Moreover, Rustin brought with him a check for $5,000.

Although the concept of nonviolence was implicit in the Christian emphasis of the MIA, thus far it had remained unarticulated. Miss Juliette Morgan, now ostracized by her friends and shortly to commit suicide, had been more perceptive than the leaders of the boycott. The arrival of Rustin and Smiley contributed to the acceleration of the MIA's construction of a philosophical framework for its tactics. The disciples of the Fellowship of Reconciliation were a remarkable lot, almost monomaniacal in their commitment to pacifism. Rustin, Smiley, Richard Gregg, James Farmer, the founder of CORE, and William R. Miller, a future biographer of Martin, and others were among its more distinguished exponents. They had a special jargon of their own—*sobornost, Satyagraha, ahimsa, hartal*—derived from their polymorphous philosophy of Indian, Christian, and humanistic pacifism. They were a loquacious and insistent group, and it is a safe assumption that Rustin and Smiley availed themselves of every opportunity to present Martin an exegesis on nonviolent passive resistance. "During all my work with Martin King," Rustin confirms, "I never made a difficult decision without talking the problem over with A. J. [Muste] first." There is more than coincidence, certainly, in the fact that, from this point on, Martin began to lace his discourses with Gandhian terminology.

Martin King was now a national figure who was particularly intriguing to the generation of young college blacks. Appropriately, Fisk University invited him to spend several days on its campus late in February, lecturing and meeting students informally. Martin's reception by the Fisk community revealed an emotional and social fissure that was frequently present in later years when he addressed black audiences. Some students were mesmerized. Others were disenchanted by what they regarded as unabashed emotionalism and pseudophilosophical pomposity. But, while Fisk students sized up his qualities, Martin was compelled to leave prematurely. A telegram from Ralph informed him that Montgomery had finally taken the long-feared step of indicting the MIA leaders for conspiracy to interfere with normal business. On February 22, Martin enplaned for Montgomery by way of Atlanta, where he had left Coretta.

In Atlanta, his father had assembled a battery of the city's black leaders—Dr. Mays of Morehouse; C. R. Yates, vice-president of Citizens Trust Bank; C. A. Scott, owner-editor of the *Atlanta Daily World*; T. M. Alexander, Sr., an investment broker; "Colonel" A. T. Walden, political spokesman for the community; Bishop S. L. Green, spiritual leader of Georgia's African Methodist Episcopal denomination; and Dr. Rufus Clement, president of Atlanta University. It soon became obvious that these gentlemen were camouflage, for the senior King's apprehensions. Two prominent Atlanta whites had telephoned Reverend King, Sr., to convey their alarm for Martin's safety. He and his wife were deeply distressed by the jeopardy in which their son heedlessly but increasingly placed himself. It was hoped that these *éminences grises* could dissuade his return. Martin politely but firmly declined their counsel. "I would rather go back and spend ten years in jail than not go back," he said. When it became clear that his resolve could not be shaken, Dr. Mays spoke up in support of Martin's position. The following day he returned to Montgomery by car with Coretta and his anxious father. When the party arrived, Martin headed immediately for the county jail with Ralph, where they were booked, photographed, bonded, and released. The photograph of Dr. Martin Luther King, Jr., with a numbered plaque (7089) hanging from his neck attracted indignant national and world attention.

The trial of the indicted MIA leaders was scheduled for March 19. Like Emile Zola's, which it strongly resembled in courtroom drama and overwhelming rectitude of the defense, the trial was a great moral victory for the black community. It was a legal triumph for the opposition. The MIA could not have won. But as the twenty-eight witnesses summoned by the defense offered their testimony, the whites felt the moral bankruptcy of their cause. Moreover, the defense was represented by a battery of lawyers whose competence humiliatingly overshadowed the opposition. Orzell Billingsley, Peter Hall, Charles Langford, Fred Gray, Arthur Shores, and the NAACP's Robert Carter (whom the judge denied the right of active participation) threw aside the customary veil of suppliant black advocacy and compelled even Mayor Gayle to refer to defense witnesses by title.

The trial was watched, and occasionally cheered, by a courtroom audience that was two-thirds black. Many wore crosses in their lapels reading "Father, forgive them." The international press was represented by correspondents from England, France, and India. Judge Eugene Carter was also aware of the presence of a black U.S. Congressman, Charles C. Diggs, whose frequent trips to a nearby telephone booth may have worried him slightly. For four days, the parade of victimized and unsuspectedly eloquent defense witnesses continued to fill the dock. There was Mrs. Stella Brooks, whose husband requested the return of his dime because the bus was too crowded to accommodate him and who was fatally shot by police summoned by the driver. There was Mrs.

Martha Walker, whose blind husband's leg was pinned by a bus door. The driver had prematurely closed it and had driven several blocks dragging Mr. Walker in tow. There was Mrs. Sadie Brooks, who related the case of a black passenger who was threatened because he lacked the correct change. There was Mrs. Della Perkins, who was called an "ugly black ape." The procession of the wronged continued. Finally, there was Mrs. Georgia Gilmore, who was left standing after she had paid her fare and dutifully disembarked to walk to the rear entrance. Turning to presiding Judge Carter, she declared ingenuously, "When they count the money, they do not know Negro money from white money."

And, finally, Martin entered the dock. He cited again the indignities to which black bus passengers had been subjected. He patiently explained the recourse to organized resistance forced upon the black community and emphasized that the *sine qua non* of MIA tactics was to avoid violence at all costs. Altogether it was a memorable performance. Nevertheless, Judge Carter found the eighty-nine defendants (originally more than one hundred persons were indicted) of the MIA guilty of violating Alabama's antiboycott law. The settlement of their fines was made contingent upon the results of Martin's final appeal. Judge Carter explained that the $500 judgment plus court costs (or 386 days' hard labor) that he imposed against Martin was minimal, because of Martin's pacific and responsible leadership. Leaving the judge's court room to the strains of "We ain't gonna ride the buses no more," Martin intuited more clearly than before that certain victory for the movement was forthcoming.

On May 11, the suit contesting the state's segregation laws relative to public conveyances was heard in Montgomery. As they listened to the exchanges between the panel of three judges and the attorneys for the litigants, Martin, Ralph, and Vernon Johns believed that the court was strongly disposed to favor the MIA. To the reiterated argument of the city that uncontrollable violence would result from the invalidation of present transportation laws, Judge Rives posed the fundamental question, "Is it fair to command one man to surrender his constitutional rights in order to prevent another man from committing a crime?" During the court's adjournment, the leaders of the MIA were encouraged by the evidence of national support. Martin accepted an invitation to speak at the Cathedral of Saint John the Divine in New York on May 17. Toward the end of the month, a heavily attended benefit rally was held in Madison Square Garden. Eleanor Roosevelt, Roy Wilkins, A. Philip Randolph, Congressman Adam Clayton Powell, Charles Zimmerman of the International Ladies' Garment Workers Union, Dr. Israel Goldstein, Sammy Davis, Jr., and Tallulah Bankhead addressed the crowd, who cheered enthusiastically when Rosa Parks and Ed Nixon were introduced. Martin was unable to attend. Shortly before departing for California to attend several conferences and enjoy their first vacation, he and Coretta learned that, with one dissent, the panel of judges had declared the city's bus ordinance unconstitutional. The city insisted, of course, upon prolonging the struggle by filing an appeal. But the Kings and the Abernathys were prepared to enjoy, as much as the companion cares of Montgomery would allow, this first trip to the West Coast.

In general, the façade presented by the MIA to the opposition appeared to be monolithic. There was fractiousness, certainly, even an undetermined number of defections after the "get-tough" policy of the city; but, owing largely to the magnetic leadership of Martin and the efficiency of the MIA staff, there was scant reason for unseemly public dispute or denunciation. Moreover, the Association was a model of participative democracy. It was staffed by persons who were well known to the community and who were required to hold themselves available by telephone and by direct encounter to their "constituents." And policymakers were continually interpellated by the Association's supporters in innumerable mass meetings. But the cumulative success of the boycott also created an area of possible vulnerability. As tens of thousands of dollars poured into the coffers of the MIA, some people were made uneasy by the leadership's unrecorded disbursement of these funds. Ed Nixon, for one, had never ceased to insist that the MIA adopt orthodox bookkeeping methods. The following year, he resigned as treasurer because of the vagueness of the financial records upon which he was compelled to base his reports. Too much money was spent under the categories of telephone calls and travel, he believed. Recalling the objection of Nixon and others, Fred Gray observes, "In any large organization, the question of money is bound to disturb somebody."

Reverend U. J. Fields was particularly disturbed, and on June 11 he told the press that he was resigning from the MIA because of the "misuse" of funds by its leaders. In the weeks immediately following the inception of the car pool, the whites had circulated rumors to this effect, specifically charging that Martin had purchased for his personal use a Cadillac and a Buick station wagon. Reverend Fields' apparent corroboration of such charges could have had fatal results in the black community. Martin returned immediately from California to Montgomery. Within hours, he had extracted from Fields the confession that he was angered by the decision of the MIA executive board not to re-elect him to that body. Fields admitted, to the packed crowd at Beulah Baptist Church on the afternoon of June 18, "I confess that I don't know a single instance of misappropriation. All of those things I made up in a moment of anger." Nor was Fields to become the Benedict Arnold of the boycott, for Martin's expiatory address in his behalf moved the congregation to applaud Fields' apologia.

Although the city of Montgomery had been underhanded and vicious in its campaign, it had been unwittingly, until

the decision of the federal court, an ideal enemy, because
of its badly timed and transparent maneuvers. The MIA had
been able to anticipate city strategy and had blinked somewhat incredulously at its slow-wittedness. The MIA had
avoided seizure of its funds by depositing them in out-of-state
banks, particularly with Atlanta's Citizens Trust. The vehicles purchased for the car pool were registered in the name
of local churches, not the MIA. Collision insurance had been
obtained from a black insurance company. And the repeated
cancellations of liability insurance, involving potential sums
that only white firms could guarantee, was solved by con-
tracting a policy with Lloyds of London.

At last, having attacked the leaders of the Association,
the city undertook to enjoin the car pool itself as a public
nuisance and an unlicensed private enterprise. This incredibly
belated gambit noticeably chilled the ardor of the black community. Many people had chosen to walk to work to ad-
vertise their resolve, but they did not walk every day. Furthermore, the car pool was symbolic of the boycott's success and efficiency. Anywhere in Montgomery, whatever the
racial composition of the neighborhood, trudging blacks
knew they had the option of riding in a spanking new MIA
station wagon or a private citizen's auto. At a mass meeting,
Martin revealed the possibility of the car pool having to fold.
He perceived then that the *élan* of the boycotters would almost inevitably diminish. An attempt to have the federal
district court enjoin the city's action was denied by Justice
Frank M. Johnson. "You know the people are getting tired,"
Martin confided to Coretta. "If the city officials get this injunction against the car pools—and they will get it—I am
afraid our people will go back to the buses." Grasping for a
straw of inspiration, Coretta told Martin that she was somehow certain that the Supreme Court would save the boycott.
"I don't know whether I really believed that such perfect
timing would ever come about," she admits now, "but Martin

and the Movement needed desperately to believe in near
miracles at this stage of the struggle."

It seemed the beginning of the end when Martin appeared
in court on the morning of November 13, 1956. Judge Carter,
who had found the MIA leaders guilty of interfering with
private enterprise, was again presiding. There was little doubt
as to his decision. Because of this crushing blow, it was almost a certainty that the black community, first in a trickle
and then massively, would return to the buses. White Montgomery would have been shaken, it would heave a sigh of relief over the closeness of its victory, and there would be, for
a few weeks, an uncharacteristic mannerliness on the part of
bus operators. Martin, Ralph, and several others would find
it appropriate to resign their responsibilities and leave the
city. To have nearly succeeded would be more paralyzing to
the black community than to have met defeat earlier in the
struggle. "You ought to knowed better," the sententious comment of the lady who had witnessed Reverend Johns' premature assault upon bus segregation, was again about to be
humiliatingly verified. The city lawyers, certain of the court's
verdict, presented their arguments with cogency and verve.
As the recess period was ending, Martin was puzzled by the
bustle in the rear of the courtroom and the worried expressions worn by Mayor Gayle, his two commissioners, and the
city's lawyers. At that moment, a reporter for Associated
Press handed Martin a note:

> The United States Supreme Court today affirmed a decision
> of a special three-judge U.S. District Court in declaring
> Alabama's state and local laws requiring segregation on buses
> unconstitutional. The Supreme Court acted without listening to
> any argument; it simply said "the motion to affirm is granted
> and the judgment is affirmed."

The trial resumed, but both parties knew they were finishing
an irrelevant ritual. At the end of the day, Judge Carter,
whose deliberations must have established a record for speed

in this area of jurisprudence, took five minutes to find the city's request for an injunction justified.

The news of November 13 marks a watershed on the terrain of indispensable legal rights for blacks, but not there alone. The parade of the Ku Klux Klan the following night elicited from Montgomery blacks reactions that less than a year ago would have been inconceivable. Hooded and awesomely caparisoned, the Klan procession of forty vehicles entered the black neighborhoods, expecting the mere news of its coming to broadcast paralyzing fear. Instead, porch lights remained lit, and a few black spectators lined the sidewalks to jeer or gesture good-naturedly. Many people went about their business as though oblivious to this intrusion. After a few blocks, puzzled and embarrassed, the procession abruptly turned into a side street and was engulfed by the darkness from whence it had come. This night witnessed a unique psychological victory, perhaps the first of its kind in the deep South.

This surplus courage persisted unabated during the subsequent days of adversity following the Supreme Court's decision. At first, Martin had believed that the federal order making the integration of Montgomery buses mandatory would arrive within the week. In fact, more than a month would elapse. Meanwhile, the MIA attorneys advised compliance with Judge Carter's injunction. The car pool was officially disbanded. But no one rode the buses. Despite the inclement weather, people continued to walk or to make arrangements through the share-a-ride plan devised by the MIA leaders. Indeed, it was not community stamina or courage that caused concern. Martin, Ralph, Glenn Smiley, and Bayard Rustin were now concerned about the black community's ability to return to the buses and withstand, positively but with restraint, the provocations of the whites.

A program of mass indoctrination in the tactics of nonviolence was undertaken. One month earlier, the Fellowship of Reconciliation had provided the money and equipment to produce a didactic film (a seventeen-minute "sociodrama"), *Walk to Freedom*, that was shown in numerous churches and supplemented by commentary from Martin, Smiley, Rustin, and others. Almost nightly, church sessions were given over to lectures and demonstrations of techniques of nonviolent resistance. Skits were prepared in which likely white abuse was dramatized by members of the congregation. Those who portrayed the insulted or assaulted black passengers steadfastly avoided undignified verbal ripostes or active physical response. It was during this period that nonviolence became a formal doctrine of professional techniques for Montgomery's black community. The MIA circular detailing appropriate bus behavior, prepared in the main by Smiley, was indicative of the new doctrinal emphasis. In its eight general and nine specific recommendations, black citizens were instructed, "If cursed, do not curse back. If struck, do not strike back, but evidence love and goodwill at all times. If another person is being molested, do not arise to go to his defense, but pray for the oppressor." "Oh, yes, I know the words by heart, now," a local matron stated after a meeting: "Though I need not *like* Engelhardt [a local segregationist], I must *love* him."

At 5:55 A.M. on December 21, 1956, Martin, Ralph, Ed Nixon, and Glenn Smiley boarded a Montgomery bus in front of Martin's home. The federal order had arrived the preceding day. Their reception from the driver was, after a twelve-month insistence on the point, completely civil. Newsmen with cameras and television equipment recorded the historic moment. For Montgomery, this commencement of a new era in race relations was far too auspicious. Indeed, the city government had encouraged likely extremism by proclaiming, in its jeremiad released on the eve of the federal mandate,

The City Commission, and we know our people are with us in this determination, will not yield one inch, but will do all

King

in its power to oppose the integration of the Negro race with the white race in Montgomery, and will forever stand like a rock against social equality, intermarriage, and mixing of the races under God's creation and plan.

One week after Martin's symbolic return to the buses, violence erupted. Buses were fired upon; a teenage girl was beaten, a pregnant woman shot in the legs. These were rehearsals for the more serious reprisals that came in the early hours of January 10. Martin and Ralph were in Atlanta to attend a two-day meeting of Southern black ministers whose deliberations were to lead, ultimately, to the founding of the Southern Christian Leadership Conference. Twice, Mrs. Abernathy telephoned her husband from Montgomery, first with the news that their home and the church had been dynamited, then to report that an undetermined number of explosions had occurred. She and the children had escaped harm. That morning, before rushing back to Montgomery, Martin and Ralph learned that Reverend Graetz's home and three other Baptist churches had been partially or totally destroyed. Damages totaled nearly $700,000.

In the exaltation of the first days of the boycott, Martin believed that "God had decided to use Montgomery as the proving ground for the struggle and triumph of freedom and justice in America." The people had followed their nonviolent script so closely that in the final triumphant act, it had never occurred to them that others would insist on writing a bloody sequel. "When I returned to Montgomery over the weekend, I found the Negro community in low spirits," Martin observed. The city halted all bus service, and Martin feared that Mayor Gayle would use the threat of violence to discontinue service indefinitely. In the deep depression of the first days of the boycott, Martin's reactions revealed something of the emotional tariff his leadership had imposed. A few months before, he had alarmed a rally by a morbid reference to his own death. Now, on Monday night, January 14, he seemed to disintegrate psychologically. "Lord, I hope no one will have to die as a result of our struggle for freedom in Montgomery," he shouted in the middle of a prayer. "Certainly I don't want to die. But if anyone has to die, let it be me." Several associates helped Martin to his chair. For the moment, he was emotionally spent, but in the end this outburst proved to have been a healthy catharsis for both himself and the community. Who could be small enough to dwell on dangers to himself, when "L. L. J." ("Little Lord Jesus," an affectionate title bestowed upon Martin by the church women) entreated God to visit the collective woes of the community upon his own person?

There was another round of bombings at the end of the month, but terrorism finally began to prove counterproductive. The city, prodded by the *Advertiser* and the business community, asserted its authority. Rewards were offered for the apprehension of the arsonists and dynamiters. More surprisingly, seven white men were actually arrested. No one was very surprised to learn that the jury that tried the first two returned a verdict of not guilty, despite the prosecution's introduction of signed confessions. Still, an important precedent had been established. Whites had been caught, indicted by a grand jury, and tried for crimes against blacks. The incidence of terrorism declined abruptly and shortly stopped altogether. Bus service resumed on an integrated basis and Montgomery, thoroughly exhausted, was pleased to pretend that the new terms of racial harmony were entirely natural. The boycott had lasted from the beginning of one December to the end of the next. Its material costs to both races had been considerable. And, if its nonmaterial consequences were not precisely quantifiable, it was certain that the black community had been the overwhelming moral and spiritual beneficiary of the struggle. From the crucible of deprivation and intimidation, it had emerged united, with an irrefrangible sense of its own power and an uncommonly provident compassion for its oppressors. The whites had not only flagrantly transgressed the Christian principles and obedience to law whose superior guarantors they had proclaimed themselves to be; more significantly, they had begun to lose the institutionalized right to tyranny based on skin color; Black Americans had manifestly taken a giant first stride toward freedom.

4

Satyagraha, *Home-grown*

> "It's no use," he said, turning to me with half
> an apologetic grin. "You can't hit a bugger when
> he stands up to you like that!" He gave the Sikh
> a mock salute and walked off.
>
> JOAN V. BONDURANT

"IT IS BECOMING CLEAR," Martin prophesied at the end of
the Montgomery struggle, "that the Negro is in for a season
of suffering." As the legal victories of American blacks accumulated, he anticipated a steeply rising curve of Southern
obstructionism on the order of that at Central High School
in Little Rock, Arkansas, and at the University of Alabama
and, tragically, of the naked violence of the Emmett Till
variety. Martin could not have realized then how completely
his prognosis would be realized. If the white recoil to black
legal gains was to be withstood, it was essential that black
leaders devise an appropriate tactic of struggle. Montgomery
was the forcing house of such a tactic. The proof that passive resistance could be made to work on a massive scale was
no longer lacking.

"Nonviolence can touch men where the law cannot reach
them," Martin believed. "It is," he added, "the method
which seeks to implement the just law by appealing to the
consciences of the great decent majority who through blind-
ness, fear, pride, or irrationality have allowed their consciences to sleep." In the years to come, nonviolence would

win tens of thousands of adherents, most of them convinced of its tactical superiority. For Martin and his associates and a far smaller number of nonviolent practitioners, more than tactics was involved. Nonviolent passive resistance was a *Weltansicht*, not merely a viable technique but the sole authentic approach to the problem of social injustice. The distinction between operational and ideological nonviolence was not always clear and not always important at first.

Viewed clinically, the origins of the philosophy of nonviolence are traceable to the numerically determined and irreversible social fact that the American black cannot utilize violence on a collective scale for more than brief and infrequent periods, without jeopardizing his existence as a member of American society, no matter how marginal that existence may be alleged to be. Such a determinist judgment in no way minimizes the catalytic and creative role of Martin Luther King, nor does it suggest that his unique interpretation of passive resistance was primarily a function of objectively assessed social limitations. Martin's deep Christian concern with the brotherhood of man and his abiding faith (until late in his career, at least) in the fundamental decency of his fellow man directed his philosophical speculations far more than cold realism could have.

In his unending struggle for dignity, the American black has had recourse to four contradistinctive ideologies. (1) The ideology embodied in the plans of the slaves Denmark Vesey and Nat Turner holds that small, elitist bands of armed militants can rally black masses to assault white power by means of guerrilla warfare. It is assumed that the terrible efficacy of these tactics and fear of racial bloodletting will compel responsible white authority to enforce drastic social change. (2) Delany-Garveyism rejects the design of racial integration outright as an unworthy chimera and calls for the formation of an authentic black culture. Pure Garveyism commanded wholesale migration of the race to Africa, but there have been later thematic variations that contemplated the creation of something like black *kibbutzim* in America. (3) Dr. Booker T. Washington's ideology, that of the "Great Accommodationist," proclaimed that the races could be as unitary as the hand in economic matters and as cleanly separate as the fingers in the domain of social intercourse. What the black needs, according to this view, is the opportunity to develop separately to such a point that, by dint of industrious labor and intelligent investment in his own enterprises, his successes will create viable social and economic activity. Washington supposed that black success would ultimately win the indulgence of the white community. (4) Finally, Frederick Douglass and W. E. B. DuBois, extremists in their own right but eschewing the programs of Vesey-Turner and Delany-Garvey, argued that, while the tenets of white society must be accepted, the individual black must actively remonstrate against his degraded status and refuse to accept the spurious doctrine of separate development. He must develop his intellectual powers fully in order to argue his case before his oppressors and inspire fellow blacks to perfect their intellectual capacities.

Violence to compel justice, rejection of the Judeo-Christian tradition in order to escape its injustice, meek provisional acceptance of both the tradition and its injustice in order to buy time to reproduce in microcosm a black reflection of the values esteemed by white America, the commendation of an individualistic and proud confrontation of the "system" by gifted and psychologically unfettered personalities—these were the recurrent ideological positions (militance, migration, meekness, merit) that have alternately attracted and repelled the black community.

Eldridge Cleaver has written that Booker T. Washington was yesterday's Martin Luther King. This judgment ignores the positive fact that Martin's conception of nonviolence pragmatically grafted the exclusive requirements of black excellence and leadership upon the pitifully limited and cowed capacities of the black masses. Of DuBois's position, Martin wrote, "Yet, in the very nature of DuBois's outlook there was no room for the whole people. It was a tactic for an aristocratic elite who would themselves be benefited while leaving behind the 'untalented' 90 per cent." Martin believed that aristocracies contrive to save themselves. His frequent, glowing references to Booker T. Washington manifested a belief that humility, forbearance, and black moral probity would triumph if combined with gifted leadership and cautiously modulated militance. As for militance in the tradition of Vesey and Turner, Martin, while ostentatiously disavowing recourse to physical violence, was to channel the feral outrage on which it fed into the massive but peaceful protests of the next half-decade. This was the unique and creative syncretism achieved by Martin Luther King.

A much more practical goad to conceptualizing the lessons of the Montgomery boycott came from Reverend C. K. Steele of Tallahassee, Florida, who issued a call for a regional conference in Atlanta of the civil rights ministry. The MIA leadership responded to Steele's suggestion and set January 10–11, 1957, for the conference. Martin's and Ralph's participation was seriously disturbed by the news of residential and church bombings in Montgomery. Nevertheless, both managed a brief appearance at Martin's father's church, Ebenezer. Out of this conclave emerged the Southern Leadership Conference on Transportation and Non-Violent Integration.

The assembled ministers voted to dispatch to President Eisenhower the request that he venture south for a major policy speech encouraging officials to abide by the decisions of the Supreme Court. Further, they suggested that Vice-President Nixon tour the South and confer with its leaders, black and white. Finally, the ministers asked that Herbert Brownell, Attorney-General of the United States, conduct a

Southern fact-finding mission to apprise himself of the region's peculiar problems. The President's *porte-parole*, Sherman Adams, explained to the ministers that Eisenhower's
schedule precluded a Southern journey at that time. Simultaneously, the Justice Department advised that the recommended regional investigation was inopportune. This polite
indifference can hardly have surprised Martin, for he had
forwarded, during the height of the Montgomery boycott, a
detailed report on voting irregularities to the Justice Department and, in return, he had received a sympathetic explanation of the Department's inability to take action.

Although disappointed, the ministers agreed to hold a subsequent meeting one month later in New Orleans. Slightly
less than one hundred ministers converged upon New Orleans in mid-February. The title of their organization underwent two rapid alterations. Changing its name at the outset
to the Southern Negro Leaders Conference, they decided
finally upon the Southern Negro Leadership Conference.
Martin was elected president, Ralph treasurer. Again the body
dispatched a request to Washington, this time asking for a
White House conference on civil rights. Again, it was advised
that the establishment found the moment unpropitious. Still,
the effort was not lost. Although none doubted the efficacy of
the NAACP or the Urban League, their deliberations had persuaded the ministers that an organization whose focus would
be exclusively Southern, capitalizing upon the national treasury of grace accumulated by Martin's Montgomery triumph,
was desperately needed. There was no thought, at least during
this period, of competing with the traditional civil rights organizations, but, rather, the aim was to supplement their
work. Martin's caution in this regard had even extended to
demanding the approval of Roy Wilkins before agreeing to
attend the 1956 national Democratic convention.

Martin's psychological state continued to worry his friends.
They could not forget his bizarre address shortly after the

rash of dynamitings in Montgomery, and they were profoundly relieved to find an excuse to remove him from the pressures in the general backwash of the boycott. A letter from the prime minister–designate of the Gold Coast, Dr. Nkrumah, inviting Martin to attend the national independence festivities during that March, provided the ideal occasion. Martin's congregation voted the sum of $2,500 for the trip, and the MIA donated an additional $1,000. It was his and Coretta's first trip abroad. It was greatly enhanced by the presence aboard their flight from New York of Representative Adam Clayton Powell. His stewardship of their brief stay in Lisbon was highly enjoyable. The party, consisting of Dr. Ralph Bunche, A. Philip Randolph, Norman Manley (the future prime minister of the West Indian Federation), and Mrs. Louis Armstrong, after a brief stop in Monrovia, Liberia, arrived in Accra on March 5.

The Kings were housed with an English family in Achimota Village just outside Accra, the site of the Gold Coast's excellent preparatory school and college. On their first evening, they attended the ceremonies marking the severance at midnight of the Gold Coast (now Ghana) from its colonial dependency upon Great Britain. "The battle is ended. Ghana, our beloved country, is free forever," Dr. Nkrumah solemnly proclaimed. For a black American, the moment was invested with all the poignancy of legendary aspirations and vicarious pride. Martin derived a special significance from the Ghanaian experience. As he told the South African prelate, Father Michael Scott, what most impressed him was that Ghana's freedom had been gained nonviolently. He was deeply impressed, as well, by Dr. Nkrumah, who invited Martin and Coretta to lunch.

Although he was beginning to feel the feverish effects of an undiagnosed Ghanaian malady, the Kings gamely attended the round of postindependence festivities. At one of them, they met Vice-President Nixon, who chided Coretta for her premarital aversion to preachers and extended a politician's invitation to her husband to visit him in Washington. Nixon had noted the February 18 *Time* article on Martin. On the morning of March 7, however, Martin was fully stricken. Michael Scott, who found him prostrate and feverish on the morning of their meeting, immediately reported Martin's condition to Lord Hemingsford, who detached a naval physician from his retinue. Later in the day, Prime Minister Nkrumah's personal physician arrived to treat him. Coretta was also ill, but Martin appears to have suffered terribly. He recovered, and they returned to the United States by way of Nigeria, Rome, Geneva, Paris, and London.

Before returning to Montgomery, Martin stopped in New York to confer with A. Philip Randolph and Roy Wilkins about the advisability of dramatizing black demands through a mass pilgrimage to the nation's capital. A subsequent meeting of these three and some seventy other civil rights leaders at the Metropolitan Baptist Church in Washington, D.C., on April 5 resulted in an appeal to concerned blacks and whites to join in a May 17 prayer pilgrimage to the nation's capital.

The modest success of the Prayer Pilgrimage has been overshadowed by the mammoth rally six years later, for which it was the indispensable rehearsal. Between 15,000 and 25,000 persons congregated at the Lincoln Memorial three years to the day after the Supreme Court's epochal decision outlawing school segregation. The retired baseball hero Jackie Robinson, black novelist John Killens, and actress Ruby Dee were presented. Sidney Poitier, Sammy Davis, Jr., and Harry Belafonte spoke, as they were to do on numerous similar occasions in the future. And, of course, the redoubtable Mahalia Jackson was there to stir the largely black crowd with song. Among those who came to address the crowd—Dr. Mordecai Johnson, Roy Wilkins, Adam Powell, Charles Diggs, Reverends Borders, Davis, Shuttlesworth, and Steele—the presence of the venerable A. Philip Randolph was particularly noteworthy. At a later time and in altered circumstances, the Prayer Pilgrimage was a partial reification of Randolph's 1941 idea to march on Washington to compel President Roosevelt to improve the conditions of American blacks in the country's defense industries. His projected avalanche of 100,000 blacks upon the capital never took place, for Roosevelt elected not to call Randolph's bluff; instead, he issued Executive Order 8802, prohibiting racial discrimination in the employment and promotion of personnel engaged in defense production. Randolph, tall and erect, alert eyes surveying the thousands before him, delivered a moving speech.

Finally, in mid-afternoon, Randolph presented Martin, whose reception by the throng made clear that it considered him as the pre-eminent civil rights leader. He scored against both national political parties for their cynical and niggardly treatment of the black man. He deplored the "silent and apathetic" conduct of the White House in the field of race relations. A fourfold strategy was essential, he continued. First, the federal government must accept its responsibility to pursue an aggressive policy of enforcement of desegregation; second, it was imperative that white sympathizers move beyond a position of "quasi-liberalism" to one of positive commitment to immediate and full rights for minorities; third, Southern white moderates, who continued to insist that they really did exist, must make their counsels heard, must insist upon a regional minimal acceptance of federal law; finally, he called on black leaders to provide the moderate but unequivocal leadership that would inspire their people and also reassure and encourage their white allies.

The crowd liked what it heard and communicated its approval through a rising chorus of "amen's." This was Martin's first truly national address, and his peroration was eminently worthy of the moment. The register of his voice deepened, its cadence undulated, and, in a spellbinding finale, he transported his audience. The problems confronting the black had one certain solution:

Give us the ballot. Give us the ballot and we will no longer have to worry the federal government about our basic rights. . . . We will no longer plead—we will write the proper laws on the books. Give us the ballot and we will fill the legislature with men of goodwill. Give us the ballot and we will get the people judges who love mercy. Give us the ballot and we will quietly, lawfully, and nonviolently, without rancor or bitterness, implement the May 17, 1954, decision of the Supreme Court.

The metrical ingredients were identical to those of the speech to be delivered from the same spot half a decade later.

The results of the Prayer Pilgrimage were mixed. It added considerably to the personal luster of Martin Luther King. His growing national role was recognized by the NAACP, which awarded him its coveted Spingarn Medal; at twenty-eight, he became the youngest recipient of this honor. Howard University, the Theological Seminary of the University of Chicago, and Morehouse College bestowed honorary degrees upon him. "See how the masses of men worry themselves into nameless graves," Dr. Mays fittingly intoned, as he completed the Morehouse ceremony, "when here and there a great soul forgets himself into immortality."

Meanwhile, the Crusade for Citizenship, intended as the practical implementation of the Prayer Pilgrimage, cranked up slowly in its program to register five million disfranchised Southern blacks. Its success would not be notable in 1957. And Martin's personal success, it was persistently rumored, was causing discord within the established civil rights leadership. Indicative of the tension were the blunt words of NAACP's chief legal counselor, Thurgood Marshall, who was quoted as saying of Martin's proposal to send black students to sit in at white high schools that to use children in the place of men lacked heroism and wisdom.

If there was a rift, Martin appears to have striven meritoriously to repair it. He presented a check for $1,000 to purchase a life membership for himself and the MIA with the NAACP. In their public pronouncements, of course, none of the civil rights organizations conceded the existence of tension. If the speculations of *Jet* and *Afro-American* were grossly exaggerated, it was nonetheless patently obvious that the school of thought inspired by Martin was in conflict with the strictly litigative approach of the NAACP or the theory of osmotic progress adhered to by the white-collar Urban League. Lerone Bennett brushes aside the circumspect disclaimers of the civil rights leadership, to uncover a major organizational crisis in the black community. "It looks simpler now than it did then," Bennett asserts. With the aid of hindsight, "we can see clearly that events were foreclosing the possibilities of the dominant Negro leadership styles. The grain of history was moving in King's direction." If his judgments are premature and harsh, Bennett correctly detects an organizational malaise in the black community. But the full measure of Martin's disagreements with Roy Wilkins, Lester Granger, and Granger's successor, Whitney Young, were not to mature until well after the SCLC crises in Albany, Georgia.

Meanwhile, the ripples of the Prayer Pilgrimage expanded. Six days after the event, Vice-President Nixon responded favorably to Martin's May 15 letter requesting a conference. Bayard Rustin, serving as his special assistant, carefully prepared a memorandum to assist Martin and Ralph in formulating a persuasive cluster of requests to present to the Vice-President. In addition to an eloquent rehearsal of the daily injustices suffered by 11 million Southern blacks and a statement of their "unshakable spirit" and determination to achieve first-class citizenship, Rustin counseled his superiors to make six specific points:

1. Convey the idea that neither party has done enough to advance the cause of civil rights.
2. Make it clear that the South cannot solve its problems without positive federal action.
3. Impress upon the Vice-President and the Secretary of Labor that the great majority of white Southerners are ready for changes but require federal prodding.

4. Ask the Vice-President to convey to President Eisenhower that the latter should take the civil rights issue to the nation as he did his struggle for the foreign-aid bill.
5. Call on Nixon to do the following: Make a trip South and speak out in moral terms for civil rights in general and voting rights in particular; urge Southerners, black and white, to obey the laws and uphold the Constitution; call together all Republican representatives and senators to impress upon them the importance of passing the civil rights bill now before Congress.
6. Indicate to Vice-President Nixon and Secretary Mitchell that something beyond logic and mind is needed at this point.

The meeting took place on June 13 at 3:25 P.M. in the White House, with the Secretary of Labor present to assist Nixon, Abernathy to support Martin. The Vice-President would have preferred to confine the discussion to pleasant reminiscences of Ghana and encouraging generalities about racial problems in America. But Martin insisted upon pinning Nixon to a definite commitment to visit the South as a show of the federal government's concern about Southern delinquency in complying with the directives of the Supreme Court. The Vice-President thought Martin's suggestion was sound but stated that, if he made the tour, he ought to contrive to avoid the impression that he was acceding to the requests of black leaders. Gracious and impenetrable, Nixon left the two leaders fairly well in the same federal limbo they had been before the two-hour interview. Ralph seemed to feel that Martin had treated the Vice-President rather too gingerly.

A rather tame civil rights bill was passed, nonetheless, early in September, 1957, the first of its kind since 1875. As Professors Blaustein and Zangrando observe, "It was not a far-reaching measure in substance, but it was a clear indication that the legislative branch was at last undertaking responsibilities that had previously been left to the executive and the judiciary." The act created a Civil Rights Commission empowered to gather information on voting rights violations and authorized the quiescent Justice Department to initiate injunctive relief in cases of proven voting irregularities.

Back in Montgomery, Martin pondered the full dimensions of nonviolent involvement. The compelling power of the example of personal physical suffering increasingly intrigued him. He remembered that the evils in society had once struck Thoreau as so overwhelming as to compel an honest man to seek imprisonment. The Mahatma's fasts and lengthy incarcerations offered even nobler guides to nonviolent resistance to evil. The example of Kwame Nkrumah's career had also become an inspiration. It was the mid-August three-day visit to Montgomery of the Gandhian disciple and scholar Ranganath Diwakar that convinced Martin that he, too, must set an example of physical suffering. Thus far, Martin's agony had been intellectual and psychological. "We began to think more deeply about the whole philosophy of nonviolence. We talked about how superficial and shallow our knowledge of the whole thing was," Coretta recalls. Martin resolved that, if the opportunity again presented itself, he would accept imprisonment rather than compromise with an evil law. He could be fairly certain that Montgomery would not deny him the opportunity.

On September 3, Martin and Coretta were in court with Ralph, who was to testify in a private suit. The mere presence of the Kings angered several policemen, who verbally abused them and ordered them to leave the building. Suddenly, one of the officers hammerlocked, trussed, and insultingly searched Martin and then carted him off to jail. "Boy, you done it now," a white officer declared with devastating grammatical insouciance. Martin posted bond and was released. A few days later, the presiding judge unsurprisingly found him guilty of the charges of loitering and failing to obey an officer. The fine was $10 or fourteen days in jail. Martin elected to serve the sentence. Instantly and mysteriously, his fine was paid and he found himself free. It was later revealed that Commissioner Clyde Sellers had dipped into his own pocket to prevent the MIA leader from using the jail "for his own selfish purposes." Upon his release, Martin vowed never again to accept liberty when convicted for the violation of what he deemed an unjust law.

Slowly and by dint of bitter experience, he was moving toward formal acceptance of Gandhian nonviolence. He received considerable encouragement from white intellectuals, politicians, and other public figures. A flood of mail flowed into MIA headquarters to commend the path of meekness and the domestication of Gandhian nonviolent concepts and tactics. Early in the Montgomery struggle, the Southern writer Lillian Smith had written two letters to Martin, the gradualist message of which was narcotic in its eloquence. In the second letter, she told the boycott leader, "You would be surprised, I believe, to know the strength of the admiration thousands of white Southerners feel for what you are doing. I hear it everywhere I go." Long ago, in Arkansas, Miss Smith continued, she had heard an evicted black sharecropper pray before a meeting of irate farmers, among whom were a large number of unionists and not a few "tough Communists." She detailed the bureaucratic impersonalism of the unionists and the revolutionary cynicism of the Communists. Only that unforgettable, evicted sharecropper remembered the point of their meeting—to turn away the evil practices of the landowners. " 'Break their hearts,' he cried, 'Oh God, give them tears . . . make them tears flow, God, make them flow . . . until a flood comes, God. Wash away their pride, God, wash away their hate; wash away their stubborn ways.' " "That's when I began to see plainly," Miss Smith concluded, "that the way of love is stronger than any other way." She enclosed a small donation to the MIA.

Many other letters of this genre followed. One from Chester Bowles, once ambassador to India, particularly affected Martin. "More than ever," Bowles wrote, "I am convinced that the only practical way out of our present dilemma is some adaptations to our present situations of the Gandhian techniques which amount to no more or no less than Christianity in action." Bowles regretted that his efforts to arrange a meeting a year previously between Prime Minister Nehru and Martin had aborted. But King, he concluded, should certainly visit India. Martin's reply to Bowles indicates how far along the road to philosophical nonviolence he had come. He was ready for a visit to India.

> It is my hope that as the Negro plunges deeper into the quest for freedom and justice he will plunge even deeper into the philosophy of nonviolence. The Negro all over the South must come to the point that he can say to his white brother: "We will match your capacity to inflict suffering with our capacity to endure suffering. We will meet your physical force with soul force. We will not hate you, but we will not obey your evil laws. We will soon wear you down by pure capacity to suffer.

In the weeks following his nearly fatal stabbing in Harlem in Blumstein's department store on September 20, the enforced inactivity permitted Martin to think seriously about a trip to Gandhi's homeland. As he had sat autographing copies of *Stride Toward Freedom*, his first book, Mrs. Izola Curry had been driven by unfathomably psychotic motives to plunge an eight-inch letter-opener into Martin's chest. His composure was incredible. As excited photographers circled about and several nearly hysterical females had to be restrained from yanking the weapon from his chest, he remained calmly seated. Later, he attributed his self-control and rapid recovery to God's use of him as an instrument: He had had "divine companionship in the struggle." At the hospital, as Coretta monitored the procession of distinguished visitors (among whom was Averell Harriman), Martin pondered the relevance of Gandhi to the American dilemma. When his physicians pronounced him recovered, but with the warning that he must husband his activities in the future, he decided to visit India.

There was a year-old invitation from Gandhi Smarak Nidhi (Gandhi National Memorial Fund) to visit India. After several months of rather tight negotiating, the American Friends Society agreed to finance the major portion of the visit of Martin, Coretta, and Professor Lawrence Reddick to India, provided that the black community raise the token sum of $500, to indicate its support of the voyage. This was easily accomplished, and, underwritten to the tune of nearly $6,000, the party enplaned for India early in February, 1959. They were expected to arrive on February 8. In fact, their complicated schedule delayed their arrival for two days. Thus, only a small crowd, swelled by a large coterie of journalists, was on hand to greet the Kings on February 10 at New Delhi airport. But, wherever they journeyed, they were enthusiastically greeted, especially Coretta, whose quasi-Indian appearance, fancy for saris, and renderings of Negro spirituals enthralled the Indians. Martin remembered, "Coretta ended up singing as much as I lectured." Their hosts were also pleased by Martin's first remarks. "To other countries I may go as a tourist, but to India I come as a pilgrim. This is because India means to me Mahatma Gandhi, a truly great man of the age." The first day, Tuesday, passed in a maelstrom of activity. The party had tea with the notable philosopher and vice-president of India, Radhakrishnan. Later, there were two receptions, the first at the Quaker Center, the second at Gandhi Smarak Nidhi.

The high point of the day was the evening meeting with Prime Minister Nehru. The boycott leader was surprised and not a little flattered by the Prime Minister's familiarity with his career. Their talk naturally turned to the alleviation of religious and racial suffering, and Nehru spoke compassionately of his government's determination to eradicate vestiges of caste. Three times during the week, Martin was to read the

pronouncements of the Prime Minister on untouchability.
He reflected upon the contrast between governmental concern in India with social injustice and the quiescence of
federal authority in his own country. He may well have reflected for a moment on the impervious congeniality of President Eisenhower the preceding June, when Martin, Roy
Wilkins, A. Philip Randolph, and Lester Granger of the
Urban League had met with him to plead for the issue of a
proclamation squarely endorsing the morality of the Supreme
Court's school desegregation decision. "Reverend," the
puzzled Eisenhower had told Martin, "there are so many
problems . . . Lebanon . . . Algeria," too many, apparently,
to bother with the explosive one of forcing the pace of racial
integration.

During Martin's interview with Nehru the Prime Minister
explained that caste discrimination was punishable by imprisonment, under the Indian constitution. Furthermore, in
the case of competition for university admission, government
institutions were compelled by law to give preference to the
untouchables. Professor Reddick asked if this was not discrimination. "Well, it may be," he was told, "but this is our
way of atoning for the centuries of injustice we have inflicted
upon these people." Nehru's words made a profound impression on Martin. They undoubtedly quickened his formulation of a program of governmentally promoted compensa-
tory treatment for American blacks. The impression of Nehru
that he carried away from this meeting was that of a public
servant who had achieved a rare union of political realism
and visionary sense of human potential. The tête-à-tête with
the Prime Minister received full coverage in the Delhi *Times*
the following morning, and this news served as a bellwether
for the country's numerous provincial and ethnic publications. Lawrence Reddick was continually surprised by the
enthusiasm and ubiquity of the Indian reception.

The King party rose early the following day to visit the

site of Gandhi's cremation; Martin and Coretta placed a wreath upon the memorial and Martin led his friends Reddick, Swami Vishwananda, and James Bristol, director of Delhi's Quaker Center, in silent prayer. Thursday, the day of their departure for Patna and Calcutta, was also memorably busy. Martin and Reddick had an enlightening discussion about Indian nonviolent concepts and tactics with the director of Gandhi Smarak Nidhi, G. Ramachandran. Before they had left the United States, Bayard Rustin had provided the party with a document containing "the latest thinking on the latest concept in the Gandhi movement. This was written (this latest material) by Gandhi's expert in basic education, Ashadevi Aryanayakam," Bayard had scrawled across the top. This document traced the origin, history, and present stage of implementation of the Mahatma's and Vinoba Bhave's idea for a *shanti sena*, an army of peace volunteers. It defined the unique characteristic of the peace army as one in which "character or soul force [*Satyagraha*] must meet everything and physique must take second place." Martin was enabled, because of Rustin's efficient homework, to explore this suggestive concept with Ramachandran and to prod for clarifications of *Satyagraha*, the primordial source of Indian nonviolence. On the day of Martin's arrival, a young lecturer at the Delhi School of Economics, Dr. R. K. Unnithan, had barged into his rooms at the Janpath Hotel and treated him to an extemporaneous and brilliant explanation of *Satyagraha*. Awaiting him upon his return to the Indian capital would be an instructive outline of Unnithan's research project, "The Sociology of Nonviolence."

Thursday wound to an exciting close with a speech to the Delhi University Student Union and a visit to President Rajendra Prasad of India. The party now began a three-week tour of the country, its rhomboidal path proceeding clockwise to Calcutta, Madras, Bombay, and back to Delhi. The pilgrims stopped at Patna and Gaya, arriving by rail in Calcuttta late Sunday. Three days later, February 18, they flew south to Madras. Racial diversity is especially interesting to black Americans, and Martin, Coretta, and Reddick were fascinated by the black complexions of Madras' Dravidian population and the contrasting whiteness of the northern Indians of Aryan descent. Outside Madras, they were granted an interview with Gandhi's aged mentor, C. Rajagopalachari, who added to the steady accrual of the party's Gandhian intelligence. Continuing to study the peoples and institutions of southern India, in the Dindigul and Madurai regions, the Kings and Reddick looked with intense interest at the political and social experiments of the Indian Government. There was the peace army contingent at Gandhi Village, the untouchable (*harijan*) village farther south, and two villages established through the efforts of Vinoba Bhave to secure land from the large proprietors for the peasantry.

The party turned northward, after a stop in Kerala, for Bombay. During their two-day sojourn there, February 26-28, R. R. Diwakar, the director of the local Gandhi center, accompanied the party, affording Martin another valuable discussion with one of India's principal authorities on nonviolence. Diwakar, reviewing the fact that Gandhi had conceived the doctrine during his struggles on behalf of the Indian minority in South Africa, explained that its most successful application to India occurred in March, 1930, near the city of Ahmedabad, when Gandhi left the banks of the Sabarmati River to go on foot with seventy-nine disciples to the banks of the Arabian Sea, 170 miles away. The Mahatma vowed he would never return to Sabarmati until the British Government abolished the salt tax. This highly publicized "Salt *Satyagraha*" was the signal for a national eruption of civil disobedience. Diwakar was anxious to draw certain distinctions between these tactics and those adhered to by similar movements. He reminded Martin of Gandhi's description of *Satyagraha*:

[It] differs from passive resistance as the North Pole from the South. The latter has been conceived as a weapon of the weak and does not exclude the use of physical force or violence for the purpose of gaining one's end, whereas the former has been conceived as a weapon of the strongest and excludes the use of violence in any shape or form.

The Montgomery pastor remarked that he had perceived during the Montgomery struggle the near identity of *agape* and *Satyagraha*: "*Agape* was love seeking to preserve and create community." Gandhi's philosophy was equally assertive in the moral sense. It surpassed the pragmatic pacifism of Thoreau (one of Gandhi's original inspirations), which preached active and armed opposition to evil after a certain point of forbearance.

Finally, Martin discussed with Diwakar, as he had with other Indian leaders and teachers, the disciplinary prerequisites for *Satyagraha*. The Mahatma's first nationwide effort in India prefigured, on a grander scale, the dilemmas to be confronted by his American disciple in Albany, Georgia, and, particularly, Selma, Alabama. This was in early 1919 when, from Ahmedabad, Gandhi's followers issued a national call for passive resistance. The British Government arrested Gandhi while its military authorities employed excessively harsh measures to break the spirit of the peaceful rebellion. Soon the rebellion erupted into open and almost uncontrollable violence throughout a large part of the country. Hastily released by the authorities, Gandhi called a halt to the *hartal*, or general strike, and publicly denounced the pacifist indiscipline of his followers. Ahmedabad, Gandhi confessed, had been a "Himalayan miscalculation." "Victory is impossible," he wrote, "until we are able to keep our tempers under the gravest provocation."

Much was learned from Ahmedabad, nevertheless, for it helped the completion of a tactical breviary for the adherents of *Satyagraha*:

1. Negotiation and arbitration

2. Preparation for direct action
3. Agitation (propaganda, mass meetings, parades)
4. Issuing of an ultimatum
5. Economic boycott and strikes
6. Noncooperation (nonpayment of taxes, boycott of schools and other public institutions, use of ostracism and voluntary exile)
7. Civil disobedience
8. Usurpation of the functions of government ("assertive *Satyagraha*")
9. The establishment of a parallel government to oppose the established regime

Martin deliberated these tactics with Diwakar, as he had with Ramachandran and Unnithan, among others. He was to restate most of them in an abbreviated and much less radical form for the instruction of his followers in Birmingham, Alabama. The film of Gandhi's life, *Voice of India*, that the party viewed at the Bombay Smarak Nidhi made the message and method of Gandhism more vivid.

On March 1, the pilgrims arrived at Ahmedabad, now rich in significance for them. From there, they journeyed to a village near Kishangarh, where they met the legendary Vinoba Bhave. The meeting took place as Vinoba Bhave was setting out on foot for remote regions. Because of Martin's health—he had been unwell for a day or so—and the cumulative fatigue of ceaseless travel, the party Americanized the occasion, Reddick recalls, overtaking the Indian leader by car, accompanying him for a short distance by foot, and then returning by car. Coretta remained behind. Martin was greatly impressed by Bhave, whom he described as "a great spiritual man, moving in a humble way to keep the spirit of Gandhiji's philosophy alive." By the end of the week, they were again in Delhi. On March 10, Martin, Coretta, and Reddick returned to the United States. His farewell words to India were warmly quoted, for he stated that he had perceived throughout the land the spirit of the Mahatma toiling to achieve the grand design of its genius.

Although he would again visit foreign countries on several occasions, the Indian trip was a unique spiritual catharsis. Reddick observed the changes in Martin. It made the difference between an emotionally based intellectual conviction that nonviolence was a morally superior and practical philosophy and certitude founded upon empirical and generalized observation of this philosophy in daily operation. Montgomery, for all its success, had been too small a laboratory to justify the Q.E.D. of universal applicability. The attention lavished upon him by the Indians both surprised him and developed within him a heightened sense of awareness of the historic significance of the Montgomery boycott. He returned to America with a much surer appreciation of the techniques appropriate to the peculiar and exigent combat of the nonviolent crusader: "I left India more convinced than ever before that nonviolent resistance is the most potent weapon available to oppressed people in their struggle for freedom. It was a marvelous thing to see the results of a nonviolent campaign." The research materials of Dr. Unnithan were to be particularly valuable in this respect, and Martin showed his gratitude by assisting the scholar in obtaining a grant from a foundation.

For many black American readers, Martin's accounts of his Indian experiences must have had a noble irrelevance. Slightly more than a month after his return, Mack Parker was lynched in Poplarville, Mississippi. Eight weeks later, the school board of Prince Edward County, Virginia, disbanded its public education system rather than comply with integration. The federal government persisted in its hands-off position. What unique inspiration he derived from India was to be fully drawn upon in the months ahead. He was pleased, certainly, to be asked by Vice-President Nixon to attend a conference of religious leaders in Washington on May 11. He was gratified to know that outstanding pacifists such as Norman Cousins, Clarence Pickett, Muste, and Linus Pauling considered that his signature weighed heavily in the scales of international *détente* and nuclear control. But liberals, whether in the government or not, were at best temporizingly sympathetic and at worst incredibly ignorant of Southern racial conditions.

By the summer of 1959, copies of Martin's detailed reports of voting irregularities, telegrams citing specific legal infractions, and messages imploring the creation and dispatch of federal fact-finding missions to the South comprised a sizable file in the MIA archives. Congressman Emmanuel Celler and Senators Kenneth Keating, Jacob Javits, and Paul Douglas, among others, were representative of the small gallery of congressional sympathizers who unfailingly responded to Martin's messages but not to the needs they cited. "I fear that to comply with your request," Congressman Celler had written, typically, early in 1957, "would only delay the enactment of the [civil rights] legislation. I am sure you realize that opponents of the legislation would welcome any action which would hamper and delay such action." This was in response to Martin's request to the Judiciary Subcommittee of the House of Representatives to conduct civil rights hearings in the South. Typical, as well, was the letter from Senator Douglas, confiding that, although he agreed with its goals, he felt constrained by senatorial etiquette to decline the cochairmanship of the 1959 Petition Campaign and Youth for Integrated Schools. But these solons at least protested their good faith. It required saintly charity to ascribe the same good faith to the executive branch. Attorney-General William P. Rogers' reply to Martin's telegram alerting the government to discriminatory practices at the Redstone Missile site in Alabama conveyed irritated indifference. Rogers' assistant sent the reply, "The Attorney-

General has asked me to convey his appreciation of the commendation and of the views expressed by you in that communication."

As federal immobility continued and white violence and
legal circumvention escalated, so did black frustration and
calls to violence. In the early months of 1958, Martin had
encountered the advance tremors of black anger and some
sharp criticism from a friend. His visit to Los Angeles, California, in mid-February provoked unbridled wrath from the
black *Herald-Dispatch*: "This paper submits that Reverend
King's philosophy reflects neither the long and stubborn
struggle of Montgomery Negroes to end bus segregation nor
the flaming heroism of Negro children braving hostile and
jeering racist mobs (Little Rock, etc.)."

At the same time, but from the moderate end of the spectrum, Representative Charles Diggs sternly lectured Martin
about the organizational weaknesses in his voter registration campaign. "Rallies and speeches are fine for inspirational
purposes," Diggs telegraphed, "but a successful registration
campaign demands skillful follow-up in the field." Beyond the
moralizing and the marching was the unglamorous and gritty
routine of educating, entreating, even physically transporting people to the registration desks and polling booths
throughout the South. The SCLC had thus far not developed
machinery to cope with this urgent problem.

There were other portents. In Monroe County, North Carolina, Robert Williams, the local NAACP president and an
ex-marine, engendered a sharp if brief crisis at the Association's fiftieth annual convention in July, 1959. Williams had
organized, drilled, and armed a band of Monroe County blacks
and persuaded them to abandon for *lex talionis* the seemingly
fruitless tactic of court appeals.

Toward the end of the year, the television program "The
Hate That Hate Produced" ("every phrase," Malcolm X
alleged, "was edited to increase the shock mood") shocked

the nation with a view of the world of the Black Muslims. Martin's prognosis of racial conditions was not optimistic. "The struggle for civil rights has reached a stage of profound crisis," he wrote.

Out of the ministerial meetings in Atlanta and New Orleans had come tentative prescriptions for treatment of the rapidly deteriorating racial health of the South. In 1958, the embryonic organization that would become the Southern Christian Leadership Conference (SCLC) had established its head-quarters in Atlanta, under the capable superintendence of Miss Ella Baker, a former field secretary for the NAACP. Late in July, 1959, the first nonviolent institute was held on the Spelman College campus in Atlanta, sponsored by the SCLC, CORE, and FOR (Fellowship of Reconciliation). More than sixty delegates attended the three-day affair and heard speeches by A. Philip Randolph, Rustin, Lawrence Reddick, Richard Gregg, Reverend James Lawson, and Dean William Stuart Nelson of Howard University. Dean Nelson's keynote address, "The Tradition of Nonviolence and Its Un-derlying Forces," traced the origins of nonviolence from Hin-duism, Buddhism, and Jainism through Christianity to Tolstoi and Thoreau. Lawrence Reddick contrasted the slowly vanish-ing caste system in India with the increasingly virulent mani-festations of bigotry in America. The practical management of nonviolence was in the hands of Abernathy, Lawson, Fred Shuttlesworth, James Robinson of CORE, and Reverend Wyatt Tee Walker. These men and other delegates drew up a five-point manifesto, the vagueness of which did not detract from its militant determination to achieve full citizenship for American blacks.

The needs of the South and the potential effectiveness of the SCLC urged Martin to experiment with nonviolence in a larger theater. Late in November, he answered a letter from the clerk of his father's church, offering him the co-pastor-ship. He would give the request "my most prayerful and serious consideration." On November 29, a Sunday, the flock at Dexter Avenue Baptist Church was much troubled. News of an impending decision that might remove their beloved pastor from them had spread through the community. And it came, emotion-choked and dramatically. Having surrendered the pulpit to a colleague minutes before, Martin again approached his congregation to give a speech that was remarkable for its mixture of hubris, grandeur, and historical prevision. He once had said that Rosa Parks was "tracked down by the *Zeitgeist*." He left no doubt that Sunday that he too was a quarry of history. For four years, he had carried upon his shoulders the work of six men. He refreshed the congregation's memory of those painful and glorious days following December 1, 1955. He had had no choice but to spend himself in the combat against injustice. But he was weary now, weary of local duties, weary of speaking engagements, weary of the general routines of responsibility; weary, as he put it, of "the general strain of being known." It was time for him to pause, to meditate. He could not always be "giving, giving, giving, and not stopping to retreat." He was in peril of losing his "creative" resources, in even greater immediate peril of becoming a "physical and psychological wreck." The young preacher had tarried long enough in "the crowd and in the forest." His peroration was commensurate with the apostolic sublimity he foresaw: "I can't stop now. History has thrust something upon me which I cannot turn away. I should free you now." Martin wept; the congregation wept and sang. In less than a month, his responsibilities at Dexter would end. He was not quite thirty-one years old.

Before moving into the SCLC's Auburn Avenue headquarters, there was quite a considerable amount of business to be completed in Montgomery. The selection of only three matters for analytical comment—the Southern Conference Educational Fund, the Henry Winston case, and the FOR speech—betrays a seeming indulgence of the arbitrary. However, their relative importance as gauges of Martin's developing political awareness and wariness speak for themselves.

The Southern Conference Educational Fund (SCEF) had obtained Martin's collaboration as chairman of its voting rights panel, to be held in Washington on January 31, 1960. SCEF was a venerable, if rather ineffective, organization that had labored doggedly for human rights in the South. The executive director, Dr. James Dombrowski, a noted labor relations expert, superintended the organization at its New Orleans headquarters. SCEF had been just sufficiently effective, nonetheless, to cause Senator James Eastland to conduct a one-man hearing for three days in New Orleans in March, 1954. His corroboration of an anonymous charge of Communism against SCEF was a foregone conclusion. The possibility of taint appears to have worried Martin. In a letter to Dombrowski, too elaborate in its reasons and too apologetic in its tone to be entirely credible, Martin begged off in the eleventh hour.

The Henry Winston case involved an appeal for clemency by a Communist purging himself of a harsh sentence for contempt and conspiracy under a law that had subsequently been voided by the Supreme Court. Benjamin J. Davis, a Communist and a black Atlantan whose father had been highly respected, interceded with Martin to have him sign a petition. After a second letter, Martin informed Davis that he had written to the chairman of the U.S. Board of Parole to urge favorable action in Winston's case. It seems fair to say that Martin's handling of these two incidents was governed by a judicious combination of political caution and moral courage.

In August, the Montgomery pastor addressed the annual convention of the Fellowship of Reconciliation. Martin's topic, "The Future of Integration," embodied an optimistic warning that "the Era of Restricted Emancipation (1863–1954)" had closed and that "the Period of Integration" would be characterized by increasingly "direct action against injustice without waiting for other agencies to act. We will not obey unjust laws," Martin stated, "or submit to unjust practices." His audience fully understood that the speaker intended to play a considerable role in the "direct action" ahead.

5

Skirmishing in Atlanta

> To protect the skull, fold the hands over the head. To prevent disfigurement of the face, bring the elbows together in front of the eyes.
>
> INSTRUCTIONS TO CLAFLIN COLLEGE
> AND SOUTH CAROLINA STATE
> COLLEGE STUDENTS, 1960

IT IS DIFFICULT, if not impossible, to find a city whose black population was more smug and more affluent than Atlanta's in 1960. Atlanta was a fount of black wealth and, *ergo*, black wisdom in the deep South. It was in its Citizens Trust Bank that the MIA had deposited a great portion of its funds. It was to Atlanta's black Brahmins that the established leadership of Albany, Georgia, had come, in 1959, to submit its plan for desegregation of public facilities. It was told to wait. The times were not right. Howard Zinn, professor of history at Spelman College, has faithfully captured the imperturbability of Atlanta's black oligarchy. Quoting a friend's account of the first meeting between the students and the oligarchy, he reports the latter's spokesman as saying, in effect,

> So you see, kids, we've been in this a long time. We want the same things you do but we know by now they can't be gotten overnight. It's our experience that you have to work slowly to get lasting results. We'd hate to see your movement backfire and spoil things we've worked so hard for. You need guidance, and we hope you'll have the vision to accept it.

Atlanta is ruled by a coalition, or power structure (the term was first applied to Atlanta), of politicians, members of the press, businessmen, middle-class whites interested in "good government," and "Negroes aiming to free themselves of disabilities that have so long held them down," a student of urban politics writes. But the owners and officers of financial and insurance institutions, enterprising druggists, realtors, physicians, lawyers, and the academic *junta* running the four colleges, the school of theology, and one university were not omnipotent in the black community. An intermediate stratum containing a wide variety of stable occupations had far less reason to be content with the refined gradualism of the black oligarchy. Moreover, the nearly four thousand college and university students were visibly restive. As Martin settled into his co-pastoral duties at Ebenezer and superintended the ordering of the Atlanta headquarters of the SCLC (ably assisted by Ella Baker and Maude Ballou) an event occurred in Greensboro, North Carolina, that portended the historic drama that he had foretold upon leaving Montgomery.

Ezell Blair, Jr., and his roommate, Joseph McNeill, were students at North Carolina Agricultural and Technical College in Greensboro, a segregated institution for blacks. Having been refused service at the lunch counters reserved for whites in Greensboro's department and variety stores, Blair and McNeill decided to undertake their own form of nonviolent protest. (They had just read the FOR comic book *Martin Luther King and the Montgomery Story*.) On February 1, 1960, they took seats at the Woolworth's lunch counter and thereafter continued this tactic on a daily basis. By the second week in February, Blair and McNeill had sparked a student revolt in other North Carolina cities. White students at Duke University and black students at North Carolina College soon joined forces to demand integrated service in Durham's department stores and bus stations. The "sit-in" syndrome spread to Tennessee, where students at Fisk University, under the leadership of Marion Barry and

Diane Nash, marched en masse to sit at counters and tables in dining facilities that until then had been gustatory sanctuaries for whites. John Lewis, a divinity student, was also there to lend his organizational abilities to the demonstrations. James Lawson, a divinity student at Vanderbilt University, was one of the movement's first martyrs; under pressure from the local press and white public, Vanderbilt dismissed Lawson for participating in the Nashville sit-ins.

Then the sit-ins reached Atlanta. Whereas they had been spontaneous in other Southern cities, the Atlanta demonstrations were meticulously plotted and almost sportingly forecast. Don Clarke, president of Clark College's student body, Marion Bennett, president of the Interdenominational Theological Center student's association, James Felder, president of Clark College's Student Government Association, Willie Mays, president of Atlanta University's Student Dormitory Council, Mary Ann Smith, secretary of Morris Brown College's Student Government Association, Roslyn Pope, president of the Student Government Association at Spelman College, and Morehouse's Lonnie King and Julian Bond caucused with Professor Sam Williams of Morehouse to determine strategy. Bond, Felder, Miss Pope, and especially King were the true masterminds of the sit-in. The students later begged Martin's support. Williams, his former teacher, advised him not to attend the first plenary meeting of the student planners. His motives and Martin's reasons for acquiescence stemmed from their sure knowledge of the Atlanta community. Its spokesmen were primed to seize upon the slightest manifestation of civic presumptuousness by the SCLC.

The student manifesto, "An Appeal for Human Rights," was prepared, therefore, in Martin's absence. It was published with funds raised by Atlanta University's president, Rufus Clement, in the *Atlanta Constitution* of March 9. Nevertheless, Martin's influence upon the document was apparent.

Proclaiming "We do not intend to wait placidly for those rights which are already legally and morally ours to be meted out to us one at a time," the manifesto demanded community action in seven areas: education, housing, jobs, voting, law enforcement, hospitals, and entertainment facilities (restaurants, movies, concerts):

> We, the students of the Atlanta University Center, are driven by past and present events to assert our feelings to the citizens of Atlanta and to the world.
> We, therefore, call upon all people in authority, state, county, and city officials; all leaders in civic life, ministers, teachers, and businessmen; and all people of good will to assert themselves and abolish these injustices. We must say in all candor that we plan to use every legal and nonviolent means at our disposal to secure full citizenship rights as members of this great democracy of ours.

At least fourteen cities in five Southern states became unwilling laboratories for student experiments in nonviolent confrontation. Ella Baker knew that the militance of the students would be short-lived and might very well run to violence if it were not soon given organizational shape and direction. She persuaded the president of her former school, Shaw University, in Raleigh, North Carolina, to make its facilities available for a plenary civil rights student conference to be held April 15-17. The SCLC appropriated $800 to underwrite the affair. The conference provided the springboard for the Student Nonviolent Coordinating Committee (SNCC). In attendance were 212 delegates, black and white students from the South, Northern students, SCLC and CORE representatives, and *doyens* of the civil rights movement.

Martin and James Lawson were the keynote speakers. Martin's message commended three points: (1) the establishment of an on-going organization to lead the struggle, (2) a nationwide campaign of selective buying to reward progressive business establishments and punish those that remained segregated, and (3) the formation of an army of volunteers prepared to accept prison sentences in lieu of fines and bail. He made it clear that nonviolence as a tactic was inseparable from nonviolence as a way of life: "There is another element in our struggle that then makes our resistance and nonviolence truly meaningful. That element is reconciliation. Our ultimate end must be the creation of the beloved community. The tactics of nonviolence without the spirit of nonviolence may become a new kind of violence."

"King touched here on a matter of extreme delicacy," Lerone Bennett observes: "Although the students honored King as a nonviolent pioneer, some of them did not think he was radical enough and many accepted nonviolence as Nehru accepted it, as a tactic." James Lawson may have articulated the innermost sentiments of the audience by restricting his observations to practical techniques of confrontation and dismissing out of hand courtly policy meetings between black and white community leaders. Whatever misgivings some students may have harbored, Martin's support was essential; moreover, it was sincerely given.

The weeks following the Raleigh conference were packed with SCLC activity. To create an organization capable of meeting the challenges of this new era, Martin imposed upon himself a regimen that would have dazed a less dedicated man. Rising at 6:30 A.M., he generally worked until 2 or 3 o'clock the following morning. There were also the periods when he got himself into furious bouts of traveling and speaking. For all the able talent sooner or later to come to the new organization, the SCLC was from its inception an extension of the personality of Martin Luther King. The public paid attention only when he spoke, followed only him, and donated because he asked. It was up to him to breathe life into the fledgling civil rights body. This was not going to be an easy task.

The tactics of nonviolent confrontation were not joyously acclaimed by the senior and most powerful of the civil rights

organizations, the NAACP and the Urban League. These
organizations had long ago carved out spheres of influence,
and each was unshakably convinced of the excellence of its
operations. During the preceding three decades, the Urban
League had attempted to inject a steady trickle of middle-
class blacks into white business, primarily through dignified
persuasion of chambers of commerce and important citizens
and by lobbying for fair-employment legislation on national
and local levels. Its paramount concern was not the masses of
blacks but their white-collar cousins. It is fair to say that,
while local offices were known to be aggressive, in general the
Urban League's dependence upon white good faith and money
gave it a conservative cast and severely limited its effectiveness.

The NAACP was less conservative and possessed a much
larger popular support. But it serviced the ambitions of the
black middle class also. The point was, however, that the
manner in which these goals were articulated by this organization encouraged a far greater number of underprivileged blacks
to share them, at least for the moment. No one could forget
that the landmark decision of 1954, *Brown v. Board of Education of Topeka*, was the fruit of the NAACP's years of long,
painstaking, and costly toil. Even so, it had already begun to
miss the pulse of the young and the destitute. Robert Williams, president of the Monroe County chapter, was fond of
quoting a laborer as asking, "Man, do you mean we can belong
to that organization?" The time had not yet come when the
youth would irreverently refer to its national director, Roy
Wilkins, as "Uncle Roy"; but it was not far away.

The NAACP placed its faith in the courts, not in coalitions
espousing direct mass assault upon segregated facilities, or
did so only in moments of extraordinary crisis. Most older
blacks, especially those whose faith and patience had been
materially rewarded, shared the aversions of the NAACP. The
Northern whites who customarily supported civil rights endeavors took their cues from the black establishment. They

respected Martin but were prone to question the wisdom of the SCLC's announced tactics. Several persons who had been asked to serve on the SCLC Advisory Committee declined. James A. Pike's declination and Herbert Lehman's were typical. The Episcopal prelate sent a donation but begged off because of his lack of intimate familiarity with Southern problems. There were affirmative replies, of course. Adam Clayton Powell did not send a donation, but he accepted membership immediately. Through the summer of 1960, the black press continued to speculate on the personality clashes and ideological differences racking the civil rights movement, despite the forceful disclaimers of Roy Wilkins, Lester Granger, and Martin. Momentarily, Jackie Robinson had believed there was a rift between the NAACP and the SCLC. His letter to Martin late in June expressed relief that the incipient "power struggle" had blown over.

That there was a cooling off of relations between these organizations is certain. A retired Boston businessman and member of the NAACP board, Kivie Kaplan, received a diplomatic refusal from Martin to a proposal made early in 1961. "A position on the board of the NAACP, while being a cherished one and one that I would be honored to accept," would require more time than his schedule would allow, Martin explained. He asked not to be nominated. No doubt the effervescent Mr. Kaplan had ignored the likelihood that the nomination of Martin would have embarrassed both sides. A letter from Martin's former professor Allan Knight Chalmers, an active NAACP supporter, appears to express disappointment over the lukewarm attitude of the SCLC. Martin's intrinsic feelings about the NAACP were conveyed to his literary agent toward the end of 1960. *Coronet* magazine had asked him to prepare an article in collaboration with journalist Louis Lomax. Lomax had recently indicted the unimaginativeness and *attentisme* of the established civil rights leadership. Besides being extremely complimentary to Martin, Lomax's *Harper's* article blistered the NAACP and accused it specifically of suppressing local leaders. "Actually, the article aroused the ire of the NAACP supporters probably more than anything in recent years," Martin explained: "While I privately agreed with many things that Mr. Lomax said . . . I feel a moral obligation to preserve a public image of unity in our organizational work."

The consensus of the black establishment was that Martin was attempting to move too swiftly and too aggressively. The word "backlash" had not yet been coined, but there was much fear that the emotions it describes might compromise the hard-won gains of the 1950's. These leaders were mindful that on May 6, only three months after the commencement of the sit-ins, President Eisenhower had signed the second civil rights bill since Reconstruction. Its primary accomplishment was to strengthen the Justice Department's power to take action on behalf of any person denied the ballot, provided a "pattern or practice" of discrimination was established. However, it was possible to construe Title II of the bill, providing stiff provisions for punishment of individuals crossing state lines to foment violence, as a Southern-inspired weapon to smite the sit-in demonstrators.

For the present, established civil rights leaders were anxious not to rock the boat. This was also an election year. Many who sought to advise Martin counseled a moratorium on demonstrations. But he knew that the students not only would not agree to unwind their movement but were absolutely adamant in believing that the times were propitious to their tactics. *Student Voice*, written and published by the Atlanta activists, made this clear in its first editorial, "Time to Take a (Firm) Stand." Bill Strong proclaimed,

> There is a time for all things. A time for thought, a time for speculation, a time for investigation, but most assuredly this is not a time for straddling the fence. The American Negro is engaged in a gigantic life-or-death struggle with the foes of

human decency. Is it possible that some of us occupying positions of leadership are trying to stay the hand of fate?

The SCLC leader was not going to be numbered among the fence-straddlers.

Meanwhile, fund-raising had proceeded slowly in 1959. Martin's visit to India had contributed to this. In April and May of 1959, he had been ubiquitous, traveling over California, Chicago, Detroit, New York, much of the South. He had rushed from the Raleigh conference to appear on the television program *Meet the Press* on April 17. Early in May, he had spoken at a luncheon of trade union leaders. The next day, Governor Rockefeller had dispatched his plane to bring him to Albany, New York, for a *tête-à-tête*. As a trustee of Spelman College, a member of a family whose donations to the Atlanta University colleges were considerable, and an active Baptist, the governor could obviously discuss much with Martin. Later, Rockefeller had made a liberal monetary contribution to the SCLC. Martin regretted that he could not recompense the governor by endorsing his candidacy for the presidency.

In this same month, the second policy meeting of the student organizers was held at Atlanta University. Again Martin, Lawson, and Ella Baker were present to address the fifteen student delegates and offer advice. Two important decisions were reached at this conference. First, the students voted not to operate as an affiliate of the SCLC but to confer separate identity upon themselves. The title Temporary Student Nonviolent Coordinating Committee was adopted. Marion Barry, a graduate student at Fisk, was elected chairman. The Committee's headquarters was to be established in Atlanta. Second, the student organization adopted nonviolence as its lodestar. Its statement of purpose read: "We affirm the philosophical or religious ideal of nonviolence as the foundation of our purpose, the presupposition of our faith, and the manner of our action. Nonviolence as it grows from the Judaic-Christian traditions seeks a social order of justice permeated by love." To assist SNCC in putting together an office, the SCLC made a small grant of $250 early in July.

Martin's appearance at the Raleigh conference and his numerous public engagements during this time constituted a triumph of duty over personal adversity. Not only was he distressed by his growing misunderstandings with other civil rights leaders; he was harassed and threatened by Southern white intrigue. In May, 1960, returning Lillian Smith to her hospital room at Emory University, he was arrested while driving through De Kalb County, adjacent to Atlanta. The charge was operating a vehicle with an out-of-state operator's license. The three-month period of grace on it had expired, and he had neglected to obtain a Georgia permit. On September 23, he was tried and convicted by the De Kalb County court and sentenced to pay a $25 fine. A fact that he had ignored—one that was to have an immense bearing on the forthcoming national elections—was that Judge Oscar Mitchell had also placed him on probation for twelve months, at the time of sentencing.

Also in May, he was compelled to stand trial on an Alabama charge was operating a vehicle with an out-of-state opera- always distressing. It is even more distressing for a black leader, because of the *a priori* guilt the black community customarily assumes. Many of its leaders, especially its spiritual counselors, historically have enriched themselves opportunistically at the expense of their followers. "But who will believe me?" Martin pleaded, after two deputies from Fulton County, Georgia, served him a warrant requested by the state of Alabama. Alabama claimed that he had filed fraudulent returns for 1956 and 1958. The reckless charges of Reverend Fields, once forgotten, would certainly seem to give credence to the accusation. Totally distraught, Martin hastily decided not to honor a Chicago speaking engagement, but, fortunately, he

changed his mind and addressed the Chicago audience after
all. Despite the bitter trials of Montgomery, Coretta had never
seen Martin so troubled. "I tried desperately to assure him
that the vast majority of people believed in him and understood the motivation of the state of Alabama." A little later,
Ralph Bunche offered similar consolation. "Look, Martin," he
said, "it's the word of the state of Alabama against the word
of Martin Luther King. There is no question in my mind
which the country will accept."

The state of Alabama charged that Martin had perjured
himself in computing his 1956 income as $9,150, his 1958
income as $25,248, whereas his actual revenue for those years
was alleged to have been $16,162 and $45,421. In the light
of the subsequently luxuriant rumors that he derived huge
personal sums from his civil rights activities, the facts presented to the Alabama court are most interesting. They revealed that, although he protested its figures, Martin had
given the state a check for the disputed amount in 1958. It
had never been cashed. Rather than embroil himself in an
undignified and possibly interminable dispute, he had in effect
made a sizable gift to the state. Attorneys Gray, Hubert Delany of New York, and William R. Ming of Chicago also
compelled a state tax official to admit that his department had
never reached a final determination of the exact sums Martin
supposedly owed. How could the defendant be charged with
a crime whose details the prosecution had failed to determine
fully? Here was logic that spoke even to the hard prejudices
of the white jurors. On May 28, they returned a verdict of
not guilty.

This trial was costly to Martin's peace of mind. He had
brooded over its consequences until the moment of the surprising verdict. The worries of this period were quietly expressed in a letter to Rosa Parks, who had written to him a
few lines of comfort earlier: "In the midst of constant harassment and intimidation because of my involvement in the

civil rights struggle," Martin wrote, "I often find myself asking 'Is it worth it?' But then a friend of good will comes along with kind and encouraging words that give me renewed vigor and courage to carry on." He was also grateful for the international support received by the Committee to Defend Martin Luther King, ably put together under the direction of Bayard Rustin and enhanced by Mrs. Eleanor Roosevelt's active participation. But even an unfavorable verdict would probably not have destroyed his leadership potential. The fact is, he was innocent; and, on numerous occasions throughout his career, he showed his complete disinterest in accumulating a personal fortune, by malversation or even honestly.

The June, 1960, issue of *Commonweal* reported that there was a strong probability that the SCLC would become a national organization and accept individual as well as affiliate memberships. Martin's actions during this period appeared to justify this prediction. He wrote to the national committees of the Democratic and Republican parties to request a hearing of the proposals that he wished to see incorporated into their election platforms. Bayard Rustin was again the principal advisor in this matter. In a long letter to Martin, dated June 15, 1960, he proposed the presentation of seven major demands. Interestingly, Rustin asked Martin not to discuss these demands with Chester Bowles until he, Rustin, had seen Martin:

1. Both parties should repudiate segregationists within their own ranks and make a forthright declaration that any form of discrimination is unconstitutional, un-American, and immoral.
2. Both parties should endorse the spirit and tactics of the sit-ins as "having the same validity as labor strikes."
3. In accordance with the Fourteenth Amendment, congressional representation ought to be reduced in those areas where Negroes are denied the right to vote.
4. Both parties should explicitly endorse the 1954 Supreme Court decision as morally right and the law of the land.

5. That Section III of the proposed civil rights legislation, empowering the federal government to bring suits on behalf of Negroes denied their civil rights, be enacted into law.
6. That Congress pass the "federal registrar" plan of the President's Civil Rights Commission and that the responsibility for the protection of voting rights be placed squarely with the President and not with Southern courts.
7. That the two parties and their candidates take a clear moral stand against colonialism and racism in all its forms, especially in Africa.

This was not a pleasant bill of demands for politicians. Senator Thruston Morton, Chairman of the Republican National Committee, replied cagily that he thought Martin should request an appearance before the Republican party's platform committee.

The position of the Democrats was tested early in July. Martin, Roy Wilkins, Randolph, and Adam Powell organized a meeting of civil rights leaders in Los Angeles to be held during the time of the party's convention. All the Democratic nominees for presidential candidacy were invited to address the civil rights gathering at the Shrine Auditorium. Oscar L. Chapman represented Senator Lyndon Johnson. Mrs. Agnes Myer read Mrs. Eleanor Roosevelt's telegram supporting Adlai Stevenson. Senators Stuart Symington and Hubert Humphrey spoke for themselves. Humphrey received an enthusiastic reception by stating that he would rather be right about civil rights than President or Vice-President. Senator John Kennedy's arrival was greeted with booing. The presiding officer, Clarence Mitchell, pleaded for courtesy. Not many minds were changed by his speech, but Kennedy did succeed in winning respectful applause at the end. But the greatest enthusiasm was reserved for two of the meeting's organizers, Martin Luther King and Adam Clayton Powell. The delegates rose from their seats, cheering, when the latter proclaimed, "Our demands for civil rights are a revolution—a revolution of passive, massive resistance." They rose again when Martin intoned, "We have a determination to be free in this day and age. This is an idea whose day has come. We want to be free everywhere, free at last, free at last." Most of the people left the Shrine Auditorium determined to support Humphrey.

As the nation readied itself for the presidential contest, other forces were steadily building up constituencies. Most blacks, even dedicated activists, had not taken the Black Muslims seriously. And, although they were a topic of conversation among whites, very few really believed that they constituted a menace. The Muslims attempted to begin a dialogue with Martin's movement on at least two occasions, in 1957 and July, 1960. Malcolm X invited the SCLC leader to deliver a speech at the 1960 Muslim Education Rally in New York's 369th Armory. The invitation was declined. Martin's opinion of these separatists was that of most Americans. "They have some kind of strange dream," he explained to Kivie Kaplan, "of a black nation within the larger nation. At times the public expressions of this group have bordered on a new kind of race hatred and an unconscious advocacy of violence." The two leaders met at least once and too briefly to discuss their differences. The gulf of misunderstanding between them appeared to be practically unbridgeable.

In mid-October, the embryonic Student Nonviolent Coordinating Committee held its last plenary conference of the year in Atlanta. Marion Barry, its president, asked Martin to deliver the principal speech, addressing himself to the topic "The Philosophy of Nonviolence." Martin was arrested on October 19, three days after the conclusion of the conference. He and thirty-six others, mostly students, were charged with trespassing, because of their insistence on being served at the lunch counter in Rich's department store in Atlanta. Unanimously, they refused to accept bonded release. The city's mayor, William Hartsfield, intervened immediately, to propose a two-month truce, during which the demands of the protestors could be reviewed fairly. The pledge was later broken, but it appeared to have achieved the immediate objective of freeing Martin.

While these arrangements were being completed, the De Kalb County authorities acted. The SCLC leader was still subject to the terms of the probationary sentence against him for his May traffic violation, and De Kalb County now demanded that he be released into its custody. Because the charge of trespassing, in Atlanta, in Fulton County, was based upon a statute of the state of Georgia, he had been detained in the Fulton County Prison rather than at the city jail. It is unlikely that the city authorities would have risked the almost certain embarrassment of judicial buffoonery by releasing Martin into the custody of De Kalb County. Martin's attorney, Donald Hollowell, worked fervishly during the next five days to prevent a change of his client's jurisdiction. Nevertheless, on October 25, Martin was transported in handcuffs to the courtroom of Judge Oscar Mitchell of De Kalb County. Attorney Hollowell's defense was exceedingly able but unavailing. Judge Mitchell construed Martin's "trespassing" at Rich's department store to be a violation of his probation. He sentenced him to serve four months of the twelve-month probationary sentence at hard labor in the Reidsville State Prison, a rural penal camp in Tatnall County. Hollowell rushed to his office to prepare a legal maneuver that would prevent the sheriff from transporting his client to the camp the following morning.

Hollowell returned to De Kalb County before 8 A.M. the next morning and was informed that Martin had been taken to Reidsville State Prison. The hours that followed Hollowell's alerting the family, the SCLC, and the press were agonizing. There was some reason to fear that the police car transporting the prisoner might be conveniently ambushed along the dusty Georgia roads. There was more reason to dread the appalling

conditions he would suffer at the prison camp. Hollowell was
rattled, because he was certain that Martin's legal predicament was far less serious than the physical peril of his confinement. Judge Mitchell's sentence was in such flagrant violation
of basic jurisprudence that it could only be a matter of days
before it was reversed. That afternoon, the attorney filed two
bills of exception in the De Kalb court. In substance, they
demanded that Judge Mitchell, in accordance with the
statutes governing misdemeanors, release his client and set
bail in lieu of imprisonment. In a case such as Martin's, this
was in fact an automatic procedure under state law. A colleague of Hollowell's was prepared to file, minutes afterward,
an identical request with the state supreme court in the event
of the De Kalb court's noncompliance.

While Hollowell prepared his brief, the wire services reported the arrest to the world. The White House was deluged
by telegrams demanding federal intervention. From virtually
every nation, messages of support from private citizens poured
into the SCLC offices. Northern governors, representatives,
and senators deplored the outrage and hoped the President
would authorize an investigation. All civil rights leaders protested. The Republican Administration was inclined to manifest its concern. The national elections were only days away.
In a moment of uncharacteristic boldness in civil rights matters, President Eisenhower contemplated making a public
statement:

> It seems to me fundamentally unjust that a man who has peace-
> fully attempted to establish his right to equal treatment, free
> from racial discrimination, should be imprisoned on an un-
> related charge, in itself insignificant. Accordingly, I have asked
> the Attorney-General to take proper steps to join with Dr.
> Martin Luther King in an appropriate application for his re-
> lease.

Several prominent black leaders were informed of the
President's forthcoming declaration. But, in principle, inter-

vention in local affairs was repugnant to Eisenhower. Richard Nixon, the Vice-President as well as Eisenhower's party's candidate, was not sure whether the statement would not do more electoral harm than good. The White House remained silent and the Vice-President declined to comment. The electoral calculations of Nixon's opponent, John Fitzgerald Kennedy, dictated a different policy. One of his Atlanta advisers, Attorney Morris Abrams, advised making a gesture of some kind. He was seconded by Harris Wofford, one of the senator's special advisors on minority affairs. After conferring with his brother-in-law, Sargent Shriver, Kennedy made a telephone call to Coretta King.

John Kennedy told Mrs. King that he knew that this was a trying period and that he would endeavor to help her husband. Robert Kennedy phoned the astonished Judge Mitchell to inquire whether Dr. King's case would allow bail. The next day, October 27, Judge Mitchell granted Hollowell's request for the release of his client. These were dramatic moments, and news of the role of the Kennedys in Martin's release was reported nationwide. Meanwhile, Hollowell, accompanied by representatives of CBS and NBC and a local network and the SCLC, flew in four small planes to Reidsville to collect the civil rights leader. More drama was to come. A press conference was held just outside the gates of the prison. As it ended and the party headed for the aircraft, a low voice cried out "Long live the King!"—a parting tribute from one of Reidsville's black inmates. But he had not left yet. The engine in the plane that Martin had boarded failed to start and, for a terrible moment, it was thought that it had been sabotaged. Finally, it sputtered to life, and Martin was free. In a telephone conversation shortly thereafter, Hollowell was chided by Thurgood Marshall with the professional joke "Say, Hollowell, they tell me that everybody got King out of jail but the lawyers." Parenthetically, Marshall promised Hollowell that the NAACP would assume the legal expenses incurred in the sit-in and the De Kalb trials.

Understandably, the lawyers may have felt that their role had been ignored in the general delirium that the Kennedy phone calls ultimately provoked within the black population. That Sunday, the senior King told his congregation that "It took courage to call my daughter-in-law at a time like this. Kennedy has the moral courage to stand up for what he knows is right." Martin's father, a life-long Republican, had openly endorsed Nixon's candidacy. It was rumored as well that he had the fundamentalist Protestant's dislike of Catholics. But he completely shed such prejudices that morning. "I've got a suitcase of votes," he shouted, "and I'm going to take them to Mr. Kennedy and dump them in his lap." Although blacks across the nation were at first ungratefully slow to appreciate the Kennedy gesture, the distribution of two million copies of Harris Wofford's pamphlet " 'No-comment' Nixon Versus a Candidate with a Heart, Senator Kennedy" corrected the oversight just in time.

Martin was less enthusiastic. "There are moments when the politically expedient is the morally wise," he reflected. Still, Kennedy had more than delivered on Martin's suggestion, made during dinner at the senator's Georgetown home, that he "do something dramatic" if he wanted to capture the black vote. Martin let it be known that he was grateful to Kennedy for his concern, but he declined to make a formal endorsement of Kennedy's presidential candidacy. Taken with the famous television debate between Kennedy and Nixon, the Kennedy intercession in the King case was a decisive element in the results of the 1960 presidential election. Theodore White, authority of the 1960 elections, observes that "the candidate's instinctive decision must be ranked among the most crucial of the last few weeks." John Kennedy carried the election by a mere 112,881 votes. Vice-President Lyndon Johnson was gracious in a letter to Martin: "I want to let you know how much I particularly appreciate having had your support," he wrote.

Martin's assumed responsibility for the victory of the Democrats was roundly denounced by many people of both races. "I am a negro [sic] from the north," one of his correspondents declared, "and I am amazed at the way Senator Kennedy put one over on the negroes of the South. Senator Kennedy was always against the negroes, but he felt he had to do something *big* to win the vote in the South." A furious Northern white wrote Martin, "You people are truly dumb when you swallow the political bait of the . . . ambitious John F. Kennedy and mistake 'political ambition' for 'moral courage.'" Martin probably shared their misgivings and sense of possible exploitation. To forestall the growing impression of naïve collusion with the Kennedys, he prepared an article for *The Nation*, challenging the new Administration to live up to its progressive slogans:

> The new administration has the opportunity to be the first in one hundred years of American history to adopt a radically new approach to the question of civil rights. . . . [It] must begin . . . with the firm conviction that the principle is no longer in doubt. The day is past for tolerating vicious and inhuman opposition on a subject which determines the lives of 22,000,000 Americans.

The federal government has the power to provide firm leadership in the crises ahead, he continued. In voter registration, it should certainly end its temporizing. Utilizing the relevant clause in the Fourteenth Amendment, the government must reduce congressional representation in states where the franchise is racially restricted. It remained to be seen whether the new Administration would heed this advice.

Among the first pertinent acts of the Kennedy Administration were, regrettably, the appointments of three notorious strict constructionists to federal judgeships in the South. Judges J. Robert Elliot of Georgia, William Harold Cox of Mississippi, and E. Gordon West of Louisiana were to serve the interests of the segregationist South loyally and effectively. Almost two years were to pass before the Kennedys telephoned again.

National developments were only part of Martin's worries. There were problems within the upper echelons of the SCLC. Some of them were exposed in James Baldwin's article in *Harper's* early in 1961. Congressman Adam Clayton Powell had accepted Martin's invitation to become a member of the SCLC board. A *prima donna* and a maverick, Powell's ideological moods were subject to sudden and mysterious oscillations. He began to see sinister influences at work within the civil rights movement. For reasons that are still obscure, he developed a profound hostility to Bayard Rustin, publicly denouncing Rustin's "control" of A. Philip Randolph. Simultaneously, Powell also condemned Stanley Levison's control of Martin. Levison is a white New York attorney of independent means who had devoted his energies to raising funds for the SCLC. Powell threatened to have Rustin's youthful connections with socialism investigated by the House Un-American Activities Committee unless Martin agreed to dismiss him from his SCLC post. Baldwin alleges that Martin "lost much moral credit . . . especially in the eyes of the young, when he allowed Adam Clayton Powell to force the resignation of his [King's] extremely able organizer and lieutenant, Bayard Rustin." An investigation of the politics of Rustin's youth, with the likelihood of a probe into his personal habits, might have been distasteful to the SCLC as well as to the victim. It is far from clear, however, that Martin passively complied with Powell's threat. Rustin denied the accuracy of Baldwin's interpretation and at least one student of the SCLC states that Rustin insisted that the SCLC release him to avoid the unsavory melodrama threatened by Powell. In any case, although their formal ties were now severed, Rustin continued to play a central part in the policy formulations of the organization.

The SCLC meanwhile continued to play an important role in the formulation of civil rights policies. In March, 1961, the decision was made by CORE, and later endorsed by SNCC and the SCLC, literally to mobilize the sit-ins. The students held the conviction that the enactment of the millennium was only a matter of total commitment and a few years. Courage and confrontation were adequate to turn the page of history. It was decided to invade the deep South by bus to compel the immediate desegregation of public facilities. In 1947, Bayard Rustin and James Peck had led a group on a "Journey of Reconciliation" through the border states to achieve this very goal. The South that had united solidly behind the Confederacy remained wholly untouched by integrationist experiments of this nature. Martin was elected chairman of the Freedom Ride Coordinating Committee. The Freedom Rides began early in May. James Farmer, CORE's director, obliged the government by forwarding a map detailing the cities to be visited by the students. Martin's organization played a secondary role, although Ralph Abernathy and Wyatt Tee Walker were arrested for their participation.

From Washington, D.C., the Freedom Riders proceeded south through South Carolina, across Georgia, to Alabama. Outside Anniston, Alabama, one of the two Freedom Buses was stopped and set afire by angry whites. The second bus reached Birmingham, where the demonstrators were set upon by local toughs, two of them brutally beaten under the benign superintendence of the police. Charles Person, a black student attending Morehouse, and James Peck, whose family owned the Peck and Peck clothing establishment, were savagely assaulted. The bus companies, Greyhound and Trailways, refused to carry the group to Montgomery, its last major stop in Alabama. Narrowly escaping further violence at the Birmingham airport, the Freedom Riders flew to New Orleans.

A second group left Nashville, Tennessee, immediately, determined to reach Montgomery. Pulling into the Alabama capital on the morning of May 20, the riders found a reception committee of 300 aroused whites. In the total absence of the police, the mob's fury heightened as its numbers rapidly increased to nearly a thousand. In the ensuing explosion, the injured included John Lewis of SNCC, James Zwerg from the University of Wisconsin, Norman Ritter, head of the *Time-Life* news bureau, and President Kennedy's special representative, John Siegenthaler, who was left sprawled in the hot tar of the highway for twenty-five minutes.

Martin rushed to Montgomery the following morning, as did nearly seven hundred U.S. marshals sent by Attorney-General Robert Kennedy and hundreds of Alabama National Guardsmen, reluctantly ordered to duty by Governor John Patterson. Martin spoke eloquently that evening to the crowd of twelve hundred, mostly black, assembled in Ralph's First Baptist Church. "The law may not be able to make a man love me," flashes of anger were in his voice, "but it can keep him from lynching me." Here was an irrefutable emendation of the Sumner-influenced thinking of many federal officials in high places. Escorted by troops and helicopters, the small band of Freedom Riders left Montgomery for Jackson, Mississippi, and more danger.

Martin undoubtedly had good reasons for declining to accompany the Freedom Riders. The spoor of repugnant physical violence that their Southern passage left may have been one reason why he remained in Atlanta. His increasingly heavy organizational duties were probably another. The financial needs of the SCLC required him to undertake an intensive speaking tour at the very moment the Alabama outrages were occurring. Furthermore, he was obliged to fulfill his duties to the Ebenezer congregation. His stature as a national race leader also may have temporarily constrained him. If he occasionally deplored some of the consequences of the students' Southern campaign, he extolled enthusiastically their right to disobey unjust laws. "I think all of this is unfortunate," he confessed, "but I think it is a psychological turning point in our whole struggle, just as Little Rock was a turning point in our legal struggle. The people themselves have said 'We can take it no longer.'" But, for the time being, Martin probably wished to maintain a posture of judicial respectability in order to be more effective in his dealings with the timid new Administration.

If this surmise is valid, not everyone appreciated its subtlety. The fiery Robert Williams, who still managed to retain his NAACP connection, wired an ultimatum to Atlanta:

> The cause of human decency and black liberation demands that you physically ride the buses with our gallant freedom riders. No sincere leader asks his followers to make sacrifices that he himself will not endure. You are a phony. Gandhi was always in the forefront, suffering with his people. If you are the leader of this nonviolent movement, lead the way by example.

Time magazine claimed that SNCC was divided over Martin's effectiveness. James Forman of SNCC confined himself to the observation that *Time*'s was "an unfortunate article." Aware of the whispering and grumbling against himself, Martin observed stoically, "These students are helping to deliver the rights that have been declared. We must overlook their impatience."

In civil rights, it was not always true that nothing succeeds like success: Success frequently embarrassed. It redoubled the visceral fury of those who had failed. In one month, CORE and SNCC stripped away the South's thin veneer of social and political benignity and the resulting murderous and seemingly incorrigible display of hatred appalled the nation. But it was not true, as the majority of the students believed, that more of the same rude surgery would compel the federal government to step in and complete the civil rights operation in a finished manner. Nor was it true that the continuing spectacle of Southern malignancy would disgust the average white citizen into uniting morally behind his fellow black Americans. It was most certainly not true that the South would be shamed by its own actions into accepting rapid and profound change. The Kennedy Administration, hypersensitive in matters of race because of its slender electoral mandate, was ready to secure black rights ultimately but demanded civil peace immediately. Attorney-General Robert Kennedy asked for a "cooling-off period" at the end of May. Outside the South, outrage and compassion over civil rights were gradually muted by doubts about the wisdom of deliberately assaulting Southern mores. The often flamboyant participation of Northern white students in these Southern sorties compounded national doubts about the Freedom Rides. Well-meaning whites in the North supposed that, given time, "responsible" whites in the South would surface if the waters calmed again. Curiously, both points of view—that of the friendly whites and that of the SNCC students—derived from the same fallacious supposition, which credited the white Southerner with a residual humanitarianism. Subsequent developments unfortunately belied this. One of the SNCC staff members, Ruby Doris Smith, an eighteen-year-old junior at Spelman College, believed that the South could be shamed into responsibility. Defending the continuation of the Freedom Rides in a rather breathless article in the student weekly, she argued, "Freedom Riders are accomplishing exactly what Dr. Martin L. King, Jr., has stated the purpose of nonviolence [*sic*]: touch the moral conscience of the nation. As the sit-ins made the south ashame [*sic*] to deny well-dressed and orderly young Negroes a hamburger, so does it feel [*sic*] about denying use of transportation facilities." The melancholy truth was, however, that there was not much shame in Alabama, Mississippi, and Louisiana and in parts of Georgia and Florida.

Martin was too close to the students not to know that a proposal to decelerate their campaign would be angrily rejected. His own reputation would most certainly by jeopardized. On the other hand, he also saw the wisdom of the Attorney-General's recommendation. He was concerned about the rising millennial pitch among some SNCC spokesmen. Propaganda, mobilization, militant protest, and then a second trial at negotiation were the pre-ordained steps to nonviolent success.

Many of the students, on the contrary, were prepared to max-imize community tensions, expecting that, in the diastolic aftermath, a radical social change would occur. Martin con-ferred with his SCLC lieutenants in Atlanta about the Ken-nedy request. They decided to reject the Attorney-General's call for a "cooling-off period," but they did suggest that the Freedom Riders might accept a "temporary lull." Semantics is an important and delicate science in which civil rights leaders learned to be expert.

The SCLC's commendation had almost no immediate effect upon the students. The kamikaze-like junkets into Ala-bama and Mississippi continued throughout June, July, and August. Behind the scenes, however, there was a gearing-up of anti–Freedom Ride forces in the weeks following the SCLC statement. In August, the SCLC and SNCC collided roughly at the Highlander Folk School meeting in Tennessee, which Martin and Ella Baker attended. The cause of this dissension was that during the June meeting of SNCC in Louisville, Kentucky, a proposal had been placed before the assembly by Tim Jenkins, a black vice-president of the National Student Association, that civil rights organizations shift their focus from militant confrontation to voter registration. Jenkins had already met with the representatives of two mammoth foun-dations, Field and Taconic, as well as with Harris Wofford, the President's special adviser on minority problems, and Burke Marshall, Assistant Attorney-General in charge of civil rights, all of whom were keenly interested in voter registration. The foundations indicated their willingness to assist in financ-ing the project.

The suspicion of an establishment conspiracy plagued the Highlander School conferees. Diane Nash and Marion Barry rallied their followers to a rigid direct-action standard. Those favoring voter registration were led by Charles Jones. Martin moved among the students, patiently listening to their con-tending viewpoints. His ability to entertain the opinions of others with what seemed genuine empathy disarmed his most hostile disputants. This quality is one of the most vivid recollections of even his most casual acquaintances. He favored the voter-registration project and his faith in the Administration and its allies was still firm; he persuaded a number of students to his point of view. Nevertheless, the Highlander crisis worsened. The militants were inconsolable and threatened to withdraw to form a separate organization. It was Ella Baker who offered the successful compromise of establishing two SNCC divisions: a Direct Action Projects Division under Diane Nash and a Voter Registration Division headed by Charles Jones. The compromise was far from being entirely satisfactory. The suspicion that they had been outmaneuvered accompanied many of the militants back to their cities. If Martin's motives had been above reproach, the linkage of Martin Luther King in their minds with racial moderation was nevertheless being forged. Another unpleasant side effect of the Highlander Folk School meeting was that it would shortly provide the extravagantly spurious basis for the charge that Martin was a Communist. He had been photographed seated near persons alleged to be active members of the Party.

Not all the bright young people were with CORE and SNCC. Reverend Wyatt Tee Walker had joined the SCLC earlier that year. A thin, tall man, Wyatt's suave air and sharp features suggest a grandee rather than a Baptist preacher from Petersburg, Virginia. His arrogance was boundless. "One big piece of evidence about the greatness of Martin Luther King is that a man as vain as I am is willing to play second fiddle to him," Wyatt once said. He was to prove a capable executive director, despite his tendency to ignore details. Fred Shuttlesworth of Birmingham, Alabama, C. T. Vivian, and Bernard Lee of Atlanta, James Lawson, and James Bevel—all Baptist ministers—were young, intelligent, and courageous. Another young minister, Andrew Young, joined the SCLC during the summer of 1961. "Andy" Young was ordained in the liberal and largely white Congregational Church. His callow appearance belied a worldliness in matters of finance and organizational techniques that had not been conspicuous among the SCLC personnel. Andy also spoke the language of Eastern foundation directors as well as the *patois* of the uneducated Southern black. Indeed, he wore two hats. He had been designated to supervise the disbursement of the Field Foundation's grant of $100,000 for voter education and registration projects. Of this sum, $40,000 went directly to the SCLC. The collaboration of the SCLC in the undertaking made his membership in that organization natural and convenient. He and Wyatt began work setting up a center for practical instruction in civic and political affairs in the abandoned Dorchester Academy, 50 miles south of Savannah, Georgia. Other such centers were later established throughout the deep South by Dorchester graduates.

If Martin's role in the Freedom Rides was first that of an inspiring symbol and banker (the SCLC donated several thousand dollars to the Freedom Ride campaign) and, later, that of a slightly tarnished mediator, neither he nor his organization had really lost their combativeness. He could argue, moreover, that the September 22 ruling of the Interstate Commerce Commission prohibiting segregation aboard buses and in terminal facilities was an important indication of the government's sincere intentions. But good intentions were not enough. Martin made it abundantly clear, in his *New York Times Magazine* article in September, that he did not believe that the government was adequately meeting the challenge of effective implementation of black rights. On the other hand, the confrontation tactics of the students were not by themselves the answer. Demonstrations must provide the stiffening for the acquisition of political and economic leverage by local communities; all else, however cathartic and dramatic, was illusory. He hoped that the SCLC would provide the methodology, combining the right proportions of common sense and militancy, that would serve as a model to other civil rights groups.

The SCLC still awaited an appropriate situation to impress further upon the public the viability of its tactics. In September, 1960, Martin had offered his assistance to the Jacksonville, Florida, NAACP in its battle against segregated facilities. The chapter president had correctly but firmly declined the offer. As the students returned to school, Martin was in search of an appropriate theater for his nonviolent program.

6

Albany, Georgia—Nonviolence in Black and White

> It's not a matter of whether I'm a segregationist or an integrationist. I'm a duly constituted law-enforcement officer, dedicated to the enforcement of the law.
>
> LAURIE PRITCHETT

IN HIS *Souls of Black Folk*, W. E. B. DuBois, the *doyen* of American historians, described Albany, Georgia, as a "wide-streeted, placid, Southern town, with a broad sweep of stores and saloons, and flanking rows of homes—whites usually to the north, and blacks to the south. Six days a week the town looks decidedly too small for itself, and takes frequent and prolonged naps." Sixty years later, DuBois's Albany remained unchanged in its essentials. With allowances made for the construction of many more buildings in brick and stone, the street and store lights made possible by the New Deal rural electrification program, and the inevitable accretion of used-car lots and drive-in restaurants, Albany was still the lethargic center of southwest Georgia's Black Belt.

Albany slept the racial and political slumber induced by a condition of sated tyranny. James Gray, editor of the daily *Albany Herald* (and once a Northerner and once slightly more liberal) voiced the thinking of the city's responsible white citizens on racial politics. On the day before the first arrests of civil rights demonstrators, Gray was moved to condemn government officials who claimed to see parallels be-

tween the independence struggles of African nationals and
the American Revolution. Referring to the African nations,
he said: "These emerging people have not yet served their
apprenticeship in the arts of responsible independence." If
pressed, Editor Gray would very likely have given the African
higher marks than the black citizen of Albany.

Southwest Georgia was spectacularly unlike the jaunty tourist's idea of America. Life was unequal, hard, and, for nonwhites, especially brutal. The counties in that part of Georgia
customarily earned such revealing adjectives as "Bad" Baker
and "Terrible" Terrell. Oglethorpe, Americus, Ellaville, Cordele, these mean little towns along the slow and twisting road
to Albany are, physically, uncannily reminiscent of the old
colonial centers in what was formerly British West Africa:
tin roofs eradiating under the merciless sun, dusty side streets
with their ditches, the administrative square with its architectural horrors, the grand white houses for white people, and
the profusion of blacks in ill-fitting and colorful garb. But
here the similarities with West Africa end. In each of these
towns stands a tree whose limbs, tradition has it, have supported the death agony of blacks at the end of a rope. There
was very little justice in such places. For whites, there was
consideration determined by social status; for blacks, there
were whimsical sanctions ruled by affection, sadism, and fear.
The minority race (which frequently outnumbered the white
population) did not vote, except for a handful of "respectable" blacks who were believed to be safely housebroken.
Naturally, blacks did not sit with whites in public or commercial places even when they were allowed to enter them. Buses,
when a town's size justified their use, were segregated. Literally, the black American survived from one generation to the
next by feigning spinelessness and stupidity.

Crossing the Kinchafoonee Creek into Albany, material
conditions could be seen to have begun relatively to improve.
Formerly a cotton capital, the city was now the financial and

cultural center of the thriving peanut, pecan, and corn economies of the region. Within a decade, Albany's population had
grown from 31,155 to more than 56,000 in 1960. Forty per
cent of its people were black. Not all of them were abjectly
poor. Besides the persons who were homeowners by dint of
superhuman effort, there was the usual fairly prosperous
stratum of professionals. The Clennon W. King family, with
its extensive real estate holdings and numerous commercial
establishments, had amassed a considerable fortune. Albany
State, a segregated college, was administered by well-off blacks
who had been chosen for their racial insouciance. Its students
were not the best. Charles Sherrod of SNCC describes the
students and faculty of the institution in the following
manner:

> They are "protected" from all seductions to think on what it
> means to be a black man in Albany or anywhere else in the
> South. . . . The campus is separated from the community by a
> river, a dumpyard, and a cemetery. And if any system of intel
> ligence gets through all of that it is promptly stomped under
> foot by men in administrative positions who refuse to think
> further than a new car, a bulging refrigerator, and an insatiable
> lust for more than enough of everything we call leisure. . . .

There was an army installation near Albany, which provided
employment for black citizens. It also provided a glimpse of
what racial integration was like, as, of course, it abided by
the presidential decree abolishing military discrimination.

   The dramatic events occurring in Montgomery and Little
Rock, the contemporary publicity of the sit-ins and Freedom
Rides, and Martin King's proximity in Atlanta began to stir
the Albany leadership. But the leadership was cautious. The
Criterion Club, an organization composed of prominent black
men, had emphasized social enjoyment rather than civic involvement. Ministers generally had preferred to dwell upon
the beatitudes or the condign punishment awaiting their
flocks in the afterlife. The local NAACP was quiescent. In

1959, Albany Attorney Chevene B. King proposed filing suit to end the city's segregated polling stations. After a conference with Atlanta's black oligarchy, the leaders decided to delay application for legal remedy. The younger men were not content to wait for outside forces to bring change to the community. Two of the King brothers (unrelated to the Atlanta Kings), Slater and Chevene, Dr. William G. Anderson, Mrs. Irene Wright, Marion Page, and the members of the NAACP's Youth Council decided to force Albany to step to the quickening beat of Southern racial progress. In February, 1961, they addressed a letter to the city commissioners calling upon them to desegregate public facilities. The reply was indirect but unequivocal. The *Albany Herald*'s editorial column exhorted the commissioners to reject the proposals out of hand. In the ensuing months, the white community pursued a tactic of admonitory violence in order to cow the blacks. Arrests for spurious traffic violations increased. A costly civil suit was instituted against Clennon W. King, whites drove through the Albany State campus, and a number of students were molested. The year was nearly over and it appeared that it would almost certainly end on a futile note.

SNCC headquarters in Atlanta had followed the Albany malaise with mounting interest. The September 22 decree of the Interstate Commerce Commission banning segregated buses and station facilities spurred the organization to action. Charles Sherrod, twenty-two, and Cordell Reagan, eighteen, were already fully acquainted with progressive leaders and the college students in the city. They had spent a considerable amount of time during the preceding months winning the confidence of the students and the common folk. Both men are easy to listen to and convincing because of their cogency and sincerity. Sherrod was more immature in appearance than most of the apparently immature SNCC types. He excelled in the Southerner's art of inviting underestimation by the unsuspecting. He had studied theology at Union Theological

Seminary in New York. He was slow and sleepy-voiced only when there was no reason to hurry. Indeed, his casual manner—careless dress and sandals—was a bit frightening to the community elders, who believed, says Chevene King, that "Charlie was a kook or a commie." It did not improve Sherrod's and Reagan's relations with the established leadership that their impact upon the NAACP Youth Council was devastating. Almost to a member, these young people swung in step behind the SNCC leaders. With a firm base in the local community, Sherrod and Reagan returned to Atlanta late in October, prepared to move to the second phase of SNCC's plan—demonstrations.

The SCLC was informed of SNCC's plan. Wyatt Tee Walker and Charles Sherrod were more than personal friends. Walker had financially assisted the younger man's education. The SCLC agreed to provide a small amount of money to the Albany campaign. On the morning of November 1, Sherrod, Reagan, James Forman, Charles Jones, and a white member of SNCC, Salynn McCollum (who was to contact the Justice Department to report the anticipated violations) boarded the Trailways bus for Albany. Atlanta police were aware of the quintet's intentions and phoned the Albany police. The Albany bus terminal was closely guarded by ten officers by the time they arrived. They decided to wait until later in the day for a try at the white waiting room. That afternoon, after Sherrod and Reagan had visited the Albany campus, nine students unobtrusively entered the station and took seats in its *sanctum sanctorum* before they could be stopped. They were ordered to leave or face arrest. Here was a patent and public violation of the ICC ruling. Miss McCollum, who observed the scene, telephoned the Justice Department in Washington upon her return to Atlanta. She was thanked for her citizen's vigilance but no action was initiated.

The bus station episode catalyzed Albany's leadership. On November 17, there was an amalgamation of the city's black organizations to form the Albany Movement, with Dr. Anderson, an osteopath, as its president. It made good organizational sense to bring together the Ministerial Alliance, the Federation of Women's Clubs, the Negro Voters League, the Criterion Club, and the NAACP with its Youth Council. One observer contends that the Albany Movement was created to insulate the friction between the students (now captained by Sherrod and Reagan) and the NAACP. "I wouldn't say we didn't want the students here," an NAACP spokesman confided, "I would say, however, that they found us not too receptive to them." Plans were readied for the second challenge of the city's codes. Five days after the formation of the Albany Movement, three members of the Youth Council entered the Trailways station dining room and were arrested by Chief of Police Laurie Pritchett. That same afternoon, two Albany State students, Bertha Gober and Blanton Hall, were taken into custody for the same offense. They were charged with disorderly conduct, failure to obey an officer, and behavior tending to create public disorder and were released on bond. The date of their trial was set for December 11. The whites began to mobilize forces at this point. City government elections took place on Monday, December 4, and the threat of a large turnout of black citizens sent white voters to the polls for a record turnout of their own. The blacks, not yet fully adjusted to taking advantage of opportunities that circumstance presents, failed to vote in large numbers. Asa Kelley and Buford Ellington were elected Mayor and Mayor pro tem, respectively. The new government would take office officially on January 11.

The blacks were also gearing up. Again the Albany police learned that Freedom Riders were arriving from Atlanta. This time, nine persons—four black and five white—were traveling by train. They sat together in the "white" car, ignoring the conductor's orders that the blacks must retire to the rear of the train. James Forman, SNCC's executive secretary, Norma

Collins, SNCC's office manager, Lenore Tait, a volunteer worker, and Bernard Lee of the SCLC were black. Robert Zellner of SNCC, Per Laursen, a Danish writer, Tom Hayden of Students for a Democratic Society, his wife, and Joan Browning from Georgia were white. The Albany Movement directors intended to reap maximal national publicity from the Freedom Train. At approximately 3:30 on the afternoon of December 10, 1961, the Atlanta train braked before the station. Several hundred blacks were there to welcome the riders. Chief Pritchett and a detachment of police were also on hand, Pritchett obviously much irritated by the widespread support that "outside agitators" had achieved, as well as by the large crowd's serious and dignified behavior.

The passengers entered the white waiting room. Chief Pritchett ordered them away, and they prepared to leave. Something deep in Pritchett's viscera snapped. He lost his cool professionalism. Following the riders outside, he bellowed, "You are all under arrest." Of the nine, all were arrested but one. Charles Jones, Bertha Gober, and a student bystander were also arrested. This was a scenario of which the SNCC and SCLC strategists had dreamed. Pritchett's action was sufficient to unite the black community around its martyrs. During the next four days, hundreds of singing, praying blacks marched to city hall to protest the November and December arrests. On the morning of the December 11 trial of the bus-station offenders, four hundred high school students demonstrated before city hall. By December 15, nearly five hundred people were in jail.

That same day, the city agreed to hold unofficial talks. A biracial committee of six was formed. The appearance of white conciliation was negated, however, by the spirit of intransigence in the air. "The teams have no authority for action," the *Herald* emphasized, "and are merely trying to see if some areas of agreement can be found." Mayor Kelley and Mayor pro tem Ellington, together with a segment of the business community, would have entertained a compromise. The Albany Movement's demands were not excessive: integration of bus and rail facilities, establishment of a permanent biracial committee, dismissal of all charges against demonstrators. As a placatory gesture, Mayor Kelley ordered the release of more than one hundred of the arrested demonstrators. But no Southern mayor could risk the epithet "nigger lover," and Kelley protected himself by simultaneously requesting that Governor Ernest Vandiver dispatch a unit of the Georgia National Guard to the city. Negotiations collapsed before the day ended, in the miasma of rumor and bad faith. Dr. Anderson offered the city a final opportunity to negotiate honestly until 10 A.M. Saturday, December 16.

It is not clear how many leaders of the Albany Movement sanctioned Dr. Anderson's next move—his telephone call to Martin Luther King, Jr., to ask that he come to Albany immediately. Sherrod and Reagan were openly hostile. They had not been impressed by Martin's conduct during the Atlanta sit-ins. "When Dr. King comes into a situation," Sherrod says, "several things happen. The power structure of the state is alerted. The federal authorities are alerted, and publicity—the public media are extra-sensitive, extra there." The SNCC generals preferred to keep their leadership and goals local rather than to see the contest inflated into a rhetorically charged and grandly symbolic struggle between the white and the black South. Nor was the Movement's secretary, Marion Page, enthusiastic about Martin's intervention. Slater and Chevene King appear to have deferred judgment for the moment. Ministers were generally more receptive to the proposal. Moreover, Anderson, whose responsibilities had begun to oppress him psychologically, was anxious to share the burden of leadership with an experienced civil rights leader. The mounting threats against his life lent peculiar urgency to Anderson's preference. Ties of friendship were factors also. Anderson had known Abernathy since their student days at Alabama State

College, and he could depend upon Abernathy to do his utmost to smooth away the misgivings of the local leadership. With the negotiations at an impasse, Anderson contacted Ralph and Martin that Friday evening, December 15.

At the Shiloh Baptist Church the next night, Martin, who had just arrived with Ralph and Wyatt, spoke to a capacity audience. "Don't stop now," he cried, "Keep moving. Don't get weary, children. We will wear them down by our capacity to suffer." In the antiphony of amens accompanying his speech, it was evident that what had been lacking—an inspiring leader—was provided from that moment on. The NAACP was represented at the meeting by Ruby Hurley, its Southeastern regional director, who spoke of the two forces that the white man understood—the dollar and the ballot. Anderson told the people to reassemble at 7 A.M. at the church for a march on the court house. "Eat a good breakfast," he advised, "wear warm clothes and wear your walking shoes." The presence of Martin and Ralph notwithstanding, the turnout the following morning was disappointing. It was one thing to chant hallelujahs in the electric but secure atmosphere of a militant prayer meeting. But those who were not students, who had jobs to protect, were hesitant about joining the march.

It was well into the afternoon before the Movement leaders and their assistants succeeded in rounding up a crowd of 257 persons. From Shiloh, they set out at 4:30 P.M. with Martin, Ralph, and Anderson in the forefront. As they marched, they gained courage, and the vigor with which they sang "We Shall Overcome" increased. A foreboding detail about this march was the conduct of Anderson. He had been under a terrible strain since his assumption of the presidency of the Movement. The *Herald* reporter noticed that he continued to repeat in a monotone the words, "God bless you. God bless each of you. Strike me first. God bless you." Close friends were concerned. There were rumors that Anderson believed himself to be in possession of supernatural powers. As the

King's birthplace, 501 Auburn Avenue, N.E., Atlanta, Georgia.

King and Abernathy ride the buses again in triumph after the Supreme Court's integration order, December 21, 1956.

King attacks Governor George Wallace after the church-bombing deaths of four Negro girls, Birmingham, Alabama, September 17, 1963.

The "I Have a Dream" speech in front of Lincoln Memorial, during the march on Washington. Whitney Young and Mahalia Jackson are among those in the foreground. August 28, 1963.

With Eisenhower after discussing the suspension of school integration at Little Rock, Arkansas, June 23, 1958.

With Kennedy and Adlai Stevenson during a meeting with the American Negro Leadership Conference on Africa, December 17, 1962.

With Johnson during the voting rights bill signing ceremony, Washington, D.C., August 6, 1965.

With Nehru and Mrs. King during the visit to India, February 19, 1959.

Accepting the Nobel Peace Prize, December 10, 1964.

With Malcolm X after announcing plans for "direct action" if Southern senators filibuster against the civil rights bill, March 26, 1964.

With family March 17, 1963. Left to right: Martin Luther King III; Dexter Scott, on Mrs. King's lap; and Yolande Denise.

Leaders in a Vietnam-war protest stand in silent prayer in Arlington National Cemetery, February 6, 1968.

During a visit to a pool hall in Chicago, February 18, 1966.

Interviewed after he was attacked at a formerly white hotel, Selma, Alabama, January 18, 1965.

A day before his assassination on the same balcony. On King's right is Jesse Jackson.

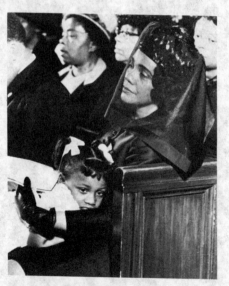

Mrs. King comforts her five-year-old daughter, Bernice, during the funeral service in Ebenezer Baptist Church, April 9, 1968.

The casket, being carried over 4 miles on a mule-drawn farm wagon, moves through the streets of Atlanta en route to the second funeral service, at Morehouse College.

marchers reached the intersection of Jackson Street and Oglethorpe Avenue, they were met by Chief Pritchett and more than a hundred police. After repeated warnings to disperse, Martin, Ralph, and Anderson were arrested along with the other demonstrators. The number of people imprisoned now exceeded seven hundred.

The arrest of Martin was a topic of national and international concern. Once again, telegrams flooded the SCLC headquarters. Politicians wondered aloud whether formal government action might not be needed. Foreign journalists hurried to the scene to join their American colleagues. The same day, December 16, Martin announced that he had refused bond. "If convicted," he declared, "I will refuse to pay the fine. I expect to spend Christmas in jail. I hope thousands will join me." Ralph called for a pilgrimage to Albany of blacks from all parts of the country. Shortly thereafter, Martin and Anderson were transferred to a model prison in another county. The militancy of the black community was rising steeply. It was learned that Mayor Kelley and Governor Vandiver had telephoned Attorney-General Robert Kennedy to plead that the Justice Department act to stop the flow into Albany of outside "subversives" and "agitators."

Faced with the imminent arrival of scores of white clergy responding to Martin's appeal, the city churlishly resumed negotiations with the Movement leaders. The leaders demanded that the city drop charges against all but eleven (the train-riders) of the four hundred still in jail and that it delay their trials for two months to allow time for a solution to the segregated-facilities debate. The city commissioners were prisoners of the escalating fury of the community's super-racists—a coalition of poor whites and the political and business forces around James Gray, the *Herald*'s editor-owner. The state's political machine, headed by former Governor Herman Talmadge, intended to prevent Albany from becoming another Montgomery, a symbol of slow but inevitable black revolt and triumph. In the midst of the negotiations, the *Herald* exhorted, "Keep on Fighting for Albany."

Meanwhile, the churches rocked in song and the waves of demonstrators rolled on toward city hall, where they broke against the "nonviolent" tactics of Laurie Pritchett. Away from the eye of the camera, in the barns and enclosed pastures taken over temporarily to accommodate the unusually large prison population, in Baker, Colquit, and Terrell counties, there were many instances of brutality. The concrete floors, beds without mattresses, inedible food, and ghastly hygiene were worse than the physical mistreatment by the arresting police officers. Nevertheless, Pritchett and his men did conduct themselves on the whole with ostentatious restraint and civility. No clubs, hoses, or dogs were ever used in Albany. "I realize I'm living in a changing world," Pritchett philosophized to a *New York Times* reporter, "You've got to adapt yourself to the situation. We are not in the old school." As Coretta observes, "He tried to be decent. He would allow the protesters to demonstrate up to a point. [He] would bow his head with them while they prayed. Then, of course, he would arrest them."

Monday morning, December 18, the world learned that a truce had been declared and that Martin had allowed himself to be released on bail. The terms of the truce were disappointingly short of the original demands. The demonstrators, including the famous eleven, were freed on bail, but the charges were not dismissed and the trial was at the discretion of the chief of police. The integration of terminal facilities was, in fact, a meaningless concession, as the September ICC ruling had taken effect on November 1. Albany merely spared itself money by agreeing not to contest the matter. Buses, parks, libraries, and cinemas remained segregated. No permanent biracial committee existed and no black police had been hired. The city agreed to discuss these matters on January 23, twelve days after the installation of the new city government. Mass demonstrations were to cease until that date. At an impromptu press conference on the steps of city hall, Martin was curiously generous to his enemies and bewilderingly sanguine about the future of Albany race relations. He complimented the Albany police department on its courteous treatment of the demonstrators and stressed that the city's problems could best be dealt with on a local level. The news reporters found these remarks jarringly at odds with the SCLC leader's statements seventy-two hours earlier. Were Albany's blacks truly oppressed amid hopeless conditions or not? they asked. Attorney Donald Hollowell interrupted, "We have to go now, Dr. King." Martin cannot have felt that his departure from Albany was premature. He was obviously straining to put the best face on the situation.

Others were greatly pleased by the compromise. Robert Kennedy telephoned Mayor Kelley to express appreciation for the orderly termination of the difficulties. Chief Pritchett announced, in martial tones: "We, the duly constituted authorities and the citizens of this city, met 'nonviolence' with 'nonviolence' and we are, indeed, proud of the outcome." One city official explained the truce by announcing, "We killed them with kindness. Apparently it was a condition M. L. King and the other outsiders had never encountered before." The *New York Herald Tribune* called Albany "one of the most stunning defeats of his career." The *Pittsburgh Courier* (a widely circulated black newspaper) advised its readers not to believe that the halt of demonstrations was the prelude to a meaningful peace. Even to Martin's friends, it seemed absurd to have invited the nation's religious leaders to share his Christmas prison only to buy his freedom two days later. "You curse first, then I will," a SNCC volunteer rejoined when asked his opinion of the truce.

Exactly what it was that transpired between his imprisonment and his release that caused Martin virtually to throw away the incremental advantages of imprisonment, international attention, and mass confrontation has never been fully explained. Martin and Wyatt were forthright in admitting error. "There were weaknesses in Albany, and a share of the responsibility belongs to each of us who participated," Martin said. The nature of these "weaknesses" has generally been left to the intuition of the intelligent reader. The Albany Movement leaders have confessed that there was friction within the organization. "There was constant war between us as to strategy," says Charles Sherrod. The students were piqued by the fixation of the press and some of the older community people upon the person and utterances of Martin. SNCC had labored unheralded in the vineyards of racial protest in Albany long before "De Lawd"—Martin's new SNCC appelation—appeared on the scene to work his miracles.

These emotions were reinforced by a more serious dissent from SCLC policy on the part of the students. Sherrod and his lieutenants believed that local leadership, the leadership that would remain after Martin and the press had gone home, must determine policy. Wyatt and his assistants had already begun to move about the community a little too haughtily and noisily, dispensing the patronage that the SCLC's sizable financial resources allowed. Bitterness against Wyatt was intense and enduring. "Why didn't Walker stay the hell in Atlanta, send us more money, let us have Martin to speak and walk with the marchers! If he had done that, we could have won," said one Movement spokesman. Ralph Abernathy's appeal to blacks across the land to pour into Albany was one of those rhetorical excesses that Martin's generals were notoriously prone to committing. The local leaders resented the implication that they needed bailing out by a national crusade. The Movement's secretary, Marion Page, said that outside assistance was welcome in principle but "as of now, we need no help."

The formulation of community demands had not been

satisfactory to many. Much more than a biracial committee and a few black police would have to be conceded, they believed, before Albany's race relations could improve. They would have had the Movement pressure the city into an omnibus agreement affecting employment as well as public facilities. Pushed by the radicals, the Movement did embark, within a few days after the truce, upon a strategy calculated, it hoped, to achieve these goals. But the whites were aware of the disunity. The *Herald* reported them. Until the truce, it had been a question of whose nerves were sounder, the Movement's or the city's. Unfortunately, the Movement's internecine conflict became so chronic after the jailing of Martin that it was in imminent danger of sundering. To an objective observer, the sins imputed to Martin, Ralph, and Wyatt were certainly venial and probably hugely exaggerated. The arrogance of Wyatt, the unsanctioned news releases of Ralph, the alleged moderation of Movement demands by Martin, and the general impression conveyed to the outside world that the SCLC was both genius and unique shepherd for the antisegregation campaign, surely these were offenses whose denunciation could be delayed for the sake of organizational unity. They were not, however, and a full explanation of why they were not verges on the bizarre.

The apology offered by several of the Movement leaders is partially illuminating. The Martin King of the Albany campaign, they recall, was still a Southern Baptist preacher. His Montgomery success was impressive, his rhetorical skills extraordinary, but he was far from being the larger-than-life leader whose dreams at the Lincoln Memorial and Nobel accolade later made awesomely splendid and unique. At this time, he was still only a man from Atlanta, a city preacher with a fine baritone and the head of an increasingly rich and powerful organization. In a word, he was merely a more successful, more renowned edition of Reverend Samuel B. Wells, pastor of Albany's Shiloh Baptist Church.

After Martin's arrest, Slater and Chevene King, Page, Sherrod, and others had conferred to determine the Movement's policy in the light of the visiting leader's vow to spend Christmas in prison. It was clear that federal and public opinion would pressure the city's white leaders. It was suspected also that, at the first sign of weakness, Martin's lieutenants would engineer a settlement that could be construed in the national press as an exclusive SCLC victory but that the locals would find thoroughly inadequate. Anderson's imprisonment in the same cell with Martin was particularly distressing to these leaders. Anderson was not considered to be a strong personality, and his deference to Martin had been noticed even in the few hours before the Saturday march. Moreover, it was said that Anderson's nervous disorder had been aggravated by confinement. In order not to be committed to a compromise authored by Martin and Anderson, the community, with its vanity and jealousy, made a pact with the city that was confused and ulteriorly motivated. It was decided to compel the jailed leaders to accept bond by arranging an inconclusive truce whose term would expire after Martin and the SCLC personalities had returned to Atlanta.

This was accomplished, and on Monday morning Martin and Anderson, no longer possessing a reason for remaining in prison, accepted release. Later, Martin explained, "I'm sorry I was bailed out. I didn't understand at the time what was happening. We thought that the victory had been won. When we got out, we discovered it was all a hoax." For a few days, it was widely reported that Page had replaced Anderson as Movement president. A large number of the Movement's people believed that it was better to accomplish almost nothing on their own terms than to sustain a modest victory with outside assistance. For Martin, this was a deeply frustrating experience. To the world, it appeared that he had capriciously abjured his prison vow for a meaningless agreement, and perhaps it would never be possible for him to reveal the true reasons for his conduct. The decision must have been one of the most painful of his career.

Fortunately, despite these complicated stratagems, community unity held, and, in the days that followed the truce, a selective boycott of white businesses was launched. Many black newsboys left the service of the *Herald*, and the number of black readers dipped sharply. The boycott of department stores received the support of between 50 and 75 per cent of the black community. The boycott worried the business community but not enough to cause it openly to brave the coalition of proletarian and politically potent whites. Incredibly, the SCLC strategists appear not to have ascertained what portion of white business trade was held by blacks. In fact, the general poverty of the blacks limited their buying power so that a boycott by them pained but did not seriously cripple the merchants. The attack against the bus company was a more realistic tactic. Ninety per cent of its passengers were black. The Movement demanded immediate abolition of racial seating and the hiring of black drivers. The bus company indicated its willingness to comply with the first condition fully and to hire one black driver as a gesture to the second. Once again back in the city, Martin asked his followers not to ride the buses until a written statement had been extracted from the city, stating that it would not interfere with this agreement. The bus company, meanwhile, observed a formula of *per diem* integration.

On January 12, 1962, the city counterattacked. An eighteen-year-old girl was arrested for disorderly conduct and, because she protested that she had paid her "damn twenty cents" bus fare, charged also with using obscene language in public. Shortly thereafter, Sherrod and Jones were arrested for "loitering" in the Trailways dining room. On January 23, the city commissioners, despite Mayor Kelley's dissenting vote, violated their promise to consider the Movement's petition of grievances. It proved impossible, of course, to obtain the city's written guarantee of the bus agreement. Martin decided to intensify the bus boycott. Many observers believed that this was a mistake. Commuting between Atlanta and Albany, it was occasionally difficult for him to distinguish between the theoretical and the practical possibilities of the Albany situation. He was applying to it the lessons of Montgomery instead of revising his ideas in the light of the present circumstances. Instead of fighting for the written statement, it would have been better to have sent the black population en masse back to the buses to sit where it pleased. The result of the intensified boycott was the bankruptcy of the company and the end of city bus service.

The months between the expiry of the abortive truce and Martin's semipermanent return to Albany early in July, to serve again as the heroic symbol of the struggle, were given over to fund-raising and political self-defense. Although the SCLC had received numerous monetary donations, some of them sizable, its financial requirements were increasing rapidly. In 1960, its budget had been approximately $65,000. The projected budget for 1962 was $200,000. Under Wyatt's direction, more than $193,000 had been raised in 1961. Perhaps one-fourth of that budget had been provided by foundations; these funds were earmarked specifically for voter education and registration projects. But the SCLC's needs were enormous and varied. It was still funding the Freedom Rides, in the form of purchasing tickets, providing shelter and food in key Southern cities, and maintaining a nonviolent training center in Birmingham, under the direction of Fred Shuttlesworth. Martin made a number of speeches to help fill the organization's coffers. Early in June, Harry Belafonte agreed to appear in Atlanta for a hastily arranged concert. This was the second time that Belafonte had donated his talents to the SCLC. In 1960, his SCLC benefit concert in Los Angeles, California, had netted $8,805. The Atlanta concert was a success. Unfortunately, Belafonte's visit was marred by the refusal of an exclusive restaurant to serve lunch to the singer and his party. Obviously, Atlanta was not nearly so progressive as it prided itself on being.

In retrospect, Martin's tactic of mass assault upon segregated institutions can be seen to have been both correct and timely. Consequently, it is too easily forgotten that, even within the black community, powerful forces looked upon him as a *provocateur* and believed that his civil disobedience campaigns were the worst possible antidote to discrimination. Almost without exception, these were the views of the older generation, and its control of many of the black community's purse strings was therefore a source of some distress. The older generation preferred, as did the rich Atlanta Life Insurance Company, to send its checks to the NAACP. C. A. Scott, editor-owner of the *Atlanta Daily World*, kept up a steady barrage of attacks on SCLC. An active figure in the community, a trustee of Ebenezer, and a devout Republican, the sincerity of his beliefs was self-evident. Obtain the ballot, work loyally within the structure of the two major national political parties, pool capital resources and invest in black enterprise, seek judicial redress when legitimate grievances were consistently ignored—this was the breviary of racial progress that he and his colleagues commended to the new generation. "Martin carried the direct-action idea a little too far, to the extent of creating, we'll say, undue antagonism toward the Negro on the part of the masses of the white community," Scott has always believed. Coming at the time of Martin's release from jail, Scott's attacks carried sting. This explains the uncharacteristic acerbity of Wyatt's denial that there was any truth in the paper's "irresponsible editorials and low-grade reporting."

The feud between Martin and another of the elders, Dr. Joseph H. Jackson, president of the National Baptist Convention, was two years old. Late in the summer of 1962, a secessionist body comprised of younger, more civic minded,

and generally more highly educated ministers was formed
with Martin's active support—the Progressive Baptist Alliance. Meanwhile, Dr. Jackson, who supposedly spoke for five
million black Baptists, attacked Martin's politics and his
character. In September, 1961, Jackson had accused him of
masterminding an invasion of the National Baptist Convention, which resulted in the death of Reverend Wright. This
minister had suffered a fatal heart attack in the momentary
confusion of a vigorous dispute between contending factions
on the convention stage. Martin was not present during the
fracas and, in fact, had had nothing to do with it. The Baptist
president sifted his facts to suit the accusation. The retrac-
tion that Martin demanded was never given publicly. One
year later, Jackson denounced the clergymen who had journeyed South to lend support to Martin's second attempt to
compel Albany to desegregate. "It is hypocrisy for a delegation to leave Chicago and go to Albany to fight segregation,"
said Jackson. To the extent that this reasoning was correct in
this instance, his motives were highly suspect. For Dr. Jackson, the role of the preacher was to bring the good news of
the Gospel to his flock, to save the members of his flock for
Jesus, and to effect change by exemplary conduct. It was a
conviction that many of the older black leaders shared.

On February 27, 1962, Martin and Ralph returned to Albany to stand trial for the December arrest. They were found
guilty of disorderly conduct and parading without a permit,
but sentencing was delayed until the last of those involved in
the demonstrations could be prosecuted. This occurred on
July 10. Martin and Ralph returned for the occasion. Their
penalty was to pay a fine of $178 or undergo imprisonment at
hard labor for forty-five days. Albany still had not learned
that a jailed Martin Luther King was a source of strength
sufficient to heal longstanding divisions and galvanize the
most apathetic of campaigns. Judge Durden would have done
well to have drastically reduced the prison terms or even to

have suspended sentence altogether. Naturally, Martin and Ralph insisted on purging themselves in prison, and once again international attention focused on this unenlightened town. The people were already primed to resume massive demonstrations, because of the city's intransigence and continued harassment. Several weeks earlier, a black café owner, Walter Harris, had been shot for "resisting arrest." Twenty-nine teenagers and adults had demonstrated before city hall and been arrested as a result. Cordell Reagan and Charles Jones, among others, had been sentenced to two months at hard labor for refusing to leave a drugstore lunch counter.

As a *New York Times* headline announced "Dr. King Is Jailed for Georgia Protest," Governor Rockefeller sent a telegram to the Justice Department, suggesting immediate investigation. Senator Joseph Clark of Pennsylvania deplored the existence of "areas of our country in which the Constitution of the United States, as represented by the Fourteenth Amendment, is not in effect." Burke Marshall, assistant attorney-general in charge of civil rights, was ordered by the President to prepare a full report on Martin's plight. Marshall also telephoned Coretta to assure her that the Justice Department would exercise all possible influence to secure her husband's release. At that moment, more than a score of young people and adults were being rounded up by Chief Pritchett as they sang on the court house steps the defiant "We Shall Overcome." It was not too late for the city to undo its mistake, however. Just as the confluence of world concern, federal intercession, and local defiance threatened to form an irresistible tidal wave, Martin and Ralph were informed that an anonymous black citizen had paid their fines. They were ordered from their cells on the morning of July 13. "I've been thrown out of lots of places in my day," Ralph told a mass meeting that evening, "but never before have I been thrown out of jail." Several members of the Albany Movement have speculated on the possibility that a role was played by the Justice Department in this unusual maneuver by the city. Perhaps, as a King biographer states, Kelley and Pritchett had found the time to read the portion of *Stride Toward Freedom* that recounts Mayor Sellers' payment of Martin's fine in Mongomery.

It was now absolutely necessary for Martin as the SCLC leader to give the Albany situation his undivided attention. He held a press conference in Atlanta to announce that he would return to Albany on the following Monday, July 16, to conduct a relentless campaign of civil disobedience, if the commissioners did not agree to a hearing of black demands. Meanwhile, complaints about his leadership were reported in *The New York Times.* "He's woefully inadequate in organizational ability," a Southern leader charged. And the normal penchant of some persons to lose faith in moments of crisis fed on Martin's strange inability to keep himself locked up in a Southern jail. Old rumors and half truths were resurrected. Had he not telephoned an official of the Federal Home Loan Bank in Washington, in order to obtain a favorable decision on the charter application of a Florida savings and loan association, an enterprise having only one black official whereas the rival applicant had three? Then there was the bizarre story that he had agreed momentarily to portray a Georgia senator in the movie version of Allen Drury's *Advise and Consent,* scarcely appropriate behavior for a minister and a civil rights leader. Inevitably, there were those who began to wonder in whispers about the reportedly huge sums of money raised but, allegedly, never spent in Albany. A few months after the Albany failure, Louis Lomax was to publish *The Negro Revolt,* which described instances of surrealistic organizational confusion within the SCLC. Unless he succeeded in Albany, Martin, his organization, and even the philosophy of nonviolent passive resistance might be irretrievably undermined.

Throughout July and August, Albany trembled above the

seismic waves of racial protest. Daily, small groups of blacks
and some nonresident whites sought service at lunch counters,
cinemas, libraries, parks, and bowling alleys. On Sunday,
July 22, delegations appeared at white churches to worship.
In every case but two (at a Catholic and at an Episcopal
church) they were turned away. Many were arrested. These
activities were enjoined, midnight, July 20, by Federal
District Judge J. Robert Elliot, one of President Kennedy's
recent appointees. Elliot was a confessed segregationist.
After conferring with city officials and the Georgia Governor, he issued a sweeping injunction that covered every
form of civil demonstration and specifically interdicted Martin, Ralph, Marion Page, Wyatt, Charles Jones, and Ruby
Hurley from further activity. It was to remain in effect until
July 30, when the city's petition for a permanent restraining
order would be heard. Martin denounced Judge Elliot for
"conspiring to maintain segregation." Chevene King immediately filed suit in the Fifth Circuit Court of Appeals to have
Judge Elliot's injunction overturned. Martin and the others
who had been cited decided, for the time being, not to demonstrate, but they encouraged the other leaders to do so. Early
the following morning, at Shiloh Baptist Church, Reverend
Samuel Wells stirred his audience of seven hundred in a
manner emulative of Martin:

> I've heard about an injunction but I haven't seen one. I've
> heard a few names but my name hasn't been called. But I do
> know where my name is being called. My name is being called
> on the road to freedom. I can hear the blood of Emmett Till as
> it calls from the ground. . . . When shall we go? Not tomorrow!
> Not at high noon! Now!

"I Ain't Gonna Let Nobody Turn Me 'Round," 160 marchers
sang, from Shiloh to the point at which Pritchett intercepted and arrested them.

Meanwhile, a steady stream of outsiders of both races continued to arrive in the city—ministers, students, volunteers

from assorted occupations. Their numbers were more than
matched by the massing outside the city of three thousand
Klansmen. An explosion was inevitable. It came on Tuesday,
July 24, as an enraged response to the savage assault, the
preceding day, upon Mrs. Slater King by a sheriff's deputy in
Camilla, Georgia. Mrs. King, who was pregnant, was kicked
into unconsciousness when she attempted to carry food to
friends being held in the Camilla prison camp. An integrated
group of forty persons attempted to protest the Camilla outrage at city hall and, of course, was arrested. The black population was no longer able to contain its emotions. By nightfall, nearly two thousand people, most of them teenagers,
were battling the police with bricks and bottles. One policeman was hospitalized. Governor Vandiver offered the help of
twelve thousand National Guardsmen to quell the disturb-
ance. Only hours before, Appeals Court Judge Elbert P.
Tuttle had set aside the Elliot injunction.

After a sustained effort, there is an inevitable contraction
in any organism, a dissipation of *élan*. The immediate aftermath of the riot was such a period. Martin's decision to declare a "day of penance" on Wednesday was an effective
brake to the momentum that had been achieved at great cost
during the past two weeks. Throughout the night and well
into Wednesday morning, he and his lieutenants spread the
word in nightspots, pool halls, and restaurants and on street
corners that no demonstrations would occur on Wednesday.
Martin was certainly shocked by the events of Tuesday night,
and he must have been deeply pained to learn that Pritchett
had wryly queried reporters present at the melee, "Did you
see them nonviolent rocks?" What had happened was not
only philosophically repugnant; it was, in Martin's eyes,
tactically stupid. Once again, as in Montgomery, he quietly
admonished his followers in the words of Booker T. Washington. "Let no man pull you so low as to make you hate
him." And, again, the example of Gandhi came to mind.

The Mahatma had confronted a similar crisis during the 1919 Punjab disturbances. Gandhi had canceled his civil disobedience campaign until nonviolent discipline was reinforced. Martin gave instructions that the incidence of demonstrations be reduced and the number of participants curtailed for a week.

Serious disagreement between the SCLC and SNCC resulted from this moratorium. SNCC had not welcomed Martin's first Albany visit enthusiastically. And, in the months after, while he busied himself raising funds, the students and local citizens had sung, prayed, gone to prison work camps, and almost miraculously kept the Movement intact. Somehow, though, by mid-July, the determination of strategy had been pre-empted by SCLC. Even the equable Chevene King recognized that the local leaders and the students had grounds for complaint, and at least one fretful meeting between Martin and SNCC leaders Sherrod, Reagan, Jones, and others was held at this time, in Slater King's back yard. For nearly three hours, they disputed with the Atlanta pastor the right of the SCLC to monopolize the Movement. Martin denied any such intent on the part of his organization and attempted to extenuate the peremptory conduct of Wyatt. Until that afternoon, he had probably not been fully aware of the extent to which his chief subaltern had alienated the local leadership.

The main objection of the student leaders was Martin's conservatism, his readiness, as they saw it, to settle for half a loaf. For them, nonviolence was not an indefectible principle but a pragmatic method. After the events of July 24, they were no longer so willing to resist passively, and the notion of penance was demeaning. Slater King was amazed by Martin's forbearance. Martin granted that he was more conservative than they and that his family and church responsibilities impinged upon what time he had for homework as a regional civil rights leader. He had made mistakes in Albany, he admitted, but he welcomed criticism by the young adults, who were the "creative antagonists who constantly push us into positions where we should go further." Sherrod and his group were not reconciled, but they left the parley with a high regard for the selfless commitment of Martin King. From his subsequent conduct, it may be inferred that Martin's decision to have himself arrested again resulted from the generalizing of misgivings such as those voiced by the students. That Friday, July 27, he, Ralph, and William Anderson were arrested, along with ten others, as they knelt in prayer before city hall.

That afternoon, the community was informed of the arrests and of the trio's intention to remain confined until tried. The sacrifice of Martin's freedom was intended to galvanize the black population. But it appeared that the formula had been tried once too often. The fears of the SNCC leaders had been justified. At Shiloh Church, Andy Young, Sherrod, and Reverend Wells encountered a new form of passive resistance. "Now friends," Andy importuned the congregation in an easy, businesslike manner, "we have the names and addresses of those who have signed their names as being ready to go. Now is the time to get our affairs in order." Wells followed, to admonish, "You cannot fail. If we do, we will lose our brothers and sisters now in jail. We would like to have you get off your seats and come down front." Even the popular Sherrod failed to move the audience. "You ought to be ashamed of yourselves for sitting on your chairs while our leaders are sitting in a filthy jail," he admonished. "What's more important—to suffer now and be free later or be a slave for the rest of our lives?" The reluctant congregation apparently believed that the point of disproportionate returns for continued sacrifice had been reached. The spring, it seemed, had finally snapped.

Martin's greatest ally—indeed, the staunchest force promoting the cause of civil rights—was invariably the tactical imbecility of the white South. The next day, while making a routine enquiry about the mistreatment of a jailed white student, Attorney Chevene King was struck on the head by the sheriff of Dougherty County. The sheriff had chased Chevene from his law offices in the Albany court house. Chief Pritchett "regretted" the incident. Coming as it did on the heels of the assault upon the wife of Chevene King's brother, it made the black community livid. Anger revived flagging spirits, and the pace of the demonstrations again quickened. News of excessive brutality in the neighboring counties, especially of the deteriorating treatment of prisoners, also played its part. In August, scores of protesters marched, clapping, singing, praying, to the city hall and the county courthouse. Daily, Pritchett called upon them to disperse, herded them into the fourteen-foot-wide alley at the side of city hall, processed them, and sent them to the inhospitable prisons in the vicinity. By the end of the first week, more than one thousand persons had been incarcerated.

Concerned voices were raised again in Washington. A bipartisan group of ten senators urged the Justice Department to employ its full resources to effect the release of demonstrators. A group of Northern ministers and rabbis motored to Washington to confer with President Kennedy about Martin's continuing imprisonment. The international press, much of it sincerely, some of it mischievously, commented upon the democratic pretensions and barbarous reality of race relations in America. Unwilling to espouse the cause of the Albany Movement, the President was nevertheless constrained to declare publicly that he failed to understand the refusal of the city's officials to confer with black leaders.

On August 5, a Sunday, a simple event took place, but it was of national significance. For the first time in ten days, Coretta and her children were permitted to see Martin. They were granted fifteen minutes together in the corridor of the prison. The three children scampered about noisily, oblivious

King

to the discomfort and latent peril of their father's predicament. The couple spoke with an almost studied composure of trivial matters—their affairs in Atlanta, church duties, the children's return to school. At one point, Coretta told her husband, "If you stay away much longer, the baby won't know you." Perhaps it was at this time that Coretta told Martin of Yokie's (Yolanda's) response to the explanation of her father's imprisonment: He was in an Albany jail so that all people could go where they wished freely, Coretta had explained. "Good," Yokie said, "tell him to stay in jail until I can go to [Atlanta's] Fun Town." The gravel-voiced warden unceremoniously announced that time was up, and Coretta and the children left Martin and were swallowed up by a crowd of jabbering reporters. Martin returned to his cell and knelt in prayer. To obtain for his fellow blacks the fundamental rights guaranteed to all citizens under the Constitution, one man, an ordained minister, was compelled to spend Sunday in jail.

Tens of thousands of Americans were reminded of this irony when they read, that very day, Martin's article in the magazine section of *The New York Times*, "The Case Against 'Tokenism.' " It was a summary of the author's deepening misgivings about the vigor of the Kennedy Administration in civil rights. That previous March, under the title "Fumbling on the New Frontier," Martin had praised the government for its work toward an international *détente* and for the bold design of Alliance for Progress but lamented that the Chief Executive and Congress had failed to attack the problem of domestic racial injustice. "The year 1961," Martin concluded, "was characterized by inadequacy and incompleteness in the civil rights field. . . . From this perspective, the New Frontier is unfortunately not new enough; and the Frontier is set too close to the rear." *The New York Times* article applied the same verdict to the expired portion of 1962. Again the government had done much too little and always belatedly. And, with specific reference to the moot question in the highest circles of the Administration—whether stateways can alter folkways—Martin cogently postulated that "while it may be true that morality cannot be legislated, behavior can be regulated." He went on to warn that his race would not be intimidated or disillusioned in its quest for dignity. Its sense of "somebodiness" was now too deeply ingrained for that. He made this same point to the Attorney-General, who had telephoned incessantly just before Martin's most recent imprisonment. "You know, they just don't understand what we're up against," Martin told Coretta. Robert Kennedy was not much interested in hearing the reasons for the low marks in civil rights that the SCLC leader gave to the Administration of the Attorney-General's brother, but Washington found Albany an acute political embarrassment. It wanted peace. A great many white Americans were beginning to share Martin's disquiet about the government's inaction. Their vanguard was represented by some thirty-five ministers and rabbis, led by Reverend Ralph Lord Roy, who arrived in Albany on August 9.

On August 10, after a rough approximation of a trial, Martin, Ralph, and Anderson (who had accepted bond in order to take Martin's place on a *Meet the Press* program on July 29) were found guilty of the standard charges of disturbing the peace and parading without a permit. Their sentences were suspended, and they were released. Three days earlier, the imperturbable Justice Department, in an *amicus curiae* brief, had formally requested Judge Elliot not to rule on Albany's request for a permanent injunction until the city had complied with federal antisegregation laws. At the same time, Martin announced that he was returning to Atlanta. He hoped that, in his absence, the city would take the opportunity to reopen "good faith" negotiations with the black community. Twice he emphasized to the press that it was expected that his departure would help bring the two sides together. This time, it appears that it was the white community that was desperate to be rid of him. It is not unlikely that the city commissioners had cynically hinted at an imminent solution, shortly before his release. In any event, Mayor Kelley announced immediately after Martin's remarks that he was unaware of any plan to negotiate. Five days later, the city did meet with representatives of the Albany Movement but only to reject its demands that the city abide by the ICC ruling, refund the cash bonds of those arrested, refrain from interfering with bus desegregation when the company resumed operations, and cease interfering with peaceful protest.

That same day, Martin was back in Albany to denounce the intransigence of the city. The Albany crisis became a truly national matter during this period. Approximately seventy-five white ministers and rabbis settled in the community to lend support. Reverends Roy and Norman Eddy and Rabbi Richard Israel, of Yale University's Hillel Foundation, took a prominent part in the ensuing demonstrations. Shortly thereafter, more than fifty additional whites, mostly students, arrived. Again there was the familiar routine of song and prayer before city hall and the courthouse, attempts to worship in segregated churches and to obtain service in restaurants, followed by more circumspect arrests by Chief Pritchett's myrmidons. But circumspection was increasingly limited to the city of Albany. As the well-meaning Northern whites departed for their parsonages and universities early in September, the Klan swung into operation.

Within a week, four black churches in nearby towns had been destroyed or heavily damaged by dynamite. Martin succumbed to an uncharacteristic feeling of bitterness when he saw the bombed churches. "Tears welled up in my heart and in my eyes. . . . No matter what it is we seek," he wrote, "if it has to do with full citizenship, self-respect, human dignity, and borders on changing the 'Southern way of life,' the Negro stands little chance, if any, of securing the approval, consent, or tolerance of the segregationist white South." Three of the churches were subsequently reconstructed with donations from labor organizations (AFL-CIO) and money from Northern liberals and religious organizations. Although token arrests were made and local white dignitaries deplored the lawlessness of white extremists, before the year ended racial conditions in Albany were more hopeless than ever. Public parks, swimming pools, and libraries were either closed or "sold" to a group of private businessmen headed by James Gray. The SCLC continued to assist the Movement, although Martin was now in the process of readying the Birmingham campaign and could not return to Albany.

"Albany was successful," Ruby Hurley has said, "only if the goal was to go to jail." Lerone Bennett writes that "Albany, by any standard, was a staggering defeat for King and the Freedom Movement." Martin was less sententious in his assessment of the struggle. Mistakes had certainly been made, but important lessons had been derived from them. Moreover, he argued that the exercise of mass resistance to social evil would ultimately be redemptive. Albany blacks would never again accept less than the total achievement of their legal and human rights. Writing in *New South*, Wyatt reiterated Martin's conviction that an inevitable change was under way in Albany. He went on to rebut the armchair strategists who dismissed the struggle as an unqualified failure: "Albany is a milepost in the early stage of the nonviolent revolution. Our nonviolent revolution is not yet full-grown. I do not know if it will ever come to adulthood, but I pray that it will." There is universal agreement among the Movement leaders that they were mistaken in simultaneously attacking all the manifestations of segregation in the city instead of concentrating on one or two—employment, bus segregation, an integrated police force, or free access to places of entertainment, for example. Slater King was one of the first to appreciate, in his *Freedomways* article, the enormity of this miscalculation.

It is undeniably true that Albany was a failure, that much can be learned from failure, and that, in part, the failure resulted from an excessively optimistic reading of the possible. What has not been admitted, however, is that the Albany experiment aborted largely because of the plangent discord among its technicians. The wrong things were demanded at the wrong time because there was too little coordination, trust, and harmony within the Movement. The tragedy of the Movement was most assuredly not that Martin and the SCLC monopolized and moderated its strength away. The intrinsic tragedy lay in the fact that Martin completely failed to take advantage of his singular gift of leadership and his organizational power to enforce unity upon an essentially anarchic and querulous mosaic of inexperienced groups. However imperious Wyatt may have been, his vice-regal powers were never sufficient to intimidate his followers to the extent that his detractors have alleged. In an almost intolerably confused situation, in which the people he was summoned to aid desired mainly to exploit his symbolic utility, Martin wavered back and forth between total and selfless commitment and humble, prudent withdrawal. His political credibility necessitated periodic return to Albany. On the other hand, his sensitive ego clearly perceived that many of his putative allies preferred temporary failure to his modest success. The performance of the SCLC in Birmingham would show how well its leaders had learned the hard lessons of Albany. The experience showed how costly it was for a civil rights organization to undertake its work on an inspirational, *ad hoc*, and uncohesive basis.

7

Birmingham—Nonviolence in Black, Violence in White

> Our judgment of Bull Connor should not be too harsh. After all, in his way, he has done a good deal for civil rights legislation this year.
>
> JOHN FITZGERALD KENNEDY

THERE WERE NEARLY 350,000 PEOPLE in Birmingham, Alabama, in 1963; almost all of those who were black would have preferred to live elsewhere. The widely held notion that burgeoning commerce and industry tend to make for social as well as economic progress was wholly inapplicable to this city. "The striking thing about Birmingham," columnist James Reston wrote after a visit, "is that it seems so advanced industrially and so retarded politically." Although it is the major center for the production of iron and steel in the South, Birmingham gave the impression of a city "which had been trapped for decades in a Rip Van Winkle slumber." "It's So Nice to Have You in Birmingham" proclaim the signs of the chamber of commerce along the principal approaches to the city. The urban centers of the deep South are notorious for the unintended irony of their salutatory billboards. Philadelphia, Mississippi, site of the hideous murder of three civil rights youth volunteers in 1964, essays to befriend the traveler by proclaiming that it is "A Nice Place to Rear a Boy."

The catalogue of injustices in Birmingham runs on for pages. Of the 80,000 registered voters in 1963, only 10,000 were black. In the midst of industrial plenty, nonwhites were rigidly restricted to menial and domestic jobs. Segregation was total and the slightest betrayal of discontent with the racial order was severely, often capitally, punished. Police brutality to blacks was the custom rather than the exception, and the Commissioner of Public Safety, Eugene "Bull" Connor, was notoriously vigilant and cruel, though far less professional than a gauleiter. The city officials took cognizance of federal law. They closed the city's parks rather than allow blacks to sully them. Some whites and a few blacks enjoyed the opera, so the city fathers removed Birmingham from the annual circuit of the Metropolitan Opera, when the Opera adopted a policy of performing only before unsegregated audiences. Whites still sipped water from designated fountains and tried on clothing in fitting rooms interdicted to blacks. But no system can survive if its guardians relax. There were moments in 1956 and 1957 when the disease afflicting Little Rock and Montgomery gave signs of spreading to Birmingham. But it was believed that the prophylactic bombing of seventeen churches had by 1963 adequately immunized the black population from the contagion. Birmingham, the whites said, was a "good" city.

A handful of blacks refused to be intimidated, however. Among them was Reverend Fred Shuttlesworth, a thin and intense man of medium height, well-defined features, and deep cocoa complexion. In 1963, he was forty-one years old and had spent all but three of those years in Alabama. His organization, the Alabama Christian Movement for Human Rights (ACMHR), had been formed in 1956 at the time of the Montgomery boycott. When the SCLC was organized, the ACMHR became one of its strongest affiliates. Its leaders were chosen from the key sectors in the black community. A. G. Gaston, the city's black millionaire, John Drew, a prosperous insurance broker, Arthur Shores, an energetic young lawyer, President Lucius Pitts of privately endowed Miles

College, Reverend Edward Gardner, the organization's vice-president, and Reverend Charles Billups partnered the development of the ACMHR with President Shuttlesworth. They worked closely, though not always smoothly, with the powerful Baptist Ministers Conference, headed by Dr. J. L. Ware.

Despite the routine terror enforced by Commissioner Connor, the ACMHR had encouraged the cautious boycott by Miles College students of local merchants early in 1962. At its annual board meeting, held in Chattanooga, Tennessee, in May, the SCLC voted to manifest support of Shuttlesworth's efforts by holding its plenary conference in Birmingham that September. The result of this announcement was a series of meetings between the Senior Citizens Committee (a white civic organization) and the leaders of the ACMHR in August. It was agreed that local merchants would remove racially offensive signs and discontinue separate drinking and lunch-counter facilities. When the SCLC convention ended, however, the Senior Citizens Committee acknowledged that the agreement had been a cynical maneuver to avoid the pressure of national publicity. The signs and the separate facilities reappeared immediately. It was at this stage that the SCLC decided to make Birmingham the next theater of its nonviolent efforts.

There were many good reasons to choose Birmingham. Aside from the organizational ties between the ACMHR and the SCLC and the warm friendship of Martin and Fred Shuttlesworth, the racism of this city was archetypal. To ameliorate the condition of the black in Birmingham would constitute a victory over Jim Crow, the repercussions of which would be felt throughout the South. It was also anticipated that the mobilization of thousands of black citizens in the city and the savage white counterreaction would compel the federal government to implement vigorously the decisions of the Supreme Court. "We've got to have a crisis to bargain with," Wyatt argued, "to take a moderate approach, hoping to get help from whites doesn't work. They nail you to the cross." The failure of Albany weighed heavily in the counsels of the SCLC as well. Student criticism and growing doubts as to Martin's effectiveness among established blacks were a source of considerable disquiet to the leadership.

After his October 16 meeting with President Kennedy, Martin's impatience to score a civil rights victory intensified. The subject of the meeting was the content of Martin's May 17, 1962, letter to the President, inviting him to review the body of discriminatory state codes on housing, employment, education, and transportation and to utilize the vast remedial executive powers that were available to him. Kennedy convinced Martin of his personal sincerity, of his desire to see Southern racism dealt a mortal blow. But the President was also conscious of the narrowness of his electoral mandate, and this fact appeared almost to paralyze his otherwise exceptional vigor of will in civil rights. "He vacillated," Martin later wrote, "trying to sense the direction his leadership could travel while retaining and building support for his administration."

Birmingham, then, held the possibility of affording solutions to a number of diverse but related problems. At the end of the year, the SCLC conducted a three-day retreat at the Dorchester center near Savannah. Two important decisions emerged from this meeting. First, it was agreed that the operations in Birmingham—known as Project C (for "confrontation")—would be launched during the first week in March, 1963, in order to cripple the business community's Easter sales. Second, the SCLC conferees decided to focus the campaign wholly upon Birmingham's business community. The dispersal of energies that had characterized the Albany demonstrations was not to be repeated. Early in January, Martin, Ralph, and Wyatt went to Birmingham to complete the planning for the March selective-buying campaign, setting up headquarters in Room 30 of the Gaston Motel, located in the heart of the black ghetto. There was, on the part of a number of Birmingham's black leaders, much lack of enthusiasm for the SCLC's plans. A. G. Gaston believed that the planned civil disturbances would be more costly than productive to local civil rights progress. Dr. Ware was even more apprehensive. The *Birmingham News* was to endeavor to exploit the differences within the ACMHR, claiming that Gaston, Drew, and even Shores and Dr. James Montgomery, a physician, were more amenable to negotiation than militants of the stripe of Shuttlesworth.

To overcome local reservations, Martin, Ralph, and Wyatt arranged ten meetings with the ACMHR leaders and others. Great pains were taken to avoid the wounding of local sensibilities that had marred the Albany effort. Some 250 volunteers were recruited to assist in training thousands of Birmingham blacks in the techniques of nonviolence. Considerable progress was made, in quite a short period of time, toward piecing together the nucleus of a nonviolent army. The date of the campaign was heatedly opposed by local leaders, however. On March 5, mayoralty elections were to be held. The candidates were Albert Boutwell, Tom King, and the infamous Bull Connor. Boutwell and King were orthodox segregationists, but both were unanimously preferred over Connor by the black community. It was decided to withdraw most of the SCLC personnel from the city until the election results were known.

Much preparation had gone into the Birmingham venture. In the first week in January, Martin, Ralph, and Wyatt had visited Anniston, Gadsden, Talledega, Birmingham, Montgomery, and the rural area around Selma as part of the SCLC People-to-People tour. Besides stiffening the resolve of Alabama blacks to have their names placed on the voter rolls (thirty-seven teachers had recently been fired after attempting to register), the tour provided needed area support and national publicity for the SCLC. In mid-January, Martin dashed through sixteen cities outside the South to raise funds for the forthcoming campaign. Twenty-eight public speeches in less than a month, not counting the impromptu talks to church elders and local professionals at countless after-banquet snacks, inspired SCLC affiliates to set records in fundraising. In Los Angeles, the Western Christian Leadership Conference raised $75,000 in one rally alone. Perhaps Martin's single most valuable fiscal asset at this time was Harry Belafonte. The success of the Los Angeles rally owed a great deal to the entertainer's work in founding the Western branch more than two years before.

As Martin wound up his speaking tour, Belafonte invited about seventy-five influential friends of the civil rights movement and members of the press (sworn temporarily to secrecy) to his New York apartment early in March to hear the SCLC head and Fred Shuttlesworth outline Project C. Unofficial representatives of Mayor Wagner and Governor Rockefeller attended, along with prominent business, clerical, literary, and film personalities. If Martin was often hortatory when it would have been more appropriate to explain precisely, the Belafonte meeting was exceptional for the didactic thoroughness with which planning, anticipation of contingencies, and clarity of goals were presented. Only at the close of the session was there a recourse to nonviolent rhetoric. At that appropriate moment, Shuttlesworth reminded the assembly of the possible violence and death awaiting the SCLC combatants. "You have to die," he said, "before you can begin to live." The seventy-five guests promised unqualified support of Project C, and Martin and Fred were able to return to Birmingham confident that the organization's projected budget of $475,000 would be met.

B (Birmingham) Day was to have been on March 6, 1963, the day following the city's mayoralty elections. While Martin had barnstormed, Wyatt completed the plan's vital staff work. He thoroughly reconnoitered the city's business district to determine priority targets, direct routes, and the numbers of counters, seats, entrances per store, and so on. Again, however, thorough preparation was to be jeopardized by events. The results of the elections had failed to give any candidate a clear majority. A run-off between Boutwell and Connor was scheduled for April 2. "Had we moved in while Connor and Boutwell were electioneering," Martin realized, "Connor would undoubtedly have capitalized on our presence." Despite secrecy, the SCLC's campaign had been widely anticipated by word of mouth. There had even been a direct reference to it in the *Chicago Sun-Times* late in January. Wisely, the leaders again ordered the total withdrawal of all SCLC staff from Birmingham. Martin also instructed the Atlanta headquarters to write confidential letters to the major civil rights organizations, the NAACP, CORE, and SNCC, and to the Southern Regional Council, fully explaining Project C and asking for their cooperation. The seventy-five religious leaders who had assisted the Albany Movement were also informed. April 2 brought the relatively heartening news that Boutwell had defeated Connor in the run-off. B Day began twelve hours later, five days after Coretta had delivered a healthy baby girl, Bernice Albertine.

B Day began in the grand style worthy of an epochal event. The *Birmingham Manifesto* is susceptible of exegesis à la Charles Beard if its several levels of meaning are to be revealed. First, the manifesto is a moving summons to action and a graphic iteration of wrongs:

The patience of an oppressed people cannot endure forever. The Negro citizens of Birmingham for the last several years have hoped in vain for some evidence of good faith resolution of our just grievances. . . . We have been segregated racially, exploited economically, and dominated politically. Under the leadership of the Alabama Christian Movement for Human Rights, we sought relief by petition for the repeal of city ordinances requiring segregation and the institution of a merit hiring policy in city employment.

The "Negro" people had "always been a peaceful people" whose demands had been reasonable. Despite this, Birmingham had callously refused to yield them their basic rights. The alternative of open protest, the manifesto continues, was the sole meaningful alternative.

Those who doubted this were reminded of the abortive negotiations in August and September of the preceding year. Martin, Fred, and their aides were uneasily aware of the lack of enthusiasm evinced by several powerful black leaders. These men feared the civil disruption and possible Albany-like impasse that would result from Project C. Equally disconcerting were the inevitable counsels of moderation from well-intentioned liberal whites and the morally astigmatic Justice Department. The document assured opponents that its composers were loyal Americans who believed in the Jeffersonian doctrine that "all men are created equal, that they are endowed by their Creator with certain inalienable Rights." As loyal citizens, they were driven to radical protest. They had exhausted available conventional remedies. This was not a precipitate action they were about to undertake:

> Twice since September we have deferred our direct action thrust in order that a change in city government would not be made in the hysteria of community crisis. We act today in full concert with our Hebraic-Christian tradition, the law of morality, and the Constitution of our nation. The absence of justice and progress in Birmingham demands that we make a moral witness to give our community a chance to survive.

The cogency of the *Birmingham Manifesto* may have impressed students of politics. Mr. Gaston and Dr. Ware, among many others, were not reconciled, however. Their reservations became more audible at the end of the first day, which saw twenty of thirty black demonstrators arrested for attempting to integrate downtown lunch counters. That evening, Martin spoke to a capacity prayer meeting. "We are heading for freedom land," he cried, "and nothing is going to stop us. We are going to make Birmingham the center of antidiscrimination activity in the nation. I have come here to stay until something is done." He intensified public pressure upon the dissidents. A week after the commencement of the demonstrations, he was proclaiming in plain language that "there are some preachers in Birmingham who are not with this movement. I'm tired of preachers riding around in big cars, living in fine homes, but not willing to take their part in the fight. He is the freest man in the Negro community. The white community can't cut off his check. If you can't stand up with your own people, you are not fit to be a leader!" Here was an indictment whose truth had the power to blackmail the local ministers.

Gradually, sullenly, most of them swung into line behind the ACMHR-SCLC coalition. Not all, however. Late in April, Dr. Ware qualified a press release that stated that his organization unanimously supported Martin and Fred, by saying: "We are against segregation in all phases, but we haven't taken a specific stand as such. . . . There is quite a bit of dissension, but we would not do anything to handicap the Movement." The ordinary people in the black community were free of doubt. The careful selection of leaders from among its own ranks, the mimetic effectiveness of the SCLC sociodrama (a standardized play directed by James and Diane Nash Bevel, James Lawson, Bernard Lee, Dorothy Cotton, and Andy Young), the devoted talent of the blind singer Al Hibbler, achieved a far higher degree of community solidarity than had been achieved in Albany. At packed church meetings, citizens listened intently to nonviolent lectures, watched their neighbors portray white merchants and policemen, and stood, arms locked and bodies swaying, to sing "Ain't Gonna Let Nobody Turn Me 'Round" and "Woke up This Mornin' with My Mind Stayed on Freedom." It was clear that the caveats of the faint-hearted would elicit few reactions. And, when Martin spoke before a march, his oratory could generate a voltaic hysteria:

I got on my marching shoes!

Yes Lord, me too.
I woke up this morning with my mind stayed on freedom!
Preach, doctor, preach!
I ain't going to let nobody turn me round!
Let's march, brother; we are with you!
If the road to freedom leads through the jailhouse, then, turn-
key, swing wide the gates!
Amen, praise the Lord!
Some of you are afraid.
That's right; that's right.
Some of you are contented.
Speak, speak, speak!
But if you won't go, don't hinder me! We shall march non-
violently. We shall force this nation, this city, this world, to
face its own conscience. We will make the God of love in
the white man triumphant over the Satan of segregation that
is in him. The struggle is not between black and white!
No, no!
But between good and evil.
That's it, that's it.
And whenever good and evil have a confrontation, good will
win!

Before dividing into small groups to visit department stores
or massing to walk to city hall, the demonstrators would each
have given a firm pledge to abide by the tenets of nonviolent
passive resistance. To solemnize their commitment as well as
to provide the organization with detailed information about
each volunteer, signed "commitment cards" were collected
in the churches:

I HEREBY PLEDGE MYSELF—MY PERSON AND BODY—TO THE NON-
VIOLENT MOVEMENT. THEREFORE, I WILL KEEP THE FOLLOWING
TEN COMMANDMENTS:

1. MEDITATE daily on the teachings and life of Jesus.
2. REMEMBER always that the nonviolent movement in Birmingham seeks justice and reconciliation, not victory.
3. WALK AND TALK in the manner of love, for God is love.
4. PRAY daily to be used by God in order that all men might
   be free.
5. SACRIFICE personal wishes in order that all men might
   be free.

6. Observe with both friend and foe the ordinary rules of courtesy.
7. Seek to perform regular service for others and for the world.
8. Refrain from the violence of fist, tongue, or heart.
9. Strive to be in good spiritual and bodily health.
10. Follow the directions of the movement and of the captain on a demonstration.

I sign this pledge, having seriously considered what I do and with the determination and will to persevere:

Name _____
Address _____
Phone _____
Nearest Relative _____
Address _____

Besides demonstrations, I could also help the movement by: (Circle the proper items) Run errands, Drive my car, Fix food for volunteers, Clerical work, Make phone calls, Answer phones, Mimeograph, Type, Print signs, Distribute leaflets.

The first three days of demonstrations were unique in Birmingham, for the civility of the police. At first, demonstrators were matter-of-factly warned away from their targets and then quietly arrested. By Friday evening, thirty-five people had been arrested by Commissioner Connor's men. Saturday, April 6, marked the second stage of Project C. That morning, forty-five carefully chosen people marched, two abreast and in silence, toward city hall. Connor intercepted them and "with amazing politeness" had them escorted to police vans. They were the vanguard of the marching army of singing demonstrators that would advance each day, for the next thirty-four days, upon the building symbolic of the institutionalized injustice of the city and the South. While they marched, the downtown stores operated almost entirely without black trade. Connor continued to behave like the comparatively benign Laurie Pritchett, although his men had been allowed briefly to show their dogs to the crowds on Sunday. The tactic might have succeeded in Birmingham as it had in Albany, but Connor's heart was not in this nonviolent police work, and he was a man of little patience. His forbearance was mainly determined by the city's expectation that a forthcoming legal maneuver would end Martin's demonstrations. On the night of April 10, Judge W. A. Jenkins issued an injunction against the ACMHR, the SCLC, Martin, Fred, Ralph, and others by name. Martin was served at 1:30 the following Thursday morning.

Martin had spoken before of "unjust" laws and the duty to disobey them when every conventional channel of redress was clogged. He had come very near to violating Judge Elliot's restraining order in Albany. It was clear that, in the next campaign, this issue would probably have to be squarely faced. The Belafonte apartment meeting had raised this dilemma, and Martin had revealed his readiness to violate a court order: "There, in consultation with some of the closest friends of the movement, we had decided that if an injunction was issued to thwart our demonstrators, it would be our duty to violate it." At times overly cautious in action, Martin was never slow in perceiving a fundamental principle. Law is the mortar of society, certainly, but the primordial source of law is justice. When the conflict between them is irreconcilable, one must strike for justice, despite the terrifying potential for anarchy in such an action. "The injunction method has now become the leading instrument of the South to block the direct-action civil rights drive and to prevent Negro citizens and their white allies from engaging in peaceable assembly, a right guaranteed by the First Amendment," Martin wrote. The law of the South, in such instances, was "pseudo" law, he reasoned. He announced to his intimates that he would compel the authorities to arrest him two days after Judge Jenkins' order—April 12, Good Friday.

There was little that was easy about Martin's Birmingham campaign. If Albany had presented a problem unique in the annals of Dixie jurisprudence—that of remaining in jail—

Birmingham nearly devised a means of preventing Martin from being locked up. Late on Thursday night, the leaders were informed that the authorities had declared that the financial resources of their bonding company were no longer adequate. According to plan, many more people were to be imprisoned after Friday. Several of Martin's lieutenants argued that only he could raise the cash needed to finance the release of scores of daily-wage earners. Sitting in Room 30 in the Gaston Motel, Martin recounted the despair that he read in the faces of twenty-four of his colleagues. "Martin, this means you can't go to jail," one of them said. "We need money." It was a terrible decision that he had to make. He rose, walked into the adjoining room, stood "in the center of the floor." "I think I was standing also at the center of all that my life had brought me to be." America was not India. Practical issues weighed decisively with ordinary people, whose paramount ambition was total immersion in the mainstream of American life. What was categorically imperative in this instance threatened to be socially irresponsible. As he pondered, Martin's mind was suddenly illumined by a vision that transcended the specific problems of Birmingham: "Then my mind leaped beyond the Gaston Motel, past the city jail, past city lines and state lines, and I thought of twenty million black people who dreamed that someday they might be able to cross the Red Sea of injustice and find their way to the promised land of integration and freedom. There was no more room for doubt." The matter was now in God's hands. Had he not recently said that when good and evil conflict, good inevitably triumphs? He would go to prison, he announced to the anxious group in Room 30. The caucus ended with a fervent stanza of "We Shall Overcome."

On Wednesday evening (while the injunction was being readied), Martin, Ralph, Fred, and Al Hibbler had gone to Zion Hill Church. The area around the church was dense with police. "Negroes are not afraid anymore," Martin told the congregation. "We are winning the struggle for which we have sacrificed, but we must even be ready to die to be free, if that is what is necessary." Ralph followed with a rousingly straightforward speech: "Tell 'em we're going to rock this town like it has never been rocked before." His request for volunteers to accompany Martin, Al, and himself to prison was answered by a forest of raised hands. Fifty persons were selected. Friday came. It was now time to go. Martin rose at dawn after a day-long fast. He prayed, then went to the Sixth Avenue Baptist Church. His father had flown to the city for the occasion. After a brief statement to the gathering, he walked with Ralph and Al Hibbler toward city hall, clad in a workshirt and denim trousers. The fifty volunteers followed behind in close order. Nearly a thousand spectators lined the way, shouting "Freedom has come to Birmingham!" Connor allowed them to proceed for seven or eight blocks before he shouted the command for his men to take them into custody.

The arrest of Martin and his lieutenants marked a turning point in the Birmingham crisis. Until that moment, Mayor-elect Boutwell and several members of the white business community had succeeded in restraining Bull Connor, who had agreed to abide by their counsels only because of the expected efficacy of the restraining order. Now, Connor's patience was exhausted. Moreover, the white community was in the throes of a leadership crisis. The old administration under Mayor Hanes availed itself of an ambiguity in the city's charter to claim that its tenure in office, despite the April 2 run-off, would not expire for another two years. The dispute would necessitate the adjudication of the state supreme court, a slow process during which Safety Commissioner Connor remained at his post. During his more than twenty-year term of office, Bull Connor had amassed a degree of power that made his department a state within the state. When, for example, the director of the city's bus terminal had dared to comply with the antidiscrimination directive of the ICC,

Connor twice arrested him. Part of the continuing undertow of black opposition to Martin's campaign derived from the conviction that demonstrations ought to be discontinued until Hanes, Connor, and his crowd were ousted. Determined to exacerbate racial enmity to the point at which his repressive tactics would compel statewide approbation, Connor began to abandon his genteel police procedures.

The policies to be followed henceforth were evident upon the arrest of Martin. He and Ralph were immediately separated, and Martin was placed in solitary confinement. Access to a telephone and even right to counsel were denied. If Connor intended to wreck Martin psychologically, his formula was diabolically sound. Even the strongest man has a weakness that may be exploited in an Orwellian manner. Jail was part of the routine of his life, and Martin was admirably free of fear for his own safety. But in Montgomery, Atlanta, and Albany, he had not been completely cut off from his trusting followers. Friday night came. Then thin shafts of light illumined his narrow, dark cell on Saturday morning, and again the sun set. Sunday, the terrible cycle was repeated:

> You will never know the meaning of utter darkness until you have lain in such a dungeon, knowing that sunlight is streaming overhead and still seeing only darkness below. You might have thought that I was in the grip of a fantasy brought on by worry. I did worry. But there was more to the blackness than a phenomenon conjured up by a worried mind.

What agonized Martin was the knowledge that there was no bail money for the other prisoners, that the Movement was denied any message of hope from its leader, that the city officials might exploit his enforced silence, and that the health of his convalescing wife might be impaired. Finally, on Sunday afternoon, Attorneys Arthur Shores and Orzell Billingsley were permitted a brief visit. Their news was not encouraging. The Movement was foundering. There was no money, and the federal government remained silent. Another night and a dimly lit morning passed. On Monday, Clarence Jones, Martin's New York attorney, paid a visit. He brought the first good news. Harry Belafonte had raised $50,000 in bail money. Jones "lifted a thousand pounds from my heart," Martin said. Still, he remained in Bull Connor's cell.

The lethargic national conscience upon which Martin relied so heavily began to rouse itself. Senator Wayne Morse likened Birmingham to Angola and South Africa. Again a flurry of importunate telegrams reached the White House. Foreign newspapers censured the American government. Meanwhile, Wyatt conferred with Coretta, and they agreed that one historic telephone call deserved another. On Sunday morning, Easter Sunday, Coretta placed a call to the President's retreat in Palm Beach, Florida. Press Secretary Pierre Salinger received her call, attempted to reassure her, then telephoned Robert Kennedy in Washington. That evening, the Attorney-General rang Mrs. King to inform her that, although he had failed to arrange for Martin to contact her, her husband was safe. On Monday morning, playful two-year-old Dexter King pulled the receiver from its berth when the phone rang and chattered into its mouthpiece until Coretta, as she puts it, "had persuaded Dexter to desist." The impatient operator explained that President Kennedy was waiting at the other end. "I heard the familiar, sincere voice of the President," Coretta recalls. John Kennedy told her that he had arranged for her husband to telephone and that agents of the Federal Bureau of Investigation were on the scene in Birmingham. A little later, Martin was able to reassure Coretta that he was unharmed. The Kennedy debt to the Kings had been, in part, repaid.

Martin's ordeal was not yet over, however. In January, eight white Birmingham clergymen had issued "An Appeal for Law and Order and Common Sense," which commended the solution of racial problems through the local and federal courts. Since the eruption of civil discord, these ministers had endeavored to restrain the black community. Such outstanding divines as Bishops C. C. J. Carpenter and Joseph A. Durick, Rabbi Hilton L. Grafman, and Reverend Drs. Ramage and Stallings were above reproach in the worthiness of their motives, and in Martin's absence they might have succeeded in halting the demonstrations for another futile interracial meeting. To counteract their "Appeal for Law and Order" as well as to occupy himself in the oppressive isolation of his cell, Martin had begun his famous "Letter from Birmingham Jail," first in the margins of a newspaper, then on scraps of paper supplied by a black trusty, and finally on a notepad provided by his attorneys. It was completed on April 16.

Every nation has its stockpile of rhetorical memorabilia, addresses, and documents, which enshrine by their passionate sincerity and eloquence a moment of curtain call in the drama of its people's maturity. Washington's farewell address, the Webster-Hayne debates, Lincoln's Gettysburg Address, the inauguration speeches of Franklin Roosevelt and John Kennedy—these are milestones in the republic's growth. To this stockpile must be added Martin Luther King's "Letter from Birmingham Jail" and his "I Have a Dream" speech. "Letter" has been described by one specialist as an American "*J'accuse.*" The document runs on for some nineteen pages. It begins directly, with a rebuttal of the charges that Martin's action is "untimely and unwise."

It was seldom that he paused to counter criticism of his ideas and work. Obviously, to rebut all of the objections to his civil rights activities would leave him little free time and swamp the secretaries of the SCLC. The criticisms of these ministers, however, seemed to Martin to be sincerely inspired by a concern for social peace. In "patient and reasonable terms," he undertook a detailed response to them.

Martin then explained the organizational responsibilities that brought him to the city and to prison. These, however, are secondary considerations, he explained.

He was in Birmingham to bring the gospel of freedom to a city of injustice. Like the prophets of the eighth century B.C., like the Apostle Paul, he had felt the urge to carry the gospel far beyond his own home. "Like Paul, I must constantly respond to the Macedonian call for aid."

Many lay readers have been astounded by the apparent immodesty of these opening sentences. Eighth-century prophets, Saint Paul—the comparisons are heady to the uninitiated. To the professional theologians to whom they were addressed, however, they were meant to have the special impact redolent of the divinity-school seminar. Before the toll of practical ministerial duties had dulled their pristine zeal, these eight clergymen, like Martin, had experienced the ineffable expectation of truly Christian service. It had been no heresy then to dream of emulating the conduct of the early saints. It was these conveniently interred memories that Martin's letter contrived to raise.

Saint Paul had commended obedience to civil authority, however unjust. Another Martin Luther had seemed to desert his principles in the wake of peasant rebellion. The *National Review* of William Buckley, Jr., had sententiously reminded Martin Luther King of the Christian duty to render unto Caesar uncomplainingly. Now, the eight Birmingham clergymen were also scandalized by the disruptive militance of the black leaders. During the Montgomery boycott, Martin had speculated upon the meaning of Jesus' message "I have not come to bring peace, but a sword." He had realized that the passive peace of Southern racism was altogether a pagan social arrangement totally repugnant to the essential meaning of the New Testament. "Positive peace" entailed wrathful social dislocation by the just. These men of God deplored the mass demonstrations in Birmingham. They appeared to be thoroughly unmindful, however, of the intolerable conditions that made these demonstrations necessary, Martin observed.

He had no doubt that they would not want to be content with a "superficial kind of social analysis" that confined itself to citing effects but avoided probing underlying causes. If civil disorder was generally a regrettable occurrence, he reminded the ministers that they ought to find it far more regrettable, nevertheless, that Birmingham's white leaders "left the Negro community with no alternative."

Martin proceeded to enumerate the Gandhian steps that precede recourse to nonviolence, revealed the fruitless negotiations with the city authorities, and revealed further that demonstrations had twice been deferred in hopes of a measurable improvement in local conditions through the ballot. He had energetically opposed "violent tension," but he had also recognised the reconstructive character of "nonviolent tension." He shared Socrates' belief that men break the shackles of mythology and half-truth and reach the "unfettered realm of creative analysis and objective appraisal" only if they are compelled to undergo "tension in the mind." Society desperately needed "nonviolent gadflies" to generate and sustain the intellectual and institutional unrest that made racial prejudice no longer blindly received dogma. It was this creative tension, he continued, that would lead men to the "majestic heights of understanding and brotherhood."

But it was not merely principle that Martin sought to defend. There was also the charge of bad timing. Every Negro was familiar with the cry of "Wait!" It nearly always meant "Never." Martin gave a graphic picture of the speed with which Asian and African countries were gaining political independence, but, he added, "we still creep at horse-and-buggy pace toward gaining a cup of coffee at a lunch-counter." The letter moves on to recite from a heart-rending catalogue of ordinary things denied the American black.

At this point, the author returned to the question of violation of laws. He seemed to feel that his response in an earlier paragraph had dealt only with the psychological legitimacy of black "lawlessness." He endeavored to resolve the question philosophically. A man-made law that was just had to match God's law. A law that was unjust conflicted with this moral law. This was the basis of Martin's argument. Any law that degraded people was a bad law. Thus, segregation laws were bound to be unjust because they injured the soul and the human being. Martin pointed out that a law was unjust if a minority bound by it had no part in making it. He gave the Alabama Legislature as an example, for it had set up the state's segregation laws even though it was not democratically elected. Finally, he reminded his fellow ministers that the laws of Hitler's Reich had been "legal."

Nearing his conclusion, Martin spoke of the bitter disappointment that the Southern white moderate had caused dedicated civil rights leaders. In effect, he stated that, whether he and his associates were right or misled, their actions were determined in large part by the silence of invertebrate liberals. Despite the courageous writings of Ralph McGill, Harry Golden, Lillian Smith, James McBride Dabbs, and Sarah Patton Boyle, courageous liberals "are still too few in quantity." Most of them raised their voices only to praise the conduct of the law-enforcement officers. And Martin ended on a note of trenchant prophecy. He wished the protesting clergymen had seen fit to commend the black demonstrators of Birmingham for their "sublime courage," readiness to accept hardship, and unprecedented orderliness and restraint despite "great provocation." The day would come, indeed, when the South would acknowledge that its authentic heroes were such persons as Mississippi's James Meredith, who braved angry mobs in his crusade for dignity. Martin's prose caught the fire of his spoken word:

> They will be old, oppressed, battered Negro women, symbolized in a seventy-two-year-old woman in Montgomery, Alabama, who rose up with a sense of dignity and with her people decided not to ride segregated buses, and who responded

with ungrammatical profundity to one who inquired about her weariness: "My feets is tired, but my soul is at rest." They will be the young high school and college students, the young ministers of the gospel and a host of their elders, courageously and nonviolently sitting in at lunch counters and willingly going to jail for conscience's sake. One day the South will know that when these disinherited children of God sat down at lunch counters, they were in reality standing up for what is best in the American dream and for the most sacred values in our Judeo-Christian heritage.

The South's real heroes were being dealt with more harshly each day by Birmingham's police. Several hours after Martin's arrest, a serious exchange of rocks, bottles, and nightsticks occurred as Reverend A. D. King and twenty-eight others were being loaded into police vans for parading illegally. (Martin's brother had entered the ministry after all.) It was certain that things would grow far worse in the city before they would begin to improve. Its climate of racial extremism was heated by the example of open rebellion against federal law set by Governor George Wallace. While he was appealing to Martin to moderate his Birmingham drive, Attorney-General Kennedy attempted to reason on Alabama soil with the Governor about integration of the state's major university. "It's like a foreign country. There's no communication," the bewildered Kennedy confessed later. "What do you do?" There was no real communication in Birmingham either, despite the unpublicized renewal of discussions between the SCLC, the Alabama Council on Human Relations, local merchants, and the mayor-elect. The industrialists, without whose sanction no agreement could survive, remained either silent or opposed to concessions. Martin began to detect the approach of an impasse that would enfeeble the mass support behind Project C. For this reason, he and Ralph decided to accept release on bail on Saturday, April 20.

Their trial took place six days later. Its outcome provided

Martin with one of the first gauges of the extent to which the whites were discomfited by his campaign. Had he, Ralph, Al, and the other defendants been tried for civil rather than criminal contempt (as the nature of their offense prescribed), they would have been required, by Alabama law, to remain in prison until they made a public apology. The city prosecutors realized that no apology would be made and that to lock up the SCLC leaders would make them martyrs. Under the criminal charge, the penalty was a fine of $50 and five days' loss of liberty. The demonstrators were speedily convicted on the lesser count, but they were permitted twenty days in which to file an appeal. Birmingham was still trying to learn from Albany. The *New York Times* correspondent believed that "the mild sentences . . . obviously came as a surprise to Dr. King and the other defendants." In one sense, the sentence was tantamount to an exoneration of the leaders' cause. On the other hand, it bought time and a slightly improved press for city hall. Time—delays, legal feints, slow negotiations —was always the nonviolent movement's greatest foe.

The strategists in Room 30 concluded that the third and most controversial phase of Project C must be launched. On May 2, a Thursday, D Day broke over Birmingham. On that day, 959 of some six thousand children, organized by James Bevel and ranging in age from six to sixteen, were arrested as they marched, singing, in wave upon wave from Sixteenth Street Baptist Church into town. Although a few broke ranks when the police approached to arrest them, the overwhelming majority maintained excellent discipline, kneeling to pray as they were rounded up. Older youths gave directions by means of walkie-talkies. More would have been taken away if the police had not run out of wagons. It was one of the most unusual spectacles since the Children's Crusade. It was graphic evidence of the commencement of a profound psychological revolution in the American black. The unmanly caution of many of their elders, the paternalism of their obsequious leaders, their own moribund ambitions—all this appeared to dissipate suddenly as sons disobeyed fathers in order to march, as six-year-old girls chanted "F'eedom!" in the front line, and as children of a generation whose quest for legal rights and cultural identity would be conceived in absolute terms defied the savage police power of an intransigent city.

The whites of Birmingham were not alone in their shock. Local and national black leaders joined them in the chorus of reproof of Martin's tactics. The use of children was, they said, cynical and cruelly exploitative. The precious commodity favorable public opinion seemed about to be compromised. The critics had no reply to Martin's question: "Where had they been with their protective words when down through the years, Negro infants were born into ghettos, taking their first breath of life in a social atmosphere where the fresh air of freedom was crowded out by the stench of discrimination?"

Martin need not have worried about criticism. Until D Day, Commissioner Connor had demonstrated, more often than not, an unsuspected judiciousness in his work. But he was a man of granite principles. He was not prepared to allow professional squeamishness to place him in the position of presiding over the dissolution of the Southern way of life. Daily his angry contempt rose. "If you'd ask half of them [demonstrators] what freedom means, they couldn't tell you," he spluttered to a correspondent. On the following day, Bull Connor abandoned his relative restraint. As nearly a thousand demonstrators of all ages prepared to leave Sixteenth Street Church, the police appeared and barred the building's exits, preventing more than half of them from leaving. Those who left the church were brutally handled. Police dogs were released to charge snarling into the marchers. At least three young people were seriously bitten. Officers waded into their midst, flailing nightsticks indiscriminately. Firemen released gallons of blistering water from their pressure hoses. Only a group of twenty managed to reach city hall. By 3 P.M., the carnage ended with large numbers of marchers bruised and two firemen and a newsman injured by bricks. The question of local criticism and national public opinion was, from this day on, resolved irretrievably in favor of the SCLC. The Kennedy Administration, still respectful of the white South's political power, questioned the "timing" of Martin's escalated campaign. The Attorney-General did admit, however, that the unjustified denial of rights to the black community would lead to more turmoil. On the following day, Assistant Attorney-General Burke Marshall and his deputy, Joseph F. Dolan, arrived in Birmingham.

The next three days witnessed an intensified repetition of May 3. Violence was not confined to Connor's men. Blacks began to retaliate, and James Bevel was sorely pressed to intercept zealous demonstrators who wished to march with knives and pistols. He was not able to prevent some marchers from pelting the police with bottles and bricks. In a crisis of this magnitude, the unusual tends to be routine. One of the most spectacular confrontations occurred on May 5. Reverend Charles Billups, a local leader, led his congregation from the New Pilgrim Baptist Church in the direction of the city's jail that evening. After a few blocks, it approached the police blockade. "Turn on your water, turn loose your dogs," Reverend Billups cried, "We will stand here till we die." "Dammit, turn on the hoses," Connor ordered. Nothing happened. To the marchers this was a providential sign. They rose from their knees and walked through the ranks of stupefied police to a park a block beyond, where they held a thankful prayer meeting.

The demonstrations and the police violence reached their peak on Monday and Tuesday, May 6 and 7. More than two thousand persons had by now been imprisoned. The city's facilities were exhausted. There remained several thousand volunteers still awaiting their turn to march. On the first day,

Comedian Dick Gregory was arrested, and the enraging photograph, internationally reproduced, of a female demonstrator pinned to the pavement by five policemen, one of whom had placed his knee on her neck, was taken. Despite the bitterness on both sides, there were moments of quasi-humorous relief, such as James Bevel in his yarmulke, negotiating the unwarranted use of fire hoses with a police captain. Bevel offered his hand to seal the pact. The offer was declined with a good-natured smile. There was no bonhommie in Burke Marshall's negotiations. After two hours with Martin, in a private home, the Assistant Attorney-General left empty handed. "I must confess," Martin stated, "that . . . I had some initial misgivings concerning Marshall's intentions." He was no more successful with Mayor-elect Boutwell and his allies. Black demands had crystallized into four conditions: (1) desegregation of lunch counters, rest rooms, fitting rooms, and drinking fountains in department stores; (2) upgrading and hiring of blacks on a nondiscriminatory basis throughout the city's business and industrial community; (3) dropping of all charges against demonstrators; and (4) formation of a biracial committee to prepare a timetable for desegregation in other areas of Birmingham. None of these terms was acceptable to the city authorities.

Tuesday surpassed Monday in violence. Two separate demonstrations involving nearly three thousand blacks flared into open riot in the city's business district during midafternoon. The hoses, which had not been used the day before, sprayed the demonstrators with water pressured to denude tree bark. Two hoses mounted on one tripod were dislodged by their water pressure and rocketed into a group of policemen; one officer's ribs and another's leg were crushed. Connor's men were no longer attempting to contain the crowds. They had been ordered to drive them brutally into the black section of the city. It is not surprising that nonviolent discipline collapsed under naked provocation. A hail of rocks, bottles, and brickbats showered the police and fire-men. As he attempted to restore discipline, Fred Shuttles-worth was lifted by a stream of water and hurled against the side of a building. An ambulance rushed him, badly bruised, from the scene. Told what had happened, Connor said, "I waited a week to see Shuttlesworth get hit with a hose: I'm sorry I missed it. I wish they'd carried him away in a hearse."

To professional observers, it was manifest that the SCLC leaders had lost control of the crowds. The churchgoing demonstrators might have responded to their appeals for calm, but hundreds of young black spectators, whose confidence in nonviolence was at best tentative, joined the fray. One prominent SCLC leader charged that SNCC was behind the disorders, one of the first of many similar public charges that would be made in the future. Earlier in the day, Martin had told a group of newsmen that "Activities which have taken place in Birmingham over the last few days, to my mind, mark the nonviolent movement coming of age." Within a few hours, the day's events had compromised this optimistic assessment. In a larger sense, however, Martin's verdict was accurate. The thrust of the Movement was unequivocally pacifist. The proximate cause of the violence was white brutality. And the proportion of black to white violence in Birmingham was finite. Although the retaliation of the demonstrators on Tuesday was deplorable from the optic of nonviolent passive resistance, it was probably indispensable to the success of Martin's objectives. Without its example and the imminent likelihood of more civil disorder, it is a reasonable speculation that neither the local white leaders nor the temporizing federal establishment would have mobilized to end the crisis in a relatively equitable manner. As in Albany, the regnant preoccupation of the Kennedy Administration was the quick restoration of civil peace in Birmingham. The legitimacy of black demands, although emotionally and ethically sympathetic, clearly enjoyed a secondary priority in the Kennedy brothers' political universe.

Sitting with the 125 white leaders at the Birmingham chamber of commerce on May 7, Burke Marshall found these gentlemen no less intransigent than during the previous two days. Several times during the morning, he left the room to telephone the SCLC leaders and the Attorney-General. The situation appeared to be at a dead end. It was only as they adjourned for lunch that the politicians and the businessmen saw, first-hand, the consequences of their obduracy. For many of them, knowledge of the events in Birmingham was derived from the press and television. On Tuesday, however, the business district was swarming with hundreds of demonstrators. "There were Negroes on the sidewalks, in the streets, standing, sitting in the aisles of downtown stores," Martin wrote. "There were square blocks of Negroes, a veritable sea of black faces." Birmingham's white leaders lunched to strains of "We Shall Overcome" and returned to the chamber of commerce, unnerved by what they had seen and heard. It was less than two hours later when the riots had begun. Frightened by Connor's stormtrooper methods and fearful of a recurrence of violence, the whites requested a truce. That evening, Connor asked Governor Wallace for and received more than five hundred state troopers. Two hundred and fifty of them, under the command of Colonel Al Lingo, took up posts within the city before nightfall. The Connor forces had every intention of engineering a slaughter. After a three-hour conference with the whites, the SCLC leaders agreed to a truce that evening. But Martin announced that demonstrations would resume on Thursday at 11 A.M. if their demands had not been met.

A month before Project C was put into operation, Martin had again complained of the Kennedy Administration's lassitude in civil rights. "If tokenism were our goal," he wrote in *The Nation*, "this administration has adroitly moved us toward its accomplishment. But tokenism can now be seen not only as a useless goal, but as a genuine menace." He went on to hope that the Administration would realize that it was at "a historic crossroad," that at stake was "its moral commitment, and with it its political fortunes." Reluctantly, by late April, the Kennedys were stumbling toward the same conclusion. The reasonableness of black demands and the egregious savagery of Southern white public officials made forthright action increasingly difficult to avoid. Birmingham was, as Martin had hoped it would be, the turning point for the Administration. In order to preclude the crisis that would make overt federal intervention mandatory, a final offstage effort was undertaken by the White House.

Shortly after Marshall's arrival, Birmingham businessmen were made aware of the keen interest in a negotiated settlement on the part of powerful Northern industrialists. Douglas Dillon, Secretary of the Treasury, contacted Edward Norton, chairman of Royal Crown Cola, Frank Plummer, president of Birmingham Trust National Bank, and William H. Hulsey, board chairman of Realty Mortgage Company, who now began to take an active part in the chamber-of-commerce deliberations headed by Sidney Smyer, a prosperous real-estate executive. Secretary of Defense McNamara was also helpful, through his business contacts inherited from his days as director of Ford Motor Corporation. Eugene V. Rostow, dean of Yale University's law school, asked one of his graduates, Roger Blough, chairman of the board of United States Steel, to intercede with the president of his corporation's Birmingham subsidiary, Tennessee Coal and Iron Company. Rostow had valuable contacts in both camps. Through Yale law professor Louis H. Pollack, the Administration was able to convey to the NAACP its determination to engineer a settlement, provided Martin and Fred could be persuaded to water their demands slightly. Pollack flew to Birmingham to assist Marshall in the final stages of negotiation.

The auguries on the day of truce were heartening—until later in the day. President Kennedy opened his morning conference with an encouraging reference to the negotiations in

Birmingham. At noon, Fred Shuttlesworth announced to the press that a tentative pact had been prepared; he expected a final accord before the deadline. Colonel Lingo's myrmidons were being deprived of their expected pretext for terrorizing the black community. Bull Connor sensed that he had been outmaneuvered in the secret negotiations of the previous day.

The Connor clique now played one of its last cards. That afternoon, Martin and Ralph were arrested and returned to jail, ostensibly to purge themselves of the sentence imposed for their Good Friday offense. Shuttlesworth gave orders to ready thousands of demonstrators to march into the heart of the city, where they would encounter nearly two thousand heavily armed law-enforcement officers. The bloody confrontation, barely avoided that very morning, now seemed a certainty. Once again, the Kennedy touch was needed. Joseph Dolan of the Justice Department rushed to see Fred, pleading with him to delay the fateful marching order until the Attorney-General could use his influence, unofficially, to obtain the release of Martin and Ralph. It took the full measure of Robert Kennedy's persuasiveness to restrain the founder of the ACMHR. Fred agreed by telephone to delay the marchers for several hours. Within minutes, the Attorney-General conferred by telephone with city officials. This time, Kennedy's persuasiveness betrayed the irritation and candor that his opponents often found both angering and intimidating. Federal neutrality, unlike Southern extremism, had definite limits, he lectured.

The tonic of the Justice Department had the desired result. When A. G. Gaston appeared at city hall that evening with $5,000 of bail money, the police agreed to release the two SCLC leaders. On Thursday morning, the white negotiators agreed to the essential demands of the black community. Lunch counters, rest rooms, fitting rooms, and drinking fountains in the large downtown stores were to be desegre-

gated. The SCLC accepted a ninety-day transition period,
however. Similarly, the hiring and promotion of black personnel in commercial and industrial establishments was to
take place over a sixty-day period. The biracial committee
was to be formed within two weeks. The nearly three thousand persons arrested were to be released immediately. The
whites refused, however, to recommend the dismissal of
charges against them, necessitating the payment of bail. For
the SCLC leaders, this last agreement constituted a serious
compromise of principle and imposed a huge financial burden.
Before the day had expired, nevertheless, the greater portion
of $237,000 in bail money had been raised through the
generous contributions of the United Auto Workers and the
National Maritime Union.

On May 20, the Supreme Court's decision legalizing sit-in
demonstrations in cities enforcing segregation nullified the
Alabama laws under which the large majority of Birmingham's demonstrators could be prosecuted, It is quite probable
that Martin and his colleagues had received assurances from
Washington and from the NAACP legal staff of the likelihood of an imminent and favorable court decision. It is also
probable that another court decision influenced the final
negotiations: The Alabama state supreme court was to rule
on the city government conflict on May 22. The Birmingham
pact's desegregation timetable conceded the white negotiators
the semblance of partial victory in delaying the inevitable by
releasing them from the intolerable responsibility of implementation before Bull Connor and his cohorts had been
defanged.

What Martin had termed a "bold design for a new South"
seemed to have survived its preliminary sketch when, on
the morning of May 10, the Birmingham settlement was
publicly proclaimed. The toll had been severe. Scores of persons had been injured. Several dozen had required either
hospitalization or recuperation at home. On the day of the

compromise, Fred Shuttlesworth collapsed during the press conference and was taken away in an ambulance. Naturally, a number of persons had been fired by their white employers. Still, the city was at peace, and tomorrow's Birmingham could be a much better place for both races. Martin's optimism and generosity—always more expansive in moments of triumph than good tactical sense warranted—overflowed at the press conference: "I must say this, too: in these recent days, I have been deeply impressed by the quality of the white persons of the community who worked so diligently for a just solution." Within hours, these "men of good will" would evince a distressing ambivalence about honoring the pact. He was on surer ground when he gave thanks to the Almighty for his interest: "When all is said and done, when this situation is seen in [the] perspective of eternity, ultimate credit and glory and honor must be given to Almighty God, for He has clearly been at work among us. And it is He alone who has finally gained the victory for all His children."

Many of God's children in Birmingham were ingrates. At approximately 11:45 P.M., the first of two time bombs demolished the home of Martin's brother, A. D. King. Miraculously, his wife and five sleeping children escaped harm. Earlier that evening, Ernest Gibson, manager of the Gaston Motel, had received telephone threats. When he reported them to Sheriff Bailey, he was told not to worry. "If you see anything," Bailey advised, "call us." What Gibson saw, one hour after the demolition of Reverend A. D. King's home, was the partial destruction by another time bomb of the Gaston Motel. Several persons were injured. Through his telephone receiver in Atlanta, Martin heard the strains of "We Shall Overcome" as his brother told him what had happened: "I marveled that in a moment of such tragedy the Negro could still express himself with hope and with faith." Some blacks found other channels for self-expression that night. It was not until 4 or 5 A.M. that riots ended in Birming-

ham. The crowds rampaged through nine blocks of the
ghetto area, immobilizing a large number of police cars. One
officer was stabbed; several were assaulted. Firemen were
prevented from approaching burning white-owned shops, and
Chief Inspector W. J. Haley's picture appeared the following
morning in the *Birmingham News*, blood streaming from his
scalp wound. It was one of the worst riots in Southern history, and the number of unreported injuries to blacks may
have been considerable.

In a moment of distracted anger, even Martin said that
the bombings justified "some tangible protests." Although
badly shaken by the bombings and their aftermath, the SCLC
personnel did what it could to restore calm. Wyatt found,
however, that he had little influence on the rioters, who were,
for the most part, young adult males (periodically or only
barely employed) for whom the black church and Kingian
vision of brotherhood were contemptible irrelevancies. They
had always existed side by side with their law-abiding, dignified, hardworking, and Christian fellows, the "decent" blacks
who, in the depths of grinding exploitation, contrived somehow to hold fast to a piecemeal version of the American
dream. The latter, especially their women, believed in Martin
Luther King. Those who rampaged and burned on Thursday
night belonged, by income or psychology or both, to that
"desperate class" observed by a James Weldon Johnson hero
during his first trip South: "They cherish a sullen hatred for
all white men, and they value life as cheap." They existed in
every Southern community, alternately ignored and slaught-
ered by the whites and an embarrassment to the black
preacher, schoolteacher, dining-car waiter, and hard-working
farmer. "I'll go to hell for the first white man that bothers
me," Johnson reports them as saying nearly sixty years ago.
Wyatt heard their descendants shouting nihilistically, "Let
the whole fucking city burn. I don't give a good goddamn—
this'll show those white motherfuckers!" This "desperate

class"—more desperate than elsewhere in the South, because of Birmingham's industrial squalor—was, in fact, staging a dress rehearsal of the more fiery summertime catastrophes that would soon rack cities outside the South.

What of the Birmingham pact? Did it still hold? Mayor Hanes spoke for the extremists: "Martin Luther King is a revolutionary. The nigger King ought to be investigated by the Attorney-General," he added. Arriving from Atlanta on Friday morning, Martin insisted to the press that he was certain that the agreement remained in force. The merchants and industrialists were less positive. Bull Connor was calling on the white citizenry to boycott downtown stores until the agreement was publicly abrogated. The fact that no signed statement had been obtained from the white negotiators made the SCLC victory even more parlous. Further disorders were being provided against by the dispatch of federal troops to the city by the President. Major General Creighton W. Abrams had established a command post in the Federal Building in Birmingham, and hundreds of municipal and state officers were patrolling the streets. Birmingham's return to order was reassuringly complete by the end of the day. The U.S. soldiers who had been transferred to two nearby bases were not needed. Nor was it necessary to federalize the Alabama National Guard, as President Kennedy had informed the protesting Governor Wallace he would not hesitate to do.

Support came from the White House as John Kennedy publicly praised the accord and pledged a federal guarantee of its fulfillment. Toward the end of the week, he finally responded to Martin's repeated plea that he tour the South and speak out positively on racial issues. At Vanderbilt University, the President lauded the heroism and justice of the cause of Birmingham's blacks. Earlier, on May 15, sixty of the 125 negotiators finally allowed their names to be published in support of the agreement. Five days later, the Hanes-Connor clique had the city board of education order the expulsion of eleven hundred elementary and high school students for participating in the demonstrations. It was another gambit calculated to provoke a renewal of conflict. It nearly succeeded. "There were some people in our ranks who sincerely felt," Martin knew, "that, in retaliation, all the students in Birmingham should stay out of school and that demonstrations should be resumed." Again returning to the city from Atlanta, he convinced the others that this was a matter best contested through the courts. In the capable hands of a team of NAACP lawyers, the case was favorably decided within two days by the Fifth Circuit Court of Appeals. Indeed, it was an exceptionally good week of legal decisions for civil rights leaders. The May 20 Supreme Court decision legitimizing demonstrations against segregated institutions has already been cited. On May 23, a Thursday, the Alabama state supreme court ruled the Hanes government out of office.

Of course, Birmingham's endemic savagery could not be exorcised by a grudging agreement between black ministers and white civic leaders and by the installation of the relatively civilized Boutwell commission. But Connor, impresario of much of the city's terror, was gone. "It would have been pleasant to relate that Birmingham settled down after the storm, and moved constructively to justify the hopes of the many who wished it well," Martin lamented. "It would have been pleasant, but it would not be true." Militant black intellectuals also knew that racial peace would not rush in upon Birmingham. The radical monthly *Liberator* (whose advisory board numbered, among others, James Baldwin, Harold Cruse, Ossie Davis, and Richard B. Moore) found little to praise in Martin's Birmingham accord. "The kindest statement which can be made about the role of Reverend Martin Luther King in Birmingham," its June editorial ran, "is that it is unusual behavior for a commander in a winning battle to urge his troops not to fight as hard and to negotiate

a surrender when victory is in sight. This so-called agreement
with nameless representatives of Birmingham financial power
. . . is a sell out."

In mid-September, the world was to be shocked by news
of another dynamiting of a black church, taking the lives of
four little girls and injuring twenty-one other Sunday worshipers. The police compounded the outrage by shooting
to death two adolescents near the scene. President Kennedy's
televised remarks the following day were compassionate in
their grief and sternly remonstrative. "This nation is committed to a course of domestic justice and tranquility," he
stated. There was praise for the "Negro leaders of Birmingham who are counseling restraint instead of violence."
Kennedy's message contained one note of hope, whose
reasonableness would have been justified in any city but
Birmingham and cities like it throughout the deep South:
"If these cruel and tragic events can only awaken that city
and state—if they can only awaken this entire nation . . . then
it is not too late for all concerned to unite in steps toward
peaceful progress before more lives are lost."

Martin King was a man of great hope as well. Standing
before the mound of flowers in which the four tiny coffins
were berthed, touching little Cynthia Wesley's casket as the
Sixth Avenue Baptist Church choir sang low and mournful,
no man could have wished more desperately that the murder
of these children might be redeemed by a moratorium on
hate in Birmingham. But, "if humane people expected the
local leadership to express remorse, they were to be disappointed," Martin confessed. No whites attended the
funeral services. Almost none deplored the psychopathic
violence. "There is little evidence that it [the bombing] has
changed the convictions of the white leaders about what
they regard as the proper (separate) relations between the
races," James Reston wrote. Instead, the city fathers sought
every opportunity to dodge the stipulations of the recent agree-

ment. Although libraries, the golf course, public schools, and department stores were desegregated, the city construed the agreement in the narrowest possible terms. It refused outright to hire black policemen. It also dragged its feet on accelerating the hiring and promotion of black personnel in commerce and industry. "I like to believe," Fred Shuttlesworth wrote in *Freedomways* several months later, "that further persistence by our Movement will finally make a City of Brotherhood." Hope, obdurate and everlasting, was the quintessence of the nonviolent movement.

In the months to come, an increasing number of less nonviolent American blacks wavered in their faith as they contemplated the spectacular disparity of the ultimate promise of Martin's doctrine with contemporary racial injustice. It is interesting to note that Martin himself initially wanted to resume demonstrations on a massive scale in the wake of the church disaster and was dissuaded by local black moderates who, quite probably, had been indirectly contacted by the alarmed Justice Department. Lerone Bennett observes that Martin "has been criticized, perhaps too harshly, for not *leading* the rebellion he had created." Such criticisms were muted, however, in the climactic months that followed the Birmingham settlement. If Albany had seemed to be the moment when, as Malcolm X declared, "the civil rights struggle in America reached its lowest point," Martin's apparent success in Birmingham nullified the mistakes and ignominy of the past, making him a singularly dynamic and glamorous black American leader.

For a few seasons, it would not matter greatly that beyond the bare right to travel, dine, read, and avail himself of public entertainment more than less unhindered, the black man's economic and political impotence remained unchanged in Montgomery, Birmingham, and even Atlanta. And, in two crucial areas of community progress, despite agreements and federal laws, whites had managed to hold the line. Black policemen and integrated public schools in the deep South were as rare as Southern white contributors to the NAACP. The final chapter in Martin's narrative of the Birmingham story, *Why We Can't Wait*, establishes his growing pre-occupation with the question of economic redress of minority group poverty through federal programs. There, he formulates sketchily a federal assistance scheme analogous to the post-World War II G. I. Bill of Rights. His knowledge of Southern racism disabused him of excessive optimism about the honorable implementation of the hard-won pledges from mayors and businessmen. Nevertheless, out of the combat in Alabama and Georgia cities—even Albany—a "New Negro" had emerged. "Am I just imagining it," a Birmingham businessman queried, "or are the Negroes I see around town walking a little straighter these days?"

There was certainly a new gait to be seen on the streets of Southern cities everywhere. Like collard greens and chitterlings among the black bourgeoisie, the ingratiating shuffle was becoming unfashionable among the ordinary people. If "Mr. Charlie" or "The Man" was becoming hysterically confirmed in his determination neither to change himself nor to suffer improvement in others, many Southern blacks (and, shortly, Northern blacks) were swept up in the euphoric vision of the Promised Land toward which Martin King vowed to lead them. "For hundreds of years," the new Moses wrote, "the quiet sobbing of an oppressed people had been unheard by millions of white Americans. . . . The lament became a shout and then a roar and for months no American, white or Negro, was insulated or unaware." The voice that had been heard only when it sang spirituals, mushmouthedly professed its pleasure over a small gratuity, or begged some small favor for its people now joined in strident chorus with thousands of others:

> It isn't nice to block the door
> It isn't nice to go to jail
> There are nicer ways to do it
> But the nice ways always fail.

This freedom song, "It Isn't Nice," youthful, Rabelaisian, and determined, captures an *élan* that scarcely existed in the Southern black community before Montgomery. True, there had always been blacks too proud to ride segregated buses and trains, manly enough to curse brackish store clerks and police (usually they were blessed with some special distinction in the community), and sufficiently emancipated to disdain the ideology of the humble and separate racial uplift espoused by Booker T. Washington. The consequence of Martin's tactic of massive, peaceful confrontation was that it democratized the attitudes that had until then been held by a special minority. Poignant testimony of this unprecedented assurance of the Southern black was given by the fifteen-year-old demonstrator Grosbeck Preer Parham before Judge Talbott Ellis of Birmingham. The judge, a compassionate man, sought to explain to young Parham the error of trying to force social change. Impatiently, the youth replied that freedom had been denied too long to justify cautious methods. Perhaps the mother could see the wisdom of his counsel, Judge Ellis hoped. "Mrs. Parham, what do you think of Booker T. Washington," he asked? "I think that he was a fine man. But his day is past. The young people won't take what we did," she replied.

"The sound of the explosion in Birmingham reached all the way to Washington," Martin said. Because blacks in the South were fighting for their rights, Northern blacks re-examined the superficiality of their liberties. The country was astir as never before since the Civil War over the dilemma of race. On June 11, John Kennedy, whose Administration had belatedly rethought its priorities, spoke to the nation to advise that he was requesting Congress to enact immediately the most comprehensive civil rights bill to date. The President's speech was by far the most positive he had made on behalf of the American black:

One hundred years of delay have passed since President Lincoln freed the slaves, yet their heirs, their grandsons, are not fully free. They are not yet freed from the bonds of injustice. They are not yet freed from social and economic oppression. And this nation, for all its hopes and all its boasts, will not be fully free until all its citizens are free.

We preach freedom around the world, and we mean it, and we cherish our freedom here at home, but are we to say to the world . . . that this is a land of the free except for the Negroes . . . ? Now the time has come for this nation to fulfill its promise. The events in Birmingham and elsewhere have so increased the cries for equality that no city or state or legislative body can prudently choose to ignore them.

Because of what Martin King had accomplished in Birmingham—however incomplete and superficial—Grosbeck Preer Parham, Albert Boutwell, and John Fitzgerald Kennedy saw civil rights issues not quite the same way as they had before B Day, April 3, 1963.

8

The Strength of a Dream

> I am, indeed, a practical dreamer. My dreams are
> not airy nothings. I want to convert my dreams
> into realities, as far as possible.
>
> MOHANDAS K. GANDHI

WHILE BIRMINGHAM SUTURED its wounds, Martin undertook
a triumphal tour from California to New York. In Los Angeles,
25,000 people turned out to hear his description of the recent
struggle and bold prognoses of grander accomplishments.
Nothing typifies better Martin's uncanny ability to weave
into his elevated speeches the arresting homilies of the un-
tutored black. "I say good night to you by quoting the words
of an old Negro slave," he told this audience: " 'We ain't
what we ought to be and we ain't what we want to be and we
ain't what we're going to be. But thank God we ain't what
we was.' " In Chicago, he addressed a crowd of 10,000 enthusiastic sympathizers. But the most impressive success of
the tour came on June 23, in Detroit, where he led 125,000
people on a Freedom Walk down Woodward Avenue. In
addition to Reverend C. L. Franklin, chairman of the city's
Council on Human Rights, which sponsored the event,
Walter Reuther walked with Martin that day to Cobo Hall.

The Detroit speech was worthy of the huge crowd, only a
fraction of which was able to squeeze into Detroit's largest
auditorium. He spoke almost mischievously of the power of
nonviolence:

We've come to see that this method is not a weak method. For it's the strong man who can stand up amid opposition. . . . You see, this method has a way of disarming the opponent. It exposes his moral defenses . . . and he just doesn't know what to do. If he doesn't beat you, wonderful! But if he beats you, you develop the quiet courage of accepting blows without retaliating. If he doesn't put you in jail, wonderful! Nobody with any sense likes to go to jail. But if he puts you in jail, you go in that jail and transform it from a dungeon of shame to a haven of freedom and unity. And I submit to you that if a man hasn't discovered something that he will die for, he isn't fit to live!

This speech was remarkable also because, several times, Martin repeated the phrase "I have a dream."

From Detroit, he flew to New York to speak at a Harlem church. The reception to his sermon-speech was tumultuous, but it was marred by an ominous incident as his limousine made its way to the engagement. Although the national media covered his movements and pronouncements as if no other civil rights leader existed after Birmingham, there were other voices to be heard if the trouble was taken to visit the alleys and pool halls in the shadows of the churches. Malcolm X and Robert Williams and a host of nameless militants were busy decrying nonviolence. The rotten eggs that splattered Martin's car windows were thrown by their spiritual disciples. The assassination of NAACP field secretary Medgar Evers, on the steps of his Jackson, Mississippi, home on June 12 nourished in some quarters the incipient disenchantment with nonviolence. If Mrs. Izola Curry's letter-opener had had any meaning, it was that urban centers beyond the South were to be unlucky for Martin King.

As Martin finished his speaking tour, the forces unleashed by the Battle of Birmingham were beginning to engulf America. Dozens of minuscule Birminghams erupted in the South—Placquemine County (Louisiana), Jackson (Mississippi), Rome (Georgia), Danville (Virginia), Cambridge (Maryland)—and, in every major city of the North, demon-

strations were mounted to protest discrimination in education, jobs, and housing. Distinguished white prelates joined
black pickets and went to jail for violating state laws. Aca-
demics joined the procession. The requests for Martin's assistance came from virtually every section of the country
where beleaguered organizations were seeking to shatter the
age-old pattern of separate and unequal social conditions. He
gave advice and put in as many appearances as his health
and pastoral duties in Atlanta allowed, but he concentrated
his energies and those of his organization upon Danville,
Virginia, the last capital of the Confederacy. Already, Fred
Shuttlesworth, along with former SCLC staff member Jack
O'Dell, had joined Reverend L. C. Chase, the local SCLC
head, to guide the Danville protests.

On Thursday, July 11, Martin arrived in Danville to lead a
demonstration in defiance of a local injunction. "I have so
many injunctions that I don't even look at them anymore,"
he declared, "I was enjoined January 15, 1929, when I was
born in the United States a Negro." Actually, he did not
head the march but left its generalship to Ralph, who dropped out of line shortly before arrests were made. Martin was
unable to remain in Danville, although he returned twice to
lend his presence to the struggle directed by Reverends Chase,
Lawrence Campbell, and A. I. Dunlap and taxi driver Julius
E. Adams, Mrs. Beatrice Hairston, Maxine Muse, and others.
Danville proved to be another Albany in many ways. There
was tension between the SCLC and SNCC. The campaign
drew a large number of nonresident whites, conspicuous
among whom was Bob Zellner. Danville's white establishment never yielded entirely to the demands of its black
citizens. The critical areas of education and employment remained virtually unchanged.

An interesting sidelight to Martin's participation in the
Danville demonstrations helps provide several important
pieces in the smudged mosaic of his personality. Increasingly,

the demands of public crises had left him so little time to be himself that even some of his friends had difficulty picturing him otherwise than immaculately dressed, behind a rostrum, churning out those round, earnest phrases. J. Pius Barbour recalls that, during this period, Martin stood before the full-length mirror in his study and confessed, " 'Doc, I am conscious of two Martin Luther Kings. I'm a wonder to myself!' " "Well, he couldn't understand his career," Barbour adds, "all the publicity he'd gotten as a civil rights leader." "There's a kind of dualism in my life," Martin sighed. Ella Baker and Charles Sherrod believed that Martin was a phantom of the news media, a symbol without more substance than that of hundreds of other Southern Baptist preachers.

Whatever the truth of these assessments, by the summer of 1963, the essential Martin Luther King was buried under tons of press copy and television film. But, in Danville, there was no equivalent of the Gaston Motel. He stayed with an intelligent, kindly, extroverted retired schoolteacher, Mrs. Beatrice Hairston, and her husband. The Hairston home was open to the community, and, although Martin had little rest there, he was able to palaver informally with a procession of refreshingly ordinary but dedicated Danvillians. They got to know him faily well. Mrs. Hairston was so unimpressed by his stature and humility at first that she mistook one of the lawyers in his entourage for Martin. He was, she recounts in her ingratiating Southern accent, "just as humble and gentle a man as you ever saw." Quite different from the bull-voiced and patrician James Farmer, whom she had also hosted. "Oh, I feel more at home here than any place I've ever been except my own home," Martin drawled. Off went the shoes, the tie was loosened, and, after a cup of her good coffee, he made his way to the Hairston refrigerator for some Southern fried chicken. Later, they talked about families they knew in Atlanta, and Martin cracked a number of the jokes that, although few can be recalled, unfailingly convulsed his friends. The young people, especially the young ladies, found nothing stuffy and sanctimonious about Martin, either. His fame had not spoiled—not yet, at any rate—the jaunty but human self-possession of his days as Tweed.

The idea of compelling national attention to social or economic grievances by marshaling the aggrieved in the nation's capital is at least as old as General Jacob Coxey's tattered army of unemployed, which descended upon Washington in 1894. Segregation in defense industries had been ended by President Franklin Roosevelt when A. Philip Randolph threatened to inundate Washington with an army of blacks. Martin's 1957 Prayer Pilgrimage and the mass delegations of subsequent years were exploratory developments of this strategy. In an address to the American Negro Labor Council late in 1962, Asa Randolph documented the slow progress and even loss of ground in civil rights achievements. The depressing facts were that, since the 1954 landmark decision of the Supreme Court, there were more blacks in segregated schools than there had been in 1952. More were unemployed now than in 1954. More serious, the median income of blacks had slipped from 57 per cent to 54 per cent of that of whites in less than a decade. Desegregation was crucial, Randolph stated. But the combat against the systematic impoverishment of unskilled labor must be enlarged from skirmishes to direct, massive assault. In November, 1962, Randolph formally proposed to the five major civil rights organizations that an army of black plaintiffs be sent to Washington to demand the enactment of fair employment legislation and the passage of an increased minimum wage to extend to the areas of agriculture and commerce presently outside the scope of federal wage regulations. The NAACP replied that it would take the matter under advisement. The Urban League declined the invitation outright. SNCC, CORE, and the SCLC responded affirmatively although they left the organizational initiative entirely to Randolph.

The critical point in the fissionable mass of American racism appeared to be approaching rapidly in 1963: the murder of William L. Moore, the white Baltimore, Maryland, mailcarrier, on his way by foot to Mississippi; the federalizing of the Alabama National Guard to provide protection for three black students entering the University of Alabama; the murder of Medgar Evers. When Randolph revived his proposal in mid-1963, it was received with considerably more enthusiasm. President Kennedy's pending civil rights bill, threatened by a filibuster by Southern senators and the collusion of Republican colleagues, was a decisive factor in the decision to rally to the march idea. On July 2, some two hundred civil rights leaders, representatives of sympathetic national organizations, and officials of Walter Reuther's UAW assembled at New York's Commodore Hotel for a day-long meeting. The heads of the five civil rights organizations were present. The planners of the March provided it with a pedigree of unparalleled liberal auspices: National Council of Churches, represented by Dr. Eugene Carson Blake, American Jewish Council, represented by Rabbi Joachim Prinz, National Catholic Conference for International Justice, represented by Mathew Ahmann, United Auto Workers, represented by Walter Reuther. Also lending support were the American Baptist Convention, the Brethren Church, the United Presbyterian Church, and innumerable Catholic parishes and Lutheran congregations. A conspicuous absence among the March sponsors was the American Federation of Labor and Congress of Industrial Organizations (AFL-CIO), headed by the conservative and irascible George Meany. This was a major blunder, Martin correctly stated. Later, Meany agreed.

Mythomania is an inevitable byproduct of extraordinary historical events. The March on Washington has been no exception. Black militants have tapped the vein of events that led to August 28, 1963, and extracted from it a rich find of conspiratorial interpretations. Louis Lomax first alerted

the militants to putative maneuverings of the white establishment in a *San Francisco Chronicle* article on August 19.
According to Lomax, the March leaders had agreed to moderate their demands for $1 million to be paid by the business
community. Taking their cue from the *Chronicle* article,
Adam Clayton Powell (perhaps smarting because he had not
been invited to assist in planning the March), Malcolm X,
and writers Julius Lester and Calvin Hernton, among others,
lamented the suborning of the March on Washington by the
omnipotent and indomitably clever Eastern business community and its allies in Washington.

Hernton, in an excess of populist fantasizing, states that

> The original idea germinated among the field Negroes in the
> ghettoes subsequent to the disillusioning bloodbath in Birming-
> ham: Negroes got mad and started talking about storming the
> White House, tying up Congress, and even lying down on the
> runways of the airports. As soon as the white folks heard about
> this, they called a meeting with the chiefs of staff of the non-
> violent Negroes in the Carlyle Hotel in Manhattan and mapped
> out plans for "shaping up" the March on Washington.

The gifted young writer Julius Lester summarizes the
March in such sententious terms as almost to intimidate cautious investigators. "People were talking about sitting-in on
Capitol Hill and the floor of Congress. . . . They were ready
to bring the country to a halt, but Jack Kennedy called in the
top 'civil rights leaders' and before the people knew what
was happening, the March was Kennedy-sponsored and proclaimed as being 'in the American tradition.'" Finally, we
have the sainted confirmations of Malcolm X. "I was there,"
he says for effect, "When they found out that this black
steamroller was going to come down on the capital, they
called in Wilkins, they called in Randolph, they called in
these national Negro leaders. . . . Kennedy said, 'Look you
all are letting this thing go too far. . . . If you aren't in it,
I'll put you in it. I'll put you at the head of it. I'll endorse

it.'" It is, perhaps, well to bear in mind James Farmer's judgment that Malcolm "was a simpler man than is usually supposed."

Without a doubt, there were movements and maneuverings by white liberals, millionaires, and politicians that lend superficial credence to the militants' charge of disingenuousness on the part of the principal civil rights leaders. It was true that the Kennedy brothers had sought to regulate the civil rights movement through a personal diplomacy calculated either to flatter or to obligate key black leaders. For example, the militants saw Robert Kennedy's dealings with James Baldwin as part of the Kennedy libretto to enchant and divert the black thrust for immediate social and economic emancipation. Late in May, the Attorney-General had invited Baldwin to confer with him at his McClean, Virginia, estate. "Who are the Negroes other Negroes listen to, do you think?" Robert Kennedy asked. He added immediately, "Not politicians. I don't mean Adam Clayton Powell. Or even Martin Luther King."

Two days later, May 25, Kennedy met a group of thirteen persons assembled by Baldwin in New York. It was a rather peculiarly composed group. In it were Rip Torn, Henry Morgenthau, and Robert Mills, who were white. Lena Horne, Lorraine Hansberry, Harry Belafonte, William Berry of the Chicago Urban League, Baldwin's brother David, psychologist Kenneth Clark, Attorney Clarence Jones, who more or less represented the interests of Martin King, and a young activist named Jerome Smith. Although there may have been an element of profitable redintegration in Robert Kennedy's later political career, the confrontation was an unmitigated failure. The Attorney-General was nonplussed by the group's composition and incensed by its irreverence for his brother's civil rights accomplishments. Baldwin's friends found Kennedy to be woefully ignorant of black conditions. Parenthetically, it is interesting to note that, later, Belafonte, along with Clarence

Jones, unobtrusively demurred from the harsh judgments that had been expressed. "I just want you to know," Jones confided in a corner of the room, "that Dr. King deeply appreciates the way you handled the Birmingham affair." The news media publicized the meeting.

Naturally, the militants were darkly suspicious. Then came the Hotel Carlyle conference late in June, the veritable Yalta of black politics, according to their lights. This too, was thought to be Kennedy inspired. The murder of Medgar Evers on June 12 stirred Stephen Currier, an exceptionally humane man (husband of a descendant of Andrew Mellon and president of the Taconic Foundation) who was deeply conscious of the social responsibilities of great wealth. On June 19, he convened a meeting of ninety-six chairmen of corporations and foundations at the Hotel Carlyle to elicit monetary pledges in order to aid the civil rights movement. Three days later, Currier attended a White House meeting of civil rights leaders at which the goals and program of the March were outlined to the President, the Vice-President, and the Attorney-General.

The President opposed the March because of its high risk of civil disruption and the likelihood of congressional backlash. "We want success in Congress," the President emphasized, "not just a big show at the Capitol. Some of these people are looking for an excuse to be against us. I don't want to give any of them a chance to say, 'Yes, I'm for the [voting rights] bill, but I'm damned if I will vote for it at the point of a gun.'" Randolph's reply, delivered with the measured dignity that had impressed Franklin Roosevelt more than two decades earlier, put the matter in a different light: "The Negroes are already in the streets. It is very likely impossible to get them off. If they are bound to be in the streets in any case, is it not better that they be led by organizations dedicated to civil rights and disciplined by struggle rather than to leave them to other leaders who care neither about

civil rights nor nonviolence?" And, while John Kennedy
pondered Randolph's argument, Martin and James Farmer
sustained the pressure. The March, said Martin, "could also
serve as a means of dramatizing the issue and mobilizing support in parts of the country which don't know the problem
at first hand. I think it will serve a purpose. It may seem
ill-timed. Frankly, I have never engaged in any direct action
movement which did not seem ill-timed. Some people,"
Martin concluded significantly, "thought Birmingham ill-
timed." "Including the Attorney-General," the President
good naturedly appended. Randolph, King, Farmer, Wilkins,
and Young stood their ground. Lyndon Johnson, Robert
Kennedy, and Currier later successfully counselled the President to support the rally.

Slightly less than a month afterward, July 17, Currier accepted the cochairmanship, with Whitney Young, of the
Council for United Civil Rights Leadership (CUCRL),
whose purpose was to solicit $1.5 million in emergency funds
for the five civil rights groups and the National Council of
Negro Women. *The New York Times* announced that the
emergency funds were to be raised by the end of the summer, "although disbursements may be distributed over as long
as three years." At the July 17 meeting, $800,000 in taxable
and nontaxable money was partially distributed among
CUCRL members in the following proportions: $225,000 to
the NAACP Legal Defense and Educational Fund; $100,000
to CORE; $100,000 to the Urban League; $50,000 each to
the SCLC and the National Council of Negro Women's
Educational Foundation. SNCC received $15,000, with the
promise that its quota would be "sharply upgraded" later.
The SCLC, according to Attorney Stanley Levison, generously had asked that its share of CUCRL proceeds be reduced because of its greater fund-raising capabilities.

Currier had no desire to direct the course of the civil
rights groups into quiescent channels. He believed in unity

and coordination, certainly, but it is a reasonable presumption that common sense and philanthropic etiquette would have precluded an endeavor to enforce standards of political conduct acceptable to white liberals upon civil rights activists. Of more significance is the fact that none of the leaders who attended the meeting believed then or later that the Currier largesse was a weapon to control the March on Washington. The offer was "definitely above board," John Lewis says, and James Farmer scoffs at Malcolm X's conjecture, observing that in any case, by July the planning and financing of the March had all but been completed. Nor was there anything sinister in Currier's insistence upon "responsible action" by "responsible" civil rights leaders. There was no need to invent a conspiracy around the March on Washington. What was happening, as President Kennedy grew more concerned about white violence and black impatience and as titans of finance and industry took time off to look at the race problem, was a natural and altogether predictable *entente cordiale* among the more enlightened in government and business. They were intervening diplomatically and obliquely to promote partial solution of a problem chronically threatening to the consensual universe of whose order they were the guardians. Nor does it make sense to charge that the black leaders of the March betrayed their followers by accepting the financial support and political endorsement of liberal whites—unless, that is, it is argued that, initially, the men and goals behind the March were revolutionary. This would make sense, but it would be completely untrue.

As August 28th, the date of the March, approached, support increased. The fourteen participating major civic, religious, and labor organizations raised almost $130,000. Approximately two thousand black New York City policemen belonging to Guardian (a fraternal order) volunteered their services as marshals. In Paris, James Baldwin led a march of some eighty American artists to the United States Embassy to present a scroll containing the signatures of three hundred supporters; on the day of the March, the number of signatures had grown to fifteen hundred. Bayard Rustin, the chief organizer, worked closely with federal officials and with civic and police authorities of the District of Columbia to ensure flawless movement into the heart of the city of the expected 150,000 pilgrims. Those arriving by train at Union Station, and marching past theater advertisements of "Stop the World, I Want to Get Off," were to proceed along Louisiana Avenue to Constitution Avenue and then follow the Ellipse (the semicircular thoroughfare behind the White House) to the assembly point on the grounds of the Washington Monument. Having been entertained by a spectacular variety of famous artists for an hour and a half, the marchers would move at 11:30 A.M. along the banks of the Reflecting Pool to the Lincoln Memorial for more entertainment and to hear the ten principal speakers. Traffic along Pennsylvania Avenue was to be diverted in order to accommodate the fleet of buses shuttling from outlying assembly points to disgorge participants arriving by car, bus, and plane. Earlier, from 9 until 10 A.M., the March leaders were to confer with the leaders of Congress. At the close of the day, the March leaders were to confer with President Kennedy.

Many people were presented to the crowds on the day of the March. The principal speakers represented the major civil rights groups and their collaborators. Cardinal O'Boyle of the Washington archdiocese would deliver the invocation. Appropriately, Asa Randolph of the American Negro Labor Council would give the opening remarks and present the speakers. Reverend Eugene Carson Blake of the National Council of Churches, SNCC's John Lewis, Walter Reuther of the UAW, Floyd McKissick (standing in for CORE'S James Farmer), Whitney Young of the Urban League, Mathew Ahmann of the National Catholic Conference, Roy

Wilkins of the NAACP, and Rabbi Joachim Prinz of the American Jewish Council would follow with brief speeches. Martin, who "was assigned the rousements," as Roy Wilkins puts it, would speak last. Dr. Benjamin Mays would conclude the March proceedings with a benediction.

In the planning conferences, Bayard Rustin had left the selection of topics entirely to the major speakers, recommending only that they adhere scrupulously to the timetable. The participants still disagree over whether or not there was an informal but implicit agreement not to indulge in egregiously anti-Administration tirades. Perhaps Martin, Roy Wilkins, Whitney Young, and Asa Randolph operated on this precept without undertaking to ascertain that it was unanimously understood and accepted. It was clear from the statement of March goals that every manifestation of discrimination was to be deplored in the most positive terms possible: The inadequacy of past legislation was to be underscored; the demand that Congress enact far-reaching civil rights laws was to be made, with the appended prediction of further civil disorders should the legislative branch temporize. But it seems equally apparent that the sense of the March required that the emphasis of the addresses be placed upon entreaty laced with optimism of better times to come. Rhetorical civility was not to be abandoned, and the muted threats were to be vague and inferential. Above all, John Kennedy was to be spared personal attack. If their principles had not been quashed by the bountiful gifts to the CUCRL, the black civil rights leaders nevertheless chose to grant the Administration and its liberal allies the benefit of the doubt for the time being.

On the evening of August 27, John Lewis' speech was circulated to the press. The text was the result of the collective effort of Lewis, James Forman, Tom Kahn, and others. Memories have dimmed as to individual reactions to the original SNCC text, but there is unanimous agreement that none of the other March sponsors dissented from the decision to insist that its contents be altered. "Those who saw it or heard reports of it," Roy Wilkins states, "felt that SNCC had taken advantage of the situation as they frequently do, as all revolutionaries do." Cardinal O'Boyle threatened to withdraw unless it were altered. Walter Fauntroy, Martin's representative, shared the alarm of his colleagues. Bayard Rustin was deputed to assist Lewis in making the necessary changes, although the speech, as given, was rewritten by John Lewis on a portable typewriter behind the Lincoln Memorial.

What Lewis intended to say was coruscatingly aggressive. "In good conscience," he proposed to declaim, "we cannot support the Administration's civil rights bill, for it is too little, and too late." The bowdlerized speech read, "True, we support the Administration's civil rights bill, but this bill will not protect young children and old women from police dogs and fire hoses. . . ." Lewis did say "We are now involved in a serious revolution. This nation is still a place of cheap political leaders allying themselves with open forms of political, economic, and social exploitation. . . . I want to know —which side is the federal government on?" Nor were Bayard Rustin's considerable diplomatic talents able to prevent Lewis from indicting the President: "Mr. Kennedy is trying to take the revolution out of the streets and put it in the courts. Listen, Mr. Kennedy, listen, Mr. Congressman, listen, fellow citizens—the black masses are on the march for jobs and freedom, and we must say to the politicians that there won't be a 'cooling-off' period." But, originally, Lewis had proposed a black *Blitzkrieg* of the South: "The next time we march, we won't march on Washington, but we will march through the South, through the heart of Dixie, the way Sherman did." The altered peroration was much gentler. "We will march through the South, through the streets of Danville, through the streets of Cambridge, through the

streets of Birmingham. But we will march with the spirit of
love and the spirit of dignity that we have shown here today."
John Lewis' speech, although altered, had only slightly less
impact upon the crowd than Martin's.

An estimated 250,000 people attended the March on Washington, between 75,000 and 95,000 of them white. Of course,
things did not happen according to Bayard Rustin's meticulous plans. Many of the professional entertainers were late in
arriving at National Airport. While, in the Military Air Transportation Terminal, Burt Lancaster read a short speech
prepared by James Baldwin, with Marlon Brando, Charlton
Heston, Sidney Poitier, Harry Belafonte, and Robert Ryan
among others standing by, the multitude at the Washington
Monument improvised its own diversion. Local school bands
extemporized brilliantly. Indeed, the crowd was so fired up
by their performance that, when several of the Danville
demonstrators (just released from jail) shouted "Move on!"
it surged forward toward the Lincoln Memorial behind the
Kenilworth Knights, a local drum and bugle corps, ten
minutes ahead of schedule. The procession to the Lincoln
Memorial was to have been a solemn occasion in tribute to
the widowed Mrs. Medgar Evers. Not only was this forgotten,
but the leaders were nearly left behind. *The New York Times*
reported that marshals and newsmen pitched in to slow the
crowd's movement until Asa Randolph and the other leaders
could force their way to the front.

It could scarcely have been otherwise. Joan Baez, in her
quavering soprano, had sung the Movement's anthem, "We
Shall Overcome"; and Peter, Paul, and Mary had asked in
song "How Many Times Must a Man Look up Before He
Can See the Sky?" And the mighty Odetta, in a fantastically
resounding voice that reached almost to the Capitol nearly
two miles away, sang "If They Ask You Who You Are, Tell
Them You're a Child of God." This was not the kind of
singing one can listen to immobile and in silence. These

were strutting and handclapping songs. They spoke to the vital core of the blacks, and they communicated the joy of pristine brotherhood to the whites. That institution of American socialism, Norman Thomas, voiced the sentiments of thousands of decent, ordinary whites when he said, with wet eyes, "I'm glad I lived long enough to see this day."

At the Lincoln Memorial, there were more songs. The leaders decided to begin the main program more than an hour early, now that the marchers had begun to move from the Washington Monument. The mood of the people was a mixture of carnival, exaltation, and prayerful dignity as the dark and lovely Camilla Williams sang "The Star-Spangled Banner." Later, Bob Dylan balladized the death of Medgar Evers. Much later came Odetta, Joan Baez, and Peter, Paul, and Mary again. And, almost at the end, the crowd, sweltering and exhausted, crackled to life with Mahalia Jackson's "I Been 'Buked and I Been Scorned." Throughout the long, hot day, the procession of celebrities continued: the first black Nobel Prize winner, Dr. Ralph Bunche, Josephine Baker in the uniform of the Free French, Marlon Brando, James Baldwin, Jackie Robinson, Lena Horne, Sammy Davis, Jr., Harry Belafonte—for each named, there were scores of others, equally, or not quite so, prominent.

Before the March, Deputy Chief of Police Howard V. Covell, expecting 150,000 people, stated "We are prepared to handle this number—peacefully. But I can tell you this— we could not handle this number if it were not peaceful." After a slow start, the number had swelled by midday to well over two hundred thousand. But there were no incidents. The March was not meant to intimidate, Martin had emphasized. It was an act of "creative lobbying." More than this, for many of the blacks the day's euphoria held the naïve promise of instant acceptability in the eyes of whites. Even the *SCLC Newsletter* was impressed, if slightly amused, by how many journalists were constrained to compliment the black marchers on their dignified bearing and dress: "It was as if they were discovering for the first time that Negroes could and did make neat, clean appearances—just like other Americans." The March's spokesmen may have alluded to radical future actions but many of the people they represented were still anxious to prove to the Americans who denied them their rights how orthodox and American they really were.

And so, with many in suits and ties in the soggy Washington humidity, the multitude listened to its leaders. The theme of the whites was guilt, belated commitment to justice, and the role of the church and the labor union in bringing about racial harmony. William Robert Miller has written of the well-intentioned performance of the white speakers that "the smell of the white liberal hung over them." Certainly, their messages paled beside the angry words of John Lewis. Despite Reuther's eloquence, they lacked the pertinence of Roy Wilkins' declaration that "The President's proposals represent so moderate an approach that if any one is weakened or eliminated, the remainder will be little more than sugar water. Indeed, the package needs strengthening." The strengthening of which Roy Wilkins spoke was outlined in the statement of March goals: a comprehensive civil rights law enacted by the present Congress, including guarantees of access to public accommodation, adequate integrated education, protection of voting rights, better housing; a Fair Employment Practices Act to bar federal, state, city, and private employers, unions, and contractors from job discrimination; broadening of the Federal Fair Labor Standards Act to include areas of employment not covered and the establishment of a national minimum wage of not less than $2 an hour; desegregation of all public schools by the end of 1963; a massive federal program to train and place unemployed workers; withholding of federal funds from all institutions guilty of discrimination; greater power to the Attorney-General to provide injunctive relief for persons denied their constitutional rights; a federal order prohibiting housing discrimination in all enterprises using federal funds; and reduction of congressional representation in states disfranchising minority groups. This was the far-reaching political side of the March on Washington that the President and Congress were being asked to consider and speedily act upon.

As the hours passed, the ties choked and the suits became incubators. At its fringes, the crowd began to unravel, releasing threads of irresolute marchers. A small number began to head home. It was then that Mahalia stepped to the microphone and slowed the defections. And then, as Asa Randolph wound up his introduction of Martin, "a man who personifies the moral leadership," the multitude burst into applause and the band struck up "Battle Hymn of the Republic."

The speech that Martin was about to give had been more carefully prepared than any he had made before, more worried over by paragraph, line, and comma than the "Three Dimensions of a Complete Life" speech. During the preceding two days and even late into the last night, he had written and rewritten his text, borrowing passages from the Declaration of Independence, "My Country 'Tis of Thee," Handel, a spiritual, and a year-old article in the *SCLC Newsletter*. Ed Clayton, the SCLC public relations agent in the Atlanta office and frequently a polisher of Martin's speeches, spent hours with his employer on Monday. That night, Martin telephoned to read Ed his latest revisions. Revision continued on the plane to Washington. He kept the refrain from the Detroit speech: "I have a dream."

"Five score years ago," the confident baritone proclaimed, "a great American, in whose symbolic shadow we stand, signed the Emancipation Proclamation." The crowd ceased its movement; it became alert, sensing the dramatic promise of the exordium. "He intended to echo some of the Lincolnian lanugage," Coretta says. "But one hundred years later," the solemn voice continued evenly, "we must face the tragic fact that the Negro is still not free. One hundred years later, the life of the Negro is still sadly crippled by the manacles of segregation and the chains of discrimination. One hundred years later," the voice was louder now, the syllables more pronounced, "the Negro lives on a lonely island of poverty in the midst of a vast ocean of material prosperity." Martin's words were a magnet for the tens of thousands of shattered black aspirations and guilt-ridden white desires for fellowship. They wanted desperately to hear this message.

"There will be neither rest nor tranquility in America until the Negro is granted his citizenship rights. The whirlwinds of revolt will continue to shake the foundations of our nation until the bright day of justice emerges."

He told them that, despite the bitter temporary setbacks and frustrations, he held fast to a dream, a profoundly American dream, of a nation radically changed. Martin described this dream to an attentive multitude.

It was that, one day, the nation would really practice its creed—that "all men are created equal;" that the children of slaves and of slave-owners would one day live in brotherhood; that one day even the state of Mississippi would become "an oasis of freedom and justice."

He had a dream that, one day, his four little children would be judged not by their color but by their character. The voice had reached a peak of powerful, controlled emotion. And the crowd responded tumultuously with amens and yes, yeses: "I have a dream that one day every valley shall be exalted, every hill and mountain shall be made low, the rough places will be made plains, and the crooked places will be made straight, and the glory of the Lord shall be revealed, and all flesh shall see it together."

This was rhetoric almost without content, but this was,

after all, a day of heroic fantasy. And so it continued with increasing effect. "This will be the day when all God's children will be able to sing with new meaning 'My country 'tis of thee, sweet land of liberty, of thee I sing. Land where my fathers died, land of the pilgrim's pride' "—here, the antiphonal response of the multitude was nearly deafening—" 'from every mountain side, let freedom ring.' " Freedom was to ring from the Colorado Rockies and the mole hills of Mississippi. And then Martin closed his dream:

> When we let freedom ring, when we let it ring from every village and every hamlet, from every state and every city, we will be able to speed up that day when all God's children, black men and white men, Jews and Gentiles, Protestants and Catholics, will be able to join hands and sing in the words of that old Negro spiritual, "Free at last! Free at last! Thank God almighty, we are free at last!"

If Gustave Le Bon is correct, "The memorable events of history are the visible effects of the invisible changes of human thought." Wednesday, August 28, 1963, was a superbly memorable event. Although less than a decade has passed since then, its apotheosis in the pantheon of national historic moments is beyond challenge. Still, it says too much of the March to credit it with a change of human thought. Hearts were touched; spirits were uplifted. But, like any masterfully produced and thematically provocative spectacle, its intrinsic and durable impact upon those who walked and those who watched was largely, though by no means totally, dissipated against the obdurate mass of prejudice, apathy, and politico-economic stasis in race relations. Senator Hubert Humphrey, who watched and listened with one hundred and fifty other members of Congress that day, remarked, with exact truth, "All this probably hasn't changed any votes on the civil rights bill, but it's a good thing for Washington and the nation and the world."

Since his June 22 meeting with the civil rights leaders, President Kennedy's position was observed to have swung full circle. Shortly before the March took place, he had expressed concern to its leaders that an insufficient turn-out might greatly damage the chances of pending civil rights legislation. As the March was ending, Kennedy issued a four-hundred-word statement praising the conduct and goals of the participants: "We have witnessed today in Washington tens of thousands of Americans—both Negro and white—exercising their right to assemble peacefully and direct the widest possible attention to a great national issue." Like most Americans, he had been deeply impressed, but it was far from clear that congressional opposition to new legislation had been similarly affected.

His hour-long conference with the March leaders was relaxed and interspersed with humor. Vice-President Lyndon Johnson, Secretary of Labor Willard Wirtz, and the Attorney-General were present. When the President complimented him on his stirring address, Martin modestly observed that Walter Reuther had also had a good reception. He had heard Walter before, John Kennedy remarked to the general amusement. Refreshments were served, and Whitney Young thought to himself that it was a pity they were nonalcoholic. The chances for a new law, the President stated, had been enhanced by the March, but it would require strong bipartisan support. He added that he was frankly not optimistic about the chances of saving Title VII (Equal Employment Opportunity) and the public accommodations sections of the bill. It might be better to settle for half a loaf. This was, of course, unacceptable to the leaders, who were certain that the cause of civil rights could not be stayed much longer. At the press conference after the White House meeting, Martin expressed this conviction in the lingering majesty of the day's eloquence. The March, he announced, had "subpoenaed the conscience of the nation before the judgment seat of morality."

The activity of the SCLC and its leader, before and after the March on Washington, was conducted at a furious pace. The highly successful speaking tour after Birmingham has been mentioned. A week before the March, the SCLC held a gala benefit in Atlanta Auditorium, featuring Lena Horne. It was a notable *coup*, because Miss Horne had recently curtailed her public appearances. Meanwhile, in Birmingham, the voter-registration drive led by Reverend Billups had added 3,650 names to the ballot within a two-month period, an unprecedented achievement. In St. Augustine, Florida, America's oldest city, Reverend C. T. Vivian, president of the local SCLC affiliate, was preparing to launch a hard-fought campaign against that city's intransigent white leadership. Meanwhile, plans were being completed for the September 24–27 annual SCLC convention in Richmond, Virginia. Senators Paul Douglas and Jacob Javits, Georgia state senator Leroy Johnson (a black man), Roy Wilkins, Dr. Samuel Proctor, and historian Lawrence Reddick, were participants. Comedian Dick Gregory was to receive the SCLC's highest decoration, the Rosa Parks Award.

Late in July, Martin had received a flattering encomium from *Newsweek*, whose poll of civil rights leaders revealed that 95 per cent regarded Martin King as the most successful spokesman for the race, while 88 per cent of ordinary blacks interviewed concurred. Of the 5 per cent of prominent civil rights spokesmen who were not greatly impressed by Martin's generalship, the majority were under twenty-five. Julian Bond voiced their skepticism when he told the *Newsweek* reporter that Martin had "sold the concept that one man will come to your town and save you." Increasingly, they referred to him, as did members of the SCLC (but affectionately) as De Lawd. This was due partly to the impetuosity of youth, partly to the SCLC's belief in the power of exemplary behavior to change the heart of the oppressor, and partly from rank jealousy.

Martin was aware of the evanescent benefits of the Washington March, of the tremendous hurdles ahead. In an article written at the end of the year for the *SCLC Newsletter*, "The Negro Revolution in 1964," he predicted that "one fact is unmistakably clear: the thrust of the Negro toward full emancipation will *increase* rather than *decrease*." He betrayed the inadequacy of his knowledge of the seething Northern black ghettos, however, when he concluded "I do not foresee any widespread turning of the Negro to violence." Martin was beginning to appreciate that the March was regarded as largely an important symbol, as clearly as the experienced Bayard Rustin, who was to write more than a year afterward that "At issue, after all, is not *civil rights*, strictly speaking, but social and economic conditions." For this reason, Martin had Wyatt speculate upon the propitiousness of a Gandhian campaign of total national civil disobedience at the SCLC convention in Petersburg. Wyatt said:

> The Negro revolution will begin to develop in structured form along national lines. It is very possible that in the next few months on some appointed day, at some appointed hour, the nation will be literally immobilized by widespread acts of civil disobedience. That day may not be far off if the nation does not act swiftly on the Negro's plea for justice and morality. Transportation centers could be strangled by the bodies of committed witnesses nonviolently insisting, "Freedom now!"

Wyatt's threatening broadside coincided with the appalling events in Birmingham on September 22. Among a small but articulate number of blacks, South and North, there was a groundswell for a total assault upon the national political and economic structure. The government was to be declared "null and void," as Gandhi had declared it, until drastic federal action had righted the endemic injustices that business and government deplored verbally but tolerated complacently. Many of his advisers counseled Martin not to lend his support to a black general strike that garnered verbal support from blacks but that, in all probability, would fizzle miserably for lack of grassroots support. He took their advice, deciding to focus on segregation in his own back yard for the time being.

Atlanta's racial conditions were far from ideal, and Martin felt compelled to force the pace of desegregation in the city. Operation Breadbasket, an SCLC-sponsored enterprise in Atlanta, had succeeded in creating some 730 new jobs for blacks. At its first annual banquet, Ralph Abernathy announced that the city's department stores were to be induced to employ and promote more blacks. On October 19, the Atlanta Summit Leadership Conference, composed of the SCLC, SNCC, and the NAACP and business and civic organizations, presented Mayor Ivan Allen, Jr., and the aldermanic board with a number of job demands under the heading "Action for Democracy." Although the city was given only until November 15 to comply, the proposed Christmas boycott was canceled in advance because of the apparent good faith of the whites. The first days of December proved how naïve this expectation had been and led Martin to organize a march on Atlanta on Sunday, December 15.

In icy Hurt Park, before a crowd of three thousand, he scored the city administration and threatened mass demonstrations. James Forman of SNCC shared the platform and, seemingly mindful of Julian Bond's admonition, proclaimed, "No one leader, no group of leaders, can get your rights. You have to get them for yourselves." Within a few days, the belated boycott was launched. In the *SCLC Newsletter*, Martin invested the campaign with the usual nonviolent arguments calculated to mollify the community's black conservatives and, at the same time, expose the bad faith of the city. It was not true, he wrote, that Atlanta was "too busy to hate." By virtue of its wealth and cosmopolitanism, the city should have evidenced a far greater readiness to put its house in order.

The Atlanta demonstrations were led by SNCC, assisted by Dick Gregory. Although Martin, Wyatt, and two ranking SCLC officers were denied service at the exclusive Heart of Atlanta Motel and three hundred students were arrested, the demonstrations would have been labeled as outstandingly peaceful elsewhere in the South. But this was Atlanta. There were several altercations between police and students that shocked citizens of both races, plunging the Summit Leadership Conference into disagreement, despite that body's unanimous endorsement of SNCC's actions a few days before. Attorney ("Colonel") A. T. Walden, the symbol of Uncle Tomism to the students, resigned as chairman, announcing that he was "not in agreement with excess, like the recent demonstrations. Disorderly demonstrations tend to drive people away." He was replaced by Martin's close friend, Professor Samuel Williams, who defended SNCC and favored a continuation of its tactics. Many of the Summit leaders and those whose advice they sought, while not condemning SNCC, wondered aloud whether a one-month cooling-off period should not be declared. This was the position of Reverend King, Sr. Dr. Mays took the position that "the demonstrations may be necessary to speed the desegregation of Atlanta. If nothing more is ever said of desegregating Atlanta, things are likely to stand still." The local chapter president of the NAACP, Dr. C. Miles Smith, concurred and exhorted SNCC and the SCLC to continue marching and sitting in.

The older leadership was confirmed in its anti-SCLC prejudices by the disorders. It became increasingly hostile to Martin King, whom it blamed for encouraging the "band of young revolutionaries" in the national SNCC headquarters just off Hunter Street N.W. Although the demonstrations fell short of the goal of immediate desegregation of Atlanta, they awakened the white community to the power of the civil rights militants and propitiated the city fathers into adopting an increasingly enlightened policy of gradual compliance with federal law. By the time the 1964 Civil Rights Bill became law, Atlanta was able to take the step to total elimination of segregated accommodations and services with little hesitation.

Grudging change was occurring elsewhere during the final months of 1963. In most large Northern cities, there were sit-in demonstrations, and in Chicago 225,000 school children boycotted classes late in October because of the avowedly segregationist policies of the superintendent of schools, Benjamin C. Willis. Four months later, nearly twice that number of school children refused to attend classes in New York City. Martin's prediction that the momentum of the civil rights struggle would accelerate was being fulfilled. Reluctantly, the federal government was being compelled to devote increasing attention to black demands and to pressuring Congress to allow the passage of a strong civil rights law. The September atrocities in Birmingham provided a further goad. Then occurred the supreme atrocity, which placed not only the progress of civil rights in question but also the integrity of American society—the assassination of President John F. Kennedy on November 22.

For Martin, this national catastrophe was deepened by a sense of personal bereavement. Although he had never entirely conquered the suspicion that Kennedy's commitment to civil rights was abstract and political, he had witnessed the growth of the President during his thousand days in office, and there was an element of proprietary pride in this. "He was at his death undergoing a transformation," Martin wrote in *Look*, "from a hesitant leader with unsure goals to a strong figure with deeply appealing objectives." From a telephone call, John Kennedy had scored the supreme triumph of his career. From a series of telephone calls initiated by the White House, Martin had sustained his greatest triumph in Birmingham. Certainly, it was no more than fitting that Martin King was among the twelve hundred mourners who attended the President's funeral in Washington's St. Matthew's Cathedral.

It was in keeping with his attempt to view the world philosophically that Martin's remarks about the death of Kennedy were addressed to the primordial causes of the assassination. In what he wrote, there was uncanny and prophetic relevance to his own death: "While the question of 'who killed President Kennedy?' is important, the question 'what killed him?' is more important." His death was caused by a "morally inclement climate":

> It is a climate where men cannot disagree without being disagreeable, and where they express their disagreement through violence and murder. It is the same climate that murdered Medgar Evers in Mississippi and six innocent children in Birmingham, Alabama. So in a sense we are all participants in that horrible act that tarnished the image of our nation. . . . We have created an atmosphere in which violence and hatred have become popular pastimes.

This was the proper note to strike for the public. Privately, Martin's reactions were more alarmist. "This is what is going to happen to me also," he told Coretta. "I keep telling you this is a sick society."

Kennedy's death created an air of deep uncertainty among civil rights leaders, and many of the militants despaired of the policies of an Administration headed by a Southern President. "Everything is in a state of suspension for the moment," Roy Wilkins said, "No one can say what our future timetable will be." Nevertheless, he was certain, as was Martin, that steady progress would continue. On Tuesday, November 26, a plenary meeting of the CUCRL took place, attended by all the heads of civil rights organizations, including Martin. Their collective press statement asked for the immediate passage of civil rights legislation as a testament to the slain President. The response from the White House surprised and gratified them, for, on the following day, President Lyndon Johnson asked Congress to end immediately the legislative deadlock and submit a strong civil rights package for his approval. Martin spoke of Johnson's "heroic and courageous affirmation of our democratic ideals." The other leaders were equally enthusiastic about the message to Congress.

Beginning with Roy Wilkins on November 29, then Whitney Young on December 1, the new President saw Martin on December 3 for a fifty-minute conference. The warmth of their relations was more genuine, initially, than had been the case with Martin and John Kennedy. "Very impressed" as Martin was by the new President's "awareness of the needs of civil rights and the depth of his concern," he appeared to have embarked with Johnson upon a durable and felicitous honeymoon. An old and persistent belief among Southern blacks that the secret corollary of Southern bigotry is a genuine and uncomplicated comprehension of the essentials of the American race problem strongly colored Martin's assessment of Lyndon Johnson. "As a Southerner," he told the press, "I am happy to know that a fellow Southerner is in the White House who is concerned about civil rights." Nevertheless, his confidence in the special empathy of Johnson did not prevent him from emphasizing to the President that the moratorium on demonstrations, declared out of respect for the murdered Chief Executive, would end shortly and protests would be resumed with escalated intensity.

For the moment, however, Martin believed that cruel chance had devised the ultimate civil rights weapon, a presidential voice that spoke in a drawl. Confidence in Lyndon

Johnson was to grow throughout the following year. In *Why We Can't Wait*, published that July, Martin was unsparing in his encomia: "[Johnson's] emotional and intellectual involvement were genuine and devoid of adornment." Furthermore, President Johnson had "seen that poverty and unemployment are grave and growing catastrophes, and he is aware that those caught most fiercely in the grip of this economic holocaust are Negroes. Therefore, he has set the twin goals of the battle against discrimination within the war against poverty." Unfortunately, Martin's trust in Lyndon Johnson was not returned, even at this early period. According to Professor Eric Goldman, one of the earliest chroniclers of his Administration, Johnson "was no great admirer of Martin Luther King, among other reasons because he questioned how well his judgment would hold up over the long pull." Within the next two years, that want of admiration was to be supplanted by rank outrage as Martin King spoke out, at first tentatively and in select company, later publicly and firmly, against the war in Vietnam.

As 1963 drew to a close, the stature of Martin King continued to grow. For some months past, he had known that the editors of *Time* magazine had selected him for their most special honor. Twice he had taken time from his busy schedule to sit for portrait artist Vickrey. On January 3, 1964, the calm, directed gaze of Martin King graced the cover of *Time* again. He had been chosen Man of the Year, the second black man since Emperor Haile Selassie to receive this honor. *Time*'s accolade was not truly a personal honor, Martin was quick to stress. "I consider it to be a tribute to the Negro's great and gallant struggle," he wrote in the *SCLC Newsletter*, "I would like to think that my selection . . . was not a personal tribute, but a tribute to the whole freedom movement." The article was flattering to Martin. "Few can explain the extraordinary King mystique," it said, "yet he has an indescribable capacity for empathy that is the touchstone of leadership. By deed and by preachment, he has stirred in his people a Christian forbearance that nourishes hope and smothers injustice." It was also critical. *Time* observed that Martin lacked the "quiet brilliance" and "administrative capabilities" of Roy Wilkins. He had "none of the sophistication" of Whitney Young. Nor was he as "inventive" as James Farmer nor as endowed with "raw militancy" as John Lewis. Naturally, he had none of James Baldwin's "bristling wit." The Albany failure was cited. The article was just slightly snide in citing a number of Martin's more infelicitous metaphors. "The word 'wait,'" he was quoted to have said, "for Negroes has been a tranquilizing thalidomide," giving birth "to an ill-formed infant of frustration." Similarly, segregation was "the adultery of an illicit intercourse between injustice and immorality" that cannot be "cured by the vaseline of gradualism." It must be admitted that not infrequently Martin's imagery was distressingly far-fetched.

Martin's detractors in the civil rights movement were quick to suggest that his favorable treatment by the press of the establishment would compromise his aggressiveness. Soon, like Walter White, a man of unquestionable courage, he would relish first-name intimacy with the nation's white leaders, water his fiery rhetoric to suit the banquet table, and begin to appreciate the "complexities" that delayed immediate racial justice. Such were the dark predictions of Malcolm X. But Martin was a long way from being flattered into traducing his principles. Early in March, he demanded in *The Nation* that an army of federal marshals be sent to the South to guarantee the right of blacks to register without intimidation. White liberals, he added, continued to limit themselves to ineffective verbal condemnations of injustice but were notoriously passive, both North and South, in applying effective pressure upon Congress and the city halls. It had been left to the black, the most denied and impotent group in the land, to mount an assault upon bigotry, unassisted by "the most powerful government in the world." He was far from quiescent during the spring of 1964.

Aside from numerous speeches, Martin and his lieutenants were becoming more deeply involved in the St. Augustine, Florida, crisis. Dorothy Cotton, one of the Atlanta headquarter's specialists in nonviolence, was sent to St. Augustine to assist Reverend C. T. Vivian and Dr. R. N. Hayling, head of the NAACP, in organizing demonstrations against one of the most thoroughly terror-ridden racist communities in the South. The oldest city in America (founded 1565), it was also one of the most unreconstructed socially. Since 1959, the courageous dentist Dr. Hayling had struggled almost alone to compel St. Augustine, a city of nearly 15,000, to desegregate its public facilities and permit the uninhibited registration of blacks. The result had been police intimidation and Klan violence. In September, 1963, Dr. Hayling and three other blacks were kidnapped by the Klan and rescued by the sheriff only minutes before they were to be incinerated with kerosene. In the following month, his home was dynamited; it had already been blasted by shotgun in July. During that same October, a number of black nightclubs were peppered with buckshot. The violence continued. Early in February, the homes of two black families who had dared to enroll their children in a white school were burned to the ground. Late in March, 1964, Mrs. Malcolm Peabody, mother of the governor of Massachusetts, and Mrs. John Burgess, wife of the first black Episcopalian bishop, were arrested, along with a number of distinguished ladies of both races, for attempting to integrate a local black church and the white Monson Motor Court.

On March 6, Martin had conferred with Dr. Hayling during an SCLC rally in Orlando, Florida, and had promised the support of his organization. Hosea Williams, who had recently conducted a successful desegregation campaign in Savannah, Georgia, was dispatched to St. Augustine three weeks later.

During the following weeks, the SCLC mounted demonstrations almost daily. Police vanished from the center of the city while local whites savagely beat black marchers. Harry Boyte, who was white and a special representative of the SCLC, was knocked unconscious, and later that same day, May 28, as he and his son parked before a motel, the windshield of his car was shattered by bullets. That day had been especially violent, because only twenty-four hours had elapsed since news of the final election returns had been received. Haydon Burns, a rabid segregationist, was now governor of the state.

Earlier in the day, a crowd of blacks kneeling in prayer near the old slave market had been attacked by Klansmen in mufti. Three days later, May 31, the local sheriff, L. O. Davis, forbade marches after 6 P.M. Martin, who had arrived shortly before the sheriff's order, instructed his attorneys to seek a federal court injunction against Sheriff Davis. On Tuesday, June 9, word arrived from Jacksonville that evening demonstrations were legal and not to be interfered with. Nevertheless, the police and vigilantes attacked the demonstrators as they approached the heart of town that night. And, once again, Martin and Ralph were arrested and imprisoned. Earlier that day, they had demanded service at the Monson Motor Court and had refused to leave until the police placed them in custody.

Spirits remained high in St. Augustine for a time. Thus far, the unrestrained brutality of the whites had only nerved the city's blacks in their conviction of heroic righteousness. The week before his arrest, Martin had galvanized them with his matchless rhetoric during a prayer meeting:

> Now they do other things, too. You know they threaten us occasionally with more than beatings here and there. They threaten us with actual physical death. They think that this will stop the movement. I got word way out in California that a plan was under way to take my life in St. Augustine, Florida.

Well, if physical death is the price that I must pay to free my white brother and all my brothers and sisters from a permanent death of the spirit, then nothing can be more redemptive. We have long since learned to sing anew with our foreparents of old, "Before I'll be a slave, I'll be buried in my grave and go home to my Father and be saved."

There were amens aplenty that night. But, as the days passed and the brutality increased, and Martin departed jail to receive an honorary degree from Yale University, enthusiasm flagged. The arrival of sixteen rabbis to participate in the demonstrations only inflamed the local whites further. Martin's request to President Johnson to dispatch federal marshals to enforce the court injunction was sympathetically declined, despite the headline news of black swimmers being beaten and chased from "white" beaches. It also appeared inevitable that the federal government would grant St. Augustine the $350,000 it needed to finance its quadricentennial. There had been tentative proposals to negotiate from the whites but only on condition that Martin and his lieutenants depart, with no assurances whatsoever that agreements reached by a local biracial committee would be binding on the city. State senator Verle Pope and bankers H. E. Wolf and Frank Harrold did promise to recommend that the city comply with what civil rights legislation was enacted into law. However, unless the white moderates were willing to denounce the Klan and vigilante lawlessness of Holsted "Hoss" Manucy and call Sheriff Davis to heel, such promises, Martin alleged, were meaningless. Manucy's forces increased daily. Nearly a thousand violent whites were in the area by the last week in June. On June 25, hooligans attacked an evening SCLC rally.

In the *SCLC Newsletter*, Martin assessed the significance of St. Augustine in portentous terms. The city "has been a testing ground. Can the deep South change? Will Southern states maintain law and order in the face of change? Will local citizens, black and white, work together to make democracy a reality throughout America?" For Martin, these were rhetorical queries: "The nonviolent movement seeks to answer with a resounding: Yes—God willing!" The facts of St. Augustine scarcely justified his resounding affirmation. In an equation in which there was an almost total absence of federal involvement and in which there was blatant support of the segregationists by the state government, the SCLC was unable to find the political values that could restore balance. That it had been deprived of the initiative was evident from its hypersensitivity over the swimming-pool incident. The Monson Motor Court manager poured muriatic acid into his pool in order to force an interracial group of swimmers to quit his property. The swimmers stayed put and, when ordered by the police to come out of the water, one of them defiantly invited the officers to come in after them. This was more in the spirit of SNCC than faithful to the unprovocative humility prescribed for the volunteers of the SCLC. The leaders were embarrassed. Naturally, the whites were delighted to be outraged by this example of black "lawlessness." And then the retiring governor ignored the federal court injunction and issued an executive order proscribing evening marches. In fact, there was little that the SCLC could do by the end of the month.

With a Southwide voter registration drive forthcoming, organizational involvement in the Mississippi Freedom Summer project already under way, strategies to be devised for the Democratic national convention in August, and the long-range planning for Selma, Alabama, on the drawing boards, Martin was understandably anxious to avoid a second Albany. Compounding the stresses upon the SCLC was the departure of the flamboyant and able Wyatt Walker to assume the vice-presidency of the newly created Educational Heritage, which proposed to publish a twenty-volume series on the history and culture of the American Negro. "I'm reluctant to let him go," Martin wrote, "but the development of the

Negro Heritage Library is so critical to the long-range goals of the Negro community that he goes with my full blessings." The situation did not constitute a total checkmate, however. Encouraged by the Florida governor, the biracial committee began secret negotiations which, it was hoped, would be influenced by the new civil rights bill that would be signed into law by President Johnson within the week. Manucy's rabble also began to disappear from St. Augustine's streets. Hoping for the best, Martin proclaimed a civil rights victory in the city on June 30 and departed immediately for Atlanta. A month later, Dr. Hayling secured a federal court order that provided the moderate white leadership with the excuse of external duress that it believed indispensable to justify compliance with desegregation.

On July 2, Martin King joined the other major civil rights leaders to witness the presidential signing of the third and most comprehensive civil rights law passed since Reconstruction. The violence of Birmingham and the March on Washington had compelled Congress to study the legislation seriously; for this, Martin's contribution was almost universally acknowledged. The death of John Kennedy shamed the bill out of the House of Representatives on February 10, and the crafty and resolute statesmanship of his successor had accomplished the extraordinary feat of cloturing the objections of Southern senators, while Martin and Ralph were under lock and key in the St. Augustine city jail. On June 10, in the favorite words of Martin, Senate minority leader Everett Dirksen sonorously proclaimed, "This is an idea whose time has come. It will not be stayed. It will not be denied." Pleased that one more crucial legal victory was behind him and his associates, Martin returned to Atlanta to confer with Ralph, Andrew Young (who was replacing Wyatt), Reverends Bernard Lee and C. T. Vivian, Randolph T. Blackwell (a new member of the staff), and Dorothy Cotton about the massive voter-registration campaign. He was also unsuccessfully endeavoring to rough out the chapters of his book *Why We Can't Wait*. There was the correspondence in connection with the annual SCLC conference, to be held late in September in Savannah, Georgia. And, shortly, he would have to attend the Democratic convention in Atlantic City. Whatever the state of national disorganization of the SCLC or the languid atmosphere of the Auburn Avenue headquarters, Martin King was far from disorganized or languid. He continued to maintain the unrelenting regimen reported by *Time* —work from 6:30 A.M. till 2 or 3 A.M.

On July 18, Martin's work in Atlanta was interrupted by an urgent appeal from Mayor Robert Wagner of New York City. Martin appreciated, with the clarity of a man who had witnessed and consoled almost daily the pent up grievances of black Americans, that expectations tend to outdistance reality at the very moment when injustices are being alleviated. In his public utterances, he had minimized the probability of race riots. In Rochester, on July 15, and now in New York, blacks had taken to the streets on a rampage of looting, burning, and assault against white police and merchants. Without consulting the other major civil rights leaders or attempting first to contact the key leaders in Harlem, Martin met with Mayor Wagner and then toured the ghetto. There were boos from the crowds and criticism from Harlem leaders, among others. "No leader outside Harlem should come into this town and tell us what to do," Adam Powell told his congregation. Kenneth Clark thought that Martin had allowed himself to be used. Wagner's invitation was construed as a maneuver—one that Martin ought to have been wise enough to parry—to divide the black community and to extract from its primary leader a statement tending to exonerate the city.

The mayor nearly succeeded. Martin was greatly troubled by what he saw and heard in Harlem, the savage destruction not only of commercial property but of the dwellings of ghetto denizens, and the strident anti-Semitism. In "Of Riots and Wrongs Against the Jews," an *SCLC Newsletter* article, he wrote with apparent emotion, "I solemnly pledge to do my utmost to uphold the fair name of the Jews. Not only because we need their friendship, and surely we do, but mainly because bigotry in any form is an affront to us all." In this same issue, he expressed the conviction that "all people of good will join me in deploring these outbreaks of violence." But, whereas the administration of his host was primarily concerned with ending the disorders and offering palliatives, Martin addressed himself to the root cause of urban black violence: "The time has come for an honest and forthright initiation of a massive program to free the Negro from the long night of economic deprivation and social isolation. Such a massive program will require millions of dollars." For the present, Martin's most significant practical recommendation to Mayor Wagner (one that Wagner lost no time in rejecting) was the creation of a civilian review board in the city's police department.

Realizing that he had allowed himself to be cast in the role of an establishment emissary to his own people, Martin left New York immediately for Mississippi, to begin another of his People-to-People tours on July 20. The majority of the headquarters staff accompanied him. There was a special urgency to enroll as many Mississippi blacks on the ballot as possible, because of the recent formation of the Freedom Democratic Party in that state. Martin's appearance was intended to provide the dramatic and publicized complement to the dangerous and relatively unheralded labors of hundreds of black activists in the state. Throughout 1964, the Council of Federated Organizations (COFO), consisting of CORE, the state NAACP, SNCC, and the SCLC, had preached the gospel of salvation through the ballot. COFO attempted to infiltrate even the smallest townships, where the preponderance of blacks over whites frequently made the act of registration tantamount to a death sentence. Dr. Aaron Henry, leader of the Mississippi Freedom Democratic Party (MFDP), Charles Evers, successor to his slain brother's presidency of the state NAACP, Robert Moses and Jimmy Travis of SNCC, and scores of other men and women of rugged courage pressed toward COFO's goals against heartbreaking odds.

During this summer, a new force was added to COFO's strength with the arrival of hundreds of ebullient, naïve, and dedicated white (and not so many black) college students, soldiers in the Freedom Summer army of 1964. Many of these young adults had gathered late in June at Western College for Women in Oxford, Ohio, to hear Mississippi's Fanny Lou Hamer sing,

> If you miss me at the back of the bus,
> You can't find me nowhere . . .
>
> Come on over to the front of the bus,
> I'll be riding up there.

"The music had begun," one of them records, "the music that would have to take the place for them, all summer, of swimming, solitude, sex, movies, walking, drinking, driving, or any of the releases they had ever grown to need; and would somehow have to come to mean enough to drive off fear." Bob Moses, who had left Harvard after receiving a master's degree in philosophy to direct SNCC's Mississippi effort, instructed them with a matter-of-fact calm that heightened the giggly tension of the volunteers: "Our goals are limited. If we can go and come back alive, then that is something. If you can go into Negro homes and just sit and talk, that will be a huge job. We're not thinking of integrating the lunch counters. The Negroes in Mississippi haven't the money to eat in those places anyway." Distributing books, helping people to read and write, running civics courses, teaching summer courses at private Tougaloo College—these were the goals of the Freedom Project. Three volunteers, James Chaney, Andrew Goodman, and Michael

Schwerner, had already arrived in Mississippi and had vanished on June 21. Chaney was black; the others were white. They were to be the martyrs of the Freedom Summer, an experiment that perpetuated and probably brought to its fullest expression the spirit of interracial comity symbolized by the March on Washington. It benefited from the final surge of color-blind religious fervor in SNCC and the simplistic issues of a civil rights movement almost two years away from addressing itself to the complex phenomena of Northern racism. That summer, everyone, white and black volunteers, was "sweets" to Howard University's Stokely Carmichael.

In little more than a week, Martin addressed more than twenty thousand black Mississippians, stopping in Greenwood, Jackson, Vicksburg, and Meridian, as well as visiting a number of rural communities. The state was tense because of the activity of the MFDP and the inundation of Northern college students. Mississippi senator James Eastland denounced them on national television, claiming, in a revealing slip of the tongue, that "We don't have any racial fiction, uh, friction." Martin's appearance, his eloquence, helped greatly to provide the necessary sensation of communal solidarity and destiny. He spoke of a "Bill of Rights for the Disadvantaged" that he intended to submit to the Democratic convention to be ratified as part of the Party's electoral program. Increasingly, economic measures were being added to the SCLC demands; the lunch-counter phase was gradually melding into the phase of poverty budgets and open housing.

Despite the general warmth of his reception in Mississippi, there was a strong undertow of disaffection. Months ago in Atlanta, Martin and Wyatt had confronted it dramatically at a Black Unity Forum at the Magnolia Ballroom. Discovering that the meeting was closed to whites, they had protested and begun to leave, when Wyatt was nearly pummeled by several young militants. In Mississippi, Sally Belfrage found Martin's speeches "flowery" and "incongruous." In Greenwood, he enjoined the workers, "If you can't fly, run; if you can't run, walk; if you can't walk, crawl! But keep on keeping on." Muted in the applause were shouts of "De Lawd, De Lawd!" And, as Martin left with a regiment of police, FBI agents, SCLC staff members, and news reporters, SNCC volunteers were observing wryly, "He didn't say what they're supposed to keep on keepin' on at." At the other end of the spectrum was the black bourgeoisie of Jackson, the state capital. Even in backward Mississippi, this class was uneasy about Martin King. The black professionals there were faithful to the NAACP, proud of their homes, hygiene, and diction. They clapped politely, without amens, and drove home in large and expensive automobiles.

While it was incipient among Southern civil rights militants, the rejection of Martin's leadership appeared to be fairly widespread in the Northern ghettos. Late in July and throughout August, rioting spread to Chicago, Philadelphia, and Jersey City. It was true that a poll conducted by *The New York Times* late in July ascertained that three-fourths of New York's blacks believed that Martin was accomplishing more than any other civil rights leader, although more than half believed that the organizational performance of the NAACP was superior to that of the SCLC. Nevertheless, the celerity with which black attitudes were changing manifestly endangered the durability of a nonviolent consensus among the minority race. Moreover, it was entirely possible to admire Martin King for his exemplary goodness while cheering the arsonists and looters.

On July 29, when the major civil rights leaders convened to decide upon a common statement about the riots, their temperamental differences and the diversity of their constituencies shattered, for the first time, the public facade of unity. The majority issued a statement calling for a moratorium on all civil rights demonstrations until after the national elections. "We see the whole climate of liberal democracy in the

United States . . . threatened," King, Randolph, Rustin, Wilkins, and Young warned. The election of Senator Barry Goldwater to the Presidency would have been the likely and calamitous result of black urban lawlessness, these five leaders believed. Despite this prospect, CORE's Farmer and SNCC's Lewis refused to endorse the moratorium. Martin would have endorsed John Kennedy, had Kennedy lived. His support of Lyndon Johnson amounted to the same thing, although an official statement was never made. "I'm not going to tell you who to vote for, but I will tell you who I'm not going to vote for," his speeches ran, late in September. In the *SCLC News-letter*, however, Hosea Williams was totally unambiguous. "SCLC Puts Might of Its Organization Against 'Goldwater-ism,' " he wrote.

Paralleling the rage of the black poor was a psychological collusiveness—embarrassed perhaps and assuredly slightly nervous, but pervasive—on the part of much of the black middle class. For blacks, South and North, a special quality of philanthropy was needed after August 4 to resist the inference that the usual wage of nonviolent labor was deceit and death. On that date, the riddled, mangled bodies of Chaney, Goodman, and Schwerner were exhumed from a cattle pond near Philadelphia, Mississippi. Two months earlier, Colonel Lemuel Penn had been fatally shotgunned in a small Georgia town while returning to Washington from reserve officer training. Colonel Penn was a prominent black educator in the District of Columbia. It was not surprising that CORE and SNCC elected to encourage the agitative and retaliatory mood in the black community.

"Movements cannot live by charisma alone," a student of the civil rights movement has written. As its most popular spokesman, Martin was also its most vulnerable. In Albany, Georgia, he once confided to Slater King the lack of competence that he experienced when grappling with sophisticated economic relationships. The ministers around him were not much help. Intelligent for the most part, dedicated to a man, their intellectual formation, if less thorough than his, had been primarily theological and philosophical, as was Martin's. Wyatt, Andy Young, and James Bevel were capable of clinically studying the ganglion of government, business, philanthropy, and labor unions and of assigning correct values to its political and social signals. But Wyatt was leaving the SCLC and Young and Bevel still had much to learn. Spiritually and intellectually, this was a desperate season for Martin. His credibility with the SNCC students was clearly beginning to slip, and his powers of suasion in the riot-racked urban centers of the North were minimal. "Martin Luther King can't reach those people," James Baldwin declared, "I think he knows it."

Martin did not know this, however. He was determined to devise a program of national scope that would answer the exigent and accumulated needs of the ghetto black. With this goal in mind, he formally submitted his Economic Bill of Rights to the platform committee of the Democratic Party. The essence of the proposal was a federal program amounting to billions of dollars that would spend the blacks out of poverty. The Johnson Administration had anticipated Martin's program by steering through Congress a $1 billion anti-poverty appropriation, signed into law on August 8. If it represented an anemic beginning, it was, nonetheless, a highly significant undertaking by the government, one that had, surprisingly, been initiated and perfected almost entirely by specialists in the Administration. Civil rights leaders, including Martin, correctly suspected that the Johnson antipoverty budget was intended to buy time against further civil disorders rather than attack the root causes of urban economic sickness. On the Southern front, Martin intended to force the pace of racial advancement by encouraging black voter potential and by conducting a massive nonviolent protest in Selma, Alabama, capital of the Black Belt.

Meanwhile, he worried. When Robert Penn Warren passed through Atlanta at the end of the summer, Martin spoke of the Harlem hostility to him almost petulantly. "I guess you go through those moments when you think about what you're going through, and the sacrifices and suffering you face, that your own people don't have an understanding—not even an appreciation, and seeking to destroy your image at every point," he said. He caught himself in this interview, however, and with a rare and philosophic smile shrugged off the *Weltschmerz* of his leadership: "You know, they've heard these things about my being soft, my talking about love, and they transfer their bitterness toward the white man to me." He was confident that his nonviolent creed would triumph. "All this talk about my being a polished Uncle Tom" would subside. And, unlike the head of the NAACP, who displayed over the riots the stuffy indignation worthy of a retired admiral, Martin never wavered in his compassionate perspicacity. In New York's Riverside Church, on August 9, he told a capacity audience of 4,100 that, while urban violence was regretable, "As long as the Negro feels himself on a lonely island in a vast sea of prosperity, there will be the ever-present threat of violence and riots." Nonetheless, the conditions upon which his success in the civil rights movement were based were rapidly altering. The viability of the coalition of Northern white sympathizers, Eastern philanthropists, Midwestern unions, and lunch-counter-oriented blacks was reaching its term. Significantly, the departing Wyatt Walker told Warren, "I agree with Adam Clayton Powell that the day has come when the white person has no role to play in the policy decisions of the Negro Movement."

The truth of Wyatt's prediction was borne out at the Democratic convention in Atlantic City, New Jersey. Initially, Martin had supported the totalistic demands of the Mississippi Freedom Democratic Party (MFDP) that its credentials, rather than those of the white and segregationist delegation composed of the Party regulars, be recognized by the convention. By the end of the first day, it was clear that the Party directorate could not accept the MFDP demand and would instead hammer out a compromise. Bayard Rustin prevailed upon Martin to lobby for the compromise. A minority of the MFDP delegation, including Dr. Aaron Henry, its leader, and the Reverend Edwin King, a white member, favored compromise. Stokely Carmichael recalls that Martin surpassed himself in quiet, eloquent persuasion in the hours before the delegates voted on the matter. At 8:30 P.M. on August 25, the convention voted to seat the regular Mississippi delegation on condition that its members sign a loyalty oath and seat two MFDP delegates. The MFDP rejected the solution. Stokely Carmichael's slogan "Black Power" was nearly two years away, but the psychological foundation for it was already being laid.

For many of the civil rights regulars, the aroma of SCLC accommodationism was unmistakable. Martin had recently suggested that there was a "third phase" to civil rights protest. Beyond protest and redress, he argued, there was a crucial test of racial worthiness. Blacks must not wait for federally engineered racial progress. Bad conditions were made considerably worse by sloth and apathy within the black community. Martin summed it up in Washingtonian terms: "If you're a street-sweeper, you ought to be the best possible." For Dr. Henry, Bob Moses, James Forman, and countless others, this was heresy. The question of black occupational responsibility and excellence was not to be touched upon until the race had achieved an optimal quota in all metiers in American society. When Martin spoke out against CORE's plan to place bodies along President Johnson's route to the New York World's Fair early in August, he must have known that his already shaky stock would plummet further. As though providence itself was conspiring against Martin's organization, the Savannah SCLC annual conference was nearly rained out. Still,

Harry Golden and Bayard Rustin appeared. Dr. Henry came to receive the Rosa Parks Award. When the conference ended, the prospect of leaving the country must have been appealing to the organization's leader.

There were invitations to Amsterdam and Berlin. But, before his European junket, he received a visit from his former doctoral supervisor, L. Harold DeWolf, who was anxious to transfer Martin's private and organizational papers to Boston University, where they were to be catalogued in a special collection in the University's new Mugar Library. On September 14, Martin and Ralph were hosted by Mayor Willy Brandt in West Berlin's new Philharmonic Hall. Martin also addressed the Evangelical Church rally in Berlin's Waldbühne amphitheater. From there, they crossed into East Berlin, where Martin preached in two churches, Sophienkirche and Marienkirche. In Rome, they were granted a twenty-minute audience with Pope Paul VI. The son of a devout and anti-Catholic Baptist preacher had traveled an incommensurable spiritual distance. Without title and without a formal ecumenical establishment, Martin Luther King, Jr., represented a mighty congregation—the universal church of the black downtrodden. With his alter ego, Ralph, he flew to Madrid for a few days of complete relaxation before returning to turbulent America.

William Robert Miller, a King biographer, has described Martin as a psychic center of irreconcilable tensions:

> When he did obey what seemed to be an occasional irresistible inner compulsion, he said that he felt seriously called to be a martyr, a suffering servant, a disciple—but he found it extremely difficult, and equally difficult to admit that he was worried about what he regarded as his inadequacy for the destiny that God had given him.

Coretta knew these tensions well. "My husband was what psychologists might call a guilt-ridden man," she states. "He was so conscious of his awesome responsibilities that he literally set himself the task of never making an error in the affairs of the Movement."

No one close to him was surprised to learn that he had entered Atlanta's St. Joseph's infirmary for a desperately needed rest in mid-October. There was nothing physically wrong. He was, as a local spokesman said, "simply exhausted." "I'm so tired," he told Coretta. He took a sleeping tablet that first night and enjoyed the first restful sleep in more than a week. The next morning, Coretta told him that he was to receive the world's most prestigious accolade, the Nobel Prize for Peace. Martin was thirty-five, the youngest recipient in history. One other black American, Dr. Ralph Bunche, had won this honor. The only other black recipient had been Chief Albert Luthuli of South Africa.

Martin was incredulous, more enthusiastically happy than perhaps he had ever allowed himself to be since the awesome responsibilities dating from Montgomery. His happiness did not prevent him from placing the honor in perspective immediately, however. To him, the man, had come a distinguished award that symbolized the international recognition of the grandeur and justice of the cause of the American black. Of the many persons who came to the hospital to congratulate Martin, the visit of Archbishop Hallinan of Atlanta was the most unusual. Having received his permission to offer a blessing, the archbishop dramatically knelt at Martin's bedside and asked the Baptist preacher to grant blessings upon him. Of the hundreds of congratulatory messages that poured into St. Joseph's, one was particularly significant, both in content and uniqueness. No Southern political figure congratulated Martin except Mayor Ivan Allen of Atlanta, himself an important symbol of the New South. "It should be recognized that Dr. King has furnished the Negro people the leadership that a white leader would have given his race should it have been a minority seeking equal rights and full citizenship," Allen told the press. The dull and churlish ob-

servation of Bull Connor—"shame on somebody"—was a far
more faithful expression of Southern white reactions.

On November 15, Martin fulfilled a long-standing promise
to preach to Adam Powell's Abyssinian Baptist Church congregation in Harlem. Afterward, he flew to Bimini, to Powell's
retreat in the Caribbean, to relax and prepare the two speeches
he would deliver for the peace prize. But the political cruelty
of the world never ends. Enjoying a well-deserved rest, anticipating the Norwegian ceremony, Martin was shocked to
learn that, on November 18, J. Edgar Hoover chose the unlikely forum of eighteen lady reporters to attack Martin as
the "most notorious liar in the country." Hoover was angry
about Martin's alleged statements that the FBI had failed to
curtail violence in the South because many of its agents were
Southerners. Despite the spectacular furor that ensued and
the obvious discomfiture that his remarks caused the President, the director was unrepentant. Several days later, he
stated of the King case that "I haven't even begun to say all
that I could about that subject."

Hours after the Hoover charge was broadcast, Martin sent
a telegram to the FBI, emphasizing that, although he had
indeed questioned that institution's effectiveness, he had
never attributed its shortcomings merely to the presence of
Southerners on its staff. With polite insinuation, Martin's
statement to the press made the point that Hoover's "inconceivable" statement must be the consequence of "extreme
pressure. He has apparently faltered under the awesome
burdens, complexities, and responsibilities of his office. Therefore, I cannot engage in a public debate with him."

In his telegram, Martin had requested an early conference
with Hoover. On December 4, with Ralph Abernathy, Andy
Young, and Walter Fauntroy, director of the Washington,
D.C., bureau of the SCLC, Martin conferred with the FBI
director in Hoover's offices. The omniscient Drew Pearson,
the syndicated columnist, and Reverend Fauntroy insist that

the meeting was entirely cordial. Hoover did most of the talking, endeavoring eloquently to demonstrate through statistics how effective the FBI had been in apprehending and maintaining surveillance of Southern civil rights violators. "What you need to do is educate the Negro and get him to vote," Hoover advised. Gratuitous advice from Hoover and sympathy-inducing histories of obstructionist maneuvers by Southern sheriffs continued until well after 4:30 P.M. The director appeared reluctant to release the civil rights leaders, although Martin was scheduled to enplane at 5 P.M. on the first leg of his trip to Europe. It was necessary to phone National Airport to hold the plane for five minutes.

An intriguing body of speculation has been engendered by the Hoover-King controversy. It has been widely reported that Martin left the FBI offices stunned and cowed by references to a mass of compromising tape-recorded evidence pertaining either to subversive political or to unsavory personal conduct within the SCLC. Attorney-General Robert Kennedy, whose fascination for electronic listening devices was widely known, had not discouraged the Justice Department from an excess of vigilance in civil rights matters. King himself appears to have been above the Attorney-General's suspicions, but it was feared that some of the personnel of the Movement were Communists. Certainly, Bayard Rustin (before he received the imprimatur of the federal establishment), Jack O'Dell of *Freedomways*, and the personnel of SCEF, maligned by Senator Eastland's investigation, aroused the security consciousness of the Administration's subversion sleuths. In the eyes of Hoover, neither a partisan of civil rights nor a liberal in politics, it is highly conceivable that the SCLC leader was dangerously tainted by his professional relationships.

That the authorized invasion of Martin's privacy uncovered a few salacious details is also a possibility. If his ideals were singularly noble and his public conduct morally resplendent, several of his intimates would scarcely regard as libelous the observation that the flesh-and-blood Dr. King knew the temptations of physical pleasure. An old friend of his claims to have received a telephone call from a New York attorney, a friend of the SCLC, alerting him that three television networks and a national weekly magazine had been contacted by persons claiming to be empowered to deliver transcripts of telephone and hotel conversations between Martin and staff members of the SCLC. There was reason to believe that, because of the pressures of organizational responsibilities, ceaseless travel, fatigue, and loneliness, the private conduct of some SCLC executives was vulnerable to sensational misrepresentation. Fortunately, the reported conference of news media representatives and dubious agents ended with a categorical rejection out of hand of the compromising information. This same friend and counselor contacted Martin, chided him for "misbehaving," and warned him of the ruthlessness of his opponents.

If there is a scintilla of truth to these rumors—and they remain no more than that—it is curious that, after an exhaustive sounding of nonattributable sources, there is perhaps only one figure, a conservative U.S. senator, who claims to have read an incriminating transcript of these tapes. Together with the Kennedy autopsy photographs and the history of Tonkin Gulf, the content of the King tapes remains a closely guarded secret.

On Sunday, December 6, Martin arrived in London for three days of speeches before continuing on to Oslo. His ideological nemesis, Malcolm X, was also in the British capital at this time, and one of Martin's press conferences was devoted to minimizing the influence of racial separatism among American blacks. "Negroes in the United States are more in line with the philosophy of integration and togetherness, and not in line with racial separation," he assured Britons. At City Temple Hall, Canon John Collins of St. Paul's Cathedral introduced Martin to a capacity audience.

Addressing himself to South African racial tyranny, Martin stated that "We must join in a nonviolent action to bring freedom and justice to South Africa by a massive movement for economic sanctions." Preparing this speech, he must have recalled the cruel plight of Chief Luthuli, restricted to a remote and primitive village and denied the right of communication with the outside world. Shortly after the publication of *Stride Toward Freedom*, Martin had unsuccessfully endeavored to forward autographed copies of this work to the Nobel laureate. Not only was the British public enthusiastically receptive; members of Parliament offered congratulations and conferred with Martin about racism in Africa.

At St. Paul's, Martin delivered an altered version of his favorite sermon, "The Three Dimensions of a Complete Life," the first non-Anglican ever to occupy the pulpit of the 291-year-old cathedral. Four thousand persons crammed into the Cathedral and into the crypt where loudspeakers carried the sermon. They heard, that evening, Kingian oratory at its fullest. He was flowery and recondite. Greek philosophers, the Bible, contemporary sages, world leaders, and Coretta were jumbled together to make an altogether unusual address for a British audience. Nor was it devoid of humor, Martin's wooden public humor. Referring to the parable of the Good Samaritan, he observed that the priest who turned away from the stricken man on the road between Jericho and Jerusalem may have been afraid or "he might have been rushing off to form a Jericho Improvement Association."

The Scandinavian public had been warmly receptive to Martin's nomination. His enthusiastic reception by the Norwegians at Gardernoen Airport, despite the heavy fog and rain, testifies to the honoree's popularity. Stockholm's Reverend Ake Zetterberg, Martin's principal Nobel lobbyist, spoke for the majority of the Scandinavian intellectual community when he said that "Martin Luther King, in our view, has long deserved the Peace Prize. He is a personality dedicated to nonviolence. . . . He has proved that he can take setbacks without losing courage or abandoning his ideals." Reverend Zetterberg added, "His unarmed struggle is a model case, a pattern to inspire colored people all over the world."

The Norwegian press corps was charmed by its audience with Martin. The twenty-six SCLC officers, relatives, and friends—the largest Nobel delegation in history—were present to lend a relaxed and family atmosphere. Ralph was introduced as Martin's "perennial jailmate." The Oslo press conference on December 9 was significant, not merely because of its quaint informality, but also because it marked the beginning of Martin's public concern with controversial international issues. His condemnation of apartheid in London was *de rigueur* and universally approved. The Norwegians pressed him to pronounce upon American action in the Congo in conjunction with Belgian paratroopers. Would he demand that his government withdraw from the Congo, he was asked. "No, I haven't gone that far," Martin said, "But the Congo civil war will not be resolved until all foreign elements are withdrawn."

These were uncharted waters, and he began his navigation cautiously. Yet, it was obvious that Martin apprehended the imminent obligation for a Nobel laureate to extend the scope of his civil rights zeal to issues of a global dimension. Charles Sherrod, who believed that Martin was the creation of the news media, and Reverend Barbour, who observed the bewilderment of his friend in the face of international renown, would have noted, had they been present, the beginnings of subtle and profound change in Martin's character: The bewilderment would soon be gone, to be replaced by the effort at wisdom appropriate for a world figure, occasionally tinged by dogmatism. And, with the closing of innocence came the likelihood of disillusionment.

Certainly one person sensed the unique past significance and future promise of Martin's life. At a birthday party for

Marian Logan, a member of the group, Martin King Sr., solemnly interrupted a champagne toast that first evening to praise his son's virtues. "I always wanted to make a contribution," Ebenezer's pastor said in a voice enforcing compliant silence, "And all you got to do if you want to contribute, you got to ask the Lord, and let Him know, and the Lord heard me and in some kind of way I don't even know, He came down through Georgia and He laid His hand on me and my wife and He gave us Martin Luther King and our prayers were answered. . . . The King family will go down not only in American history but in world history as well because Martin King is a Nobel Prize winner." They were so moved by Martin's father's words, it is reported, that even "Bayard Rustin forgot to drink his champagne."

On Thursday, December 10, the dignitaries who filled Oslo University's auditorium, among them King Olav V and Crown Prince Harald of Norway, awaited the presentation of the short, dark man, attired in an impeccably tailored frock coat, striped cravat, and pin-stripe trousers. "We had quite a time getting him ready," Coretta recalls. "Martin kept fussing and making funny comments about having to wear such a ridiculous thing." He vowed never again to be dressed in such unusual and uncomfortable garb. In the sea of white Nordic faces were more than a score of enraptured and moist-eyed black countenances. Martin, Sr.'s strong features and his wife's, broad and noble, were transfigured by the emotion of unalloyed pride, whose intensity seemed to derive, in part, from the vicarious pride of twenty-two million black Americans. As Dr. Gunnar Jahn, chairman of the Norwegian Parliament's Nobel Committee, concluded his introduction—"an undaunted champion of peace . . . first person in the western world to have shown us that a struggle can be waged without violence"—Martin swallowed repeatedly and reflexively wiped his eyes several times. Then silence as he prepared to speak and as television cameras relayed the event throughout Europe. "Your Majesty, Your Royal Highness, Mr. President, Excellencies, ladies and gentlemen," Martin began:

> I accept the Nobel Prize for Peace at a moment when twenty-two million Negroes of the United States of America are engaged in a creative battle to end the long night of racial injustice. . . . I am mindful that debilitating and grinding poverty afflicts my people and chains them to the lowest rung of the economic ladder.

He asked himself why this prize was being bestowed upon a movement that was beleaguered and, despite unrelenting struggle, still was a long way from winning the very peace and fraternity that "is the essence of the Nobel Prize." He surmised that he was considered to be the "trustee" of a movement that provided definite and viable nonviolent answers to the urgent moral and political dilemmas of modern times. The history of nonviolence, from Montgomery to Oslo, proved its efficacy. Martin's sense of positive progress and long-term optimism expressed themselves in an abiding faith in his country and an "audacious faith" in mankind's future. He knew there were imposing hurdles ahead, but he refused to accept the idea that the distressing "isness" of human nature was so firmly cast as to deny it the moral capacity to pursue the "eternal 'oughtness' " that beckoned it. Man was not mere flotsam and jetsam in the river of existence but an active agent in the unfolding events by which he was surrounded. Similarly, Martin denied the cynical notion that the nations of the world "must spiral down a materialistic staircase into the hall of thermo-nuclear destruction." It was Gandhi and Rauschenbusch, not Niebuhr, who were prompting Martin on this historic day. "I believe," he continued, "that unarmed truth and unconditional love will have the final word in reality." Here were some of the first public words on the subject of world peace, and the sincerity of their author's convictions (henceforth of increasing world significance) clearly portended further pronouncements on international peace. Martin's conclusion was in keeping with his interpretation of Nobel trusteeship. He spoke compellingly of the millions on whose behalf he had come to Oslo. Most of them would never deserve a headline, and their names would not be found in *Who's Who*.

> Yet when the years have rolled past and when the blazing light of truth is focused on this marvelous age in which we live—men and women will know and children will be taught that we have a finer land, a better people, a more noble civilization—because these humble children of God were willing to suffer for right-eousness' sake.

The audience rose to its feet, applauding. Appropriately, the Norwegian Broadcasting Orchestra played selections from *Porgy and Bess*. The prize money, approximately $50,000, was divided among the major civil rights organizations and the SCLC.

9

Crisis and Compromise— The Walk to Selma Bridge

> There's a town in Mississippi called Liberty. There's a Department in Washington called Justice.
>
> Sign in a SNCC Headquarters Office

"You see, most of your Selma Negroes are descended from the Ibo and Angola tribes of Africa," Circuit Court Judge James Hare told a visiting journalist by way of explaining the city's history of terrible racial oppression: "You could never teach or trust an Ibo back in slave days, and even today I can spot their tribal characteristics. They have protruding heels, for instance." The heels of Selma's blacks were a costly anatomical peculiarity indeed. Fourteen thousand four hundred whites, by legal ruse and naked force, had limited the number of black voters to 1 per cent of the registration rolls, although the nonwhite population amounted to more than fifteen thousand. Selma was a Black Belt city over which the stench of slavery hung densely, as yet undisturbed by the winds of change that were sweeping through other parts of the South and even Alabama. James "Jim" Clark, the "best-dressed sheriff in the Black Belt," forty-two years old and tipping the scales at 220 pounds, was exceedingly able in maintaining Selma's apartheid. Blacks suffered their economic exploitation stoically, addressed their superiors obsequiously, tried to avoid trouble with the law, and spawned children whose lot, it seemed, would never be better than their parents'.

For all this, Selma had begun to change, barely, imperceptibly, although, for its blacks, almost irrelevantly. Cotton and agriculture no longer provided adequate revenues for the wealthy. The new administration of Mayor Joseph T. Smitherman, thirty-five, represented the interests of the "Progressives," a coalition of businessmen and enlightened old families whose aim was to attract Northern industry by modernizing the style of Selma's racism. One of Mayor Smitherman's first acts was to appoint Wilson Baker to the post of chief of police, to undermine the authority of Sheriff Clark. Baker was out of the mold of Laurie Pritchett, a highly professional law officer whose distaste for excessive police brutality was capable of evoking the sympathy of Northern journalists.

Returning from Scandinavia by way of Paris, Martin's party deplaned in New York, where its leader received an extraordinary welcome. Mayor Wagner, Governor Rockefeller, and Vice-President-elect Humphrey attended a monster reception for Martin at Harlem's 369th Artillery Armory on December 18, 1964. More tributes and receptions followed in the days ahead. On January 2, Martin was in Selma to announce the voter-registration drive that would center on that city. During the following ten days, he journeyed West, to address religious and civic organizations, stressing the need for additional guarantees of black voting rights and outlining the immense task still remaining in the South of obliterating racism. On January 18, 1965, he was in Selma again, registering at Hotel Albert, the first black man ever to enter the antebellum replica of the Venetian Doge's Palace as a guest.

This symbolic event was dramatized by an assault upon Martin by a local white tough in the hotel lobby. SNCC's John Lewis pinned the assailant, and an angry Wilson Baker dragged the man off to the police station. Battered but still resolute, Martin and his friends took lunch at Hotel Albert and then led a crowd of four hundred in freezing weather to the Selma courthouse to register. For the first time, he came face-to-face with his most brutal future adversary, Jim Clark, who announced that no local registrars were on duty and instructed the assembly to return later. Both men knew that there would be another such rendezvous shortly. The voter-registration campaigns of the SCLC, SNCC, CORE, and the NAACP had tremendously increased the number of black voters. In 1947, there were only 6,000 in the entire state of Alabama. By 1964, there were 110,000. But 370,000 eligible blacks still were not registered. The SCLC had decided to use Selma as the fulcrum for a final thrust to move Alabama and the federal government to end barriers to registration.

Before the Selma campaign shifted into high gear, Martin returned to Atlanta to receive the tribute of that city's notables. Perhaps the finest editorial that the *Atlanta Constitution*'s Ralph McGill did not write—yet it would have been in character for him to have done so—would have observed that, in recent years, most of the South's most gifted citizens had been black: Frederick Douglass, Booker T. Washington, George Washington Carver, Walter White, Richard Wright, and Martin Luther King, Jr. The world had honored Martin King; Atlanta, prisoner of its own propaganda of cosmopolitanism, could not escape a similar obligation. Mayor Allen, Dr. Mays, and Rabbi Jacob Rothschild, among others, undertook the delicate task of preparing an interracial testimonial banquet. White resistance to the idea was considerable, but only somewhat more so than numerous examples of small-mindedness on the part of black notables. Both Allen and Mays were philosophically amused by the frantic eleventh-hour response of Atlantans, black and white, when it appeared that the affair might be a success.

On January 27, at the Dinkler Plaza Hotel, fifteen hundred citizens, about equally divided racially, feted their Nobel Prize winner. He was presented a Steuben bowl bearing the inscription "To Dr. Martin Luther King, Jr., Citizen of Atlanta, recipient of the 1964 Nobel Peace Prize, with respect and admiration." Martin observed that the ceremony was "quite a contrast to what I face almost every day under the threat of death and it's a fine contrast to have people say nice things. I wish I could stay on the mountain, but the valley calls me. I must return to the valley. I must return to the valley all over the South and in the big cities of the North —a valley filled with millions of our white and Negro brothers who are smothering in an air-tight cage of poverty in the midst of an affluent society." The metaphor may have been flawed but surely not the renewed resolution by which it was inspired.

While Martin divided his energies between Selma and speaking engagements, his lieutenants stoked the furnaces in Selma. Nearly two hundred blacks had been arrested by the time he returned from Atlanta. Mrs. Amelia Boynton, a prominent civic leader, was roughly handled by Sheriff Clark on January 19. In the following days, waves of blacks led by John Lewis, Hosea Williams, and others were carted to police wagons with as much indignity as possible. Time and again, Sheriff Clark barked to the demonstrators assembled to register at the courthouse, "You are here to cause trouble; that's what you are doing. [To the leader:] You are an agitator and that is the lowest form of humanity. If you do not disperse or go in as I have directed you, you will be under arrest for unlawful assembly." Wilson Baker strongly disapproved of Clark's high-handed manner, and soon the two officers were refusing to communicate with each other except through subalterns.

Albany had proven that Martin could be defeated, but the formula demanded intelligent direction from city hall and deft police work. Clark's methods invited more militance, national notoriety, and martyrdom. On January 22, a demonstration was mounted that confirmed the fears of Chief Baker. More than one hundred black teachers assailed the courthouse in two waves while School Board Chairman E. A. Stewart remonstrated from the steps of the building. "This is the first time in the history of the movement," Andy Young proudly announced at Brown Chapel African Methodist Episcopal Church that evening, "that so well organized and dramatic a protest has been made by any professional group in the Negro community." The black community was readying itself for a season of suffering. At the beginning of January, Martin had warned the city authorities, stiffening the black audience listening to him, that "If they refuse to register us we will appeal to Governor Wallace. If he doesn't listen, we will appeal to the legislature. If the legislature doesn't listen, we will dramatize the situation to arouse the federal government by marching by the thousands by the places of registration. We must be willing to go to jail by the thousands."

Three days after the march of the teachers, Jim Clark was punched in the face by an irate female responding forcefully to his provocation and that of his deputies. "She walloped hell out of me," Clark said. Later, he stressed that she outweighed him. On February 1, Martin led a giant demonstration toward Selma courthouse. Martin and Ralph along with 770 of the demonstrators were arrested. On the following day, 550 more demonstrators were imprisoned; the great majority, as the day before, were school children. Defiantly, they sang "Ain't Gonna Let Jim Clark Turn Me 'Round" and "I Love Jim Clark in My Heart." The white mechanics at Ted Gentry's Chevrolet dealership came out to watch and one of them ominously predicted, "There's going to be some niggers killed here before this is over. They'll be killed like flies." They seemed perversely ready to die. And, if many whites expected a bloodletting, Malcolm X, who arrived two days after Martin's imprisonment, professed to desire it. Yet, the apostle of black retaliation appears to have been undergoing, even then, a controversial ideological change, for he confided to Coretta that he counted on his militant reputation to scare whites to her husband's cause. Malcolm told Coretta that he wanted "Dr. King to know that I really didn't come to Selma to make his job more difficult. I really did come thinking that I could make it easier. If the white people realize what the alternative is, perhaps they will be more willing to hear Dr. King."

In the midst of the singing, marching, and jailing, Martin was released, on February 5. He announced immediately that he was requesting that the Administration introduce a new and stronger voting law in Congress. Meanwhile, he demanded that the federal court instruct the Selma voting registrars to maintain daily hours to facilitate a rapid enrollment of black voters. A federal court order had arrived that morning instructing Dallas County voting registrars to meet "more often" than twice monthly. A "pitiful and disappointing" decision, Andy Young called it. The arrival of fifteen congressmen to investigate the Selma situation strengthened Martin's leverage with the President. These twelve Democrats and three Republicans, led by Michigan's Charles Diggs, could be counted on to utter eloquent and quite categorical sounds of despair over local racial conditions. Shortly thereafter, on Tuesday, February 9, Martin conferred with Vice-President Humphrey and Attorney-General-designate Nicholas de B. Katzenbach and was given firm assurance that a strong voting act would be sent to Congress "in the near future."

But the concerned visit of congressmen and the firm intention of the President were irrelevant to Jim Clark. On the day after Martin's Washington conference, Clark's henchmen were compelling 165 youngsters to trot for nearly three miles while they themselves rode in cars and trucks, electric cattle prods dangling from the windows. Returning that evening to Selma, Martin told the throng at Brown Chapel, "Selma will never get right and Dallas County will never get right until we get rid of Jim Clark." Two days later, the blacks learned that they had almost done so. The daily shouting into a bullhorn and the three-mile ride had been too much for the sheriff. He suffered a mild coronary. According to Mrs. Clark, Jim used to give his worn shirts to black trusties and had treated their black housekeeper with faultless kindness. After all this trouble, he wouldn't do that again, she told the *New York Times* correspondent.

To love one's enemies was the cardinal principle of the nonviolent philosophy, and yet even Martin may have been surprised by the response of Selma's blacks to Jim Clark's indisposition. Perhaps Dostoevski rather than Christ or Gandhi better explained their reaction. They genuinely missed their would-be executioner. Two hundred black youngsters knelt in prayer before the absolutely puzzled deputies ringing the Selma courthouse, to pray for Clark's recovery "in mind and body." A *New York Times* reporter was told by one of them that demonstrating "just wasn't the same without Jim Clark fussing and fuming. We honestly miss him." That these emotions, entirely right and human in a sane world, were surrealistic in Selma was soberly underscored by the sadistic treatment at that moment of James Bevel, an SCLC lieutenant who was chained to a hospital bed, despite a severe cranial concussion suffered at the hands of one of Clark's zealous deputies. Yet the seeds of redemption that Martin believed to be present in every unjust experience did bear fruit—if only briefly—even in Selma. On Saturday, March 6, a group of seventy white ministers, led by Reverend Joseph Ellwanger of Birmingham, marched to Dallas County courthouse to manifest its disapproval of white violence.

The clerical demonstration notwithstanding, as yet there was no sign of fissure in the militant white establishment. More demonstrations were needed. "King's 'Master Plan' for Selma May Be Fizzling," James Free wrote in the *Birmingham News*. Despite a severe head cold, Martin returned from Atlanta to lead a march of 2,800 people on February 15. "My voice is about gone," he said hoarsely, "but my feet are in time." And off they went from Brown Chapel to their inhospitable reception at the courthouse. From Selma, Martin drove to the town of Camden, the seat of Wilcox County, where no black had ever succeeded in registering. "How's the registration coming?" he asked the curious crowd approaching his car. "You all want to vote, don't you?" The response he received from Monroe Puttaway (a name only adventitiously significant) might well have been submitted to the Field and Taconic foundations at the end of any year's SCLC financial statement: "I filled out the form like I have three times before, but I cannot get nobody to vouch for me." When Sheriff P. C. "Lummy" Jenkins, a public servant of twenty-six years, was asked why he would not serve as a reference for the solid black citizenry of the county, he told Martin, "I'm in politics myself and that wouldn't look right. Maybe some other white would vouch for them." It would be a long time before things changed in Camden.

Martin drove on to Marion, the seat of Perry County. Things were pretty desperate there, too, and he left almost immediately to return to Selma. But his presence in the county was sufficient to provoke a demonstration of blacks who were angered by the imprisonment of a civil rights activist in the Perry County jail. Colonel Al Lingo's troopers were alerted, and the night march of some four hundred blacks on February 18 was savagely disrupted. One of them, Jimmie Lee Jackson, was shot in the stomach.

While Jackson lay dying, another black man, far more significant, met a violent end. Malcolm X was gunned down three days later in a Harlem auditorium. Martin and Malcolm appear to have met only once, on March 26, 1964, in Washington, D.C. The civil rights propaganda value of this meeting was considerable, as both men pledged to concert their efforts to pressure Congress into passing the pending civil rights legislation. Practically, however, it represented little in the way of intrinsic collaboration. Ideologically they still appeared to be antithetical personalities. But Malcolm X was a mind in flux, finally liberated from the cult of white deviltry preached by Elijah Mohammed, and profoundly troubled by the light-skinned Algerian and Egyptian revolutionaries whom he had encountered during his recent roving tour of Africa. Had he lived, his enigmatic confidence to Coretta King might have presaged the formulation of a coherent black militancy that would have supplemented Martin King's nonviolence.

Jimmie Lee Jackson was dying, and Selma's blacks were still marching. All the conditions for an externally enforced solution were materializing in Selma, just as they had in Birmingham. One week after Jackson's shooting, Selma's Progressives met *in camera* to thrash out a solution. The highly respected Federal Judge Daniel Thomas from Mobile was in the city that day. He denied, but not very firmly, that his visit was connected with the deliberations of the city fathers. The following day, February 26, Jimmie Lee Jackson died of his wounds. Here was a politically useful tragedy for the SCLC. A few days later, Martin was on hand to lead three hundred blacks—far fewer than had been expected—to the courthouse to be registered. The procession took place in a driving rain, and Martin pleaded "in the name of humanity" that the demonstrators be allowed to enter the building. Sheriff Clark, who had taken to wearing a gigantic lapel button with the word "Never" emblazoned upon it—his response to the "We Shall Overcome" anthem—rejoined, "In the name of common sense, they will have to stay out there until their numbers are called."

The Selma campaign was rapidly approaching a condition of checkmate. Martin was prepared for this contingency. He proposed a massive march from Selma to Montgomery, where the grievances of the blacks would be presented to the steadfastly oblivious governor, George Wallace. Assuredly, Martin counted on profiting from the barbarous reaction of Alabama's executive branch to present before the world that state's incapacity to fulfill the canons of racial justice prescribed by federal law. The day before, Martin delivered a stiffening speech at Brown Chapel: "I can't promise you that it won't get you beaten. I can't promise you that it won't get your house bombed. I can't promise you won't get scarred up a bit. But we must stand up for what is right." He left for Atlanta immediately. It is significant that this was an SCLC idea and that SNCC's initial response was unfavorable. SNCC argued that the completion of a thorough voter-registration drive should be given preference. The reservations of SNCC were overcome and the march was set for March 7. Equipped with knapsacks filled adequately to sustain them all the way to Montgomery, the marchers, more than five hundred strong, set out for the capital, John Lewis and Hosea Williams leading them quietly two abreast from Brown Chapel.

Martin was not present on that fateful Sunday. He and Ralph had returned to Atlanta to minister to their respective congregations. Both preachers had neglected their churches during the last few weeks. There had been the Nobel Prize activity, speaking engagements, and then the commencement of the Selma campaign. Both felt guilty about this. Furthermore, Nicholas Katzenbach, the new Attorney-General, had pleaded with Martin not to lead the Selma-Mongomery march. Also, there was Governor Wallace's directive proscribing the march. Understandably, the importance of the Selma campaign was such that Martin may not have wanted to be imprisoned again while it remained unresolved. Several counselors stressed the element of risk that he might run. His own SCLC personnel advised him to delegate the affair to subordinates. Finally, it seemed that the march would not be as large as had been anticipated. Selma's blacks were beginning to lose enthusiasm; their demonstrations had become less numerous, less vigorous.

Martin and Ralph preached good sermons on Sunday morning in Atlanta. Later that day, in Selma, a body of more than five hundred of their followers left Brown Chapel African Methodist Episcopal Church and headed down Broad Street toward U.S. Highway 80, leading to Montgomery. It sang all the songs that had inspired courage in civil rights marchers since the Montgomery boycott nine years ago. It maintained an unprovocative discipline along the route. It was non-violently impeccable as it approached Jim Clark's vigilantes poised on either side of the Pettus Bridge, leading out of town. The vanguard crossed the bridge and advanced within fifty feet of the blue line of Alabama's state troopers, commanded by Major John Cloud. Cloud gave the marchers two minutes to disperse. When Hosea Williams asked twice for a word with Major Cloud, Cloud snapped, "There is no word to be had." Less than two minutes elapsed before the command to attack was given. Then the marchers were set upon from the rear by Clark's myrmidons.

First there was gas, then the posse on horseback galloped into the swarm of fleeing blacks with cattle prods and clubs flailing maniacally. The marchers were driven back across the bridge and into their houses and those of friends who dared to open their doors to shelter them. John Lewis, his skull fractured, and Hosea Williams performed the superhuman task of leading many of the exposed participants back to the church. At one point, a number of blacks retaliated, hurling rocks and bricks at the police, even forcing Clark and his men momentarily to retreat. But the combat was unequal. While the white spectators whooped approval of the rout and gave the piercing rebel yell, Sheriff Clark bellowed, "Get those God damn niggers!" Protected by masks, the police and troopers hurled tear-gas cannisters into the panic-stricken mob. Charles Mauldin, a high school student, recalls that "the gas was so thick that you could almost reach up and grab it. It seemed to lift me up and fill my lungs and I went down. At least seventeen of the marchers were seriously hurt and another forty were given emergency treatment at the local black hospital.

Doctors from New York who had accompanied the caravan were prevented from attending the injured. A Southern newsman saw Clark repeatedly charging the demonstrators who had retreated to the church, even though he was bloodied by a rock. With their anger rising, and feeling more secure in this section of town, many of the marchers were becoming belligerent, seizing whatever objects could be made to serve as weapons. Clark's men were regrouping for another charge that almost certainly would have caused several deaths, when the almost forgotten Wilson Baker intervened. First, persuading the marchers to enter the church, Baker argued Clark into withdrawing his men. More shocked and outraged than he ever had been or would be again in his civil rights career, Hosea Williams told seven hundred Brown Chapel refugees that night that he had "fought in World War II and I once was captured by the German army, and I want to tell you that the Germans never were as inhuman as the state troopers of Alabama." Before entering the hospital earlier in the day, John Lewis had had his say before an angry crowd: "I don't see how President Johnson can send troops to Vietnam. I don't see how he can send troops to the Congo . . . and can't send troops to Selma, Alabama. Next time we march," he added, "we may have to keep going when we get to Montgomery. We may have to go on to Washington."

In Atlanta, Martin was stunned. "When I made a last-minute agreement not to lead the march and appointed my able and courageous associate, Hosea Williams, for this responsibility, I must confess that I had no idea that the kind of brutality and tragic expression of man's inhumanity to man as existed today would take place." He promised to return on Tuesday to lead a second march that same day and to request a federal injunction to prevent state interference. On Monday morning, Judge Frank M. Johnson, Jr., of Montgomery heard the pleas of two civil rights attorneys that the Alabama ban be voided and that a restraining order be issued to guarantee the safety of the marchers. John Doar, chief of the Justice Department's civil rights division, was present to indicate the concern of Washington. It is ironic that the legal initiative of the SCLC was to result in a federal injunction against its own march. According to *The New York Times*, it was generally known that Judge Johnson customarily enjoined both sides in a situation like this. Had they tested the Alabama ban on the Pettus Bridge and not in a federal court, the SCLC and SNCC strategists quite probably would have avoided the agonizing dilemma presented by Judge Johnson's decision. Meanwhile, Martin was delayed in returning to Selma by strategy meetings in Montgomery. When he arrived on Monday night, he knew of the injunction. Apparently, however, he was prepared to defy federal authority, something he had never before done. "We've gone too far to turn back now," he told a rally: "We must let them know that nothing can stop us—not even death itself. We must be ready for a season of suffering."

There appeared to be no lack of readiness to suffer. The local population was embittered and emboldened by Clark's recent savagery. It looked forward anxiously to Tuesday's return match. "I had the flu yesterday," an old man told James Bevel, "and wasn't able to march, but I'm going to be out there tomorrow." Throughout the nation, there was an eruption of support for Selma's downtrodden. The NAACP asked President Johnson to send troops to the city. Again the personalities and organizations that had helped in the past rushed to Selma. Methodist Bishop John Wesley Lord, Msgr. George L. Gingras of the archdiocese of District of Columbia, Rabbi Richard G. Hirsch of the Union of American Hebrew Congregations, Reverend David K. Hunter representing the National Council of Churches, Fred Shuttlesworth, James Farmer, and Jim Forman arrived by Tuesday morning. Middle-aged ladies, for whom demonstrations had once suggested only operations performed in model kitchens, came to Selma. There was Mrs. Harold Ickes, widow of a secretary of the interior, Mrs. Paul Douglas, wife of the Illinois senator, and

Mrs. Charles Tobey, a senator's widow. Then there were scores of participants like the black minister from California whose decision was taken suddenly, at the last moment. "Buy as much insurance as possible," his wife sensibly advised as he hurried to his plane. Thousands of those who did not come joined sympathy marches, such as the one held in Toronto and the Detroit march, where Governor George Romney and Mayor Jerome Cavanaugh led ten thousand down the city's main artery.

The crisis of national proportions that Martin needed to unleash federal intervention in Selma and accelerate the passage of the promised voting legislation could not have been more consummately realized had the SCLC planned the moves of Wallace, Clark, and Lingo. The scenario was perfect: intractable segregation in a small Southern city, courageous black common folk demanding their overdue minimal rights, and police officials whose every sadistic act reified the demonology of the South. Understandably, Wilson Baker was rumored to have called Mayor Smitherman "gutless" and threatened to resign. Before Judge Johnson's injunction was issued, Lyndon Johnson had pleaded with the SCLC leader not to lead Tuesday's march. Now, the government was applying pressure on the SCLC to abide by the injunction. The prospect of a seriously injured Dr. King and Reverend Abernathy, not to contemplate the fate of hundreds of participants, gravely troubled the White House and the Justice Department.

In the face of the injunction, the increasingly urgent pleas from the government caused Martin the deepest spiritual travail. If not more just, the Selma cause was as just as any he had championed before. The cohesiveness and enthusiasm of the people he was leading and the continued support of the militant students might be irreparably jeopardized if the march were canceled. On the other hand, the vital White House sympathy and indispensable collaboration of the Jus-

tice Department might not survive the incipient white backlash if he ignored Judge Johnson's restraining order. Yet
there was Martin's deep conviction that, while one suffered
the consequences of their violation, obedience to unjust laws
was the cardinal sin of the righteous. Johnson's was "an unjust order," he stated later. Moreover, although he was aware
of the federal injunction, he had stated unequivocally on
Monday evening that the march would take place.

His decision was not made easier by the fact that several
of the persons intimately connected with the SCLC were
also employees of the federal government's new Community
Relations Service (CRS) and hence agents of the Justice
Department. Max Secrest, Fred Miller, and James Laue, un-
questionably sincere friends of the Movement, found their
loyalties split in this crisis. At the home of Dr. Sullivan
Jackson, a local dentist, Martin strove to decide upon the
next day's strategy while Miller and Laue, communicating
at intervals with John Doar, prevailed upon him to accept
a compromise solution. Andy Young (whom Martin had
affectionately taken to calling "Tom" because of his frequent
readiness to conciliate) was also beginning to doubt the
wisdom of federal defiance. While Martin pondered, the Administration undertook a final assault. Early Tuesday, former
Florida governor Leroy Collins, head of CRS, arrived in
Selma aboard the President's plane. After conferring with
John Doar, Collins was driven to Dr. Jackson's, where Martin
received him in robe and pajamas. There are two versions of
this confrontation.

The CRS personnel claim that Martin accepted Collins'
proposal that the marchers limit their demonstration to crossing the Pettus Bridge, whereupon both sides would disperse.
The SCLC vigorously denies that it entered into any agreement. Rather, Martin's position is alleged to have been that
the demonstration would continue until forced to cease by
the Alabama law officers. The weight of the available evidence

supports the government's position, however, and it seems indisputable that Martin's interpretation of a forced discontinuation of the Selma–Montgomery march corresponded exactly to the marching several yards beyond the Pettus Bridge that was prescribed by the CRS compromise. "We agreed that we would not break through the lines," Martin said. Fred Miller states that he delivered to Andy Young the map designating the point of origin, route, and cessation of the march agreed to by the Alabama authorities.

In defense of Martin's consistent denial of an agreement, it must be observed that he had regularly adopted a policy of absenting himself from discussions of a controversial tactical nature, delegating his authority to trusted subordinates. None of the marchers and perhaps none of the SNCC and CORE leaders were privy to the decisions reached in those final-hour negotiations. James Forman believed, until the order to return to the church, that the destination that Tuesday was Montgomery. It has been conjectured that the small number of knapsacks in evidence indicated that word had spread that the march was to be confined to Selma. The truth is that the relative absence of equipment for a fifty-mile march was evidence of a widespread anticipation of more violence on the order of that of the previous Sunday. Martin arrived at the departure point at 2:25 P.M. More than three thousand people were at Brown Chapel. "We have the right to walk the highways," Martin told them, "and we have the right to walk to Montgomery if our feet will get us there. I have no alternative but to lead a march from this spot to carry our grievances to the seat of government. I have made my choice. I have got to march. I do not know what lies ahead of us. There may be beatings, jailings, tear gas. But I would rather die on the highways of Alabama than make a butchery of my conscience." Allowing a moment of dramatic pause, Martin ended, "I ask you to join me today as we move on."

They moved on, five abreast down Sylvan Street, Martin

arm in arm with Reverend Robert Spike and Bishop John
Wesley Lord. In the forefront also was A. D. King, Fred
Shuttlesworth, James Bevel, James Farmer, and James Forman, among others. "We Shall Overcome" alternated with
stanzas of "Ain't Gonna Let Nobody Turn Me 'Round" as
the huge interracial crowd turned into Broad Street. The
weather was bright, clear, and cold, and the marchers saw,
well ahead of them on the other side of Pettus Bridge, the
phalanx of grim-faced troopers standing with legs apart and
braced with clubs positioned at waist level. They trudged
on through stanzas of freedom songs until the vanguard
reached the bridge, where Federal Marshal H. Stanley Fountain intercepted it to read Judge Johnson's restraining order.
Martin told Marshal Fountain that the march would continue, and the federal agent stepped aside. There was no singing now as the marchers crossed the bridge; the Alabama
troopers were approximately one mile ahead. Fifty feet from
the troopers, they halted on command of Major Cloud. "This
march will not continue. It is not conducive to the safety of
this group or the motoring public," the major barked. They
wished to kneel in prayer, Martin said. His request was
granted. When they had finished praying, the marchers rose
to their feet. At that precise moment, Cloud ordered his
men to break ranks and move to the shoulders of U.S. Highway 80, leaving the road to Montgomery open to the nonviolent army. Mayor Smitherman had already charged that
Martin was cautious to the point of cowardice, and the unexpected behavior of the troopers was intended to discredit
him.

One can only tantalize over the question of what would
have happened had the SCLC leader exploited the maneuver
of the Alabama troopers. The marchers might still have been
attacked. Worse, the snipers who were rumored to have been
positioned by the Klan along the highway might have
decimated their ranks before federal officers could act. Nor is

it clear what penalty the federal court would have imposed for Martin's violation of its injunction. These hypotheses were not to be tested that day, however, for Martin turned to his followers and instructed them to retrace their steps. With an irony that must have graven itself into the minds of the SNCC students, the three thousand demonstrators headed back to the church, many of them singing "Ain't Gonna Let Nobody Turn Me 'Round." At the church again, Martin justified the aborted march somewhat lamely:

> At least we had to get to the point where the brutality took place. And we made it clear when we got there that we were going to have some form of protest and worship. I can assure you that something happened in Alabama that's never happened before. When Negroes and whites can stand on Highway 80 and have a mass meeting, things aren't that bad.

A decisive turning point in his relations with the militants had now been reached. By the end of the summer, the racial explosion in Watts would place Martin on the opposite side of the ideological barricade from his SNCC and CORE collaborators. He was already deeply concerned about the Pettus Bridge allegations. "It is important to stress once again that no prearranged agreement existed," he wrote early in April, "All I do know is that just as we started to march, Governor Collins rushed to me and said that he felt everything would be alright. He gave me a small piece of paper indicating a route that I assume Mr. Baker, Public Safety Director of Selma, wanted us to follow. It was the same route that had been taken Sunday." But this was not true. The memoranda in the files of the CRS prove conclusively, as his testimony at the hearing in Judge Johnson's court of March 11 inferentially establishes, that he had agreed to curtail the march. Questioned by Attorney Maury Smith, representing the state of Alabama, Martin admitted that he had never intended to march to Montgomery, submitting a sworn statement to that effect before the court that heard his explanation immediately after he crossed the bridge. It would have been better if Martin had forthrightly confessed that he was unwilling to forfeit the cooperation of the federal establishment by defying a judicial injunction or that he gravely feared the savagery to the marchers by the police and the Klan.

Such a confession, however unsatisfactory to the militants, would at least have had the virtue of avoiding a transparent misrepresentation of the facts. The issue could then have been joined at the fruitful level of strategy, and the debate would have centered on whether or not the spectacle of distinguished white ministers and public figures marching arm-in-arm with black laborers—and possibly attacked by Southern rabble— would not have precluded the likelihood of subsequent federal disgruntlement. Eldridge Cleaver's argument is incontrovertible. Martin "denied history a great moment, never to be recaptured," he contends:

> If the police had turned them back by force, all those nuns, priests, rabbis, preachers, and distinguished ladies and gentlemen old and young—as they had done the Negroes a week earlier—the violence and brutality of the system would have been ruthlessly exposed. Or if, seeing King determined to lead them on to Montgomery, the troopers had stepped aside to avoid precisely the confrontation that Washington would not have tolerated, it would have signaled the capitulation of the militant white South.

Thus far there were no deaths and no pilgrims on the highway. But Southern extremism could be counted on to provide the first condition. Among the numerous whites who had come to Selma were three Unitarian clerics, Reverends James Reeb and Clark Olsen of Boston and Orloff B. Williams of Berkeley, California. The three men had taken meals in a black restaurant after the march. As they were leaving, several white roughnecks attacked them. All were injured, but Reverend Reeb, his skull smashed by a club, lay close to death. Two days later, Thursday, March 11, despite desperate efforts to prolong his life, Reverend Reeb died at 6:55 P.M. Wilson Baker drove to Brown Chapel to deliver the news. While Reeb was dying, marches led by nuns from Saint Louis, Missouri, and local high school students took place almost hourly in Selma. The SCLC lieutenants attempted to dissuade further demonstrations until Judge Johnson's ban could be overturned. In this connection, the federal government had filed suit to void the march ban.

Meanwhile, the widespread distress over Selma was anarchically manifested by a White House sit-in of ten male and two female students. On the following day, a more restrained delegation of sixteen clergymen presented itself at the White House, where it was granted a two-hour discussion with the President. Johnson's insistence that he was deeply concerned about the Selma conditions, that the Administration was wholly behind the voting-rights legislation, and that seven hundred federal troops were on standby alert to intervene in Selma failed to reassure the clergymen, who deplored government inaction later that evening at a rally of more than three thousand persons at the Lutheran Church of the Reformation on Capitol Hill. In Selma, conditions were at a dangerous impasse, with demonstrators insisting upon defying the interdiction on marches and the city administration adamantly rebuffing the compromises worked out between the CRS personnel and Chief Baker.

The climax of Selma occurred between Saturday, March 13, and Monday, March 15, 1965. In Washington, Governor Wallace met with the President in a vain effort to persuade him that his state's difficulties were caused by local and interstate provocateurs. But it was Wallace who did the listening during the three-hour conference. Johnson spoke to the Alabama governor with all the candor and bonhomie of one self-made Southerner to another. "If I hadn't left when I did," Wallace joked with his Montgomery cronies, "he'd have had me coming out for civil rights." At his press conference that day, the President spoke eloquently of the injustices to the black man and of the immediate necessity to right the wrongs of generations: "I think all of us realize that at this stage of the twentieth century there is much that should have been done that has not been done. . . . I am particularly sensitive to the problems of the Negro." In Selma, blacks and whites were determined to hold a prayer meeting for Reverend Reeb on the steps of the courthouse. At first it appeared that a small group would be permitted to do so, but Mayor Smitherman's council vetoed the plan. Later, about one thousand demonstrators broke through the police barriers and ran in the general direction of Dallas courthouse. A group of twenty blacks and whites reached its steps before being halted.

Surprisingly, the conduct of the police was noticeably restrained. The next day, Mayor Smitherman allowed the demonstrators to assemble in the city stadium to honor Reverend Reeb. Governor Wallace's office issued stringent instructions that public demonstrations were to be prevented until a federal judicial decision on the matter had been reached. That the decision would be favorable and presently forthcoming was clear from the tone and content of President Johnson's address to Congress on Monday, March 15. Interrupted by two standing ovations and thirty-six intervals of applause, the President announced that a voting bill would be sent to Congress on the following Wednesday. Speaking of the impoverished minority students whom he had once taught in Texas, Johnson, his voice rising firmly, proclaimed:

> It never occurred to me that I might have the chance to help the sons of those students and people like them all over the country. But now that I have this chance, I'll let you in on a little secret—I mean to use it. . . .
>
> What happened in Selma is part of a far larger movement which reaches into every section and state of America. It is the effort of American Negroes to secure for themselves the full blessings of American life.
>
> Their cause must be our cause, too. Because it's not just

Negroes, but really all of us who must overcome the crippling legacy of bigotry and injustice. And we . . . shall . . . overcome.

No President, not even Lincoln, had ever spoken so feelingly of the overdue rights of the American black or pledged more unequivocally to cause their fulfillment than Lyndon Johnson. To the cynical and dubious in the civil rights movement, who charged inadequacy and opportunism, it could be countered that nearly as many white Americans opposed as approved the President's action. Martin, of course, gave the President's speech an enthusiastic endorsement, writing in *Saturday Review* that Johnson "made one of the most eloquent, unequivocal, and passionate pleas for human rights ever made by a President of the United States. He revealed a great understanding of the depth and dimension of the problem of racial justice. His tone and his delivery were disarmingly sincere."

Hours before Lyndon Johnson spoke, Judge Frank M. Johnson persuaded Jim Clark, by telephone, to allow an integrated march along a prescribed route in Selma. Limited to two thousand, the crowd that gathered at Alabama Avenue included such distinguished personalities as Walter Reuther, Archbishop Iakovos, primate of the North American Greek Orthodox Church, and Dr. Dana McNeal Greeley, president of the Unitarian Universalist Association of America. Martin addressed them. It was his first public appearance in Selma since Tuesday's march. When he finished, and as Jim Clark watched from a window of the city jail, Martin placed a wreath at Sheriff Clark's door. This was an impressive gesture but not nearly as impressive as the one that the SCLC leaders had been planning during the preceding week in Montgomery. They were only waiting for a federal court ruling on the right to make the Selma–Montgomery march. The decision of the federal court in Montgomery on March 11, finding Martin innocent of violating the Johnson injunction, was a good omen.

Two days after the President's speech, Judge Johnson

authorized the Selma–Montgomery march and specifically enjoined Governor Wallace, Colonel Lingo, Sheriff Clark, and other state officials from interfering with it. It was scheduled for 10 A.M., Sunday, March 21. Thousands converged on Selma, and the roster of distinguished citizens and organizations rivaled that of the March on Washington. Asa Randolph, Ralph Bunche, and Walter Reuther participated. Bevel, Shuttlesworth, John Lewis, Forman, Andy Young, and a score of other Movement regulars were charged with last-minute preparations. Right Reverend Richard Millard, suffragan bishop of California's Episcopal diocese; Rabbi Abraham Heschel of the American Jewish Theological Seminary; Alexander Aldrich, Governor Nelson Rockefeller's special representative; Paul Screvane, president of the New York City Council; Mrs. Constance Baker Motley, Manhattan borough president; Mrs. Ruby Hurley, Southeastern secretary of the NAACP; Cager Lee, Jimmie Lee Jackson's grandfather; Professor John Hope Franklin, one of a prestigious galaxy of historians—joined this time by the AFL-CIO, the persons and bodies supporting the march were far too numerous to identify completely. Judge Johnson's approval of the march restricted the number of participants on the highway to three hundred. Four thousand federal troops were dispatched to the area, and an army field hospital was established. FBI agents were everywhere in evidence.

The mistrust and fractiousness of the preceding days were not entirely submerged, however. The SNCC generals were on the verge of open revolt against the SCLC—"Slick," as they now called the organization. Five days earlier, James Forman, who had publicly doubted the President's sincerity, mounted a demonstration in Montgomery that had resulted in a cavalry attack by the city police. Although the city officials formally apologized for the "mistake," Martin had rushed to Montgomery to prevent Forman, who was said to be furious, from encouraging his followers to acts of retaliation. Martin was told that SNCC would order a boycott of the march. During the next four days, Martin's lieutenants—Andy Young, James Bevel, Hosea Williams—caucused feverishly with Forman, Lewis, Tom Kenny (a white Iowa State University graduate student), and other members of SNCC in an attempt to save at least the appearance of unity. CRS agents also served as mediators.

Finally, SNCC agreed to permit its members to join the march as individuals, although the organization declined its official support. In return, the SCLC agreed to take part in a Washington, D.C., demonstration to protest the nonrepresentative electoral mandates of Mississippi congressmen. But there was still a good deal of bile left by the morning of the march. Tom Kenny stated that "We didn't want to bring in all these outsiders and we wanted to keep marching on that Tuesday when King turned." The uncooperativeness of SNCC may explain, in part, the preliminary languor and disorganization of the march. Or perhaps the delays were due to the cavalier conception of time that one student labeled CPT—Colored People's Time. At last, Martin and Ralph arrived, a little after noon. More than two thousand people had congregated between the George Washington Carver Homes and Brown Chapel.

Martin gave the people a rendition of his finest marching oratory: "Walk together, children; don't you get weary, and it will lead us to the Promised Land. And Alabama will be a new Alabama, and America will be a new America." But it was almost impossible to hear the speech because of the whirring of army helicopters overhead. The uncoordinated surge forward of the crowd at 12:47 P.M. was momentarily slowed by the choking exhaust fumes from a television truck. There was also some harassment from Alabama National Guardsmen, whose units had been federalized by Washington. But they were moving, finally, and the pressure from those in the rear and the rising strains of the grand anthem

"We Shall Overcome" supplied a momentum that would expire only at their destination fifty miles away, and only then in a morning of sublime triumph. As they proceeded from Sylvan into Broad streets, the marchers joyously ignored the cold fury in the eyes of the white spectators, as well as the forest of obscene placards lining their route. People who could do no better than scrawl signs reading "Nigger Lover," "Bye, Bye, Blackbird," and "Martin Luther Coon" were almost pathetically outclassed by the moral, compassionate, and generally law-abiding conduct of the King-directed and King-inspired civil rights forces. When the marchers crossed Pettus Bridge, they quickened their step and sang louder.

By evening, they reached the first campsite on the land of David Hall, a black farmer. They had marched 7.3 miles along U.S. Highway 80, familiarly known as Jeff Davis Highway. Only a portion of those who had walked from the city spent the night; the rest were bused back to Selma. At 8 A.M. on the next day, the marchers broke camp for the second and much longer walk. They were entering hostile territory now: Lowndes County was one of those benighted pockets of psychosis where the overwhelming ratio of blacks to whites had fostered a racism scarcely exceeded elsewhere in the South. The marchers were peppered by insulting leaflets dropped from a light aircraft belonging, as it was labeled, to the "Confederate Air Force." The government chose to indicate its support by having Governor Collins there and Martin advertised his confidence by having Coretta join the marchers. There was no violence along the route, and the caravan rested that evening at Rosa Steele's farm, twenty-three miles from Selma. Martin walked into camp, exhausted, sunburned, and limping from his blisters.

The third day, March 23, the pilgrims passed the midpoint and rested that evening on a farm owned by Birmingham millionaire A. G. Gaston, thirty-three miles from Selma.

Martin did not spend the night at the campsite. He was
driven to Selma and left the next morning for Cleveland,
Ohio, to receive an award. On the following day, the marchers reached the outskirts of Montgomery, stopping about
three miles from the city limits. They were led by James
Letherer, a one-legged white laborer from Saginaw, Michigan,
who had hobbled the entire distance from Selma on crutches.
Standard-bearers on each side of him, one black and one
white, carried the American flag. Len Chandler, a young
black man from New York, his head bandaged in the style
of 1776, marched with them, playing "Yankee Doodle" on a
fife. It was an apparition never to be forgotten.

That night, they were all entertained by more than a
platoon of famous performers on the athletic field of the
St. Jude center, a forty-acre Catholic complex for the
education of blacks. Ten thousand citizens of Montgomery
and early arrivals for the final march to the state capitol
walked and motored to the athletic field. Mike Nichols
burlesqued Governor Wallace's telegram to Lyndon Johnson.
Peter, Paul, and Mary sang an appropriate song from their
album "Blowin' in the Wind." The crowds heartily cheered
James Baldwin, who had flown from Europe for the final
leg of the march. Speaking, singing, or simply saluting the
audience briefly, Harry Belafonte, Leonard Bernstein, Joan
Baez, Tony Bennett, Leon Bibb, the Chad Mitchell Trio,
Sammy Davis, Jr., Bobby Darin, Ruby Dee, Ella Fitzgerald,
Dick Gregory, George Kirby, Alan King, Mahalia Jackson,
Elaine May, Odetta, Anthony Perkins, Floyd Patterson,
Nipsy Russell, Nina Simone, and Shelley Winters were
among those who made the final evening of the Selma–
Montgomery march a spectacularly memorable affair. Return-
ing from Cleveland, Martin catechized the crowd with
"What do we want?" It responded repeatedly and deafen-
ingly: "Freedom!"

It rained hard on Thursday morning, but, even if a hurricane had passed near the city of Montgomery, very likely it would not have dissuaded many of the nearly thirty thousand people who walked with Martin, Ralph, Asa Randolph, Roy Wilkins, Whitney Young, Bayard Rustin, Ralph Bunche, John Lewis, and others along the last three miles into the city. It was a miniature March on Washington, but it was no less epochal in terms of symbolism and national attention. They sang their way up the once-forbidding road to Alabama's extraordinarily white capitol building, Martin in the vanguard and Coretta by his side, singing the Movement's anthem. The mammoth demonstrations engineered by the SCLC always succeeded—at least, until the advent of Memphis—in imparting an illusion of what Martin frequently called "historical concretion," the Hegelian process by which the World Idea would become reality. As America and Europe watched by television and the rest of the globe avidly read about it during the next few days, the fulfillment of a race's destiny seemed at hand. As the marchers surged up Dexter Avenue with their petition for George Wallace, who closed his office and nervously squinted through the slats of his venetian blinds, it required a special kind of dispassion to disbelieve that any force would ever again turn the black American around. And this was not the moment for political dispassion: This was hallowed ground.

He had returned to Montgomery many times since the bus boycott, but, this Thursday, the familiar cityscape along Dexter Avenue must have been transformed for Martin into an Armageddon of triumph. Despite the earlier skirmishes of a valorous minority and the long-standing methodical labors of the NAACP, it is undeniable that the awakening of the black masses began in Montgomery. It was there that the technique was devised that transmuted their very weaknesses into seemingly irresistible strength. As Martin, Ralph, and Coretta passed the little brown church at the intersection of Dexter and Decatur, their eyes watered. Almost ten years later now, the dividends from more than half a dozen major struggles were about to be paid. "As the speeches began, I looked at Rosa Parks," Coretta writes of this occasion, whose historic importance she savored as the wife of a man now larger than life, the animate symbol of black progress. "I sat there and began to think back over the years of struggle from 1955 to 1965. I realized we had really come a long way from our start in the bus protest, when only a handful of people . . . were involved."

Had Martin never delivered his address on the steps of the Lincoln Memorial or had it fallen flat, the speech on the grounds of the Alabama capitol could easily have replaced it. "Last Sunday more than eight thousand of us started on a mighty walk from Selma, Alabama," Martin commenced. "We have walked on meandering highways and rested our bodies on rocky byways." He recited a familiar anecdote from old Montgomery days: "I can say as Sister Pollard said . . . who lived in this community during the bus boycott. One day she was asked while walking if she didn't want a ride, and when she answered 'No,' the person said, 'Well, aren't you tired?' and with ungrammatical profundity, she said, 'My feets is tired, but my soul is rested.' " Here was the catalyst prescribed for audience response. The approbative "amens" and "yessuhs" catapulted from numerous blacks in the crowd:

> They told us we wouldn't get here. And there were those who said that we would get here only over their dead bodies, but all the world together knows that we are here and that we are standing before the forces of power in the state of Alabama, saying, "We ain't goin' let nobody turn us around." . . .
>
> Our whole campaign in Alabama has been centered around the right to vote. . . .
>
> The threat of the free exercise of the ballot by the Negro and white masses alike resulted in the establishing of a segregated society. They segregated Southern money from the poor whites; they segregated Southern churches from Christianity; they

segregated Southern minds from honest thinking, and they segregated the Negro from everything.

He told them that they were on the move now and that no amount of church burnings would stop them. It was an irrepressible movement that neither beating and killing of clergymen nor maiming of young people could possible divert.

My people, my people, listen! The battle is in our hands. . . . I know some of you are asking today, "How long will it take?" I come to say to you this afternoon however difficult the moment, however frustrating the hour, it will not be long, because truth pressed to earth will rise again.

How long? Not long, because no lie can live forever.

How long? Not long, because you will reap what you sow.

How long? Not long, because the arm of the moral universe is long but it bends toward justice.

The repetition of this syncopated question mesmerized the thirty thousand listeners. Few of the whites smiled at the display of rhetorical magic, and few black militants called out "De Lawd" in the ecstasy of the moment. Martin's peroration was simply spendiferous, although equally unoriginal: "How long? Not long. Because mine eyes have seen the glory of the coming of the Lord, trampling out the vintage where the grapes of wrath are stored. He has loosed the fateful lightning of his terrible swift sword. His truth is marching on." And so forth.

Proving again that they were their own worst enemies, Southern whites virtually guaranteed that a voting-rights act would be passed by Congress, by gunning down a white Detroit housewife and mother of five, Mrs. Viola Liuzzo, while she was returning to Montgomery from Selma with a young black man in her car. Mrs. Liuzzo had been one of the many transportation volunteers. She was fatally shot through the head in Lowndes County. The nation was appropriately horrified. In San Francisco's Grace Episcopal Cathedral, Martin proclaimed defiantly to a crowd of three thousand that "If physical death is the price some must pay to save us and our white brothers from eternal death of the spirit, then no sacrifice could be more redemptive." Shortly thereafter, he appeared on the television program *Meet the Press*, where he asked for a nationwide boycott of Alabama products. Religious, labor, and industrial concerns were asked to liquidate any Alabama-derived assets that they might possess.

Within the next few weeks, the focus of the SCLC boycott centered on Hammermill Paper Company of Erie, Pennsylvania, which had planned to construct a $25-million subsidiary near Selma. Despite the adverse national publicity authored by the SCLC, Hammermill went ahead with its plans. Although *SCLC Newsletter* claimed that 144 companies had agreed to cancel or withhold Alabama investments, it seems clear that the business of these firms cannot have constituted more than a slight fraction of the total aggregate of revenues derived from Alabama-based activity by out-of-state corporations. Neither Whitney Young nor Roy Wilkins was receptive to Martin's "economic withdrawal" scheme—the Administration was equally nonreceptive—and, though the SCLC continued to champion the tactic, it was never more than a stillborn idea.

While Martin traveled in the North on speaking engagements, the Alabama situation dragged on. Governor Wallace had finally deigned to receive the Selma–Montgomery petition at the end of March, but he was thoroughly noncommittal when Reverend Joseph E. Lowery, the delegation's chairman, pressed him for a response. Meantime, in Camden, Alabama, black school children were routed by tear gas and smoke bombs when they attempted to march into the city without a permit. And, on April 1, three bombs were planted in Birmingham. Fortunately, no lives were lost, but the home of T. L. Crowell, a black public accountant, was demolished. The other devices were discovered and disarmed on the grounds of Mayor Boutwell's home. The officials of the state of Alabama professed consternation and disapproval, and Governor Wallace visited the damaged property. Out of this latest outrage and the spirited protests of white moderates throughout the state came the slim promise of racial progress in Selma. Local black ministers and SCLC representatives began meeting on Wednesdays with white merchants to devise a solution that would terminate the highly effective black boycott of downtown stores. On April 16, a three-judge district court at Mobile enjoined Sheriff Clark from using his possemen and ordered him to provide, henceforth, protection to local demonstrators. It would require a municipal election in Selma, however, before there was a superficial compliance with federal law on racial desegregation.

The exhilaration of the Selma-Montgomery march had affected Martin as well as his followers. He was confident that the voting bill would be enacted, even that it would be strengthened by congressional amendments, before receiving the President's signature. Those who listened carefully to his speeches after Montgomery—their tone as well as their content—realized that the imminent passage of a voting law would begin to close the books on Martin Luther King's role as an internationally acclaimed combatant for the rights solely of Southern blacks. Preaching in Demopolis, Greensboro, and Eutaw, Alabama, on May 11, his theme was that the fight of the Black Belt poor was part of the quickening worldwide class struggle. He would still be intensely preoccupied with voter registration in the South, but, at the annual SCLC board meeting in Baltimore, Maryland, April 1–2, he had already revealed new areas of concern.

At this meeting, it was decided that the SCLC would concentrate on 120 rural counties, spread from Virginia to Louisiana, in order to cajole and march the black population to the registration desks. The board members approved the drive, which was to be directed by Hosea Williams. They

approved, less enthusiastically, Martin's three-tiered eco-
nomic-withdrawal program for Alabama. They were not at
all receptive to his proposal that the SCLC mount a campaign in the Northern ghettos. Although it had received less
emphasis in his public statements than desegregation and
conquest of the ballot, Martin's concern with economic
uplift was as old as Montgomery. Plans were completed at
that time to create black businesses in the city, whose
financing, in part, would come from Federal Savings and
Loan Association of Birmingham, presided over by A. G.
Gaston. Bayard Rustin's *Commentary* article of February,
1965, and the concluding chapter of *Why We Can't Wait*
presaged a much greater concern with programs to alleviate
urban poverty.

Free access to lunch counters and voting booths was a
constitutional right whose denial in the South the SCLC
had learned to dramatize masterfully. Total removal of practical infringements was perhaps a generation of bitter persistence and legal initiatives away, but Martin gauged that
the momentum against legally enforced racial disabilities
would prove irresistible. On the other hand, the institutionalized poverty of the Northern black compelled the admission
that legal rights were merely preliminary and modest pos-
sessions, if stable jobs were not to be had. Legally, the black
outside the South could vote, work, seek entertainment, and
live where he wished. But, for the most part, his universe
was confined to places such as Harlem, Roxbury, Watts, the
South Side. The black man in the North "lives in a schizo-
phrenic social milieu," Martin wrote later in *Saturday Review*. "The real cost lies ahead," Martin was to write in
Where Do We Go From Here? "Jobs are harder and costlier
to create than voting rolls. The eradication of slums housing
millions is complex far beyond integrating buses and lunch
counters." However, if the SCLC board members could
understand the wisdom of coupling the now traditional tactic

of mass demonstrations for legal rights with Northern-centered economic projects, they were certainly not prepared to countenance the effervescence of civil rights into the domain of foreign policy. They voted that, if Martin was to speak out against the war in Vietnam, he must do so as a private citizen and a clergyman and not as president of the SCLC. For the first time, he was beginning to move too rapidly, too abstractly, for the folk who supported him, whether dirt-farmer, Southern city-dweller, or middle-class professional.

10

The Fire Next Time

> Negroes sweet and gentle,
> Meek, humble and kind,
> Beware the day
> They change their minds.
>
> LANGSTON HUGHES

THE PERIOD BETWEEN THE SELMA and the Chicago campaigns is an amorphous one. *SCLC Newsletter* reported a Midwestern People-to-People tour, an appearance at the White House, an SCLC plenary convention, European awards and speaking engagements, rallies—a maelstrom of activity for which not even the excitement of Martin's rhetoric would overcome the tedium of narration. Beneath this explosive activity was that impregnable region of Martin's psyche that brooded, pondered, and conceived in isolation. Now that the lunch-counter era was closing, he was feeling his way to new positions.

There were four issues that he needed to consider carefully: (1) the growing conviction among whites that the blacks, with federal backing, were moving too rapidly; (2) the fierce expostulations of black militants that racial progress had not only been too slow but was being subtly manipulated by powerful whites; (3) practical programs to deal with urban and, largely, Northern black poverty; and (4) the extent to which the nexus between federal assistance to the poor and spending for the Vietnam war could profitably be exposed.

Each offered dangerously unfamiliar terrain for the SCLC, and, in the interest of dealing effectively with the three other dilemmas, most of his advisers argued that Martin ought to forgo the role—advisable ideally for a Nobel laureate but disastrous practically—of spokesman for peace in Southeast Asia. It was true, certainly, Martin knew, that most middle-class blacks showed little inclination to criticize the war at that time.

He continued to explore this fourfold challenge in the months ahead. Late in April, he addressed the New York Bar Association, forcefully defending the right of the oppressed to disobey "unjust" laws. The predicate of law in a democracy, he reminded the audience, was that of representative sanction of legal obligations. Black Americans had not been asked their opinions of voting restrictions or restrictive covenants. They had the right, therefore, to withhold their obedience. Martin reminded the temperamentally conservative lawyers of their historic origins as advocates of justice, dwelt on his own "maladjustment" to segregation, religious bigotry, and the "madness of militarism," and, in a half-serious vein, urged the formation of an "International Association for the Advancement of Creative Maladjustment."

In Boston, he deplored the living conditions of the black poor in the Roxbury ghetto, warned of the seething discontent in America's enclaves of urban poverty, and condemned nuclear atmospheric contamination. *Time* gleefully seized upon this anachronism to point out that, had Dr. King kept abreast of the news, he would have known that the Nuclear Test Ban Treaty had long since anticipated his alarms. Governor Volpe of Massachusetts was obviously anxious to acquit himself faultlessly during Martin's visit, and, in addition to proposing a Martin Luther King Day, he invited his prickly guest to address the state legislature. "Well, it may be that you cannot legislate morality," Martin drawled to the legislators, aware of the incipient Northern resistance to further civil rights legislation, "but behavior can be regulated. It may be true that the law cannot make a man love me, but it can restrict him from lynching me, and I think that is pretty important also." Before leaving Massachusetts, he led eighteen thousand people to Boston Common in a driving rain to deliver a forty-minute speech on racial injustice.

Attacks upon Martin and the SCLC were not new. Success invited dissension, and Selma, like St. Augustine, was a success of perspective only. For those to whom parades in the name of dignity and the meliorism of federal assistance were contemptuously pithy achievements, Selma was a cruel hoax. Pettus Bridge maddened them, and the helicopter-escorted march to Montgomery demeaned the Movement, they believed. The benefit of the doubt, which they had allowed Martin before Selma (influenced, certainly, by the financial power of the SCLC), was rapidly reaching its term. *Time, Progressive,* and the SNCC-influenced *Atlanta Enquirer* suggested, with varying degrees of malice and certainty, that the militants and the SCLC were verging on an irreparable rift. SNCC and the SCLC made an announcement on April 30 that was an obvious attempt to quash such rumors. With Harry Belafonte, Jim Forman and Martin called a press conference in Atlanta to announce that their two organizations were uniting forces to manage all future projects. "To further our joint efforts, we have this day established a joint committee with representatives from both organizations, which has been charged with the responsibility of meeting periodically to discuss programs and to continue the work we began here," they said. In fact, the day of the "joint efforts" was ending. Shortly, Stokely Carmichael would call the tune, and the philosophy of nonviolence would battle for its life against an excess of racist shibboleths.

But Martin's critics were not confined to militant students. The intellectual community had its doubts as well. From Paris and Berkeley, James Baldwin pitied Martin's moderation and ghetto myopia. Many reasonable scholars such as John Hope Franklin, meditating their experiences in Selma, were distressed by the heavy-handed attempts to apothesize the SCLC leader. Wyatt Walker had sinned egregiously in this respect, but his successors, it appears, were equally guilty of an offensively misguided devotion. One of the historians who marched with the Selma demonstrators later wrote a devastating appraisal of Martin:

> In a movement in which respect is accorded in direct proportion to the number of times one has been arrested, King appears to keep the number of times he goes to jail to a minimum. In a movement in which successful leaders are those who share in the hardships of their followers, in the risks they take, in the beatings they receive, in the length of time they spend in jail, King tends to leave prison for other engagements.

The author concluded that Martin was a "Conservative Militant."

If militants and civil rights scholars found fault with Martin, it is scarcely surprising that many among the black bourgeoisie uncovered grievous shortcomings. Why had he not remained in Selma, or Birmingham, for that matter, to see the battle to its end? Were there not compromising coincidences between SCLC campaigns and the replenishment of its annual $1-million budget? This latest thrust into the North, was this not a play for more publicity and additional revenue? And what about his preaching in Atlanta and re-crossing that bridge in Selma? One had only to stop in at a few of the house parties then being catered for the well-to-do blacks (summer was approaching) in Chicago, Durham, Atlanta, and Houston to measure the spreading cynicism about the man and his organization.

The reverberations of Selma were still not spent. President Johnson was determined to heave the weight of his office on the side of full political citizenship for the American blacks. His next gesture was carefully planned. On June 4, 1965, he would deliver the graduation address at Howard University, the nation's most prestigious largely black center of higher learning. Martin, Roy Wilkins, and Whitney Young were each presented an advance copy of the speech at the White House, which they enthusiastically approved. The civil rights leaders were completely ignorant of the fact that the speech had been inspired by Daniel Patrick Moynihan, the assistant secretary of labor, who had just then completed his controversial and confidential report on the Negro family.

On the appointed day, Lyndon Johnson spoke to the Howard University graduating class. The address bears the title "To Fulfill These Rights," a fitting sequel to the "We Shall Overcome" address to Congress. The 1965 graduating class at Howard heard the most perceptive talk on racial injustice, its causes, tragic consequences, and practicable cures, that any American President had ever given. There were undoubtedly passages whose sociological burden the President could never have unraveled, concepts whose complexity this Texan only dimly perceived, promises whose instant realization his Administration would recoil against in a matter of months, and statistics whose human import he would know absolutely nothing of, as his limousine returned him to 1600 Pennsylvania Avenue:

> There is no single easy answer to all of these problems. Jobs are part of the answer. They bring the income which permits a man to provide for his family. Decent homes in decent surroundings, and a chance to learn, are part of the answer. Welfare and social programs better designed to hold families together are part of the answer. Care of the sick is part of the answer. An understanding heart by all Americans is part of the answer.
>
> To all these fronts—and a dozen more—I will dedicate the expanding efforts of the Johnson Administration. But there are other answers still to be found. Nor do we fully understand all of the problems. Therefore, I want to announce tonight that I intend to call a White House Conference of scholars and experts, and outstanding Negro leaders—men of both races—

and officials of government at every level. This White House conference's theme and title will be "To Fulfill These Rights."

How well Johnson comprehended the implications of the Howard speech was a valid question. For the moment, Martin was intensely gratified. The disintegration of the impoverished black family and the paralyzing poverty of the Northern ghetto had been glimpsed by a President.

While Congress debated the voting-rights bill, Martin continued to travel. Late in June, the SCLC's operation SCOPE, part of its global voter registration drive, was held on the Atlanta campus of Morris Brown College. Nearly one thousand volunteers assembled for orientation in the college's Joe Louis Gymnasium. During their orientation by Hosea Williams and Bayard Rustin, Martin gave them a typically rousing speech. Later in the summer, sometime in July, came an SCLC rally in Petersburg, Virginia.

The board meeting in Baltimore had indicated that there was considerable organizational resistance to a statement Martin had made about the Vietnam war. He felt that he had contained his feelings too long, however. As far back as the summer of 1959, in answer to a question put to him by the editor of an Italian magazine, he had stated that, if he were to add a chapter to *Stride Toward Freedom*, it would be concerned with adapting nonviolence "not merely to the local level in struggles between relatively small groups, but even between nations." A black man acutely aware of the costs of war to domestic poverty programs, a minister who found all wars abhorrent, and a Nobel laureate for whom the espousal of international peace was a consequence of the honor, he believed that he could no longer restrain himself. "I'm not going to sit by and see war escalated without saying anything about it," he proclaimed. "It is worthless to talk about integrating if there is no world to integrate in," he added. "The war in Vietnam must be stopped. There must be a negotiated settlement even with the Viet Cong. . . . The long night of war must be stopped." In the same month, CORE was agitated by the same insistence upon connecting issues of war and race at its annual conference in Durham, North Carolina. By majority vote, a resolution condemning the war was voted, only to be rescinded after considerable politicking by James Farmer.

There were problems aplenty—domestic and familiar—to occupy Martin during this period. Chicago needed him. He agreed to lend his person to a three-day effort in that city to protest the *de facto* segregation of its public schools. On July 24, 25, and 26, he conducted a People-to-People tour there that was highly successful. Already the Coordinating Council of Community Organizations (CCCO) had been established by the dynamic Al Raby and others. In his short visit, Martin delivered at least thirty speeches and led nearly thirty thousand people down State Street to Chicago's city hall to protest the racist maladministration of Superintendent of Schools Benjamin C. Willis. "Chicago will never be the same now that the people here see what [King] brought," Bill Berry, the local director of the Urban League, stated.

On August 6, Lyndon Johnson invited civil rights leaders King, Farmer, Wilkins, and Young to be present for the historic signing into law of the voting-rights bill. Rosa Parks, now a secretary in the office of Michigan Congressman John Conyers, was also on hand to witness the grand event. Immediately after the ceremonies, Martin asked the President for a formal signal that he backed also the eradication of the economic disfranchisement of the Northern black man. But, by this time, the polls, which Lyndon Johnson held as sacred, strongly indicated that a period of federal relaxation was in order. Moreover, the President was increasingly preoccupied by the American involvement in Southeast Asia. A malfunction in the transmission of political signals occurred at this moment, one that was never to be repaired in the next two years. Quite probably, no intercessor could have prevented the hostile misunderstanding that was to arise between Lyndon Johnson and Martin King. Martin seems to have sized up John Kennedy the politician far better than he did Lyndon Johnson the man. Only much later did he speak of "this ego thing" when referring to Johnson.

To persist in denouncing Johnson's Vietnam policy was unwise, from the point of view of most civil rights leaders. Congress had responded more quickly on the voting-rights bill than it had ever done in similar matters. The President had expostulated the socio-economic disabilities of the black more trenchantly than ever before. Surely this was the moment for a grateful pause. Martin disagreed. Visiting Atlanta, his former professor, Harold De Wolf, an active member of SANE, encouraged him to take a strong stand. At Birmingham's Municipal Auditorium, he spoke of his conviction, before an audience of four thousand, that immediate negotiations between U.S. diplomats and the Viet Cong should be opened. At the SCLC annual convention, August 9–13, he received the organization's qualified endorsement to advocate this position. Martin's friends (Bayard and Bill Berry, for example) continued to caution him. The Administration had already begun to bridle, and, behind the scenes, pressures were being applied to silence him.

George Weaver, the assistant secretary of labor and a black man, spoke out sharply at the annual Masonic convention against civil rights leaders who presumed to pass foreign-policy judgments. Martin was not mentioned, but the direction of the Administratively inspired message was clear. The Urban League and the NAACP granted Martin his private right to worry about the war, but they were adamant about maintaining the priorities of domestic civil rights issues. Martin himself was stunned by the disfavor that his antiwar speeches aroused in the black community. While there was approval in SNCC circles, the articulate middle class was cool to bitter. But their disapproval bothered him far less than their demeaning counsels that a "Negro ought not speak out on such matters." He was to say later, to David Halberstam, that many of the economically advantaged blacks were "hoping the war will win them their spurs. That's not the way you win spurs."

But he had begun to waver, probably not so much because of the unpopular public reaction, or even the firing of a broadside by the White House, but because he was not yet certain of his own position. Lyndon Johnson, still capable of a friendly chat with Martin, requested that he withhold further antiwar statements until he had conferred with U.N. Ambassador Arthur Goldberg. His greatest comfort at this time was provided by Coretta, an active member of Women Strike for Peace, one of the speakers at SANE's June rally, and, since her Antioch days, an adherent to pacifism. She had never had a moment's doubt about Martin's position and always encouraged him to persist. Her counsel also served to blunt somewhat the complete disapproval of Martin's father of his anti-war position. Harold De Wolf and A. J. Muste also believed that Martin's conjoining of the civil rights and peace movements was ultimately a sound position. Their support compensated somewhat for the surprising opposition of Bayard to his Vietnam war stand. Nevertheless, Martin backed away from the position for the time being. He continued to refer to the war in the months ahead, to deplore it, but it was clear that it was no longer the main issue that he had earlier intended to make it. In fact, this was probably no longer possible, for domestic racial violence shortly upstaged the programs of the established civil rights organizations.

Martin was in San Juan, Puerto Rico, attending the world convention of the Disciples of Christ, when news of the Watts riots reached him. "It is probable that future historians will regard it as significant a turning point in Negro-white relations in the United States as John Brown's raid on Harpers Ferry," Robert Conot has written. The arrest of Marquette Frye for drunken driving on August 11 had touched off the most de-

structive and sanguinary race riot in American history. Martin
reached Los Angeles on August 15 and toured a section of
the beleaguered black enclave. He was astonished to find that
most of the people there had never heard of him. Almost all
were hostile to his attempts at mediation. As he, Andy Young,
and Bayard walked through the ruins, a group of young blacks
boasted to them "We won." "How can you say you won,"
Martin asked, "when thirty-four Negroes are dead, your community is destroyed, and whites are using the riots as an excuse
for inaction?" "We won because we made them pay attention
to us," they told him. He, Andy, and Bayard had not thought
of that interpretation. "We must hold ourselves responsible
for not reaching them," Bayard Rustin confessed. ". . . Roy,
Martin, and I haven't done a damn thing about it. We've
done plenty to get votes in the South and seats in lunch
rooms, but we've had no program for these youngsters."

Martin agreed. It had been a miscalculation to concentrate
so exclusively upon Southern problems over the last ten years,
he wrote in *Saturday Review*. There was not the large measure
of derivative Northern progress that had been expected. The
illusion of freedom in the North had masked its hideous economic conditions—matriarchal families whose morality was
vitiated by perpetual dependence upon welfare programs,
levels of unemployment that had actually risen in the
decade since Montgomery, and agglutinations of the impoverished in substandard housing that had few equivalents
even in the South. Moreover, Northern civil rights leadership
had been largely apathetic, when not corrupted by city bossism. Los Angeles could have expected the Watts riot, he
stated. Its conditions fitted the pattern of urban poverty in
the North; its ghetto population density was among the worst
in the nation; the level of employment there was only
slightly higher than during the Depression. Even the distant
hope of breaking out of the ghetto had burst with the state's
repudiation of open housing in 1964.

If Martin spoke out forthrightly on immediate restoration of order by the police and the military, he left no doubt about the source of blame and the broad obligations of American society to attack the causes of ghetto unrest. "The atrociousness of some deeds may be conceded by legal ritual," he wrote, "but their destructiveness is felt with bitter force by its victims. Victor Hugo understood this when he said, 'If a soul is left in darkness, sins will be committed. The guilty one is not the one who commits the sin, but he who causes the darkness.' " Martin's sober appraisal of the causal conditions of the Watts riot provided an interesting contrast to his earlier written statements that violent racial combat would be rejected by the American blacks. If he had been wrong, he was astute enough to seek the reasons honestly. Watts accelerated his appreciation of the superficiality of civil rights gains. His national role as a champion of massive federal assistance to the urban poor was henceforth a moral necessity. It was going to be necessary to select shortly a Northern city in which to mount a massive program of nonviolent disobedience—probably Cleveland or Chicago. An SCLC task force was already at work on the problem.

Meanwhile, there was the Vietnam issue. On September 10, with Bayard Rustin, Bernard Lee, and Andy Young, Martin conferred with Ambassador Goldberg. Goldberg assured him that, while his Vietnam position was commendable, the American Government was equally resolved to effect a negotiated settlement and that, in fact, a peaceful settlement was imminent. Lyndon Johnson had instructed Goldberg to convey the impression that resolution of the Vietnam war would occur in the very near future. Martin was stymied, and perhaps relieved, in his peace efforts. A private citizen, not privy to the sensitive discussions in Saigon and Geneva, he was, certainly, constrained to respect his government's good will.

Five days later, Vice-President Humphrey was assigned the

responsibility of getting to know the civil rights leaders informally. The presidential yacht *Honey Fitz* sailed down the Potomac with Martin King, Whitney Young, Floyd McKissick (the new director of CORE), Clarence Mitchell (head of the Washington, D.C., chapter of the NAACP), and Andy Young, for a pleasant cruise. Humphrey's stock among civil rights leaders was high. His personal charm was legendary. This boat ride was intended to seal the romance between the Administration and the spokesmen for the blacks. Poverty budgets and Vietnam, it was hoped, would pleasantly dissolve in a maritime consensus of mutual conviction that black organizations and federal agencies together were doing their best, concertedly, to ameliorate the lot of the urban, and largely black, poor. The stratagem failed. "They almost turned the boat over," one of Humphrey's assistants revealed. The attempt of a Humphrey aide to turn the discussion to the Moynihan report was rebuked with the demand, probably McKissick's, that the group confine itself to "realistic" problems. Watts had made them angry, if belatedly. Comity with the Administration was no longer so desirable.

The forthcoming White House conference on civil rights was not being planned to accommodate the opinions of carping dissidents or of spokesmen whose consciences were stimulated by the war in Southeast Asia. The series of planning sessions in July, 1965, directed by ten White House assistants, had requested the testimony of only one civil rights leader, although the academic community was impressively represented by Kenneth Clark, Talcott Parsons, Urie Bronfenbrenner, Eric Erickson, Robert Coles, James Wilson, and other distinguished scholars. Bayard Rustin was invited, but he was in Europe at the time. Shortly thereafter, the contents of the Moynihan report were beginning to appear in the press, its sections dealing with the alleged disintegration of the black family rather sensationally presented. Two experts, Elizabeth Herzog and a Howard University sociologist, Hylan Lewis, countered the report's statistics with their own, indicating that the report presented an exaggerated picture. Whichever set of statistics was more correct, both confirmed a nonetheless alarming state of affairs in the black ghetto. Bayard Rustin's observation that the disorganization of the poor white family was probably comparable and that the matriarchal family could be construed as a positive adjustment of the black poor to the ecology of the ghetto only begged the question. Unfortunately, the gravamen of the report and the accuracy of its statistics were soon to succumb to ideological sensitivities. Martin anticipated this danger in an October speech in Westchester County, New York. He approved the report, provisionally, but added the *caveat* that "The danger will be that problems will be attributed to innate Negro weaknesses and used to justify, neglect, and rationalize oppression."

The Moynihan report and the White House conference were politicized even more by the Watts riot and the Vietnam war. Late in August, the President had used the White House conference on equal employment opportunities to speak out against urban violence. Civil rights leaders, equally attentive to national polls, interpreted this as a signal of the Administration's intention to adopt a go-slow policy and to stress law and order above racial equity. One year had elapsed since the passage of the $1 billion poverty-program budget, and the black response, so voices in Congress grumbled, was Watts. The enemies of civil rights affected to believe that the Moynihan report offered a large part of the explanation. Lyndon Johnson was more concerned about the outspokenness of civil rights leaders against the war. Floyd McKissick saw a direct connection between urban unrest, an inadequate poverty program, and the more than $20 billion being spent in Vietnam.

Martin was no less distressed by the Administration's priorities. For the January 1 issue of the *Chicago Defender*, he composed the most exhaustively reasoned argument—until

his Spring Mobilization speech in New York the following
year—for his opposition to the Vietnam war. If this piece, in
his weekly column titled "My Dream," escaped general public
notice, it was almost certainly brought to the attention of the
White House. "Some of my friends of both races and others
who do not consider themselves my friends have expressed
disapproval because I have been voicing concern over the war
in Vietnam," he wrote in the black weekly, "They have alleged that Martin King is 'getting out of his depth.'" There
were three overriding reasons why he had chosen to broach
the matter. First, as a minister of the Gospel, formed in the
"prophetic Judeo-Christian tradition," he was compelled to
honor his calling by condemning war. "I believe that war is
wrong"—it was that simple. That he lacked the expertise of
the student of international relations, that he possessed no
more knowledge of the government's peace maneuvers than
the average informed citizen, Martin readily conceded. "Yet,
at bottom," he said, "I am expert in recognition of a simply
eloquent truth. That truth is that it is sinful for any of God's
children to brutalize any of God's other children, no matter
from what side the brutalization comes."

His second reason was equally passionate, if slightly self-
conscious: "I must involve myself in the long-fought effort
to change the jangling discords of war into meaningful and
measured rhythms of negotiation and reason—and ultimately
to fuse a marvellous symphony of peace." Martin's final reason revealed a quality of disinterested humanitarianism and
racial enlightenment that set him apart from the overwhelming majority of civil rights leaders of the period. "I am an
American," he stressed. But he construed love of country as
synonymous with love of democracy, justice, and peace. The
destruction of Vietnamese villages proved, he said, "that we
still believe that might makes right." It would be heresy for
the American black to compartmentalize his ideals, to demand
the full measure of human dignity for himself while ignoring

its denial to others elsewhere. "That same idealism, that same nonviolent spirit and courage which brought embattled men to the conference table in the Montgomery of the South might well achieve identical victory with Moscow," Martin wrote. "The Negro must not allow himself to become a victim of the self-serving philosophy of those who manufacture war that the survival of the world is the white man's business alone."

It was this conviction that compelled Martin to speak out early in January in defense of SNCC alumnus Julian Bond, deprived of his elective seat by the Georgia legislature because of his endorsement of SNCC's anti-Vietnam platform. The unpopularity of the Bond-King position among blacks was borne out by the surprising position taken by the once pro-SNCC *Atlanta Enquirer*. "We believe the views espoused by SNCC have the potential of comforting and aiding our enemies," one of its editorials proclaimed. The president of the Chattanooga, Tennessee, branch of the SCLC, Reverend J. L. Edwards, and his assistant, Reverend Robert Richards, tendered their resignations as manifestation of their disapproval of their leader's recent pronouncements.

Eric Goldman's statement that Lyndon Johnson mistrusted the political judgment of Martin can scarcely be doubted. The forthcoming civil rights conference reflected the President's uneasiness. Lyndon Johnson had no intention of risking embarrassment from civil rights ingrates. The control by the White House of the final planning for the civil rights conference increased. The list of the 2,400 guests was examined at the very highest level. The original cast changed markedly. The intellectuals who had participated in the planning stages disappeared from the list. Bronfenbrenner, Parsons, Michael Harrington, Frank Riessman, Nathan Glazer, Lewis Killian, Charles Silberman, Herbert Gans, and others, who had been consulted earlier, were now scrupulously ignored. On the other hand, the proportion of businessmen and industrialists was greatly augmented. Ben Heineman, president of Chicago and Northwestern Railroad, was appointed conference chairman. Asa Randolph was made honorary chairman. The number of District of Columbia participants rose considerably, as well. Howard University President James Nabrit, Jr., was designated chairman of one of the eight research panels, to handle the anticipated awkward Vietnam resolutions. Despite the fact that SCLC's Walter Fauntroy was one of the conference's vice-chairmen, the role of Martin King was carefully minimized. His antiwar position had now completely alienated Lyndon Johnson.

The civil rights conference met on the first two days in June, 1966. It was a highly controlled affair. Lyndon Johnson made an unscheduled appearance before the body and called its attention to the fact that he was making the unprecedented gesture, for an American President, of introducing a speaker who was not a head of state, Thurgood Marshall. The President spoke warmly of the impressive career of the new solicitor-general, Thurgood Marshall, who in turn spoke enthusiastically of the civil rights gains made under the present Administration. Whitney Young remarked to the press that the "Negro was more concerned about the rat at night and the job in the morning" than he was about the war in Vietnam. Dr. Nabrit handily repulsed McKissick's anti-Vietnam resolution in committee. And Martin King was totally ignored. Indeed, his wife came nearer to making a contribution to the proceedings when she was asked to sing. Among the participants, Martin lobbied for Asa Randolph's freedom budget of $100 billion to be spent over a decade to eradicate poverty. Wisely, he rejected the advice of some of his staff members to withdraw at the end of the first day. It was undoubtedly painful to be calculatedly shunted aside, but he kept his aplomb, hoped that the conference report would be acted upon, and was all the more determined to pursue the ungrateful path of advocacy of world peace.

11

The Pied Piper of
Hamlin Avenue—Chicago
and Mississippi

> Nonviolence might do something . . . but a bullet didn't have morals and it was beginning to occur to more and more organizers that white folks had plenty more bullets than they did conscience.
>
> JULIUS LESTER

THERE ARE DOZENS of cities in America blighted by bossism, poverty, crime, corruption, police brutality, and civic indifference to the poor and the racially disadvantaged. Probably none of them rivals Chicago in the perfection of these evils collectively. Of its 3.5 million people nearly 1 million are black, and almost half of these are impoverished. Of those who are not, not many are well above the poverty line. And the overwhelming majority are concentrated in the appalling residential sumps located on the city's south and west sides. "I have never seen such hopelessness," Hosea Williams confessed after a month in the city, "The Negroes of Chicago have a greater feeling of powerlessness than any I ever saw. They don't participate in the governmental process because they're beaten down psychologically. We're used to working with people who want to be freed."

To attack the problems of poverty and racism in Chicago seemed to presuppose an almost quixotic valor. Mayor Richard Daley's political machine was probably the most ruthlessly efficient in the nation. Its use of patronage and pressure were consistent proof against the periodic half-hearted calls for reform. City hall's control of the black population was abetted by the machine within the political machine, directed by aging black Congressman William Dawson, inevitably re-elected to his seat session after session. Shortly before Martin established headquarters in the city, the Committee for Independent Political Action (comprised of radical whites, several local civic groups, SNCC, and CORE) had completely failed to agree on a strategy to mount a campaign against the Vietnam war and segregation. Nor had it agreed to support the candidacy of comedian Dick Gregory for Chicago mayor in the forthcoming primary. There were nearly as many battle plans as civil rights and community organizations in Chicago, a divisiveness readily exploited by the city establishment. Even the Coordinated Council of Community Organizations (CCCO)—consisting of the West Side Federation, the Woodlawn Organization, the local Urban League, the local NAACP, CORE, SNCC, and the SCLC—which invited Martin to come to Chicago, was divided. The younger members, led by Rev. Albert A. Raby, the CCCO president, favored a frontal assault on Daley's machine, while many of its senior members advised the route of diplomacy and entreaty.

If the civil rights leadership of Chicago lacked the measure of cohesion indispensable to the success of its projected campaign, the national SCLC approached the challenge with its wonted sense of destiny and indifference to planning. Warned by a CRS agent that Chicago might become the Waterloo of the SCLC, Andy Young replied that the Lord would provide. It was true that Andy Young, Bernard Lee, James Bevel, and Walter Fauntroy already had begun and would continue in the weeks ahead the preparation of a detailed report on Chicago social and economic conditions. If they were "out of their depth," as Charles Sherrod told Martin, they showed great determination to master the currents of urban politics and ghetto problems. Nevertheless, the SCLC did not do a sufficiently thorough job of homework. It was not so much ignorance of statistics or, eventually, failure to uncover the labyrinthine channels of municipal control and federal collusion and the tremendous power of the Midwestern business community that would defeat them. Rather, it was a combination of these and the SCLC's Southern and fundamentalist Gestalt. "They can run a big Baptist church," Louis Lomax observed, "but faced with the task of administering the affairs of a complex and diffuse organization, particularly a secular one, the men molded in the fashion of Martin Luther King, Jr., tend to flounder." Bill Berry, director of the Chicago Urban League and an admirer of Martin, corroborates Lomax's statement. "It is true," he confides with a visible degree of pain, "that a good many of Martin's people did not understand what is required in the way of organization in a big city. It is true that some of the people who worked—the field workers and the young people—did not understand that the methods of Selma are not transferable intact to Chicago."

On Sunday, January 23, 1966, the nation's news media reported that Martin Luther King had installed himself the day before in a Lawndale slum tenement at 1550 South Hamlin Avenue. When Bernard Lee, in whose name the apartment was leased, had arrived with an associate on Friday to inspect the premises, he found four plasterers, two painters, and two electricians furiously working to transform the apartment so that it would meet the standards of the municipal housing code. Despite the new tenants' secretiveness, the landlords had learned at the last minute that it was Martin and two colleagues who were to be the new residents. Even so, the transformation left much to be desired, as the *Chicago Tribune* reporter wrote after an inspection. When Coretta joined Martin, she found that the smell of urine was overpowering. Three days later Martin informed the press that his occupation of the apartment was meant to serve notice to landlords that, unless they undertook immediate improvement of their properties, he intended to lead a rent strike. He stated, however, that, before doing so, he intended to direct an intensive study of the city's housing and job conditions during the month of February.

On that same day, he met with Superintendent of Police O. W. Wilson and his staff. The good will of this meeting was to contrast with the later relations between the police and Martin's demonstrators. Martin warned them that "It may be necessary to engage in acts of civil disobedience in order to call attention to specific problems. Often an individual has to break a particular law to obey a higher law, that of brotherhood and justice." He went on to say that he had three objectives in Chicago: (1) to educate people about slum conditions, (2) to organize slum-dwellers into a union to force landlords to meet their obligations, and (3) to mobilize slum tenants into an army of nonviolent demonstrators.

City hall followed Martin's maneuvers carefully. It was not yet alarmed, but it took the precaution of cranking up its public-relations machinery. On February 10, the huge *Chicago Tribune* headlines pushed much of the usual volume of news off the front page to announce, "Plan New Drive on Slum-lords." The paper stated that fifty housing inspectors were being added to the city's force and that landlords guilty of housing-code violations were to be vigorously prosecuted. Already, twenty-five of the worst offenders were marked for punishment. The same edition recalled to Chicagoans of both races the advice of Abraham Lincoln in 1838 when, while championing the repeal of unjust laws, he had insisted that they be obeyed so long as they remained in effect. The impression of grave concern and conciliative openness was being cleverly nurtured by the city's rulers.

It almost appeared that the SCLC was striving to regain

the initiative when, two days later, it held a meeting, closed to the public and the press, at the Jubilee Temple Christian Methodist Church, to rally the city's ministerial leadership to a program of "economic penalties" against the business concerns that had been laggard in hiring and promoting blacks. Martin told the ministers that this drive must begin immediately under the auspices of Operation Breadbasket. The objective was to increase the income of Chicago's blacks by some $50 million. If the sum seemed unrealistic, he said, he was able to cite the remarkable accomplishments of the Atlanta Operation Breadbasket, which had augmented minority incomes by nearly $20 million over a two-and-a-half-year period, although this was probably due not entirely to the labors of the SCLC, but to the remarkable growth of Atlanta. At about the same time, Martin conferred with Elijah Muhammed, leader of the Black Muslims. Both leaders announced a collaborative effort to end discrimination in the city.

The Chicago Movement and city hall were shadow-boxing. If the example of boxing had occurred to Martin, he would have thought of his seizure of a slum tenement on February 23 as tantamount to a sharp jab. Announcing that they were placing the building in "trusteeship," three civil rights groups (the SCLC, the CCCO, and the West Side Federation) assumed the responsibility for the collection and application of the rents of the four families residing in the slum building owned by John Bender at 3738 North Kenmore Avenue. "I won't say that it is illegal," Martin scholasticized, "but I would call it supralegal. The moral question is far more important than the legal one." The action certainly provided widespread publicity. Photos of Martin, Coretta, Al Raby, and others in overalls, shoveling away refuse, were nationally reproduced. The city adopted a bifurcated attack upon the trusteeship gambit. On the one hand, it announced, through the Assistant Corporation Counsel, that it had nearly completed a dossier on the landlord that would lead to a court investigation; as for the legality of the trusteeship, it professed to regard this as a private matter between the parties concerned. On the other hand, city hall instructed its allies to attack the legality of the trusteeship. Federal District Court Judge James B. Parson, a black, vigorously denounced the seizure. "I don't think it is legal; it is theft," he fumed, "This is a revolutionary tactic. Laws that might be suspected to be unconstitutional because they are discriminatory should be attacked in the courts." The prestigious Committee of One Hundred, an interracial body of distinguished Chicagoans, expressed regret at Dr. King's precipitate militancy and stated that it could have sympathetically reviewed a detailed catalogue of putative grievances. An editorial in the *Tribune* dismissed the seizure of the Bender building as a "grandstanding" act. Judge Richard A. Napolitano had already allowed two slum tenants, supported by the city's lawyers, to file suit to have a receiver appointed for the property of a recidivist landlord. This was long before Martin King came to Chicago, the paper stated. Undoubtedly, it would have been better for public image if the organizations concerned had investigated the building's owner. It turned out that Bender was very old, very sick, and almost as poor as his tenants.

On March 18, Mayor Daley conferred with twenty-five black ministers for nearly three hours at city hall. Martin was absent, fulfilling previous speaking commitments. Progress reports of the city's labors against housing and professional discrimination were distributed to the conferees. Mayor Daley was convivial and sympathetic. The ministers were invited to draw up a list of constructive proposals and to return shortly for another palaver. At the end of the month, the ministers returned with their proposals. Martin was unable to attend this conference also. He was in Europe with Harry Belafonte, where they succeeded in raising more than $100,000 through his speeches and Harry's concerts for the Chicago Movement.

Martin's absences may have been unavoidable, but he may well have been grateful that his itinerary was so demanding. There was absolutely no evidence that Mayor Daley was sincere in his deliberations with the local ministers, and Martin's presence at these meetings might conceivably have compromised the Chicago Movement, because of Richard Daley's determined pose of affable give-and-take. The twenty-five ministers were not so well contented after the second meeting with the mayor. Reverend Edgar H. S. Chandler, their leader, had serious doubts about the mayor's willingness to end *de facto* school segregation in the city.

Martin was not devoting his complete energies to Chicago. Aside from the innumerable national and even international commitments that arose during this period, he insisted on spending at least three days of the week in Atlanta. Nobel laureate, international figure, and cross-country civil rights leader, he insisted, nevertheless, that he was equally the humble co-pastor of Ebenezer Baptist Church. There was a psychological necessity in this. If he was humanly proud of his achievements, he also craved at times the simple peace of the modest pastorate and the affection of the family foyer. Moments with Coretta and the children were becoming increasingly rare, and the pleasure of an unmolested stroll down Auburn Avenue to the Beamon Café for lunch were equally rare. It was also true that the Chicago Movement was making less headway than had been anticipated. This was due, in part, to the trenchant apathy of the people, in part, to the continuing policy disagreements among those who were advising Martin.

The Agenda Committee was his principal non-SCLC advisory body. John McDermott of the Catholic Interracial Council, Don Benedict of the Chicago Renewal Society, Charlie Hayes of the Packing House Workers, Al Raby, Art Brazier, Bill Berry, and Hale Williams of the American Friends Service Committee comprised the Agenda Commit-

tee. Rev. Brazier (director of Woodlawn Organization) spoke
for those who opposed the traditional nonviolent tactic of
massive demonstrations, especially into white neighborhoods,
on the grounds that this would prematurely mobilize the
whites. He proposed an extended period of thorough community ghetto organization and application of economic pressure
to firms recalcitrant in their black hiring and promotion
policies.

While the Chicago strategists dickered and planned, Martin, after his return from Europe, received several civic awards
and attended the annual SCLC convention in Miami. He
delivered an exigent speech to the delegates, calling for American withdrawal from Vietnam. Despite the mumblings of the
SCLC board members and the predictions of his experienced
fund-raisers, Martin garnered the official support of his organization. It voted as a body to approve its president's denunciation of the Southeast Asian war. Late in May, he
accepted the cochairmanship of the Clergy and Laymen Concerned About Vietnam and sent a message of support to Dr.
Benjamin Spock and Chaplain William Sloane Coffin, of
Yale University, on the occasion of their Washington, D.C.,
war-protest rally.

The shooting of Fred D. Hubbard at the end of April, a
black candidate opposing Congressman Dawson in the forthcoming primary, angered the black community. Martin was
now about ready to launch a series of rallies and demonstrations. On May 26, he announced plans for a march on city
hall, to take place on June 26. "Chicago has the finest organizations working together that I've ever seen anywhere in the
country," he told a rally, "We've been studying to see exactly
what's needed and now we've emerged with concrete demands.
Chicago will have a long hot summer, but not a summer of
racial violence. Rather, it will be a long hot summer of peaceful nonviolence." That same day, Chicago's papers carried
news of a large government loan to the city, negotiated
through Secretary Robert Weaver's Department of Housing

and Urban Development, to renovate five hundred substandard apartment units. Mayor Daley's office proclaimed that slums would be eliminated by the end of the decade. The simultaneity of the two announcements was scarcely coincidental. The city had again appeared to match the concern for poverty of the Chicago Movement leaders. That same day, however, seventeen-year-old Jerome Huey, looking for employment in the all-white suburb of Cicero, was beaten to death on a street corner by four white youths. Here was a *cause célèbre* of the Birmingham or Selma variety, which the SCLC endeavored to use to galvanize the black community. Martin's lieutenants busied themselves with preparations for mass demonstrations, and he himself lent his unusual oratorical gifts regularly to the enterprise. On June 6, however, a calamity struck the nation that forced the cancellation of the projected course of civil rights activity for most of the remainder of the summer.

The highly individualistic and rather inscrutable James Meredith, the University of Mississippi's first acknowledged black student, was shotgunned on Highway 51 just a few paces within the Mississippi state line. Meredith had undertaken this perilous march by foot to Jackson, the state capital, as a symbolic act to establish the black man's right to move freely about the Deep South. The next day, Martin, McKissick, and Stokely crossed from Tennessee into Mississippi along the route taken by Meredith. The state troopers were considerably less than hospitable, although Governor Paul Johnson announced that he would provide police protection "to see that these demonstrators get all the marching they want." Carmichael and McKissick were pushed about and Martin stumbled over SNCC's project director, Cleveland Sellers, who had been pushed to the ground. They were ordered to walk along the shoulder of the highway, which they did for three miles.

They returned that evening to Reverend James Lawson's

Centenary Methodist Church in Memphis, vowing to continue the march to Jackson the next day. A few days before
the Meredith affair, Martin had been interviewed by *The New
York Times* in his dingy Lawndale flat. Reservedly, but un-
ambiguously, he had spoken out against the black separatists
of the Carmichael stripe and had regretted the a priori denunciation of the White House Conference on Civil Rights
by many militants. A few days later—almost exactly one year
after Johnson's "To Fulfill These Rights" address—Adam
Powell told the graduating class at Howard that black militancy and the exclusion of whites from civil rights activity
ought, henceforth, to be the order of the day.

The wounding of Meredith caused a moratorium on
these disputes. It was apparent, however, that it was to be
very temporary. At Lawson's church, Stokely's suave, slightly
shrill voice cried out for blacks to seize power in areas of the
South where they outnumbered whites. "I'm not going to
beg the white man for anything I deserve," he said, "I'm going
to take it." McKissick was in a grim humor also. Speaking of
the Statue of Liberty, he said "They ought to break that
young lady's leg and throw her into the Mississippi." Martin
pleaded for renewed intensity of the struggle but not to the
exclusion of interracial collaboration and temperance. Among
themselves, the ideological debate continued until early the
next morning in a black motel. "I tried to make it clear that
besides opposing violence in principle," Martin explained, "I
could imagine nothing more impractical and disastrous than
for any of us, through misguided judgment, to precipitate a
violent confrontation in Mississippi. We had neither the resources nor the techniques to win." The people from CORE,
SNCC, and the Deacons for Defense were not convinced.
They also agreed with Stokely that whites ought to be ex-
cluded from the march. After much earnest and eloquent
pleading, Martin, Whitney, and Roy, aided by Floyd McKissick's eleventh-hour conversion, succeeded in extracting an

agreement that the march would be nonviolent and interracial.

The manifesto issued the next day revealed additional disunity. Neither Wilkins nor Whitney Young were signatories, and Charles Evers, the director of the Mississippi NAACP, protested later that he had not authorized the use of his signature. He objected to the unfriendly remarks about the Johnson Administration. Evers also doubted the soundness of the march objectives: "I don't want this to turn into another Selma where everyone goes home with the cameramen and leaves us holding the bag." The manifesto stated that "This march will be a massive public indictment and protest of the failure of American society, the Government of the United States, and the state of Mississippi to 'fulfill these rights.'" Lyndon Johnson was asked to send federal registrars to Mississippi. The signatories also called on the government to accept the $100 million Randolph Freedom Budget. Martin must have had misgivings about signing. He did so, quite likely, as a gesture of solidarity and in an attempt to tamp down the more extremist elements that he feared would capture the march after his departure for Chicago.

During the next few days, Evers continued to grumble about the value of the march. "I don't see how walking up and down a hot highway helps: I'm for walking house to house and fence to fence to get Negroes registered." On June 11, the march leaders, agreeing with him, proclaimed that their main objective was to register the state's black population. And so they did. In Panola, they led fifty citizens to the courthouse to register. The hero of that day was a 106-year-old farmer who gleefully stated, after being registered, "It's alright. Registering is alright." They pressed on. In Grenada, where only 697 of a black population of 8,000 were registered, the marchers led 1,300 to the courthouse, where they were received by four black registrars, appointed on an emergency basis the day before. The Grenada officials wanted no trouble from the jubilant crowd. Bradford Dye, the city attorney, met with Martin and agreed to his demands that racial voting restrictions would be dropped. Planting an American flag between the arms of Grenada's Confederate Memorial, the marchers moved on to Greenwood. Forty-eight hours later, on June 15, the black registrars vanished as quickly as they had appeared and life in Grenada reverted to the traditional pattern.

This was an exceedingly frustrating time for Martin. The criticisms by the Urban League and the NAACP bothered him. It seemed that the unity of civil rights leadership was fragmenting along the lines of approval and disapproval of the Johnson Administration. The quixotic Meredith had withheld his sanction from the march. He took exception to Martin's anti-Vietnam position and made statements about the conduct and goals of the march which, if bafflingly unclear, were unmistakably critical. Even more disconcerting was the racist spirit that the younger participants in the march manifested. "We Shall Overcome" was still sung, but there was frequently silence when the song's line "Black and white together" was reached. Many preferred the words "We shall overrun":

> Jingle bells, shotgun shells,
> Freedom all the way,
> Oh what fun it is to blast
> A trooper man away.

Lyrics such as these, sung by youths who showed none of the humility of nonviolent marchers of the past, alarmed Martin. The mood of Stokely and his followers was becoming less nonviolent by the hour. In Greenwood, where he had been arrested for defying an order not to have his tents pitched in a restricted area, the new SNCC leader later stirred up a rally of six hundred marchers, yelling "This is the twenty-seventh time I have been arrested—and I ain't going to jail no more." And, for one of the first times, the shout "Black

Power!" filled the Mississippi night. Stokely issued instructions that, from Greenwood on (the marchers had entered deep into SNCC territory at Greenwood), the shibboleths of nonviolence were to be exorcised. At the Greenwood courthouse, Hosea Williams got carried away by Black Power rhetoric. "Get that vote and pin that badge on a black chest. Get that vote. . . . Whip that policeman across the head!" he shouted. "He means with the vote," Martin impatiently amended. Stokely fired back, "They know what he means." Martin was uneasy. He had been shuttling back and forth between the Mississippi column, Chicago, and Detroit. On Sunday, June 12, violence erupted in the Puerto Rican section of Chicago when a youth was shot by the police. Police cars were burned and nineteen persons were hospitalized. On the following day, new disorders occurred in which seven persons were wounded in gunfire exchanged between rioters and police. It appeared that Chicago's "long hot summer" was to be violent after all.

Returning from Chicago to Mississippi, Martin caucused for five hours with Carmichael, McKissick, and several others in a small Catholic parish house in Yazoo: "I pleaded with the group to abandon the Black Power slogan. It was my contention that a leader has to be concerned about the problem of semantics. Each word, I said, has a denotative meaning . . . and a connotative meaning. . . . Black Power carried the wrong connotations." To Martin's rather academic thesis, Stokely rejoined, "Power is the only thing respected in this world, and we must get it at any cost." In his final major work, *Where Do We Go from Here: Chaos or Community?*, Martin detailed the course of this lengthy ideological confrontation. He stated that, as they were winding up, Stokely told him that he had purposefully selected Greenwood to launch the slogan, "in order to give it a national forum and force you to take a stand for Black Power." Carmichael denies the implication of premeditated exploitation. He made the plea for Black Power because of the rightness of the idea and propitiousness of the occasion, he states. They reached a compromise that shortly evaporated. SNCC and CORE would cease shouting "Black Power" and the SCLC people would not chant "Freedom Now."

Summing up his reservations about Black Power, Martin made it abundantly clear that the philosophy was thoroughly unacceptable to him: "In spite of the positive aspects of Black Power, which are compatible with what we have sought to do in the civil rights movement all along without the slogan, its negative values, I believe, prevent it from having the substance and program to become the basic strategy for the civil rights movement." The *ultima ratio* of opposition, however, was not its ostensible radicalism and jolting color content. Martin saw Black Power as irrationally defeatist: "Beneath all the satisfaction of a gratifying slogan, Black Power is a nihilistic philosophy born out of the conviction that the Negro can't win. It was born from the wounds of despair and disappointment."

Some of the marchers had booed him in Yazoo. And, despite the increasing insulation provided by his sometimes overly solicitous staff, Martin was keenly aware of the growing conviction, South and North, that he had reached an impasse, that his charisma was failing as the months after the post-Montgomery decade passed. Hostility, ingratitude from those he loved and tried to serve, always hurt him. Still, he strove to understand clearly what was happening:

I went home that night with an ugly feeling. Selfishly I thought of my sufferings and sacrifices over the last twelve years. Why would they boo one so close to them? But as I lay awake thinking, I finally came to myself, and I could not for the life of me have less than patience and understanding for those young people. For twelve years, I and others like me had held out radiant promises of progress. I had preached to them about my dream. . . . Their hopes had soared. They were now booing because they felt we were unable to deliver on our promises.

The Meredith march, without Meredith, moved deeper into the state. On June 21, it arrived at Philadelphia, Mississippi, where Sheriff Lawrence Rainey had arrested Goodman, Chaney, and Schwerner, who were never seen alive again. Governor Johnson, succumbing to local pressure, had sharply reduced the marchers' police protection several days before, stating, "We aren't going to wet-nurse a bunch of showmen all over the country." Philadelphia was a dangerous place to be without adequate police protection. Thus far, there had been little or no violence, although the pursed lips, fierce stares, and crimson complexions of the whites along the route bespoke murderous emotions just barely under control. The intention of the marchers to hold a memorial service for the slain civil rights workers evoked a predictably violent response from Philadelphia's white citizens. As Martin was speaking, the marchers were attacked in the main street by a crowd that threw cherry bombs while the police turned their backs. It was only when the marchers began to return the blows of white teenagers that the police intervened. That evening, shortly after 8 P.M., the marchers' campsite was fired upon. Before the morning, three more attacks occurred. Twice, armed marchers returned the fire. Martin vowed to lead a second march to Philadelphia within a few days. Meanwhile, he appealed by wire to Lyndon Johnson to dispatch federal marshals to the city—a request that went unanswered, although the Attorney-General did phone Governor Johnson to request protection for the marchers.

Canton, Mississippi, the next stop, was a calamity. Veterans of Pettus Bridge said that it was worse than Selma. Martin, Floyd, and Stokely decided to ignore the order of the police and troopers not to erect tents on the grounds of the black school. The SNCC leader appears to have been more adamant about defying the proscription than his colleagues. As the group prepared to pitch tents, the police laid down a dazing barrage of tear gas, then sliced into the two thousand marchers with the standard arsenal of clubs, sticks, and whips. John Doar, chief of the Justice Department's civil rights division, handkerchief over his nose, stumbled into the mayhem in a futile effort to restrain them. "Take it easy, take it easy," he kept repeating to the troopers. Stokely believed for a few minutes that the marchers would be fired on and he lost his usual composure. Police gunfire would certainly be possible if the panic was not quickly controlled. Martin and Floyd got the people moving in the direction of a nearby black church. As the day ended and the marchers licked their wounds, a mood of angry despair settled over a large number of people. The conduct of the police power of the state was as unsurprising as it was reprehensible. What galled was the cynical attitude of Washington, which limited the federal presence to a CRS agent, several neutral FBI men, and the well-intentioned Justice Department chief. The slogan Black Power, born up the road in Greenwood, was weaned in Canton.

It would be difficult to sing "We Shall Overcome" from now on, even to believe in the potential reality of Martin's dream. When the Attorney-General of the United States deplored the violence in the same breath with which he noted the marchers' provocation by their disregard of the police instructions, it was assuredly questionable whether "black and white together" any longer had meaning. "The meek shall inherit the earth," James Baldwin wrote, after returning from Mississippi: "This presents a very bleak image to those who live in occupied territory. The meek Southeast Asians, those who remain, shall have their free elections, and the meek American Negroes—those who survive—shall enter the Great Society."

Martin was bewildered, angry, and perhaps somewhat frightened by the turn that events were taking. His telegram to Lyndon Johnson after Canton was not answered. Attorney-General Katzenbach washed his hands of the matter; a delegation of concerned clergymen was politely heard and then dismissed from his office. Martin knew that this was the mulct for his Vietnam position. The indifference of the Administration also reflected the generalized resistance of American whites to further unrest, demonstrations, and demands by their black cousins. "It undermined Dr. King at a time when his strength within the movement was being tested," *Nation* observed. The psychological costliness of the Meredith march is revealed by Martin's irascible tongue-lashing of Charles Evers at one of the many rallies along the route. Usually a cautious man, the Mississippi NAACP head had been affected by the Black Power rhetoric and he made a speech that struck Martin as irresponsibly violent: "Look here, Charles, I don't appreciate your talking like that. If you're that violent, why don't you just go up the highway to Greenwood and kill the man who killed your own brother." This flash of temper in public was extremely rare.

Mississippi had said that it was able to provide adequate protection and, on June 24, King and some of the marchers were back in Philadelphia, after being harassed by motorists who repeatedly sped within inches of the column. State troopers were present to maintain order while Martin approached the courthouse to pray. "You can't go up those steps," Sheriff Rainey told Martin. "Oh yes," Martin queried, "you're the one who had Schwerner and the other fellows in jail?" Sheriff Rainey was proud to say he was. "I believe that the murderers are somewhere around me at this moment," Martin said under his breath, preparing to pray. But "I sure did not want to close my eyes," he said later. He and Ralph prayed with their eyes closed anyway.

Martin was now definitely on the defensive. In the weeks ahead, he reiterated his opposition to Black Power. At the same time, the SCLC attempted to convey to the nation the depth of white complicity in the new extremism and to black militants the subsisting compassionate understanding of those in the nonviolent camp. Nonviolence was not a doctrine of suicidal passivity, Andy Young protested: "Even Gandhi preached that he would rather a man be violent than be a coward. Dr. King has never said that a man didn't have the duty to defend his person or home against attack. But we insist on nonviolence in demonstrations because it works." Martin pointed out later that "fewer people had been killed in ten years of nonviolent demonstrations across the nation than in one night of rioting in Watts." It simply was not true that urban violence was a more efficacious means of forcing racial progress. Besides being "blatantly illogical," from the optic of a program, the exponents of Black Power had started from a totally false premise, Martin believed: "They fail to see that internal revolution has never succeeded in overthrowing a government by violence unless the government had already lost the allegiance and effective control of its armed forces. Anyone in his right mind knows that this will not happen in the United States."

To those who argued that separatism was the essential portion of Black Power, Martin answered that "this was no time for romantic illusions and empty philosophical debates about freedom." "What is needed," he explained, "is a strategy for change, a tactical program that will bring the Negro into the mainstream of American life as quickly as possible." Nonviolence alone could provide that tactic. When Lyndon Johnson told the press, "We are not interested in Black Power. And we are not interested in white power. But we are interested in American democratic power with a small 'd,'" he was expressing Martin's sentiments exactly. If the two men spoke the same language at this point, unfortunately, it was certainly not to each other. It required a special kind of moral irresponsibility and political arrogance for a President to write off the single civil rights leader who combined the virtues of mass appeal, however diminished, and ideological responsibility at the precise moment when racial polarization in the United States was rapidly accelerating. Lyndon Johnson was that kind of President.

The complications arising out of the Meredith march gave the delayed Chicago campaign a new meaning. If the SCLC could implement its program of prying jobs and housing out of the city administration, that success would serve as an effective foil to the blandishments of Black Power. What really ought to matter for the black man—economic advancement engendered by highly organized and forceful manifestations of popular political power—the SCLC was now almost desperately determined to achieve. Andy Young put the matter baldly. "We have got to deliver results—nonviolent results in a Northern city—to protect the nonviolent movement." There was almost no time left to the SCLC. At Baltimore, Maryland, the delegates to the annual CORE convention voted in July to accept Black Power. Anticipating the development, Martin canceled his scheduled address to the convention. It was easy to justify nonattendance; the SCLC was in the opening phase of direct assault upon housing conditions in Chicago. Martin had asked Mayor Daley to meet with him on July 11. Daley agreed, and it was anticipated that the atmosphere of the meeting would favor the Chicago Movement because of the large rally scheduled for Sunday, July 10, at Soldiers Field. One year ago, Martin's three-day appearance in the city had been climaxed by a rally and march of nearly twenty thousand people to city hall. The Sunday demonstration was intended to increase that number fivefold.

It was an impressive affair, even if the turnout was less than the leaders anticipated. Chicago Park officials estimated 23,000, the SCLC, 65,000, in attendance at Soldiers Field. Before the speeches began, Dick Gregory and Mahalia Jackson entertained. It was a hot, humid day, the temperature rising into the stultifying nineties in parts of the center city. Labor representation was indicated by the numerous AFL-CIO and UAW placards. Chicago's black youth gangs were there, most notably represented by the Blackstone Rangers, who held aloft their Black Power signs. An impressive panoply of civic and civil rights organizations covered the speakers' platform. Archbishop John P. Cody sent a message of support: "Your struggles and sufferings will be mine." James Meredith, still sullenly collaborative, gave the crowd a brief greeting. Martin's words, at the rally and at city hall, inveighed against two prevalent misconceptions in the black community. Riots were futile. "The ultimate weakness of a riot is that it can be halted by superior force. We have neither the techniques, the numbers, nor the weapons to win a violent campaign"—his omission of the usual ethical arguments against violence probably reflected momentary concession to the angry spirit of young militants, for whom any appeal to morality would be resented as weakness. For the older generation—the humble and the bourgeois optimists—he dashed cold water on its hopes that things would get better automatically: "We will be sadly mistaken if we think freedom is some lavish dish that the federal government and the white man will pass out on a silver platter while the Negro merely furnishes the appetite. Freedom is never voluntarily granted by the oppressor. It must be demanded by the oppressed."

Then he directed his message to the city of Chicago:

> This day we must decide to fill up the jails of Chicago, if necessary, in order to end slums. This day we must decide that our votes will determine who will be the next mayor of Chicago. We must make it clear that we will purge Chicago of every politician, whether he be Negro or white, who feels that he owns the Negro vote.

About five thousand of the crowd left Soldiers Field and walked three miles to city hall where Martin, emulating his sixteenth-century spiritual mentor, posted several sheafs of demands upon the door of the city's government center. Specifically, the Chicago Movement made eight demands of the city: (1) refusal of real-estate agents to handle property not available to all races and a pledge of nondiscrimination from banks and loan associations, (2) the construction of public housing outside the ghetto, (3) restriction of city purchases to firms with "full-scale" fair employment policies, (4) publication by business and local government of racial-employment statistics and the acceptance by organized labor of four hundred black and Latin American apprentices, (5) recognition by the county public-aid department of the unionized welfare recipients being promoted by the civil rights groups, (6) establishment of a citizens review board for the police department, (7) adoption of an immediate desegregation plan by the city, (8) the boycotting of discriminatory businesses.

Many whites derided and some militants criticized the fact that Martin chose to lead the procession in an air-conditioned limousine. The *Chicago Tribune* had given exaggerated coverage to the denunciation of Martin's rally by his consistent adversary, Dr. J. H. Jackson, president of the National Baptist Convention. A more worthwhile criticism of that Sunday would be the failure of the CCCO and the SCLC to produce a larger representation of Chicago's poor. Paul Good's statement in *Nation* that Martin "had small talent for organizing outside or inside his own group" is the key to the limited success of the day. The Chicago operation was costly, of course. In its beginning stages, it ran in excess of $10,000 monthly. It seems axiomatic, however, that the number and size of demonstrations and the strategy based upon them ought to have been adjusted to the fiscal and organizational limitations of the Movement. Russ Meek, a prominent black militant and a radio and television personality, consistently argued that, for nonviolence to be effective in Chicago, huge numbers of people would have to be regularly mobilized. "If you've got ten thousand people in your demonstration, you can afford to be nonviolent—just walk on over anybody who opposes you. But none of his marches numbered that many," said Meek. The Soldiers Field rally, despite its numbers, failed in the same way—relatively, that is. If fifty thousand blacks could not be mobilized on a clear Sunday, Mayor

Daley need not be troubled by the proposed suburban marches during the week. He was correct, because the number of march participants thereafter never rose above two thousand.

An additional and intriguing critical observation that Meek and the militants of CORE and the West Side Organization made is that the timing of the Soldiers Field rally precluded its hypothetically maximum effectiveness. If several tens of thousands of marchers had converged upon city hall on a Monday, for example, Mayor Daley's administration would have derived a powerfully instructive lesson from the spectacle of a near-total disruption of traffic and commerce. This idea periodically occurred to members of the Movement, but it faltered before the organizational complexities and the votes of moderate members. Yet, an inundation of the streets, municipal buildings, transportation centers, and selected business enterprises would certainly have been in the finest tradition of Gandhi. Lerone Bennett subscribes to this interpretation. "The pity is," says Bennett, "that Martin never went as far as his mentor, Gandhi."

Returning to the city on Monday, Mayor Daley received Martin's eleven-man delegation that afternoon. It arrived fifteen minutes early. This was their second conference since the launching of the Chicago Freedom Movement. Five months earlier, the civil rights leader and Daley had met to thrash out Movement demands. Then, Daley had cleverly recommended that the civil rights organizations encourage the formation of nonprofit construction and rehabilitation corporations, availing themselves of federal government funds amounting to 100 per cent coverage of mortgages. Martin can hardly have supposed now that the most adroit city boss in America would meet his demands, especially in view of the preceding day's modest rally. City officials were predictably polite and noncommittal. Martin was also predictably polite after the meeting. Daley was not a bigot, he told the press, but he did not comprehend "the depth and dimension of the problem we are dealing with." The mayor appeared on the steps of city hall to comment. He feigned consternation. Dr. King had been prodigal in his demands and mute about solutions, he said. Asked about the threat to fill Chicago's jails with demonstrators, Daley replied, "This will not be tolerated as long as I am mayor. I don't think Dr. King would violate any law. He said he was not for violence."

But more of the violence that Martin disapproved of and had predicted would not occur took place twenty-four hours after the Daley meeting. A group of children on the West Side had illegally activated a fire hydrant (the weather was still in the nineties), and the arrival of police to turn it off led to an altercation that blazed into a three-day riot. The damage was considerable. A 140-square-block area was affected. On the third night, there was a prolonged period of sniper fire, which the four thousand National Guardsmen returned. At least six dozen people were injured, two of them by gunfire. Daley accused anarchists, Communists, and the SCLC of provoking the riots. Later, he modified his statement to suggest that, although Dr. King was above suspicion, the filmed presentations by SCLC staff members of the Watts riots had materially influenced the civil disorder. If the charge had really been provable, there is no doubt that city hall would have hauled the SCLC leaders into court. Curiously, however, Daley met with Martin shortly after his accusation and agreed to a superficial five-point proposal to improve ghetto conditions. Sprinkler attachments were to be attached to hydrants near fire stations and maintained by firemen; the park and district police were to enforce equal treatment and access to the city's parks and pools; precinct workers would encourage residents to obey the law and remain at home; more swimming pools and playgrounds were to be constructed immediately; a citizens' committee was to be appointed to investigate the police department and make recommendations to the mayor on improving police relations with citizens. "We've had a very fine meeting," Martin said. But he was disappointed that the mayor declined to appoint a police civilian review board.

Like the young Watts militant who had exulted that "Every day of the riots was worth a year of civil rights demonstrations," there were many Chicago blacks (perhaps a majority) who approved or sympathized with the motives of the rioters. The pervasive feeling that "whitey" needed "shaking up" and that nonviolence played into the establishment's hands (when it came to challenging the iniquitous economics of the North) made Martin increasingly vulnerable to facile charges of accommodationism, "Tomism." During the three-day riot, he and his staff rushed to corners, to meeting places, to churches, and to nightspots, imploring the people to surrender their weapons and return home. The fact that he and Al Raby allowed themselves to be conducted by police cars on the final night was duly noted by militants. Because of the riot leadership provided by three youth gangs— the Cobras, the Vice Lords, and the Roman Saints—Martin, Andy, and several Movement leaders called their chiefs in for a lengthy conference. The technique that had proven effective in Albany and Selma appeared to work once again. Martin listened patiently to a four-hour outpouring of anti-white, anti–city hall vituperation, allowed that he understood their indignation, and persuaded the youth leaders to agree to try nonviolence experimentally. It was to be an experiment of brief duration.

Immediately after the Chicago riots, Cleveland, Ohio, erupted. It appeared that the currency of nonviolence had limited circulation in the North. Critics of the stripe of Dr. J. H. Jackson and Ernest E. Rather, a black man and head of the Committee of One Hundred, alleged that nonviolence was a premeditated stratagem to trigger civil disruption. They urged Martin to return to the South, where there was a fertile terrain of flagrant injustice for which his tactics were ideally suited. Martin's rejoinder was that the Movement would demand the "structural changes necessary to transform Chicago into a metropolis where all can be men with full worth and dignity."

Meanwhile, he continued to deplore the increasing fashionableness of Black Power among his race. He and Bill Berry appeared late in July on television's "The Today Show," to label the term "unfortunate." The nation "does not need black power or white power, but striped power," Bill Berry offered. And, a few days before the Cicero march, Martin stated to Chicago civil rights workers that "Even if every Negro in the United States comes to think that Negroes ought to riot, I'm going to stand as that lone voice and say, 'it's impractical, it's unsound, and we'll never get our own way that way.'" It is obvious that Martin was not "scarred and flawed by the ghettos" as David Halberstam later wrote in *Harper's*, but this did not mean that he understood only in an abstract manner the vile conditions that produced violent situations. If almost half his time was spent away from Chicago during the campaign, brief periods of residence in the Lawndale apartment afforded frighteningly intimate insights into ghetto life. Speaking of one of the occasions when his children were with him, Martin wrote that "Their tempers flared and they sometimes reverted to almost infantile behavior. As riots raged around them outside, I realized that the crowded flat in which we lived was about to produce an emotional explosion in my own family. It was just too hot, too crowded, too devoid of creative forms of recreation." He now knew that Watts, Chicago, Cleveland, would soon be reproduced in dozens of urban centers if rising black extremism and the white backlash were not countered by vigorous state and federal antidotes.

Immediately after the Soldiers Field rally, the UAW had collaborated with the Movement by dispatching 125 paid or-

ganizers into the city's slums for four days, during which they
endeavored to organize tenants into unions for the purpose
of compelling landlords to bargain with them. With the sub-
sidence of the riots, the Movement launched a series of
demonstrations in white neighborhoods late in July that continued through the major part of August. To those who now
denounced further demonstrations as an invitation to violence,
Martin repeated the answer he had given in 1965: "We do not
seek to precipitate violence. However, we are aware that the
existence of injustice in society is the existence of violence,
latent violence. We feel we must constantly expose this evil,
even if it brings violence upon us."

The violence came. Frank Ditto, chairman of the Oakland
Committee for Community Improvement, led more than one
group of demonstrators to Mayor Daley's home, which led to
his arrest along with several of his followers. Ditto's two
demonstrations were unmarred by incident. The week before,
however, Martin's lieutenants had led pickets against several
real-estate agencies in the all-white Belmont-Cragin community. More than a dozen cars were overturned and set afire
(most of them belonging to the demonstrators) by the white
mobs, and police made liberal use of their clubs to disperse
them. Martin and Al Raby issued a joint statement of reproval
and demand for adequate police protection of marchers. "We
shall continue to demonstrate in every all-white community
in Chicago in our nonviolent effort to open housing for all
men," the statement read, "In the process, we demand the
full and active protection of the local police."

The test of full local police protection was to come on
Friday, August 5. Al Raby and Mahalia Jackson led seven
hundred demonstrators to Marquette Park. At first, the
crowd of several hundred whites confined itself to jeering
epithets. When Martin arrived, however, it was infuriated.
As he left his car, he was stunned to his knees by a rock.
"I have to do this—to expose myself—to bring this hate into

the open," he quickly stuttered to his anxious colleagues. The police, 1,200 of them, were on hand to contain the whites, who otherwise would certainly have killed a number of marchers. Martin led the cavalcade to its main target, the Halvorsen real estate agency at 3145 West 63rd Street, where it knelt in brief prayer. The hecklers now numbered nearly four thousand and the demonstrators felt much relieved when they returned to a safer quarter of the city. "I have seen many demonstrations in the South," Martin said, "but I have never seen anything so hostile and so hateful as I've seen here today." These words contrasted with his encouraging biblical buoyancy of earlier in the day. "We are bound for the promised land," he had said. "We shall taste the milk of freedom and the honey of equality. I have a place. My place is in the sunlight of opportunity." The mood had decidedly altered.

The march the following Sunday to the Belmont-Cragin neighborhood also invited decimation. Al Raby, James Bevel, and Jesse Jackson led two thousand demonstrators, nearly one-fourth of them white, into the segregated community from the Hanson Park stadium. As they marched along Fullerton Avenue toward intersecting Linder Avenue, more than three thousand jeered and pelted them through the girdle of some six hundred police. Attacks on policemen were described as "vicious" by the major newspaper. As they knelt to pray at Grove Lutheran Church, more than one marcher must have thanked providence for the rain that had just begun to fall. "I wish I were an Alabama trooper," the mob's chant dinned in the marchers' ears:

> That is what I would truly like to be;
> I wish I were an Alabama trooper
> 'Cause then I could kill the niggers legally.

During the next week, the demonstrations continued. On Wednesday, August 10, 240 civil rights workers, in a surprise

maneuver, marched into the Loop. Two days later, 700 black
and white demonstrators walked to Bogan Park, where 800
officers superintended the affair without incident. Seven black
aldermen who had been invited to participate failed to appear. That Sunday, the Movement escalated its activities by
mounting three simultaneous protests in the Gage, Bogan,
and Jefferson parks communities. The ensuing disorders
claimed five wounded policemen, and disturbances lasted
until late in the evening. The city officials were beginning to
become nervous. Although no definite announcement had
been made of a march to Cicero—the impregnable suburban
enclave of Slavic exclusivism—Raby and Bevel had dropped
disturbing hints. A Cicero march, it was feared, would result
in uncontrollable violence.

If Martin King did not entirely grasp the complexities of
Chicago, it is equally true that Richard Daley had failed to
take the measure of Martin King. Until now, Daley's opponents had fetched conventional prices—monetary or political rewards. Others had recoiled before the terrible prospect of not-very-mentionable forms of intimidation. The
trouble with Martin King was that he appeared to believe
that his moral demands were only honorably negotiable.
Early in August, an emissary from the mayor delivered a
compromise proposal to Martin's Lawndale apartment, which
reflected the disparity of their political ethics. In return for
cancelling the demonstrations, the city promised three hundred instant jobs for blacks by offering to hire housing-project
guards from the ranks of the tenants, construct a few hundred
new apartment units, and hire one black journeyman glazier
for the Housing Authority. The gambit completely failed.

The following week, the city mounted another conciliatory
operation. Miss Chuchut, the high school principal who,
along with Superintendent Willis, had become a hated symbol of Chicago's *de facto* school segregation, was removed
from her post for "health reasons." At the same time, Arch-

bishop Cody, who had supported the Freedom Movement, asked for an end to demonstrations. The Archbishop was opposed, however, by important members of his own flock. John McDermott of the Catholic Interracial Council supported the Movement's tactics. Meanwhile, the mayor conferred with seventeen prominent labor leaders, including William A. Lee (president of the Chicago Federation of Labor) and Robert Johnston (Midwest director of the UAW), prodding them to use their influence with the Freedom Movement leaders. To put the very best front on its machinations, the dutiful *Tribune*, on August 12, reported the city's urban renewal plan in type even larger than it had used for the Speck murder of seven nurses. In twenty-two areas of Chicago, $500 million was to be spent to eradicate slums by 1968. The marches continued, but Martin agreed to meet with city and real estate officials on the following Wednesday, August 17.

The Wednesday confrontation lasted more than eight hours. Among those present were Martin, Al Raby, Bernard Lee, and William Robinson of the Movement; the mayor, the archbishop, Ben Heineman (the chairman of the June White House conference on civil rights), Rabbi Robert Marx, Robert Johnston, and Alderman Charles Chew, Jr. The CCCO-SCLC demands were threefold: (1) city enforcement of its open housing law, (2) suspension of the licenses of real-estate brokers guilty of discriminatory sales, and (3) withdrawal by the Chicago Real Estate Board of its suit before the Illinois supreme court contesting the legality of the state's open occupancy laws. Although these demands amounted to a drastic de-escalation of those of July 10, they were still unacceptable to the other side. All that was agreed upon was that another meeting would be held on Friday. That meeting also failed to produce an accord, and the absence of Daley indicated on the city's part the lack of faith that such discussions could be fruitful. The city had other plans. At 10 A.M., the mayor appeared on television to appeal for calm and to announce that Chicago was seeking legal remedies against the demonstrators. Judge Cornelius J. Harrington of the chancery court, after a brief hearing, granted an injunction against eight individuals, their associates, and three organizations. Demonstrations were to be limited to one per day, their numbers restricted to five hundred, and a twenty-four-hour advance notice, submitted in writing to the police superintendent, was required. In addition, night marches were proscribed, as well as marches between the hours of 7:30 and 9 A.M. and 4:40 and 6 P.M.

"The city's move is unjust, illegal, and unconstitutional," Martin contended. He was in a truculent mood, "We are prepared to put thousands into the streets if need be. The city hasn't seen the number of people we can put there." But would he defy the injunction? "It is possible we will violate the injunction," he said. But, after conferring with his legal advisers, among whom was NAACP's James Nabrit, III, he stated the next day that he would fight the order in the courts. The city could make a strong prima facie case for having been motivated solely by a desire to preserve public order. Various fanatic white organizations were appearing in greater numbers at the demonstrations. The Fuehrer of the American Nazi Party, George Lincoln Rockwell, had arrived with his henchmen to fan the flames. And the sale of arms in white communities was frighteningly brisk. There was also to be considered the hardening disaffection of the North to black protest. Within a few months, Professor C. Vann Woodward's article "What Happened to the Civil Rights Movement?" would draw a parallel between the course of civil rights after Reconstruction and during the mid-1960's. "We accepted tokenism," a Justice Department official was quoted as saying, "What more do they want?" In its coverage of the Chicago crisis, *Newsweek* felt constrained to advise Martin of the provocative character of his demonstrations.

Even if the Vietnam issue had not strained relations almost to the breaking point, there was virtually no possibility of White House assistance in Chicago. The political power of the Daley machine within the Democratic Party, the socio-economic thrust, as opposed to the formerly legalistic, of the SCLC's Northern campaign, the complex interrelationships of Eastern finance, Midwestern industry and labor, and federal power—all these constituted built-in restraints upon pro-civil rights intervention by Washington outside the South. Even sympathetic observers were beginning to believe that Martin was heading for a Donnybrook in Chicago. Andy Young was openly worried: "We're not too hopeful. We haven't been able to put on enough pressure yet. In Birmingham and Selma we almost needed martial law before we got anywhere." Meanwhile, in Congress, legislation was introduced to curtail civil rights demonstrations by Representative Roman Pucinski, an Illinois Democrat and formerly a consistent supporter of civil rights legislation.

The Movement finally concluded that, if success could come only through the peril of supreme social crisis, it must euchre out city hall with a final dangerous play, the Cicero march. Martin announced on August 21 that he would lead his people to Cicero the following Sunday. Cook County Sheriff Richard B. Ogilvie said the march was "suicidal." Daley pleaded with Martin not to go through with his plan. Jerome Huey. whose martyrdom the SCLC busied itself recalling to the black community, had been killed there late in May. Fifteen years before, Cicero had discharged into one of the nation's worst race riots, as the result of the purchase of a single home by one black family. Still completely white and composed of tidy, lower-middle-class Slavic homeowners, Cicero could easily become Martin's Golgotha. Contacted by the press by phone in Atlanta, he solemnly replied, "We fully intend to have the march. We have talked with Ogilvie about this and announced our plans last Saturday." Governor Otto Kerner placed the National Guard and the state police on ready alert. Martin thanked the governor for his precautions but also made the point that it "was tragic that we can march into Southern bastions of segregation, such as Mississippi, without armed military protection, but we cannot march peacefully into a Northern suburb such as Cicero without armed escort of guardsmen." The Cicero officials granted a march permit, and the chief of police, Joseph Barloga, made the encouraging statement that he did not anticipate trouble from Cicero residents.

On Thursday night, Martin revved up the audience at New Liberty Baptist Church: "No one is going to turn me around at this point." The people responded in a gallimaufry of approvals: "We can walk in outer space, but we can't walk in the streets of Cicero without the National Guard." His verbal armaments were as complete as ever. The shouting crowd was ready to tramp off to Cicero that very night. For the most part, these were older people, religious folk whose Southern agrarian roots still showed in the bitter soil of the urban ghetto. But what the Cicero march gave Martin —really for the first time—was the unanimous support of the young militants. Russ Meek remembers his excitement when it was first announced. He and Chester Robinson, head of the West Side Organization, prepared to collaborate totally with the CCCO. Robert Lucas of CORE and Monroe Sharp of SNCC were also enthusiastic, as was Frank Ditto. From the beginning, the Chicago Freedom Movement had been riven by internal feuding. Reverend Carl Fuquah of the local NAACP continually expressed a lack of confidence in SCLC leadership. Any movement embracing such a wide range of personalities and large number of disparate organizations would have escaped dissension only by a miracle.

The major source of disagreement, however, centered around two issues—the cast of the leadership, which the militants charged was fatally middle class (and vitiated by its reliance upon white advisers), and the tactical sanity of alarming and arming the white community with no realistic achievement other than forcing it to suffer marches and prayer vigils in its streets. The marches "made many people who perhaps would at least have been maybe neutral, because of social pressure, to become anti-Negro," Russ Meek argued. Open housing was a chimera, the miltants contended. Until the economic situation of the ghetto-dweller improved, necessarily only a small number of middle-class blacks and the exceptionally frugal slum family could move to better neighborhoods. And those neighborhoods, because of the psychoses invariably triggered in integrated situations, would expeditiously turn themselves into substandard, all-black ghettos. More to the point, token open housing diverted the black community from the crucial task of improving conditions in the places where the overwhelming black majority would continue to live for an indefinite period of time. Finally, the militants argued, were it even possible, the dispersion of black people to white suburbs would destroy their potential political power base.

Such misgivings notwithstanding, Cicero created a black *union sacrée*. More than a dozen marches had already taken place, and the white communities were now polarized; the damage was already done. The innate combativeness of youthful activists now found the Cicero challenge irresistible. To savor the psychological satisfaction of penetrating this bulwark of white racism, they were prepared to submit to the grating discipline of nonviolence—provided, of course, the "honkies didn't get too rough." As the fateful day approached, the exhilarating spectacle of the SCLC, CORE, SNCC, CCCO, the youth gangs, three or more other organizations, and a sprinkling of whites marching to Cicero with Martin King in the lead gripped the people's imagination and appalled city hall. Andy Young's martial law conditions were materializing. But the Selma bridge syndrome was embedded in the psychopolitical constitution of the SCLC. Two days before the march, a compromise was reached with the city administration and the business community.

"The total eradication of housing discrimination has been made possible," the *Tribune* rhapsodized, "Never before has such a far-reaching move been made." Mayor Daley said it was a "great day" for Chicago. Martin was equally effusive. Later, he wrote, "Our nonviolent marches in Chicago . . . brought about a housing agreement which, if enacted, will be the strongest step toward open housing taken in any city in the nation." At the time, he cautioned that "We will watch this day by day, week by week, and month by month. We will begin this week." What had happened was that, on Friday, August 26, a plenary meeting of all parties, black, white, civic, business, and official, met in the Monroe Room of Palmer House to conclude what became known as the "Summit Agreement."

The seventy-nine participants presented an array of considerable distinction. Archbishop Cody, caparisoned in his ecclesiastical raiment (and affectionately dubbed "Louisiana Fats" by some of the civil rights conferees) lent a special splendor to the deliberations. The drama of the occasion was heightened by the underlying fact that the Summit Conference represented essentially the achievement of an entente between America's most powerful private citizen and America's most powerful city boss. The agreement consisted of ten points. Real estate brokers were to be required by the Commission on Human Relations to post in a prominent place a summary of the city's policy on open housing, and the city, in addition to processing housing complaints within forty-eight hours, compacted to redouble its surveillance of housing conditions and to encourage the adoption of appropriate state housing legislation. The second point, obscured in a thicket of partially self-contradictory legalese, conceded no more than the promise by the city Board of Realtors to "withdraw all opposition to the philosophy of open occupancy legislation" but categorically not to withdraw its appeal before the Cook County circuit court against the city's fair housing ordinance. The Chicago Housing Authority committed itself to striving to provide a communally wholesome dispersal of public-housing projects in the future; recipients of county aid were to be encouraged to seek accommodations without regard to discriminatory practices by communities; the Department of Urban Renewal, in addition to vigilantly reporting cases of discrimination to the Commission on Human Relations, was bound to assist families in relocating in every area of the city; both the Cook County Council of Insured Savings Associations and the Chicago Mortgage Bankers Association agreed to provide "equal service and to lend mortgage money to all qualified families, without regard to race." It was noted that the CRS pledged itself to investigate discriminatory practices by banking and mortgage institutions within the purview of federal agencies; the Chicago Conference on Religion and Race (comprised of prominent Catholic, Protestant, and Jewish organizations) committed itself to aid, by suasion, information centers, and money, minority groups in acquiring improved housing; the Chicago Association of Commerce and Industry, the Commercial Club, the Chicago Mortgage and Bankers Association, the Chamber of Commerce, the Metropolitan Housing and Planning Council, the Chicago Federation of Labor, and the Industrial Union Council agreed that "their organizations have a major stake in working out the problems of fair housing and would do their utmost to promote this goal." The final article called for a "continuing body," comprised of the major "leadership organizations" in the city, to undertake the responsibility of mounting education and "action" programs in order to facilitate all these goals.

Like his spiritual predecessor, Martin Luther King had launched the militant phase of his Chicago drive by posting theses on the door of city hall. With the Summit Agreement, he had seemed almost to duplicate Martin Luther's document denouncing the peasants. Chester Robinson was bitter: "This agreement is a lot of words that give us nothing specific we can undertake. We want it to say: apartments should be painted once a year; community people should have jobs in their community . . . The situation is just pathetic. We're sick and tired of middle class people telling us what we want." Monroe Sharp stated that "We reject the terms of the agreement that Martin Luther King made. The rank and file Negro is a new breed of cat who rejects this." For the militants, the Cicero march was henceforth a *sine qua non* of ideological independence and racial manhood. They were not alone in their disappointment. Martin's trusting followers were restive, and he felt the need to speak brazenly of the consequences of the city's bad faith or failure. At Stone Temple Baptist Church, he told them that, if the Summit compact was "not carried out, Chicago can get ready for a real demonstration." Apparently, he was relying heavily upon the unwritten portion of the agreement. He promised that the unions, particularly the UAW, would locate many of their black members in white neighborhoods. Furthermore, and still unwritten, he posited the minimal gauge of the Summit Agreement to be a 1 per cent integration of all of Chicago's white communities by April 30, 1967.

"His morality derives from where *he* is, not from where his followers are," a contributor to the clubbish *New York Review of Books* wrote, with Chicago very much in mind. Martin's morality was rattled in its sinews by Chicago. He had frankly been "running scared." His organization came within a suburb of humiliating failure, and that failure would have engulfed not only the prophet of nonviolence but also the single remaining populist force capable of containing black proletarian anguish. Numerical inferiority was always supposed to provide an ultimate safeguard against perpetual insurgency by black Americans. But, after Watts, it was not at all clear that black Americans understood the mathematics of urban violence. Certain forces within the white establishment sensed the danger. The August 22 *Newsweek* attempted to fend off this danger in an issue entirely filled with color photos and wishfully optimistic commentary on racial progress. *Christian Century* also knew how important it was to boost Martin. Fortunately, Martin knew how to support Martin far more adroitly than the sympathizers. If there was a touch of disingenuousness and more than a drop of self-deception in his assessment of the Chicago treaty, there would also be some redemption in the fact that he went away from this experience with a much clearer understanding of the forces he was up against. More important, he began to identify lucidly the forces that the impoverished black American was up against. The period of rhetoric—"jive," as the militants called it—was closing and a brief season of political realism had begun.

Realism is inevitably deflationary. The long months of federal insouciance, ghetto apathy, and city unscrupulousness had finally brought Martin to a plateau of new awareness mixed with touchy self-protection and political sagacity. His words delivered to an excited church audience immediately after the Summit Agreement bear out this contention. Martin's lieutenants had been afraid to announce that, for at least several months, there would be no more demonstrations. They spoke of more mass agitation and of continuing rent strikes. "Let's face the fact," Martin told them when he arrived, "Most of us are going to be living in the ghetto five, ten years from now. But we've got to get some things straightened out right away. I'm not going to wait a month to get the roaches out of my house." He did not mention that his solicitous property managers had done so before he moved into the Lawndale apartment nor that, even then, he was looking for more congenial accommodations. "Morally, we ought to have what we say in the slogan, 'Freedom Now.' But it all doesn't come now. That's a sad fact of life you have to live with"— never before had he openly imposed such practical limits upon the struggles of the disadvantaged. Certainly it was true—no diploma in urbanology was needed to know it— that, unless and until American society accepted the challenge and the cost of eradicating poverty, slums and slum culture would be governed by an iron law of self-perpetuation. The tragedy of the ghetto was that the progress of civil rights in the South and the national concern for black deprivation in the abstract were reaching a peak more than a decade too late for mobilization into effective antipoverty programs.

Martin cannot have ignored the overwhelming limitations upon a program calculated to force the white business and political establishments into significant material concessions to an economically marginal community. Simply put, how could Chicago's ghetto blacks, with average family incomes of $4,700, purchase homes ranging from $15,000 to $30,000 in white areas? The comparable incomes of the whites in the neighborhoods targeted by the SCLC were between $7,500 and $8,500. Nevertheless, Martin had earlier promised to lead them through the white *cordon sanitaire* to the promised land of suburbia. And he had not hedged his promises then with sober reservations. The walls were supposed to come tumbling down, weakened by the seismic tramp of thousands of poorly shod feet and crumbled by the reverberations from thousands of voices singing "We Shall Overcome." He knew better, of course. His tactic of incendiary rhetoric and mass demonstrations was determined in part by his canny Sorelian appreciation of the efficacy of mythology among the ignorant and the destitute. One must believe that Jericho would founder if there was ever to be a reasonable possibility of getting to Cicero.

Mythology by itself, however, incorporated its own disillusioning antidote. It predetermined just that situation in which the mythologizer would have to preach the "sad fact of life which you have to live with" to his followers before returning to Atlanta. He had not—nor had the SCLC, the Agenda Committee, or the CCCO—done the required homework in Chicago. The Movement leaders cannot be excused for not having, while they marched, simultaneously endeavored to construct a political front in the city in order to educate the community people to the indifference of the Daley machine. Despite the inevitable charges of outside interference and organizational self-seeking, the major task of the SCLC should have been to assist in the selection and financing of aldermanic candidates to oppose city hall. What they had done so well in the South—educating and registering black voters (black voting levels in the city had declined in recent elections)—should have been duplicated in Chicago. The unionization of nearly ten thousand slum tenants by November, to be formally affiliated with the AFL-CIO, and their recognition by the real estate agencies was a considerable achievement and a step in the direction of ghetto political and economic power. But this postdated the Summit Agreement and seemed to be appreciated more for its propaganda value by the SCLC than for its practical long-range potential.

Mayor Daley had said that the Summit Agreement was a "great day" for Chicago. The *Christian Century* article on the settlement was titled "Still King." Most black Chicagoans regarded it as a sell-out. Most of the SCLC staff admitted that the Movement failed to achieve its goals. The black bourgeoisie of Chicago conceded the insufficiency of the agreement but stressed the significance of the precedent of compelling the mayor to come to the conference table to admit that drastic improvement of housing conditions caused by racial discrimination was long overdue. It praised the symbolism of the Palmer House accord and expressed a willingness to await its implementation in the fullness of time. Meanwhile, the militants prepared to lead the march to Cicero, postponing it once. It finally took place on September 4, with 2,700 National Guardsmen and 700 police alternating in the task of escorting the 205 angry participants. Thirty-nine people were arrested, fourteen seriously injured, and the return from Cicero took place under a steady downpour of bottles and rocks. Frank Ditto second-thought himself out of the march and, through James Bevel, the SCLC stated that the march "would not have any effect one way or the other." Those who went to Cicero—Lucas, Meek, Sharp, and the organizations they led, CORE, SNCC, the Brothers for Afro-American Equality, the League of Labor and Education, and assorted others—considered the march an impressive antinonviolent success. It was almost exclusively black and memorably combative.

The coruscating debate around the value of the Summit Agreement obscured two highly relevant historical facts. If the Agreement omitted any mention of a timetable and amounted to little more than a good-will pledge from the city, business, and realtors, it was no less specific and considerably more comprehensive, by comparison, than any of Martin's previous accords. To judge his Chicago campaign solely on the strength of the final paper compromise was to apply a standard to nonviolent activity that had not been applied in the past, or only secondarily. If Birmingham was a triumph, then Chicago certainly ought not to have been assessed as a virtual rout. Segregation did not end in Birmingham after Martin left the local leadership with an incomplete and vague agreement, in the same measure as integration was not much advanced by the time he left Chicago. It had always been Martin's position that, after the articulation of a community's demands and the mobilization of its people, the onus of effective implementation was the responsibility of the local civil rights leadership. His *modus operandi* in Chicago was entirely consonant with that in Montgomery, St. Augustine, Selma, and Birmingham.

The storm of criticism and rebuke after Chicago reflected the altered climate of civil rights after Selma and the particular exigencies of a Northern ghetto. First, Martin had been upstaged by the Black Power exponents and was more vulnerable than in the past. Second, the crux of the Chicago dilemma was that the city machine's emasculation of the political power of the ghetto precluded the kind of local implementative sequel that was characteristic of the South. The prevailing belief among Chicago blacks was that what the SCLC did not accomplish probably would remain undone for an intolerably indeterminate period of time. In large measure, these harsh judgments and unrealistic aspirations and the debilitating reliance upon charisma were the unwitting responsibility of Martin King. One man cannot come to town —certainly not to Chicago—and always save its people, as Julian Bond had wisely admonished.

12

Killers of the Dream

> The philosophers have interpreted the world.
> The point, however, is to change it.
>
> MARX

"FOR YEARS I LABORED with the idea of reforming the existing institutions of the society, a little change here, a little change there," Martin said in the summer after Chicago. "Now I feel quite differently. I think you've got to have a reconstruction of the entire society, a revolution of values." This social reconstruction and revolution of values entailed at the barest minimum, he added, the rebuilding of the cities, the nationalization of "some" industries, a review of America's foreign investments, and a guaranteed annual income. J. Pius Barbour has always maintained that Martin was a revolutionary, that he found more of value in the methodology of Marxism than his clerical and civil rights responsibilities ever permitted him to divulge. One need not, of course, attribute this new economic and political radicalism to Marxian predilections. Martin's fascination for the socialist ideas implicit in the Social Gospel was probably more relevant. And the Chicago debacle was undoubtedly the immediate stimulus of what might be termed nonviolent populism.

Immediately after the Summit Agreement, Martin began to emphasize the economic enfranchisement of the poor far more sedulously than in the past. A few days after the

Palmer House meeting, he addressed some two thousand
people at Liberty Baptist Church, two-thirds of them black.
Jobs were henceforth the paramount goal, and Operation
Breadbasket was to carry the major responsibility for achieving
breakthroughs in the hiring of the disadvantaged by commerce
and industry. "Where Negroes are confined to the lowest
paying jobs," he stated, "they must get together to organize
a union in order to have the kind of power that could enter
into collective bargaining with their employers." Here was
the first public expression of the tactic that Martin would
utilize in Memphis nineteen months later. If large department stores failed to hire blacks, it would be necessary to
enter the stores and "try on clothes all day long." He was
coming to this position not a moment too soon, for Chicago's
militants were in a rancorous mood. The Liberty Baptist
Church speech was interrupted by SNCC's Monroe Sharp,
whose followers demanded that he be given the microphone.
Sharp's speech was bitter but not devoid of sound criticism.
He excoriated the black aldermen, blasted the Summit Agreement, and took Martin to task for his counterproductive
marches into white communities. Martin was visibly shaken
by Sharp's attack, and, although his rebuttal brought applause from the audience, this was far more a tour de force
of rhetoric than a reasoned refutation of the SNCC leader's
charges.

The manifest inadequacies of the Summit Agreement and
the unconventional position on Vietnam resulted in an open
hunting season on Martin King and the nonviolent movement in 1967. White liberals were a special disappointment.
His Southern experience should have inured Martin to their
fecklessness. If he had formerly said repeatedly that there were
legions of Ralph McGills in Dixie who would denounce the
extremists at the right moment, by now he had learned that
those denunciations almost never came. It was masochistically
optimistic, therefore, but altogether typical of Martin King

to suppose that Northern liberals would remain faithful once
he shifted his operations from the South and extended the
terrain of nonviolent combat to encompass national economic and international policy issues. And there was irony in
the results of his strategy for the nonviolent movement was
predicated upon the conviction that dramatization of social
and racial evils would puncture the dike of white indifference,
releasing white guilt feelings. The delta of bigotry, to im-
provise a Kingian metaphor, would be irrigated by the Nile
of Judeo-Christian morality. Instead, many tough-minded
liberals paid increasing attention to the mumblings of Black
Power advocates, and, the more violent the actions, the more
inattentive these liberals were to Martin Luther King's movement.

When *Where Do We Go from Here?*, his last book, was
published, *New York Review of Books* carried a virtual epi-
taph. "He has been outstripped by his times," Andrew Kopkind wrote, "overtaken by the events which he may have
obliquely helped to produce but would not predict." This was a
middle-class tome, Kopkind continued, replete with enumera-
tions of clocks, threshing machines, and blood plasma that unknown black geniuses had first devised, but devoid of hard
programmatic content for the black destitute: "Conventional
commentators these days like to speak of King's 'nobility' and
the purity of his humanism, and they sigh that the world is
not ready for him. But it is more accurate to say that King is
not ready for the world." According to this optic, Martin was
already consigned to the pantheon of civil rights immortals,
along with Frederick Douglass, Booker T. Washington, and
Walter White, to name but a very few. The cameras of
mobile television units had no place for nonviolent leaders.
The media yielded to a monopoly of Stokely Carmichael,
Floyd McKissick, H. Rap Brown, and burning cities; the
news delectated over every lugubrious pronouncement of the
Black Power militants.

One by one, Martin's traditional allies were deserting him. The faint-hearted liberals concluded that the pace of civil rights had become improvidently rapid. Now was the time for a pause, they said, and for consolidation of the remarkable gains made by American blacks. The Chicago director of the NAACP charged that Martin's intemperate campaign in that city had cost Senator Paul Douglas, a venerable champion of civil rights, his seat. The national headquarters of the NAACP and the Urban League went on record as opposing the conjunction of civil rights and the war in Asia. As early as October, 1965, Dr. Ralph Bunche, another Nobel laureate, stated that Martin "should positively and publicly give up one role or the other," that of civil rights leader or that of international conciliator. The knife was given another agonizing twist by Bayard Rustin, who insisted that the spill-over of civil rights into international diplomacy would hobble the progress of total black citizenship. Some SCLC personnel were prepared to read into Bayard's opposition to Martin the insidious power of the superpatriotic George Meany, head of the AFL-CIO, whose organization provided the bulk of the funds for the A. Philip Randolph Institute, of which Bayard was the executive director. Rustin's maverick career makes this hypothesis quite implausible, however. A difference of principle with his sponsors would undoubtedly have resulted in his severing connections with the institute.

Attorney Stanley Levison, charged with much of the fund-raising and most of the superintendence of SCLC stock investment, advised Martin that his Vietnam position would bankrupt the organization. "I don't care if we don't get five cents in the mail," Martin told him, "I'm going to keep on preaching my message." In fact, the revenues of the SCLC slightly increased after his forthright statements on the war in March and April. But this was one of the rare elements of encouragement. On March 25, he was in Chicago to call for an immediate negotiated settlement of the Vietnam war in the coliseum. This was the first time Martin had led a peace march, a patent indication of the quality of his commitment. "We must combine the fervor of the civil rights movement with the peace movement," he told the crowd.

The desertion of the civil rights leadership was embarrassingly manifest at a fund-raising banquet in Great Neck, New York, attended by Dr. John Morsell of the NAACP and Whitney Young, among others. At the conclusion of the speeches, Martin and Whitney came together to talk about Vietnam. In a matter of minutes, they became unaware of bystanders. It was the most heated public exchange that any of Martin's friends recall. "Whitney," Martin shouted, "what you're saying may get you a foundation grant [which it later did], but it won't get you into the kingdom of truth." Young angrily dismissed Martin's recent preoccupation with urban poverty as a sham. He, Young, had the key to viable urban programs, not Martin. Looking at King's expensive suit and burnished alligator shoes, he shot out, "You're eating well!" Friends separated the eminent leaders before more damagingly quotable words could be exchanged.

Martin's popularity continued to slip. In January, the Gallup Poll revealed that he was no longer in the category of the ten most admired persons. He may have been consoled by the findings of the *Chicago Defender* survey late in 1966, which claimed that he was preferred to Dr. Jackson by Chicago's blacks 21.5 to 1 and that he surpassed Elijah Muhammed and Stokely Carmichael each by a rough 70 per cent. Vietnam, despite the condemnations of Bunche, Young, Wilkins, and Jackie Robinson, was now a moral fixation. He spoke of it on nearly every public occasion. James Bevel was also deeply involved in the peace movement. After the Chicago campaign, Bevel was granted a leave of absence from the SCLC in order to devote his energies to recruitment of black youth for the developing antiwar front. Martin's antiwar stance now found an official vehicle in the Spring Mobilization campaign, mounted by a variety of pacifist organizations and presided over by A. J. Muste, vigorously assisted by Dr. Benjamin Spock and Yale University Chaplain William Sloan Coffin.

On April 4, he appeared once again in New York's Riverside Church to speak to an overflow crowd about Vietnam. For two years now, he had been speaking out against American policy in Vietnam from the rostrum and the printed page. There was nothing new in what Martin was to say that Tuesday evening. In essence, it was a repetition of his *Chicago Defender* apologia of early 1966. Nevertheless, news coverage and public attention seized upon the Riverside address as a special semaphore of his position. Martin himself referred to the "spring of 1967, when I first made public my opposition to my government's policy," as though this was the date of a new departure on foreign policy. The ferment in the country, the accelerating course of the war, and the special significance of a New York speech obviously influenced his own historical optic.

He confessed to being "perplexed" by the war; he had no godlike certitude about the wrongness of the American position or panacea for swift resolution of the conflict. Yet, there were certain imperatives involved that he could not sidestep —his primary calling to the ministry and the brotherhood of mankind that that commitment entailed. The pragmatic reason for his denunciation of the war, however, brought him back to the pressing dilemma of black emancipation, where his expertise should have been beyond reproach. He wrote, during this period,

> Perhaps a more tragic recognition of reality took place when it became clear to me that the war was doing far more than devastating the hopes of the poor at home. It was sending their sons and their brothers and their husbands to fight and die and in extraordinarily high proportions relative to the rest of the population. . . . I could not be silent in the face of such cruel manipulation of the poor.

At Riverside Church, he reiterated his three reasons for opposing the war, more eloquently than ever before. "The Great Society has been shot down on the battlefields of Vietnam," he told the audience. If a negotiated settlement were not soon reached, Chinese involvement would become certain and world war equally inescapable. He struck again the chords of his ministerial and nonviolent message: "It would be very inconsistent for me to teach and preach non-violence in this situation and then applaud violence when thousands and thousands of people, both adults and children, are being maimed and mutilated and many killed in this war, so that I still feel and live by the principle, 'Thou shalt not kill.'" If the war continued, the next phase of civil disobedience, he promised, would be massive antiwar protest. Martin's Riverside speech made at least one very important convert immediately. The Senior King's certainty until that moment that his son was making a terrible mistake was overcome. "When he finished his great speech, I knew—the whole audience knew—the man was right," Ebenezer's pastor admitted.

A composite of Martin's admonitions during the early months of 1967 reveals a political maturity and courage possessed by no other national civil rights leader and, with such exceptions as the Periclean Senator William Fulbright and, later, the quixotic Senator Eugene McCarthy, unexpressed by the great majority of national political leaders. "We are committing atrocities equal to any perpetrated by the Vietcong. . . . The bombs in Vietnam explode at home—they destroy the dream and possibility for a decent America," he said in Chicago, late in March. "Honestly," he told the Overseas Press Club late in April, "if I had to confront this problem, I would be a conscientious objector. I would not even serve as a chaplain." At the end of May, in Geneva, he called again for an immediate negotiated termination of the "immoral" war. At Riverside, he spelled out a five-point program for peace in

Vietnam: an end to all bombing, North and South; the declaration of a unilateral cease-fire to prepare a climate for negotiation; a curtailment of military build-ups throughout Southeast Asia, to prevent new editions of Vietnam; realistic acceptance of the popular preponderance of the National Liberation Front; establishment of a definite date by which all foreign troops would be withdrawn from the Vietnam theater, in accordance with the 1954 Geneva agreement.

On April 15, Martin, with Benjamin Spock and Harry Belafonte, was one of the leaders of a monster demonstration of pacifists numbering in excess of 125,000, moving from Central Park through New York City's streets to the United Nations Plaza Building. Before the speeches began, Martin, with five others, delivered a formal note to Ralph Bunche, U.N. undersecretary-general: "We rally at the United Nations in order to affirm support of the principles of peace, universality, equal rights, and self-determination of peoples included in the charter and acclaimed by mankind, but violated by the United States." During the parade, a group of seventy youths burned their draft cards in Central Park, and, before the end of the day's speeches, Floyd McKissick and Stokely Carmichael mounted the podium to rage against the genocidal policies of the American Government in Vietnam. It is certain that Martin was not privy to the first event and was far from enthusiastic about the second.

His address was not in the category of the "I Have a Dream" speech, perhaps because he was much less a dreamer by this time. It was, nonetheless, the highlight of the rally, ending in a deafening ovation. He deplored the burden upon the black and the poor, imposed by this war. Movingly, he drew a word-picture of the indiscriminate American devastation of life and property in Vietnam. The people "watch as we poison their water, as we kill a million acres of their crops. . . . They must weep as the bulldozers roar through their areas preparing to destroy the precious trees. They wander into the hospitals with at least twenty casualties from American firepower for one Vietcong inflicted injury." Out of this rally came the proposal, which he enthusiastically endorsed, of a Vietnam Summer, a proposal to put thousands of pacifist volunteers to work pricking and canalizing American consciences about the war.

He had not signed the manifesto of the Spring Mobilization campaign because of the reference to genocide that it contained. His basic nature and long experience in civil rights remained proof against the genre of passion that overwhelmed common sense. But his identification with the cause was now beyond question. The students at Berkeley clamored for his appearance at their Spring Mobilization affair, and, late in April, he arrived on the campus, guided by one of the university's black deans and followed by an impressive cross-section of the world press. The reception passed with flawless enthusiasm, and his informal chat with the "Afro-American" students was a success. As Martin was leaving them to address a group of white students, he was stopped cold by a student, a white youth, who extemporized a plea that moved him visibly:

> Dr. King, I understand your reservations about running for President, but you're a world figure, you're the most important man we've got, you're the only one who can head a third-party ticket. And so when you make your decision, remember that there are many of us who are going to have to go to jail for many years, give up our citizenship, perhaps. This is a very serious thing.

Spock was not the answer, the student continued, as Martin stood motionless, apparently waiting for the young man to stir him even more. "I have watched King with dozens of people as he nods and half-listens, and this is the first time I have ever seen anyone get to him," David Halberstam wrote. Later, in the limousine returning to the airport, Martin admitted to Halberstam that this encounter had penetrated.

The sound and fury of the militants and the parochial optic of the civil rights leadership was no longer adequate for him, he added. He still had no intention whatsoever of running for President, but the April experiences had convinced him that his charismatic force was desperately needed to maximize the power of the peace movement and, by a process of political capillary action, the civil rights movement.

There is no reason to dignify by rebuttal those who argue that Martin's Vietnam position was merely an egocentric maneuver to recoup the prestige lost in the encounter with Black Power and the credibility damaged by the Chicago debacle. Still, the less cynical critics—those who believe in Martin's sincerity but also believe that he began to doubt the efficacy of his solutions to the post–lunch-counter and polling-booth crises of the late 1960's—are not so readily dismissed. He was in serious danger of being written off by the two established civil rights organizations (the NAACP and the Urban League) and by young black extremists. "The Movement is back where it began," an Urban League spokesman said, after the United Nations Plaza speech, "It's us and the NAACP." "The main function of the nonviolent Negroes," Calvin Hernton wrote, "appears now to be that of keeping the other Negroes in their places." Hernton went on to make the astute comment that "The species of the non-violent Negro, as a progessive social force towards the liberation of black people in America, has been eclipsed by the very forces that have called the species into being and yet prevail against it—the forces of compromise, corruption, hate, and violence." Eldridge Cleaver's *Soul on Ice* denounced Martin's "self-flagellating" policy, articulating in virile prose the attitude of the very angry and very desperate young ghetto male. The verdict was that Martin was finished.

If Vietnam was a matter of conscience antedating the Chicago experiment, after the Summit Agreement it provided an issue now grander than Southern desegregation and more palpable than the hypothetical solutions to urban poverty. Whatever escapism was involved, the emphasis upon Vietnam was primarily an indication of Martin's careful appraisal of the relationship between racial unrest, economic destitution, and the spiraling national investment in a war whose dividends were patently marginal to the American people.

In December, 1966, Martin, Coretta, Bernard Lee, and Dora McDonald, Martin's personal secretary, went to Jamaica for a three-week period of relaxation and writing. Away from the abrasive debates over the war and civil rights ideology, he swam with Coretta in the swimming pool of their rented villa, walked along the deserted beach, and ordered his thoughts for the final chapters of *Where Do We Go from Here: Chaos or Community?* He intended to answer for himself and his critics some of the divisive questions that afflicted the black man as well as American society. The editor of all his books, the late Mrs. Hermine Popper, was distressed when she received his manuscript. Martin had reproduced much of the text of *Why We Can't Wait* and portions of well-worn sermons and speeches. Mrs. Popper was to spend the next two months editing and rewriting these pastiche materials. Although he enjoyed himself in Jamaica, Martin was obviously a tired man. His originality seemed spent.

Nevertheless, his fatigue did not preclude a quantity of incisive observations in *Where Do We Go from Here.* Whereas he had placed great faith in the basic decency of white America's conscience after Montgomery, now he forswore the earlier optimism, without committing the opposite philosophical excess of despairing of the positive attitudinal and institutional changes that could be nonviolently forced upon the majority of whites. It was certain that racial discrimination in America was a "congenital deformity. . . . Historically it was so acceptable in national life that today it still only lightly burdens the conscience." No doubt there were militant theorists who would argue that Martin's admission of a "congenital" condition of racism placed him in the illogical quandary of accurately diagnosing a malignancy and then unscientifically prescribing placebos against it. But realism for Martin could never mean thoroughgoing cynicism about human nature. He still had faith in the redemptive power of moral witness. Conceding the pervasiveness of racism, he was driven to question the conduct of white liberals. He had inveighed before against their quiescence in the South, and the retreat of his Northern allies continued to surprise him: "The white liberal must escalate his support for the struggle for racial justice rather than de-escalate it. This would be a tragic time to forsake and withdraw from the struggle. The need for commitment is greater today than ever." These were sage words, but for sagacious people. Nor did his appeal for common sense make the slightest headway among the black militants. He mused provocatively about the militants' aversion to nonviolent discipline. People whose entire lives had passively been spent in the rat-infested squalor of urban tenements and under the sealed sphere of violent social and economic exploitation now derived a strange sense of manhood, he wrote, in loudly refusing to reject the opportunity to strike a white bystander or policeman. This point was much too cerebral to interest the bitter young militants.

In July, three months after the publication of *Where Do We Go from Here*, racial disturbances flared in Newark, New Jersey, and Detroit, Michigan. The loss of life and the property damage in Detroit surpassed everything of its kind in American history. There no longer appeared to be any place for the sincere, "creative" moderation of a Martin Luther King, his nonviolent abstractions and gratuitous preoccupation with a remote war. Louis Lomax states that Martin even began to accept the "undeniable fact that violence paid off."

The truth is that Martin became even more opposed to violent social action after the July riots. But he also recognized the general public impression of nonviolent bankruptcy that had been fostered by the riots. Since Chicago, nonviolence had not demonstrated the capacity to play a "transforming role," he admitted later. Indeed, a review of the accomplishments of the SCLC in Chicago, after the Summit Agreement, were not impressive. Fewer than two thousand families had organized into tenants' unions and compelled landlords to recognize them officially and to make firm commitments. An SCLC-sponsored union-to-end-slums rent strike, lasting six months, achieved concessions for six hundred tenants in the Lawndale section of the city. Two grocery corporations, Hi-Low and National Tea, agreed to carry products of black corporations and to deposit in black banks the income from their stores located in the ghetto. These accomplishments, although symbolically impressive, left the surface of the problem barely scratched. Moreover, the labors of the SCLC staff in organizing a political machine in the ghetto aborted miserably. It was only in the wake of the July chaos that the readiness of the national business community to invest in the ghetto made it propitious for Martin's Chicago lieutenant, Reverend Jesse Jackson, to announce that Operation Breadbasket, focusing on jobs, would henceforth be a national undertaking.

Meanwhile, the barrage against Martin's foreign-policy position continued. In an article published posthumously, Martin stressed the underlying connection between racism and diplomatic unwisdom. "The American Marines might not even have been needed in Santo Domingo," he speculated, "had the American ambassador there been a man who was sensitive to the color dynamics that pervade the national life of the Dominican Republic." After all, black men would neither trade with South Africa nor perpetuate the species of economic exploitation characteristic of American investment in Latin America. In April, the *Detroit News* had coined the term "peace hawk" to describe Martin and warned in chorus with dozens of other papers that "he risks his credentials as an influential civil rights leader on the questionable merits of his foreign policy statements." *Life* was less diplomatic in decreeing that the SCLC leader "goes beyond his *personal right* to dissent when he connects progress and civil rights here with a proposal that amounts to abject surrender in Vietnam, and suggests that youths become conscientious objectors rather than serve." *Newsweek* observed neutrally that his and John Kenneth Galbraith's war pronouncements were portentous of the destruction of Lyndon Johnson's "vaunted consensus." Senator Edward Brooke, the sole black man in that august chamber, took issue with Martin on Vietnam. It remained for professional journalist Carl Rowan to write the most effective criticism. Rowan, a black man, had formerly been an ambassador to Finland and a chief of the United States Information Agency. Rowan's lengthy *Reader's Digest* article "Martin Luther King's Tragic Decision" was a masterly piece of political assassination. The cagey reservations of Martin's followers about Vietnam, the egotism of King, his frequent departures from prison to receive honors, his gratuitous alienation of the White House, the alleged infiltration of the SCLC by Communists—all this was carefully rehearsed in order to diminish the reliability of Martin as a representative leader.

The Supreme Court, the mainstay of civil rights, had begun to reflect the satiety of the nation with black demands and civil disobedience. In November, 1966, Justice Byron White, who had consistently voted with the Warren court's majority, cast his vote to uphold the conviction of civil rights demonstrators in a lower court for trespassing in Tallahassee, Florida. It was the first judicial reverse of this nature suffered by the Movement since Montgomery. In June, 1967, the justices decreed that Martin's conviction by a Birmingham court for demonstrating without a permit was valid. He and eight others, including Fred Shuttlesworth, Ralph Abernathy, and

Wyatt Tee Walker, were to spend four days in a Birmingham jail in October. A week before surrendering to the authorities, Martin submitted his Bill of Rights for the Disadvantaged to the recently established Kerner Commission, charged by the President with the task of uncovering the causes of urban racial explosions. In prison, he made profitable use of the time to hammer out, with Ralph and Wyatt, his cellmates, the main outlines of an interracial coalition of the poor that would pressure the government into enacting legislation benefiting those below the poverty line. At an SCLC meeting in Atlanta in December, Martin presented his plan for a poor-people's march on Washington, to take place in April, 1968. Three thousand poor whites, American Indians, Americans of Mexican descent, and blacks (who would comprise the majority) were to converge on the capital and demonstrate nonviolently until Congress acted.

The following weeks were turbulently busy. No proposal could have been more unwelcome than Martin's poor-people's march to the capital. Having legalized the right of blacks to integrated hamburgers and polling booths, having designated more than $1 billion for their uplift and accepted the desirability of open housing if not the legal apparatus to enforce it, the white community was consterned by the planned inundation of Washington by thousands of proletarians. Professor C. Vann Woodward's heuristic question "What more do they want?" (in the *Harper's* article "What Happened to the Civil Rights Movement?") caught the dominant national mood. Speaking of black ambitions, *Christianity Today* lamented much later that "Their tragic misconception that the only barrier to a Negro heaven on earth—conceived in terms of national plenty—is lack of legislation and appropriation shows where modern welfare and government propaganda have brought us." Martin's position was that only a return to nonviolent demonstrations, on a scale grander than in the past, could prevent worse disasters during the summer of 1968: "I think we have come to the point where there is no longer a choice between nonviolence and riots. It must be militant, massive nonviolence, or riots." In 1964, he had stated that

> White Americans must be made to understand the basic motives underlying Negro demonstrations. Many pent-up resentments and latent frustrations are boiling inside the Negro, and he must release them. It is not a threat but a fact of history that if an oppressed people's pent-up emotions are not nonviolently released, they will be violently released. So let the Negro march. Let him make pilgrimages to city hall. Let him go on freedom rides. And above all, make an effort to understand why he must do this. For if his frustrations and despair are allowed to continue piling up, millions of Negroes will seek solace and security in black-nationalist ideologies.

Repeatedly, he had warned the nation (and militants had scathingly reproached him for it) that a rhythm of political and, later, socio-economic concessions had to be maintained in order to avoid black violence and permanent alienation. But the whites were not ready to understand, and pleas such as this merely confirmed his accommodationism in the eyes of the militants.

The SCLC leadership was not sure that the second march on Washington would not be counterproductive. Before the final plan was completed in mid-February, Martin summoned a January meeting of ministers in Miami, Florida, to obtain official sanction. The ministers voted to follow their leader, but it was obvious that they would have preferred to have been excused from this commitment. Bayard Rustin's frank statement to them that Martin now lacked the economic resources and federal forbearance characteristic of his past demonstrations and that he, Rustin, would not support the Poor People's Campaign further shook their confidence. For the moment, the Urban League and the NAACP refrained from public comment, but no special powers of divination were required to know that they disapproved. Martin threw himself into the campaign all the more determinedly, as his intimates and the public doubted or opposed it. He spoke of the "crisis we face in America" with more intensity and foreboding than before. "The stability of civilization, the potential of free government, and the simple honor of men is at stake," he proclaimed. He praised those who dissented from the easy consensus of uninquisitive patriotism and limited social meliorism. His Massey lectures, recorded for delivery over the Canadian Broadcasting Corporation, reflected this redoubled sense of urgency when he declared that "Nonviolent protest must now mature to a new level to correspond to heightened black impatience and stiffened white resistance." This "higher level is mass civil disobedience."

Regularly, he announced from the pulpit of Ebenezer and from a forest of rostrums the latest figures on civilian and military casualties, obliteration of villages, and compounding of economic costs of the Vietnam war. Whitney Young, at the request of Lyndon Johnson, and Senator Brooke, on his own initiative, went to Vietnam and returned, to plead that the conduct of the war be left to the White House and its experts. Patriotism, both suggested, commanded that the government be given the benefit of the doubt. "Our loyalties must transcend our race, our tribe, our class, and our nation," Martin countered, "and this means we must develop a world perspective." It was absurd to expect peace to emerge from a conflict in which American "integrity" was no longer credible. His government had supported the "murderous reign of Diem," poured gallons of napalm over the Vietnamese countryside, cynically distorted the goals and composition of the National Liberation Front, and then spoken of "aggression from the North" as if there were nothing more essential to the war. Although aggrieved by the asocial extremism of "hippie" youth, he interpreted its conduct as the result of the tragic debasement of American life and approved the diagnosis of Paul Goodman's *Growing Up Absurd*. The slaughter in Southeast Asia understandably reinforced the alienation of Americans younger than twenty-five. Martin saw that "in many respects their extreme conduct illuminates the negative effect of society's evils on sensitive young people."

For him, as for the youth, Lyndon Johnson was becoming the embodiment of inflexible, outmoded cant and political deviousness. In his final months, he believed that Johnson was devoid of statesmanship, in part because he had been trapped by the "military-industrial complex." But, mainly, it was a failing of character of the kind that had not afflicted John F. Kennedy. Kennedy could admit error, as he did after the Bay of Pigs—"But Lyndon Johnson seems to be unable to make this kind of statesmanlike gesture in connection with Vietnam." The President's domestic record was impressive and rested upon a realistic response to the racial crisis and superlative skill in guiding legislation through Congress. The ultimate credit for civil rights legislation, however, belonged a fortiori to the American black man, said Martin. More significant, unimplemented legislation was an embittering hoax. President Johnson had shown little diligence about implementing the very legislation that he had authored. Congress was now determined to play "Russian roulette with riots" rather than fund comprehensive poverty programs.

Martin rejected the depth and the durability of the much-discussed racial "backlash." A poll of black Americans in *Fortune* revealed an encouraging 80 per cent preference for his methods, and a slightly lower percentile of admiration for him personally. The Lou Harris poll indicated that most white Americans were ahead of the White House and Congress in believing that some measure of economic redress was owed the blacks. The march of the poor to Washington, Martin was certain, would very likely be the final positive prophylactic endeavor to avert a racial holocaust. "The flash point of Negro rage is close at hand," *Look* quoted him as saying. Obviously the White House was not listening, for it refused to accept the findings of its own National Advisory Commission on Civil Disorders, released late in February. The Commission's report directly charged white America with racism and predicted the rapid development of two separate, hostile, and unequal American racial societies, if drastic reforms were not undertaken. Vice-President Humphrey dutifully regretted the Kerner Report's harsh judgments.

Civil rights as a political issue now had limited and diminishing national appeal, but criticism of American entanglement in Southeast Asia suddenly became immensely appealing and viable at the close of 1967. In mid-October, the Conference of Concerned Democrats had met in Chicago under the chairmanship of Allard K. Lowenstein, to seek an alternative candidate to Lyndon Johnson. On November 30, Senator Eugene McCarthy announced his candidacy. Although his campaign was distressingly white and "metro-American," and although it made not the slightest curtsy in the direction of Martin King, whose months of painful unpopularity had been such an important force in shaping the anti-Vietnam position, McCarthy's New Hampshire Primary victory was an implicit and deeply rewarding vindication. On March 15, Robert Kennedy became an official candidate. The junior senator from New York also vigorously opposed the Administration's conduct of the war. Martin's position became much more respectable nationally and within the black community. He declined to endorse either candidate, although he congratulated the California Democratic Council on March 16 for backing McCarthy, adding that "Both men have the ability of grappling meaningfully and creatively with the problems in the cities and with racism." The important thing was to prevent the renomination of Lyndon Johnson.

If Martin had been right about Vietnam, it was possible that the people would come to see that he was also right in his appraisal of domestic poverty and racism. The candidacies of Senators Kennedy and McCarthy were certainly an encouragement, but his plans would not have altered if neither of them

had entered the presidential contest. Despite the continued
opposition of his top adivsors—Bayard Rustin, Michael Harrington, and others—at the January planning session in New
York he virtually forced the acquiescence of the SCLC in the
Poor People's Campaign. On February 12, 1968, his staff
finished the master plan for the Poor People's March. The
initial cadres would be drawn from ten cities and five rural
districts located in the East, Midwest, South, and Appalachia.
From Roxbury (Boston's ghetto), Chicago's Lawndale community, Mississippi, and West Virginia, three thousand volunteers would travel in caravan to a shanty town erected in
the capital. From there they would make daily sorties over a
three-month period (from April 20) to the Senate, the House
of Representatives, and the headquarters of cabinet agencies
such as Agriculture, Health, Education, and Welfare, and
Housing and Urban Development. "We will place the problems of the poor at the seat of government of the wealthiest
nation in the history of mankind," Martin wrote, "If that
power refuses to acknowledge its debt to the poor, it will have
failed to live up to its promise to insure life, 'liberty, and the
pursuit of happiness' to its citizens."

The core of their demands was to be a $12-billion "eco-
nomic bill of rights," guaranteeing employment to all the
able-bodied, viable incomes to those unable to work, an end to
housing discrimination, and the vigorous enforcement of integrated education. The demands were intentionally vague, not
restricted to specific legislation, in order to guard against the
seductions of empty promises and legislative feints. The intensity and size of the campaign would be determined by
congressional response. An unfavorable response would result
in thousands more converging on Washington, with the original contingent acting as nonviolent marshals. The plan also
envisaged sumultaneous demonstrations of the poor on the
West coast.

The stratagem was bold and imaginative. It provided, at

least theoretically, a solution to fundamental problems in non-violence. If, for the first time since leaving the South, Martin was looking to the Poor People's Campaign and beyond, toward a national political base, as the evidence supports, he might have achieved the leverage with white activist groups that had consistently eluded his grasp. "Our challenge," he wrote now, "is to organize the power we already have in our midst." The black poor—domestics, sanitation workers, victimized tenants, seasonal laborers—organized into unions across the nation would, he thought, have a powerful appeal. Until now, the involvement of the white liberal and the white labor unions in civil rights had been voluntary, patronizing, and governed in enthusiasm and duration by pre-emptive sets of cultural, organizational, and politico-economic values. A true community of interests existed at only the most superficial level. If the cries of "burn, baby, burn!" exhilarated black youths and gave a measure of vicarious satisfaction to a majority of their elders, they appalled *bien pensants* whites. Similarly, Vietnam at first was never a spontaneous and passionate issue among the majority of blacks. Conversely, the issues by which white students justified their anti-establishment insurgency really made sense only to those whose middle-class existences drove them to become *déclassés*. If jobs and housing did mean the same thing to the unions and the black workers, it was only more necessary that the unions appear at civil rights rallies while ubiquitously refusing to open their ranks to blacks or encouraging their members to open their neighborhoods to them.

The movement that Martin envisaged must be "powerful enough, dramatic enough, morally appealing enough, so that people of goodwill, the churches, labor, liberals, intellectuals, students, poor people themselves begin to put pressure on congressmen." He had refused to consider running for the presidency on a third-party peace ticket, but the offer proved his value to the political dissidents. He might shortly have a

poor-people's front prepared to march with the antiwar legions, which would give him a different caliber of support—
one based no longer on the vagaries of pure humanitarianism
but on specific mutual benefit. Such a coalition would be
proof against the Gresham's law of Black Power and violent
or separatist ideologies. To those who accused him of remov-
ing himself from the eye of the civil rights hurricane, Martin
could answer that a knowledge of meteorology was much
more relevant. He began to speak more of the class struggle
in addition to the racial.

This new vision of domestic problems held considerable
danger. There were deadly charges and political slogans that
Martin's opponents would draw from a radical, working-class
political movement. When questioned about the SCLC's
nonviolent populism, Andy Young's habit was to appear
dumbstruck. "I don't know about that. I am doing what I
joined the ministry to do!" and he would cite a relevant
parable from the teachings of Jesus. Martin knew that middle-class blacks and many of the simple church people would
recoil at the prospect of an occupation of the capital. He was
nevertheless prepared to lose their support. He was equally
realistic about the response from Congress. "It is a harsh
indictment," Martin believed, "but an inescapable conclusion, that Congress is horrified not at the conditions of Negro
life but at the product of these conditions—the Negro himself." Martin added, with obvious relish at the turn of phrase,
"For two years we have been discussing philosophy. We have
been bogged down in the paralysis of analysis." Henceforth,
he intended to be action personified.

After preaching one of his most unusual sermons to the
Ebenezer congregation on February 4, he and Ralph were in
Washington on Monday and Tuesday to attend a memorial
service for the fallen of the Vietnam war and a peace rally
where he spoke of the contemporary conditions of the black
worker, which were worse than the plight of his white coun-

terpart during the Great Depression. After Washington, they went South, combining a people-to-people tour and talks with SCLC staffers about the poor-people's undertaking. February 15 was spent in Birmingham, the next day divided between speeches in Selma and Montgomery. Before the final drive began, Martin, Coretta, and Andy flew to Jamaica for a quick rest. A week later, February 23, he was in New York to participate in a Carnegie Hall tribute to W. E. B. DuBois, along with James Baldwin and Ossie Davis. An old ally, James O'Dell, now with *Freedomways*, had handled much of the planning for the occasion. Martin's speech was eloquently moving. In his reference to DuBois the man—"He confronted the establishment as a model of militant manhood and integrity. He defied them and though they heaped venom and scorn on him, his powerful voice was never still"—there was a vibration of his own severely tested manhood. O'Dell must have been gratified to hear the speaker declare that "So many would like to ignore the fact that DuBois was a Communist in his last years. . . . Our irrational, obsessive anti-Communism has led us into too many quagmires." The ovation drowned out the words that followed. On March 17, he interrupted a Southern recruitment drive for the campaign to speak in the barony of Detroit's wealthy, Grosse Pointe. He was outrageously heckled for his Vietnam views. The next day, he answered James Lawson's appeal to come to Memphis.

Eight days before his staff finalized the plans for the Poor People's Campaign, Martin had spoken more poignantly than ever to his Ebenezer congregation of his mission to save a racially sick society. It was this sermon that Coretta was to replay at his obsequies in April. Since his childhood, death had shadowed Martin King. He spoke of it frequently, both in public and privately. "I just don't worry about things like this," he had remarked early in his career, "If I did, I just couldn't get anything done. . . . The quality, not the longevity, of one's life is what is important. If you are cut down in a movement that is designed to save the soul of a nation, then no other death could be more redemptive." It was never physical death that greatly worried him. Rather, it was the moribund condition induced by spiritual despair. Given to moods, sensitive to malicious criticism, and used by his unrelenting schedule, he was on the outskirts of disillusionment that Sunday, February 4. "Dr. King's faith was draining," Andy Young admits, "because even people inside the organization were running around the country spouting talk about violence. . . . More damaging to Dr. King was the flak we were getting from friends. They kept telling him he was failing."

And so Martin was low on that February 4, saying about the day of a man's death: "Every now and then I guess we all think realistically about that day. . . . If any of you get somebody to deliver the eulogy, tell him not to talk too long." That familiar, instinctual antiphony of "yesses" and "amens" advanced and receded as Martin increased the volume of his fine voice, till finally it swept over his pulpit in a piercing, grief-stricken chorus. His eulogy need not mention his Nobel Prize and the three or four hundred other awards. What was important was that "Martin Luther King, Jr., tried to give his life serving others. I'd like somebody to say that day [that fateful day of reckoning] that Martin Luther King, Jr., tried to love somebody. . . . I want you to be able to say that day that I did try to feed the hungry. I want you to be able to say that day that I did try in my life to clothe the naked. . . . And I want you to say that I tried to love and serve humanity." He could best be remembered, Martin cried, as a "drum major" for justice, peace, and righteousness.

The reaction of several of Martin's friends and many of his sympathizers to this sermon was unfavorable, for it appeared to blend the egotistic and the lugubrious. But he had not been speaking to a national audience that day. He was sermonizing the emotional and lower-middle-class blacks who provided the bulk of Ebenezer's congregation. And they understood him.

Early on the first day of February, two black Memphis garbage crewmen were crushed to death when the automatic compressor of their truck was accidentally triggered. Grief for their comrades gave way to anger later in the week, when white sewer-workers were paid for a full day's labor although black workers employed on the same job received a reduced wage. Meanwhile, New York City's garbage collectors went on strike. It would have been surprising if the membership of Memphis Local 1733 of the American Federation of State, County, and Municipal Employees (affiliated with the AFL-CIO) had not voted to strike on February 12. Mayor Henry Loeb's administration qualifiedly acceded to several of the union's nine demands, such as institution of a fair promotion policy, an adequate hospital and life insurance program, a uniform procedure for processing grievances, and a pension fund. It refused, however, to sign a written agreement. The city was wholly inflexible in its rejection of the union's three major demands, official recognition as the exclusive bargaining agent for sanitation workers (pratically all of whom were black), a 10 per cent wage increase over a two-year period, and payroll deductions of union dues. On Wednesday, Mayor Loeb, having shouted down one of the city council's moderates the previous day, issued an ultimatum. Employees who failed to return to work by Thursday morning would be fired. Meanwhile, the mayor had already managed to mobilize twenty-three of the city's garbage trucks. By Friday, the union's continued defiance gained the support of Professor Jesse Turner, president of the local NAACP.

More than 80 per cent of Memphis's black voters had opposed the election of Mayor Loeb. The ministers, led by Dr. Ralph Jackson, an African Methodist Episcopalian prelate, and Reverend James Lawson, grasped immediately the broader political potential of the garbage strike and set about organizing community support for it. During the next four weeks, the city officials generally remained a jump ahead of the strikers, whose invasion of city hall, light skirmishes with the police, and marches down Main Street were ignored by the white citizens and finally enjoined by the chancery court. Through the use of nonunion workers escorted by police, garbage collection was re-established on a regular basis in white neighborhoods. Jerry Wurf, national president of the American Federation of State, County, and Municipal Employees, arrived in the city and defied the injunction on marches, as did Tom Powell, head of the Memphis AFL-CIO Central Labor Council.

Walter Reuther stated that his organization was deeply concerned and would lend material assistance to Local 1733's fight. Additional support and publicity came with the visits of Bayard Rustin and Roy Wilkins on March 14. A crowd of nine thousand jammed Mason Temple Church that evening to hear the two leaders encourage people to fight even harder but avoid violence. Although several councilmen had wavered on two occasions, Mayor Loeb rejected out of hand any discussion of union recognition and written contract. Evidently, the city was unimpressed by the threat of increased help for the strikers from outside.

The local ministers concluded that the missing catalyst could be provided by Martin Luther King, whom James Lawson had regularly kept informed. Memphis did appear to offer the classic preconditions for a desperately needed nonviolent victory. Desegregation had been superficial. The mayor was widely disliked by the black community. This was Southern terrain where ministerial leadership was respected and where the reactions of black people—middle class or poor—fell within the range of manipulable predictability. "We Shall Overcome" was still sung in Memphis and there was no coalition of CORE and SNCC to shout down those gentle lyrics. It would have been better, certainly, if Henry Loeb had been a foul-mouthed racist of the stripe of Birmingham's Mayor Hanes; and, if the director of fire and police, Frank Holloman, had earned a reputation worthy of Bull Connor, the people might have sung, marched, and self-immolated the Memphis establishment to its knees. Thanks to Martin, however, there were far fewer Connors and Haneses left in the South. But, if Memphis was not exactly Birmingham, it was certainly not Chicago. That, at least, is how Martin saw the matter, and his advisers confirmed his view.

In the full swing of his Poor People's Campaign recruitment, Martin decided to make an exploratory trip to Memphis. He arrived on the evening following his unsettling reception in Grosse Pointe, Michigan, and spoke to a crowd of nearly fifteen thousand. Ralph, Andy, and James Bevel came with him. In effect, he called for total support by all classes in the black community of a general strike. "They will hear you then," Martin cried, "The city of Memphis will not be able to function that day." His address reflected the nonviolent revisionism of the last few months:

> Along with wages and other securities, you're struggling for the right to organize. This is the way to gain power. Don't go back to work until all your demands are met. There is a need to unite beyond class lines. Negro haves must join hands with Negro have-nots. Our society must come to respect the sanitation worker. He is as significant as the physician, for if he doesn't do his job, disease is rampant.

It was Monday. Martin promised to return to Memphis to lead a giant demonstration that Friday. An unusual snowfall compelled the organizers to defer the date of the march to March 28, a Thursday. Amongst the ministers, the older population, and most of the sanitation workers, there was elation at the prospect of a major nonviolent operation personally conducted by Martin King. But the pollen of Black Power had reached Memphis after all. Militant teenagers were generally not impressed. The organization purporting to speak for them, the Invaders, only half-listened to the advice of nonviolent staff members. Although they had succeeded in gaining representation on the committee of key clergymen and strikers, the Invaders were usually patronized and then scrupulously ignored. "Man, you know, we want to get something done," one of their leaders protested, "I mean all this stuff about marching downtown, all these bourgeoisie wanting to march downtown and get their pictures on national television doing their civil rights thing, man that's nothing. That ain't digging. That ain't going to help my brothers." The Invaders were explicit about how to "help the brothers." "If you expect honkies to get the message," one of them said, "you got to break some windows." Martin was never made sufficiently aware of the barely constrained rebelliousness of the teenagers by his staff. This oversight was to prove disastrous to him personally and to compromise gravely the credibility of nonviolent passive resistance.

Martin's commitments in New York, a series of speeches eliciting enthusiastic responses, delayed him. He arrived in Memphis two hours late on March 28 and, after a hurried conference with Lawson and others, went directly to the march assembly area at Clayborn Temple. What actually happened three blocks later is unclear. At the first sounds of breaking glass shortly after 11 A.M., the leaders halted the march and Martin's aides hurried him to a waiting sedan. Most of the six thousand marchers retreated along Main and Beale streets to the church or their homes. The militants continued, however, and, in the ensuing melee, the police fatally shot a sixteen-year-old boy. Fifty persons were injured and approximately 120 were arrested. The *Memphis Commercial Appeal* described the events as a "full scale riot," claiming that sniper fire occurred in the Handy Park area shortly after 9 P.M. Three thousand eight hundred National Guardsmen entered the city and a dusk-to-dawn curfew was imposed. This display of police and military power contrasted peculiarly with the limited amount of property damage. Less than a hundred store windows were broken and only about sixty businesses reported loss of merchandise, the great majority of it taken from window display cases. By most accounts, the police were more indiscriminately violent than were the small number of looters.

At a press conference that evening, Martin implored the press to draw a clear distinction between the conduct of the marchers—"I thought the march itself was basically a very dignified one"—and that of the militant interlopers. He was disappointed, deeply regretful of the day's developments, he continued. Important consultations in Washington pertinent to the Poor People's Campaign would have to be delayed for at least a day while he attempted to sort out the troubles in the black community. His regret and disappointment were much deeper than the press was permitted to know. "That was the last straw," one of the SCLC executives told *Look*'s George Goodman a year later, "He couldn't sleep. He agonized over the march as though he had committed the violence with his own hands." Stanley Levison telephoned from New York to share his frustration and to deplore the exaggerated accounts of the "riot" by the news media. "The way it should be presented," Levison said, "is [that] eight thousand people showed magnificent discipline, and maybe thirty or forty lost their heads—but look at the eight thousand!" Martin's reply came with such muffled slowness, Levison recalls, that it might have been relayed from another galaxy instead of twelve hundred miles away: "Yes, Stanley, but we'll never be able to get that story through."

Kierkegaard distinguished the tragic hero from the knight of faith by saying that the tragic hero is flawed by his incapacity to transcend his adversity by a leap of faith, an act of superlative irrationality and supreme religious sanity. In the days following the Memphis Donnybrook, Martin's spiritual resiliency declined sharply. A thousand times, he had preached hope to frightened or disillusioned disciples. Through perils and reverses in nearly a hundred cities, his calm voice and firm counsel had inspired tens of thousands of people of all races. Crumpled into his couch at the expensive Holiday Inn–Rivermont in Memphis, almost impervious to the well-intentioned efforts of his aides to cheer him up, what Martin King needed on the afternoon of March 28 more than anything else in the world were the spiritual ministrations of another Martin Luther King, Jr.

From New York came word that Adam Clayton Powell was referring to him as Martin "Loser" King and that Roy Wilkins advised cancellation of the Poor People's March because of Martin's demonstrated inability to mount peaceful rallies. Middle-class blacks and whites joined the chorus of deprecation, incredibly blind to the irony of chastising the single national figure whose nonviolent witness might still buffer the emboldened sallies of black racists. Black militants took the failure of the Memphis demonstration as an incontrovertible sign of the impotence of nonviolence. The situation was extremely serious. He had been involved in riots before. Those in Albany and Birmingham were at least as destructive, if not more so, as the Memphis disorder. The magnitude of the Memphis events was not determined by the Black Power slogans of the teenagers or the windows they broke and the merchandise they purloined. What made Memphis such a disaster was the opportunity it afforded the Administration and the *bien pensant* coalition of white prelates, civic leaders, businessmen, intellectuals, and news commentators to abhor the invitational violence of Martin's activities. The President appeared on national television on March 28 to condemn "mindless violence."

It has been suggested that a man of less stature than Martin King would have "written Memphis off." He announced immediately that he would lead another march on the following Friday, this one far more carefully planned than the last. Before leaving for Atlanta the next day, he spent several hours locked in his hotel room with the leaders of the Invaders, desperately pleading with them to give nonviolence a chance to prove itself in Memphis. Although he was shaken and depressed, his tactic of intelligent indulgence of youthful anger paid dividends again, as it had in Slater King's back yard in Albany and before Selma bridge. The Invaders, doctrinally unconvinced but deeply impressed by the man, promised him that they would cooperate. He returned to Atlanta to rest and prepare himself.

Ralph had never before seen him in such a state: "I was worried about him. But he told me he would be all right and said, 'I'll pull out of it, Ralph.'" By telephone, Coretta had tried to relieve Martin's anxiety. She had not been too successful. But when he returned to Atlanta, she rushed to embrace him as he entered the house. "He was still sorrowful and disturbed," she recalls. She led him upstairs, and she gave all the comfort that she knew how to this extraordinary man, her husband, that night. "I was very glad that we had shared it quietly," Coretta says. He did seem to be better by the time that he and Ralph flew to Washington for his Passion Sunday sermon at Washington Cathedral on March 31. At Dean Francis Sayre's invitation, Martin spoke to an unprecedently large gathering about racism and poverty and promised that the Poor People's Campaign would be far more than a "histrionic gesture." Carefully planned and devotedly led, it would awaken the halls of Congress to the shameful conditions of institutionally enforced misery, which blighted almost one-third of the American population.

It appears that Martin made a surprising decision upon returning to Atlanta. That evening, Lyndon Johnson announced to a stunned nation his decision not to seek reelection. *Mirabile dictu*, the resolution of the Vietnam war, the earnest reappraisal of domestic poverty, and the alarming predictions of the Kerner Commission were suddenly freed of their taboos. A Democratic victory in 1968—whether by Humphrey, Kennedy, or McCarthy—would almost certainly result in a national rededication to the issues Martin was courageously expounding. He decided to postpone the march of the poor on the capital. "If Dr. King had lived, there would never have been a Poor People's Campaign," Ralph Abernathy has admitted recently. Just as he had called for a moratorium on racial demonstrations during the 1964 elections, in order to insure a Johnson victory, four years later Martin concluded that the risks of unruly conduct by marchers in the nation's capital would certainly promote the cause of Richard Nixon as the nominee of the Republican Party or complicate the electoral presentation of the Democratic standard-bearer. His decision not to lead a proletarian assault on Washington would also explain the curious omission of any discussion of the campaign in what was published as a posthumous article in *Playboy*.

Returning to Memphis on Wednesday, Martin learned that the city had been granted a federal court injunction against demonstrations. "We are not going to be stopped by mace or injunctions," he told the press. The skeptics recalled that he had said much the same in Selma. This time, however, he certainly meant to defy the federal court order. "We stand on the First Amendment," he said. "In the past, on the basis of conscience, we have had to break injunctions, and if necessary we may do it. We'll cross that bridge when we come to it." As Martin spoke, SCLC attorneys were petitioning the court to set aside its ruling. It seemed unlikely that this would be done and U.S. Attorney Thomas Robinson minced no words about the order being strictly enforced. City representatives asked Martin to abide by the injunction. Frank Gianotti, Memphis city attorney, stated that his employers were "fearful that in the turmoil of the moment someone may even harm Dr. King's life, and with all the force of language we can use we want to emphasize that we don't want that to happen." The threats of the judiciary and the pleas of the city left him unmoved. However, Bayard Rustin's suggestion that the march be deferred until Monday, in order to allow time for labor union delegations to reach the city, was granted.

The rains came on Wednesday night. Memphis was having unseasonably poor weather. From a wealth of past experience, the SCLC president knew that the black community seldom gave a good account of itself in inclement weather. He asked Ralph to take his place in the speaker's chair at Mason Temple. Meanwhile, he half-read the text of the sermon that he intended to deliver the next Sunday at Ebenezer, "Why America May Go to Hell." Less than half an hour later, Ralph telephoned the Lorraine Motel to say that the church was packed. The people wanted to hear Martin. He left for that final sermon with less enthusiasm than at any time in his life. It is probable that Ralph phoned him to come to the church not so much to satisfy the congregation as to give his friend the needed uplift of addressing a thoroughly sympathetic audience. For the past month, Martin had not been himself. Andy Young told CRS's Jim Laue that Martin had developed the disturbing habit of looking about him as though he expected to spot an assailant. Coretta, too, had wondered about the nature of Martin's premonitions when she received a bouquet of artificial carnations more than three weeks before. "I wanted to give you something that you could always keep," Martin had explained.

He had given premonitory orations before, had contemplated his own mortality and the eternity of the thrust for racial and human justice on many more than a dozen occasions. But his final public words at Mason Temple were uniquely timely and eloquent:

> I left Atlanta this morning, and as we got started on the plane—there were six of us—the pilot said over the public address system, "We're sorry for the delay, but we have Dr. Martin Luther King on the plane, and to be sure that nothing would be wrong on the plane, we had to check out everything carefully. And we've guarded the plane all night."

The check of the plane revealed nothing amiss, and the party had flown to Memphis. Then Martin spoke of the rumors of threats against his life, from rabid whites and militant blacks. One could not dismiss these rumors out of hand. "Well, I don't know what will happen now," Martin spoke as much to himself as to the audience, "But it really doesn't matter with me now. Because I've been to the mountaintop. I won't mind." He had his preferences, of course, "Like anybody, I would like to live a long life. Longevity has its place. But I'm not concerned about that now. I just want to do God's will. And He's allowed me to go up to the mountain. And I've looked over, and I've seen the promised land."

Curiously, the congregation intuited the special character of this sermon and remained fairly silent. Ralph, Andy, James Bevel, and James Lawson exchanged glances whose meaning they would only comprehend the following evening. Martin was stirred up in a way they were unaccustomed to seeing. "I may not get there with you," he went on, "but I want you to know tonight that we as a people will get to the promised land. So I'm happy tonight. I'm not worried about anything. I'm not fearing any man. 'Mine eyes have seen the glory of the coming of the Lord.'" On the steps of Mason Temple, a cluster of SCLC people gathered after the sermon. "What got into Martin?" one of them queried. His words had registered with the congregation, brought tears to the eyes of every person there. But the professionals felt that he had overdone it. Andy Young said Martin was almost macabre.

Most of Thursday was spent in Room 306 of the Lorraine Motel, planning the Monday demonstration. The Invaders sent word that they were sticking to their agreement, and Martin was nerving himself to defy a federal injunction for the first time. He had accepted a dinner invitation from Reverend Samuel Kyles that evening. Slightly more than 205 feet across from the Lorraine Motel, there is a seedy transient hotel, located at 422½ South Main Street. At 3:15 P.M., according to the sign-in sheet, a man calling himself John

Willard rented Room 5B overlooking the balcony of Martin's room at the Lorraine. Approximately one hour later, he purchased a pair of Bushnell binoculars and took them to his room, along with a Remington 30.06 telescopic rifle and a box of soft-point bullets. Next to Willard's room was a bathroom whose window granted an almost unobstructed sight of Martin's balcony. Slightly off to the side was a tree whose foliage, but for the unusual Memphis weather, might have partially obstructed the view of the Lorraine. If Martin King were to appear on his balcony, an assassin would easily be able to fire on him.

Shortly before 6 P.M., Solomon Jones, Jr., a chauffeur for a prominent black mortician, arrived at the Lorraine to drive the civil rights leader to the Kyles residence. Martin was almost ready but could not find his favorite tie. Ralph pointed to a chair: "There it is, Martin." Martin knotted the tie around the collar of the shirt that Ralph had carefully washed that same day. He joshed with Kyles about his wife's ability to prepare soul food. Reverend Kyles reassured him; his wife knew the traditional recipes. Martin pushed aside the plate-glass sliding door and stepped outside onto his balcony. The party would have left the hotel minutes sooner, but Ralph wanted time to sprinkle himself with his favorite toilet water. His friend waited on the balcony. In the courtyard below were the chauffeur, Jones, Jesse Jackson, Andy Young, and Ben Branch, a local musician. "Do you know Ben?" Jesse asked. "Yes," Martin said, doing a superb job of appearing to slide into a mood of folksy comradeship. "Ben, be sure and sing 'Precious Lord, Take My Hand,'" he requested. After the dinner there was to be another church rally. "Sing it real pretty," he added. Solomon Jones shouted up to him to wear his top coat. It was chilly. "OK, I will."

The sound of the shot was so loud that James Laue, who had Room 308 at the Lorraine, thought initially that it must have come from the tarpaulin-covered swimming pool in the courtyard. He had just tuned in the TV to the national news when he heard the shot. Andy and Ralph were already leaning over Martin, who was on his back, one leg caught in the balcony railing. Blood gushed from a facial wound three inches in diameter. "Martin, Martin, it's Ralph," his alter ego kept repeating. But already the flow of blood had ceased, exposing several layers of tissue. Laue looked at his watch. It was 6:08 P.M. He went to his room for a towel, which he placed over the wound. Andy continued to feel for a pulse. At first there was nothing, but, in a few seconds, Andy believed that he felt a slight heart beat. But in any case, Martin King was dead before he reached the hospital. Below the balcony, dozens of uniformed whites arrived to ask what had happened. SCLC aides mistook them for police officers. In fact, most of them were firemen who had rushed from the stationhouse diagonally across from the Lorraine. The army of police arrived somewhat later. At the flophouse, the occupant of room 5B stumbled and fell down the stairs into the street, dropping his rifle against the door of the Canipe Amusement Company, and gunned his white Mustang down South Main Street.

Epilogue: Free at Last

> If a man hasn't found something he will die
> for, he isn't fit to live.
> MARTIN LUTHER KING, JR.

MARTIN LUTHER KING, JR., had told them that he wanted a simple and brief service when he died. Instead, his last rites were protracted, elaborate, and fussily confused. The Vice-President of the United States, the chief contenders for presidential nomination, fifty members of the House of Representatives, thirty senators, a regiment of mayors, and at least a platoon of foreign dignitaries, not to mention the legion of distinguished private citizens, attended his funeral. The news reporters described Ebenezer as a humble little church, giving the impression of a rickety simplicity that was pointlessly erroneous. It is not, of course, a cathedral, but by any standards Ebenezer is a fair-sized edifice. And, if Martin's wishes had been followed, it would have been quite adequate for his obsequies.

Even if the family and leadership of the SCLC had desired otherwise, the pressure upon them to make the final rites of the deceased a quasi state occasion probably could not have been withstood and certainly would have been misunderstood by much of the public. The nation's capital was still under martial law, and, throughout the land, fire brigades and army troops were attempting with varied success to preserve property and life in the black *Götterdämmerung* following

Martin's death. When attorney Charles Morgan said of Georgia's governor, Lester Maddox, that his refusal to pay tribute to the martyred civil rights leader spared the ceremony a gesture of flagrant hypocrisy, he had also in mind the politically inspired commiseration of the very same elected officials, federal and state, whose cynicism, foot-dragging, and hypocrisy had fostered, condoned, or finessed the rising opposition to Martin's activities during the past three or more years.

The service at Ebenezer deserved the crayon of a Daumier. In order to manifest their solidarity with the black community in its wild and explosive grief, in order to mollify the reproaches of civil rights leaders, and in order to repatriate valuable publicity to their constituencies, the nation's mighty endured an excruciating experience. The agony of discomfort, unsuccessfully repressed on the faces of the presidential contenders, is almost delicious. Crushed together in the narrow pews, pinned against the walls, and sweating terribly in the sticky heat of the church, the white politicians and public figures almost earned the credibility they sought that day. But they were made to pay dearly for it, for, thanks to Ralph Abernathy, the service went along interminably. Finally, at 12:15 P.M., the ordeal ended and the sweltering three-and-a-half-mile march to Morehouse College began.

The cortege did not arrive until slightly after 2:30 P.M. The services at the campus also threatened to surpass the endurance of even the hardiest Baptist fundamentalists. Altogether the ceremony lacked dignity and somehow missed the pitched emotionalism that might have made it nevertheless memorable. The mule cart bearing the remains of the fallen leader was almost capsized by the excitable crowd as it stood before the speakers' platform behind Atlanta University's administration building. An uneasy competition seemed to reign about the speakers' microphone, a contest invariably won by Ralph. Singers without talent warbled the favorite hymns of the deceased, while the merciless Georgia sun beat down upon the gathering of fifty thousand. In an unprecedentedly off-handed manner, Martin's successor summoned first Robert Kennedy and then "the other dignitaries" to the platform. It was Martin's day and that of the SCLC. The dignitaries might well have been allowed to remain, exhausted, in their places near the front of the equally exhausted crowd. Even Mahalia failed to spark the assembly. People whispered that she was unwell, recovering from a heart attack.

On another day, perhaps, a cooler one, and assuredly at an earlier hour, Dr. Mays' eulogy would have registered with great impact. "We all pray that the assassin will be apprehended," he said:

> But make no mistake, the American people are in part responsible for Martin Luther King, Jr.'s death. The assassin heard enough condemnation of King and of Negroes to feel that he had public support. He knew that millions hated King. . . . Morehouse College will never be the same because Martin Luther came here; and the nation and the world will be indebted to him for centuries to come.

That day, however, the words of the president emeritus of Morehouse College fell flat. It was late in the day, time to bring the long folk agony to a close. The throng was asked to sing the anthem of nonviolence, "We Shall Overcome." Almost suspiciously, the first verses were hummed and mumbled. But few of the blacks could bring themselves to sing the "black and white together" part, and the whites who tried to carry the words soon gulped into silence. Shortly before 4:30 P.M., Bishop William Wilkes of the African Methodist Episcopal Church offered the benediction. They took Martin to Southview Cemetary, to lie under a marble monument whose inscription eloquently proclaims the emotions of his final days: "Free at Last, Free at Last, Thank God Almighty, I'm Free at Last."

In some ways, the manner in which Martin King was laid to rest reflected the circumstances of his public life: organizational inefficiency, limited and revocable white support, fervor for the man and gnawing doubts about the doctrine among the poor, artificially generated homage by the black middle class, and, once again, the voyage of the leader to a new place when, although he had brought the message and pointed the way, his followers were sore and afraid.

Martin Luther King failed for the same set of reasons that, for almost a decade, had promoted his success, and also because he was killed at the climacteric point at which he might have helped to create a coalition of racial, populist, intellectual, and national groups. This last is at least a legitimate hypothesis. He was a rare personality, endowed with an ample intelligence, great courage and convictions, and an arresting presence. It is nevertheless an inescapable truth that his singularity of leadership initially, and almost until the end, also derived from forces external to himself. This is not to say that the historical King was not a better preacher than most, not more dynamically moral than most spokesmen for justice and righteousness, or that one could imagine a large number of substitute figures in the place of Martin Luther King. He was an unusual man—who lived in an extraordinary time. In his own cyclone-like references to the *Zeitgeist*, perhaps he came closest to explaining his career. It struck in Montgomery and picked him up and swirled him into fame across the South in a succession of blinding touchdowns. In Selma its velocity slowed, and in Chicago and Mississippi it stopped almost completely. But perhaps in Memphis, or perhaps shortly thereafter, Martin would have demonstrated that he had learned the cyclone's secret, that he possessed within himself the power sufficient to sustain the motion of all that nonviolence had come to embody.

If the world is at all capable of candor, if the need by blacks and whites to apotheosize Martin Luther King (if for dissimilar reasons) does not exclude objective assessment, then it must surely be admitted that his nobility, his charisma, derived principally from the fact that, initially, he moralized the plight of the American black in simplistic and Manichaean terms whose veracity the enlightened Southern white was grudgingly compelled to concede and the Northern white was generally relieved, if not delighted, to champion. He was the echo chamber of the racially oppressed but an echo chamber whose reverberations were rounder, more intelligible, and much more polite than the raw cries that it transformed. Whether dreaming on the steps of the Lincoln Memorial or triumphally announcing, at the conclusion of the Selma–Montgomery march, that black people could no longer be turned around by Southern intimidation, Martin's message—in the language of the prophets and the revivalists—never directly threatened, probably never really disconcerted, and always, until near the end, evoked, in its aftermath of white guilt and black self-pity, deeply pleasurable emotions.

Martin's recitation of their tricentenary crimes against black humanity finished, it would have been psychologically perverse if whites had not felt noble in their guilt and superior in their compassion when Martin preached that they were also vouchsafed the infinitely comprehending love of the oppressed, when he insisted that the black man accept doctrinal restraints upon the urge to violent countermeasures, when he construed the whites' vilest deeds as being somehow ultimately redemptive, and when he doggedly foretold the Beulah land of racial harmony, the cruel news of the daily newspapers notwithstanding. Similarly, Martin's evocation of the terrible sufferings of American blacks tended to become muted in the ritual of repetition. What stood out was not the incredible socio-economic destitution and the anguished hopelessness engendered by a system in which the black tends to be marginal, but rather the joyous expectancy that, by putting on walking shoes, by singing to the courthouse, by suffering for a season in jail or out of work, not only would Pharaoh's social system change but his heart would change as well. Almost until the end, the meliorism of the Social Gospel—

and, more viscerally, that of the black bourgeoisie—stayed with Martin, despite the instructive lessons in Marx and Niebuhr.

It was not that Martin told whites what they wanted to hear. Rather, his generous nature and biblical imprecision provided the ideal material for ulterior interpretation. It was not that his impatience with injustice and his mass demonstrations were not fired by a passion as intense as that of the black militants. Rather, it was that in the strength of the technique of nonviolent passive resistance inhered the exploitable limitations of compromise and gradualism. So long as the civil rights campaign followed the scenario of a morality play set in the South, replete with vicious dogs and sheriffs and brutalized black women and children, it was in the interests, the moral as well as political interests, of the civilizing forces in the nation to enhance the role of Martin King. For nearly a decade, that same scenario tended to satisfy the majority of American blacks. On August 28, 1963, men had choked back their emotions as they listened to Martin speak over the television receivers in Harlem bars. In the summer of 1965, in the Black Belt, people registered to vote, trekked miles to protest, and began to use white facilities. The lunch-counter and bus-riding phase was characterized by straightforward objectives whose partial attainment, after a period of courageous demonstrations, lay comfortably by the roads of legal redress and federal assistance. But the avenues of economic equity remained free of black traffic.

As that era ended in white backlash and Black Power, Martin's moral consistency and tactical sanity became an embarrassment and a burden to the most disappointed blacks and to a considerable segment of the most powerful whites. His power in Washington, influence in the business world, and appeal within the black community dipped sharply. And, as this was happening, partly from bewildered frustration but principally because of a more sophisticated appreciation of the springs of social action, he enlarged his campaign from one of civil rights to one of human rights. Black Americans were confused by Martin's intellectual growth. White Americans generally did not care to appreciate it. His tragedy was that he increasingly developed an intellectual capacity to penetrate the veil of American plenty-poverty but seemed incapable of overcoming bourgeois reflexes that would have allowed him to translate that knowledge into an appropriate politics. It is only in the months after Chicago that one perceives the gestation of a program going beyond the social cosmetics of civil rights to second-layer economic and political reform. The Johnson Administration, business, and the right wing of the labor movement gauged the danger to their interests of Martin's groping toward a new program. Having come to grips with the inevitability of mounting black unrest in the 1950's, the establishment had assiduously promoted Martin to the center of the civil rights stage. It was naturally much alarmed that he intended now to discard the script he had been encouraged to follow for a decade. Nor could the artificially resuscitated Urban League and the charming leadership of Whitney Young be made to obscure sufficiently the residual appeal of Martin and the SCLC.

If Martin King worried powerful white interests, they could draw considerable comfort from divisive black reactions to the SCLC leader's evolving ideas, particularly the minority group's parochial attitude to the Vietnam war. The antithesis of war and the alleviation of poverty became a national commonplace only since Martin's assassination, a fact that is much too easily overlooked. For American blacks—certainly for those whose opinions were deemed worthy of sounding by the media—patriotism has generally been akin to salvation. Lyndon Johnson, whose Southern upbringing particularly equipped him, was uncannily able to exploit black patriotic sensitivities, as when he brought Senator Edward Brooke to tears after the Senator reversed his antiwar position upon returning from Saigon and made a spirited defense of the

American war effort on a national television program. Johnson's telephone call immediately after the program deeply moved Brooke.

Having sat with Martin in a parked car sometime early in 1966, several blocks from the Atlanta SCLC headquarters, Harold DeWolf recalls the tremendous spiritual turmoil his former student underwent in deciding how strongly he should oppose the war. The decision to go ahead and denounce the war and disregard the anticipated costs measures the Martin Luther King who had emerged from earlier civil rights battles to proceed by his own instruments into the uncharted weather of international warfare. It offers the truest measure of a morally autonomous man who was also a black man daring to place the struggle of American blacks on a plane where their authentic victory would contribute to a radical change of not only American race relations but also international relations. For a time, this new populist and internationalist approach of Martin's had made and would have continued to make him almost a pariah. But, within weeks after Memphis, it had become fashionable to decry the war in Southeast Asia; already Johnson had felt compelled to decline to succeed himself. The potential for change was immense.

Those who accept Martin's philosophy must believe that his death, like the deaths of countless American blacks felled by racism, will be redeemed somehow, someday. The militants who reject the King creed are prevented from censuring its genius too harshly, for there remains the inchoate and contradictory appendix of the last months of his life. To imagine a Martin King surviving the electoral summer of 1968 raises plausible speculations whose promise and pain are stupefying.

Notes

Page numbers in left-hand column.

CHAPTER 1 DOCTOR, LAWYER—PREACHER?

8   *more nearly with wealth:* Horace Cayton and St. Clair Drake, *Black Metropolis* (New York: Harcourt, Brace & World, 1945), esp. ch. 4.

8   *black upper class:* August Meier and David Lewis, "History of the Negro Upper Class in Atlanta, Georgia, 1890–1958," *Journal of Negro Education* (Spring, 1959), pp. 128–39.

10 WERD: Robert Alexander, "Negro Business in Atlanta," *Southern Economic Journal* (April, 1951), pp. 451–64.

12 *Bennett observes:* Lerone Bennett. Jr., *What Manner of Man*, 3rd rev. ed. (Chicago: Johnson Publishing, 1968), p. 21.

13 *idea of having them:* Coretta Scott King, *My Life with Martin Luther King, Jr.* (New York: Holt, Rinehart & Winston, 1969), p. 80. Referred to hereafter as *My Life.*

16 *angry in my life:* "Man of the Year," *Time* (January 3, 1964), p. 14.

24 *with no morals:* In *Maroon Tiger* (1948), p. 10.

CHAPTER 2 THE PHILOSOPHER KING

29 *moribund religion:* Martin Luther King, Jr., *Stride Toward Freedom* (New York: Harper & Row, 1958), p. 73. Referred to hereafter as *Stride.*

30 *twentieth century:* For the development of the Social Gospel movement, see Marquis Childs and Douglass Cater, *Ethics in a Business Society* (New York: New American Library, Mentor Books, 1954); Henry S. Commager, *The American Mind: An Interpretation of American Thought Since the 1880's* (New Haven: Yale University Press, 1950); and Charles H. Hopkins, *The Rise of the Social Gospel in American Protestantism, 1865–1915* (New Haven: Yale University Press, 1940).

30 *private taxes:* Walter Rauschenbusch, *A Theology for the Social Gospel* (New York Macmillan, 1917), p. 79.

30 *moral endeavors:* Reinhold Niebuhr, *Christianity and Power Politics* (New York: Scribner's, 1940), p. 7.

31 *Rauschenbusch observed:* William E. David, "A Comparative Study of the Social Ethics of Walter Rauschenbusch and Reinhold Niebuhr" (Ph.D. diss., Vanderbilt University, 1958), p. 16.

34 *eliminate social evil: Stride,* p. 73.

34 *Gandhi's life and works: Ibid.,* p. 78.

35 *through the years:* Nat Hentoff, *Peace Agitator: The Story of A. J. Muste* (New York: Macmillan, 1963), p. 18.

35 *no longer appealed: Stride* p. 73.

36 *Mike wrote: Ibid.,* p. 75.

36 *Mike admitted:* Ibid., p. 79.
36 *collusion with evil:* Niebuhr, *Christianity and Power Politics*, pp. 6 and 28.
37 *inflicter of it:* Stride, p. 80.
37 *philosopher reminded:* Harry David and Robert C. Good (eds.), *Reinhold Niebuhr on Politics: His Political Philosophy and Its Application to Our Own Age* (New York: Scribner's, 1960), p. 135.
37 *Protestant liberalism:* Stride, pp. 80–81.
37 *His mercy:* W. E. David, "A Comparative Study," p. 218.
37 *evil as well:* Stride, p. 81.
39 *active spiritually:* Ibid., p. 84.
39 *qualifying examination:* Martin Luther King, Jr., Collection, File Drawer #1, Mugar Library, Boston University, Boston, Mass. Collection is designated henceforth as BUColl.
39 *relativistic and finitistic:* Examination Booklet, BUColl.
40 *human personality:* Stride, p. 82.
42 *get married soon:* Coretta King, *My Life*, p. 65.
43 *divergent theisms:* Martin Luther King, Jr., "A Comparison of the Conceptions of God in the Thinking of Paul Tillich and Henry Nelson Wieman" (Ph.D. diss., Boston University, 1955), pp. 1–10, 166, and 225.
43 *sought the advice:* King to R. Niebuhr, December 1, 1953, BUColl.
43 *Tillich wrote:* Tillich to King, September 22, 1953, and November 3, 1954, BUColl.
44 *impersonal God:* King, "A Comparison of the Conceptions," p. 270.
44 *distortions and rationalizations:* Contained in (but later deleted from) original draft of "How My Mind Has Changed in the Last Decade," BUColl, I, 21A.
45 *doctrinal lands:* Ibid.
45 *literary ferment:* Lawrence Reddick, *Crusader Without Violence* (New York: Harper & Row, 1959), p. 4.

CHAPTER 3 STRIDE TOWARD FREEDOM

50 *generations yet unborn:* Stride, p. 29.
50 *spearhead a boycott:* E. D. Nixon, "How It All Started," *Liberation* (December, 1956), cited in William Robert Miller, *Martin Luther King: His Life, Martyrdom, and Meaning for the World* (New York: Weybright & Talley, 1968), p. 36.
51 *special problem:* Stride, p. 20.
51 *of his face:* Ibid., p. 55.
52 *for a white man:* In Nat Hentoff, "A Peaceful Army," *Commonweal* (June 10, 1960), p. 276.
52 *further instruction:* This text differs slightly from that of the first leaflets. This one was prepared during the Friday-evening meeting. In Stride, p. 33.
53 *selected to preside:* Ibid., p. 31.
53 *South on fire:* Daniel Guérin on Nixon, cited in Lawrence Reddick, *Crusader Without Violence* (New York: Harper & Row, 1959), p. 125.

55 *activities that day:* Stride, p. 34, refers to a Saturday announcement, which in fact did not appear, as does Miller, *Martin Luther King*, p. 37.

55 *impending boycott:* Joe Azbell, "Negro Groups Ready Boycott of City Lines," *Montgomery Advertiser*, December 4, 1955, pp. 1 and 6.

55 *Fred Daniels:* Joe Azbell, "5000 At Meeting Outline Boycott," *Montgomery Advertiser*, December 6, 1955, p. 6.

56 *think it through:* Stride, p. 42.

58 *freedom and justice:* Ibid., pp. 47–48.

60 *come back to earth:* Ibid., p. 53.

61 *personnel:* Stride appendix has a complete list.

62 *not stand for:* Stride, p. 93.

63 *military precision:* Ibid., p. 59.

64 *saved Paris:* Juliette Morgan, "Tell It to Old Grandma," *Montgomery Advertiser*, December 12, 1955, p. 4.

64 *different race:* Montgomery Advertiser, December 15, 1955, p. 4.

67 *his doubts:* Stride, pp. 103–104.

68 *headline account:* Montgomery Advertiser, January 22, 1956, p. 1.

68 *riding the buses again:* Joe Azbell in *Montgomery Advertiser*, January 24, 1956, p. 2.

69 *stronger than ever before:* Stride, p. 111.

69 *in the struggle:* Ibid., p. 116.

70 *battle it out:* Ibid.

70 *do to us:* Joe Azbell, "Blast Rocks Residence of Bus Boycott Leader," *Montgomery Advertiser*, January 31, 1956, pp. 1 and 2. Cf., Stride, p. 117, for King's version, which is somewhat more polished.

71 *Nothing to do with that mess:* Joe Azbell, "Five Negroes Attack Segregation," *Montgomery Advertiser*, February 2, 1956, p. 1.

72 *what else could I do?:* Stride, p. 63.

72 *telegram:* Bunche to King, February 22, 1956, BUColl, II, 27B1.

72 *[Muste] first:* Nat Hentoff, *Peace Agitator: The Story of A. J. Muste* (New York: Macmillan, 1963), p. 17.

74 *witnesses by title:* See Reddick, *Crusader*, pp. 142–44, for an eyewitness account.

76 *committing a crime?:* Stride, p. 132.

77 *moment of anger:* Ibid., p. 135.

78–79 *would ever come about:* Coretta King, *My Life*, p. 141.

79 *judgment is affirmed:* Ibid., pp. 139–40.

81 *pray for the oppressor:* Ibid., pp. 144–45.

81 *I must love him:* Reddick, *Crusader*, p. 13.

82 *justice in America:* Stride, p. 51.

83 *let it be me:* Ibid., p. 155.

CHAPTER 4 *Satyagraha*, HOME-GROWN

85 *season of suffering:* Stride, p. 196.

85 *consciences to sleep:* Ibid., p. 192.

87 *Douglass and W. E. B. DuBois:* See Harold Cruse, *The Crisis of the Negro Intellectual* (New York: Morrow, 1967), for an incisive and provocative analysis of the styles of black protest.

87 *Cleaver has written: Soul on Ice* (New York: McGraw-Hill, 1968), p. 79.

89 *sympathetic explanation:* A. B. Caldwell for Warren Olney, III, to King, October 2, 1956, BUColl, III, 20D.

90 *letter from the prime minister:* Kwame Nkrumah to King, January 22, 1957, BUColl, III, 33B.

90 *nonviolently:* Homer A. Jack, "Conversation in Ghana," *Christian Century*, (April 10, 1957), p. 446.

91 *decision of the Supreme Court:* "Crowd Chants for the Ballot," *Washington Post*, May 18, 1957, p. 131.

93 *heroism and wisdom:* Lerone Bennett, Jr., *What Manner of Man*, 3rd rev. ed. (Chicago: Johnson Publishing, 1968), p. 93.

93 *presented a check:* King to Thurgood Marshall, February 6, 1958, BUColl, IV, 19 "M" A.

94 *in King's direction:* Bennett, *op. cit.*, p. 90.

94 *Vice-President Nixon responded:* Nixon to King, May 23, 1957, BUColl.

94 *prepared a memorandum:* King, June 13, 1957, BUColl, I, 29B.

95 *meeting took place:* Lawrence Reddick, *Crusader Without Violence* (New York: Harper & Row, 1959), p. 202.

95 *and the judiciary:* Albert Blaustein and Robert Zangrando (eds.), *Civil Rights and the American Negro: A Documentary History.* (New York: Washington Square Press, 1968), p. 471.

97 *stubborn ways:* Lillian Smith to King, April 3, 1956, BUColl.

98 *Christianity in action:* Bowles to King, October 10, 1957, BUColl, III, 10B.

98 *capacity to suffer:* King to Bowles, October 28, 1957, BUColl, III, 10B.

98 *in the struggle:* Martin Luther King, Jr., "Advice for Living," *Ebony* (December, 1958), p. 154.

100 *Eisenhower had told Martin:* Reddick, *Crusader*, p. 223. Cf. "Negro Leaders Ask Ike to Act," *Washington Post*, June 24, 1958.

100 *Nehru's words:* Martin Luther King, Jr., *Why We Can't Wait* (New York: Harper & Row, 1963), p. 135.

101 *This document:* Rustin to King, February, 1959, BUColl, I.

101 *second place: Ibid.*

101 *Janpath Hotel:* T. K. Unnithan to King, February 15, 1959, BUColl, I, 5H.

103 *shape or form:* M. K. Gandhi, *Non-Violent Resistance* (New York: Schocken, 1961), p. 6.

103 *create community: Stride*, p. 87.

103 *"Himalayan miscalculation":* Gandhi, *op. cit.*, p. 74.

104 *less radical form:* A composite of *Satayagraha* precepts based on Joan V. Bondurant, *Conquest of Violence: The Gandhian Philosophy of Conflict* (Berkeley: University of California Press, 1965), pp. 40–41, and Krishnalal Shridharani, *War Without Violence* (Bombay: Bharatiya Vidya, 1962), pp. 30–37.

104 *Gandhi's philosophy alive: Hindustani Times*, March, 1959, BUColl, I, 5.

104–5 *warmly quoted: Ibid.*

105 *nonviolent campaign: Ibid.*

106 *outstanding pacifists:* Linus Pauling to King, December 17, 1960; A. J. Muste to King, January 4, 1960; Norman Cousins to King, September 26, 1961 BUColl.

106 *delay such action:* Celler to King, February 15, 1957, BUColl, IV, 4 "H" A.

106 *decline the cochairmanship:* Paul Douglas to King, January 20, 1959, BUColl, III, 20D.

106 *sent this reply:* Joseph Ryan to King, November, 1959, BUColl, III, 23A.

107 *(Little Rock, etc.):* Editorial, *Herald-Dispatch*, March 6, 1958, pp. 1 and 3.

107 *in the field:* R. Williams to King, March 13, 1958, BUColl, III, 20B.

107 lex talionis: Julian Mayfield, "Challenge to Negro Leadership: The Case of Robert Williams," *Commentary* (April, 1961), pp. 297–305.

108 *profound crisis:* Martin Luther King, Jr., "The Social Organization of Nonviolence," *Liberation* (October, 1959), cited in William Robert Miller, *Martin Luther King: His Life, Martyrdom, and Meaning for the World* (New York: Weybright & Talley, 1968), p. 83.

108 *Reddick contrasted:* Press release, BUColl, I, 15A.

109 *serious consideration:* King to P. O. Watson, November 19, 1959, BUColl, III, 27B.

110 *eleventh hour:* King to Dombrowski, December 9, 1959, BUColl, III, 20.

110 *Martin informed Davis:* Davis to King, August 20, 1959; King to Davis, April 23, 1960, BUColl, III, 20.

111 *unjust practices:* August 21, 1959, BUColl, I, 32B.

CHAPTER 5 SKIRMISHING IN ATLANTA

112 *to accept it:* In Howard Zinn, *SNCC: The New Abolitionists* (Boston: Beacon, 1965), p. 31.

112 *Atlanta is ruled:* Edward C. Banfield, *Big City Politics* (New York: Random House, 1965), p. 18.

115 *democracy of ours:* "An Appeal For Human Rights," *Atlanta Constitution* (March, 1960).

116 *as a tactic:* Lerone Bennett, Jr., *What Manner of Man*, 3rd rev. ed. (Chicago: Johnson Publishing, 1968), p. 114.

118 *sent a donation:* J. A. Pike to King, December 30, 1959, BUColl.

118 *His letter:* Jackie Robinson to King, June 29, 1960, BUColl.

118 *appears to express:* A. K. Chalmers to King, October 12, 1961, BUColl, VII, 2 "C" B.

119 *suppressing local leaders:* Louis Lomax, "The Negro Revolt Against 'The Negro,'" *Harper's* (June, 1960), pp. 41–48.

119 *organizational work:* King to Marie Rodell, November 30, 1960, BUColl, I, 40.

120 *hand of fate: Atlanta Enquirer*, August 5, 1961, p. 2. Originally published in the same paper July, 1960.

121 *permeated by love:* Reproduced in Zinn, *op. cit.*, p. 34.

122 *the country will accept:* Coretta King, *My Life*, p. 186.

123 *to carry on:* King to R. Parks, April 12, 1960, BUColl, IV.

123 *seven major demands:* Rustin to King, June 15, 1960, BUColl, I, 29C.

124 *platform committee:* Thruston Morton to King, July 9, 1960, BUColl, IV, 31P.

124 *party's convention:* Doris E. Saunders (ed.), *The Kennedy Years and The Negro: A Photographic Record* (Chicago: Johnson Publishing, 1964), p. 3.

124 *applause at the end:* Ibid., p. 4.

125 *369th Armory:* Malcolm X to King, July 21, 1960, BUColl, II, 2E.

125 *advocacy of violence:* King to Kivie Kaplan, March 6, 1961, BUColl, I, 5.

128 *allow bail:* Theodore White, *The Making of the President, 1960,* (New York: New American Library, 1967), p. 386, and Anthony Lewis (ed.), *Portrait of a Decade: The Second American Revolution* (New York: Random House, 1964), pp. 99–100.

128 *De Kalb trials:* D. Hollowell to King, November 3, 1960, BUColl, IV, 2.

129 *dislike of Catholics:* Chuck Stone, *Black Political Power in America* (New York: Bobbs-Merrill, 1968), p. 49.

129 *just in time:* Harris Wofford's pamphlet, in Lewis, *op. cit.,* p. 100.

129 *he reflected:* Martin Luther King, Jr., "It's a Difficult Thing to Teach a President," *Look* (November 17, 1964), p. 61.

129 *"do something dramatic":* Ibid.

129 *last few weeks:* White, *op. cit.,* p. 387.

129 *Johnson was gracious:* Johnson to King: November 28, 1960, BUColl.

130 *vote in the South:* Unsigned letter to King, November 11, 1960, BUColl, VII, 21.

130 *moral courage:* E. O. Reitz to King, November 7, 1960, BUColl, VII, 21.

130 *22,000,000 Americans:* Martin Luther King, Jr., "The President Has the Power," *Nation* (February 4, 1961), p. 91.

131 *Baldwin alleges:* James Baldwin, "The Dangerous Road Before Martin Luther King," *Harper's* (February, 1961), p. 42.

131 *Rustin denied:* Rustin to King, February 6, 1961, BUColl, VII, 39 "R" A.

132 *flew to New Orleans:* James Peck, *Freedom Ride* (New York: Simon & Schuster, 1962), pp. 125–27.

134 *wired an ultimatum:* Williams to King, May 31, 1961, BUColl, VII, 51.

134 *"an unfortunate article":* James Forman, "Deny Students Have Lost Faith in King," *Atlanta Enquirer*, January 6, 1962, p. 12.

135 *transportation facilities:* Ruby Doris Smith, "Nonviolence Can Work in United States," *Atlanta Enquirer*, August 5, 1961, p. 10.

136 *financing the project:* Zinn, *op. cit.,* pp. 58–59.

137 *Wyatt once said:* Robert Penn Warren, *Who Speaks for the Negro* (New York: Random House, 1965), p. 223.

139 *declined the offer:* J. H. Goodson to King, September 2, 1960, BUColl, IV, 1.

Notes

CHAPTER 6   ALBANY, GEORGIA—NONVIOLENCE IN BLACK AND WHITE

140 *prolonged naps:* W. E. B. DuBois, *Souls of Black Folk* (New York: Fawcett, 1961), p. 91.

141 *responsible independence:* James Gray, "Our Revolution and Africa," *Albany Herald,* December 10, 1961, p. 4.

142 *military discrimination:* For a general and knowledgeable discussion of Albany, see Slater King, "Albany, Georgia," *Freedomways* (Winter, 1964), pp. 93–101.

145 *Albany Movement was created: Ibid.*

145 *record turnout:* "Record Ballot Noted in City," *Albany Herald,* December 5, 1961, p. 1.

146 *agreement can be found:* "Negro Committee Demands All Violators Be Released," *Albany Herald,* December 15, 1961, p. 1.

148 *God bless you:* Vic Smith, "Peace Prevails," *Albany Herald,* December 17, 1961, p. 1.

149 *thousands will join me:* Vic Smith, "Trials Delayed," *Albany Herald,* December 18, 1961, p. 5.

149 *"agitators":* Vic Smith, "Demonstrations, Boycott Called off by Negroes Here," *Albany Herald,* December 19, 1961, p. 5.

150 *old school:* "Determined Police Chief," *New York Times,* July 23, 1962, p. 13.

150 *he would arrest them:* Coretta King, *My Life,* p. 204.

151 *go now, Dr. King: Albany Herald,* December 19, 1961, p. 5.

151 *Robert Kennedy telephoned: Ibid.*

151 *defeats of his career:* David Miller, "Loss for Dr. King," *New York Herald Tribune,* December 19, 1961, p. 1.

151 *meaningful peace:* Trezvant Anderson, "Negroes in Albany Sitting on Powder Keg," *Pittsburgh Courier,* January 20, 1962, p. 1.

152 *us who participated: Why We Can't Wait,* p. 43.

154 *all a hoax:* "Man of the Year," *Time* (January 3, 1964), p. 14.

157 *low-grade reporting:* See C. A. Scott, "The Albany Situation Hurts All America," *Atlanta Daily World,* December 17, 1961, p. 6, and "Let Albany Have Its Chance," *Atlanta Daily World,* December 19, 1961, p. 6. See also "Walker of SCLC Attacks Daily," *Atlanta Enquirer,* December 23, 1961, p. 13.

160 *a Southern leader charged:* "Spokesman for Negroes," *New York Times,* July 16, 1962, p. 47.

160 *Federal Home Loan Bank:* "What's MLK Role in Bank Dealing?" *Pittsburgh Courier,* June 30, 1962, p. 1.

160 *confusion within SCLC:* Louis Lomax, *The Negro Revolt* (New York: New American Library, 1963), pp. 98–99.

161 *maintain segregation:* Claude Sitton, "Dr. King Denounces U.S. Judge," *New York Times,* July 23, 1962, p. 1.

161 *Not at high noon! Now!:* Claude Sitton, "Negroes Defy Ban," *New York Times,* July 21, 1962, p. 1.

164 *rest of our lives:* Claude Sitton, "Dr. King Is Jailed Again," *New York Times,* July 27, 1962, p. 44.

166 *Fun Town:* E. Dunbar, "A Visit with Martin Luther King," *Look* (February 12, 1963), p. 92.

166 *"The Case Against 'Tokenism' ":* In *New York Times Magazine*, August 5, 1962, p. 11.

166 *close to the rear:* Martin Luther King, Jr., "Fumbling on the New Frontier," *Nation* (March 3, 1962), p. 191.

167 *can be regulated:* "The Case Against 'Tokenism,' " *New York Times Magazine*, August 5, 1962, p. 49.

169 *segregationist white South:* Martin Luther King, Jr., "The Terrible Cost of the Ballot," *SCLC Newsletter* (September, 1962), p. 2.

169 *Freedom Movement:* Lerone Bennett, Jr., *What Manner of Man*, rev. ed. (Chicago: Johnson Publishing, 1968), p. 130.

169 *pray that it will:* Wyatt Walker, "Achievement in Albany," *New South* (June, 1963), p. 4. Cf. Walker, "The Congo, U.S.A., Albany, Georgia," *SCLC Newsletter* (September, 1962).

170 *this miscalculation:* Slater King, "Our Main Battle in Albany," *Freedomways* (Summer, 1965), pp. 417–23.

CHAPTER 7   BIRMINGHAM—NONVIOLENCE IN BLACK, VIOLENCE IN WHITE

171 *Rip Van Winkle slumber: Why We Can't Wait*, p. 47.

172 *capitally, punished:* See Fred Shuttlesworth, "Birmingham Shall Be Free Some Day," *Freedomways* (Winter, 1964), pp. 16–19. See also, *New York Times*, September 16, 1963, p. 26.

174 *to the cross: I Have A Dream: The Story of Martin Luther King in Text And Pictures* (New York: Time-Life, 1968), pp. 37-38.

174 *for his administration: Why We Can't Wait*, p. 143.

175 *stripe of Shuttlesworth:* James Stillman, "Current of Compromise," *Birmingham News*, April 14, 1963, p. A2.

177 *on our presence: Why We Can't Wait*, p. 56.

179 *handicap the Movement: Amsterdam News*, April 20, 1963, cited by William Robert Miller, *Martin Luther King, Jr.: His Life, Martyrdom, and Meaning for the World* (New York: Weybright & Talley, 1968), p. 138.

182 *violate it: Why We Can't Wait*, p. 70.

182 *First Amendment: Ibid.*

183 *brought me to be: Ibid.*, p. 72.

185 *worried mind: Ibid.*, p. 74.

187 *j'accuse:* Haig A. Bosmajian, "Rhetoric of Martin Luther King's 'Letter from Birmingham Jail,' " *Midwest Quarterly* (April 16, 1963), pp. 66–67.

188 *render unto Caesar:* Will Herbert, "The Religious 'Right' to Violate the Law?" *National Review* (July 14, 1964), p. 579.

191 *'What do you do?':* Claude Sitton, "Robert Kennedy Unable to Budge Alabama Governor," *New York Times*, April 26, 1963, p. 1.

192 *other defendants:* "Dr. King Convicted," *New York Times*, April 27, 1963, p. 9.

193 *stench of discrimination: Why We Can't Wait*, p. 97.

193 *spluttered to a correspondent:* Claude Sitton, "Birmingham Jails 1,000 More," *New York Times,* May 7, 1963, p. 33.

194 *more turmoil:* Foster Hailey, "Dogs & Hoses Repulse Negroes," *New York Times,* May 4, 1963, p. 1.

194 *thankful prayer meeting:* Foster Hailey, "Birmingham Talks Pushed," *New York Times,* May 6, 1963, p. 1.

195 *good-natured smile: New York Times,* May 7, 1963, p. 33.

195 *Marshall's intentions: Why We Can't Wait,* p. 103.

196 *in a hearse:* Claude Sitton, "Rioting Negroes Routed by Police," *New York Times,* May 8, 1963, p. 28.

196 *in the future: Ibid.*

196 *coming of age: Ibid.*

197 *sea of black faces: Why We Can't Wait,* p. 104.

198 *political fortunes:* Martin Luther King, Jr., "Bold Design for a New South," *Nation* (March 30, 1963), p. 260.

198 *Pollack flew to Birmingham:* See Michael Dorman, *We Shall Overcome* (New York: Dell, 1965); Anthony Lewis (ed.), *Portrait of a Decade: The Second American Revolution* (New York: Random House, 1964), pp. 160–61; and Foster Hailey, "The Birmingham Story," *New York Times,* May 26, 1963, p. 58.

201 *a just solution:* Claude Sitton, "Birmingham Pact Sets Timetable," *New York Times,* May 11, 1963, p. 8.

201 *all His children: Ibid.*

201 *hope and with faith: Why We Can't Wait,* p. 107.

202 *"some tangible protests":* Claude Sitton, "U.S. Sends Troops into Alabama," *New York Times,* May 13, 1963, p. 24.

203 *Mayor Hanes spoke: Ibid.*

204 *demonstrations should be resumed: Why We Can't Wait,* p. 107.

204 *would not be true: Ibid.,* p. 112.

205 *a sell out:* "Profiles in Courage," *Liberator* (June, 1963), p. 2.

205 *relations between the races:* James Reston, "Tragedy in Birmingham," *New York Times,* September 20, 1963.

206 *City of Brotherhood:* Fred Shuttlesworth, "Birmingham Shall Be Free Some Day," *Freedomways* (Winter, 1964), p. 19.

206 *he had created:* Lerone Bennett, Jr., *What Manner of Man,* rev. ed. (Chicago: Johnson Publishing, 1968), p. 164.

207 *insulated or unaware: Why We Can't Wait,* p. 112.

208 *Grosbeck Preer Parham:* "Facets of Strike Emerge in Court," *New York Times,* May 9, 1963, p. 17.

CHAPTER 8 THE STRENGTH OF A DREAM

210 *we ain't what we was: Time* (January 3, 1964), p. 27.

212 *so many injunctions:* "After King Talks and Negroes Walk," *Danville Register,* July 12, 1963, p. 1.

216 *the March on Washington:* Calvin Hernton, "Dynamite Growing out of Their Skulls," in LeRoi Jones and Larry Neal (eds.), *Black Fire: An Anthology of Afro-American Writing* (New York: Morrow, 1968), pp. 99–100.

216 *American tradition:* Look Out, Whitey! Black Power's Gon' Get Your Mama! (New York: Dial Press, 1968), pp. 12–13.

217 *I'll endorse it:* Malcolm X Speaks: Selected Speeches and Statements (New York: Grove Press, 1966), pp. 14–15.

217 *is usually supposed:* James Farmer, Freedom—When? (New York: Random House, 1965), p. 93.

217 *even Martin Luther King:* cited by Fern Marja Eckman in The Furious Passage of James Baldwin (New York: Popular Library, 1967), p. 158. See also Victor Lasky, Robert F. Kennedy: The Myth and the Man (New York: Trident Press, 1968), p. 188; Arthur M. Schlesinger, Jr., A Thousand Days (Boston: Houghton Mifflin, 1965), p. 962; and New York Times, May 25, 1963.

217 *Baldwin's friends:* Eckman, op. cit., p. 158.

218 *Birmingham affair:* Ibid., p. 167.

218 *point of a gun:* Schlesinger, op. cit., p. 969.

219 *Birmingham ill-timed:* Ibid., pp. 969–70.

219 *fund-raising capabilities:* See Peter Kihss, "Joint Negro Council Allocates," New York Times, July 18, 1963, p. 10.

224 *shown here today:* Cf. original and altered texts in Joanne Grant (ed.), Black Protest: History, Documents, and Analyses from 1619 to the Present (New York: Fawcett, 1968), pp. 375–77.

224 *to the front:* "200,000 March For Civil Rights," New York Times, August 29, 1963, p. 16.

225 *were not peaceful:* Nan Robertson, "Capital Is Ready," New York Times, August 28, 1963, p. 1.

226 *like other Americans:* "250,000 Make History in Huge Washington March," SCLC Newsletter (September, 1963), p. 3.

226 *hung over them:* William Robert Miller, Martin Luther King, Jr.: His Life, Martyrdom, and Meaning for the World (New York: Weybright & Talley, 1968), p. 163.

226 *needs strengthening:* New York Times, August 29, 1962, p. 16.

227 *"Battle Hymn of the Republic":* See Benjamin Muse, The American Negro Revolution: From Nonviolence to Black Power, 1963–1967 (Bloomington: Indiana University Press, 1968), p. 16.

227 *written and rewritten:* For the SCLC Newsletter article, see Martin Luther King, Jr., "Oxford, Mississippi, 1962," SCLC Newsletter (December 1962), pp. 1–2.

227–28 *the Lincolnian language:* Coretta King, My Life, p. 236.

229 *changes of human thought:* Gustave Le Bon, The Crowd, (New York: Viking, 1960), p. 13.

230 *nation and the world:* Anthony Lewis, Portrait of a Decade: The Second American Revolution (New York: Random House, 1968), p. 217.

230 *Kennedy's position:* Schlesinger, op. cit., p. 972.

231 *unprecedented achievement:* "Purpose of March," SCLC Newsletter (August, 1963), pp. 2–3.

232 *Negro to violence:* Martin Luther King, Jr., "The Negro Revolution in 1964," SCLC Newsletter (January, 1964), p. 7.

232 *economic conditions:* Bayard Rustin, "From Protest to Politics," Commentary (February, 1965), p. 26.

232 *"Freedom now!":* "If Not Now—When?" *SCLC Newsletter* (June, 1964), p. 5.

233 *get them for yourselves:* "March Leaders Talk of Open Protest," *Atlanta Enquirer,* December 21, 1963, p. 1.

234 *house in order:* Martin Luther King, Jr., "The Danger of a Little Progress," *SCLC Newsletter* (February, 1964), p. 7.

234 *drive people away:* "Atlanta Negroes Speak out on Demonstrations," *Atlanta Enquirer,* February 8, 1964, p. 5.

234 *stand still:* Ibid.

235 *appealing objectives:* Martin Luther King, Jr., "It's a Difficult Thing to Teach a President," *Look* (November 17, 1964), p. 61.

236 *a sick society:* Coretta King, *My Life,* p. 244.

236 *timetable will be:* "Negroes Ponder Next Step," *New York Times,* November 24, 1963, p. 12.

237 *democratic ideals:* "Negroes Praise Johnson Speech," *New York Times,* November 28, 1963, p. 21.

237 *felicitous honeymoon:* "President Spurs Drive for House to Act," *New York Times,* December 4, 1963, p. 39.

237 *about civil rights:* Ibid.

237 *escalated intensity:* Ibid.

238 *war against poverty: Why We Can't Wait,* p. 146.

238 *long pull:* Eric F. Goldman, *The Tragedy of Lyndon Johnson* (New York: Knopf, 1968), p. 312.

238 *whole freedom movement:* Martin Luther King, Jr., "The Negro Revolt in 1964," *SCLC Newsletter* (January, 1964), p. 1.

240 *government in the world:* Martin Luther King, Jr., "The Hammer of Civil Rights," *Nation* (March 9, 1964), cited in Miller, *op. cit.,* p. 181.

242 *local whites further:* "Why We Went," *Christian Century* (August 26, 1964), pp. 1061–62.

243 *God willing:* Martin Luther King, Jr., "Of Bigotry and Hate," *SCLC Newsletter* (June, 1964), p. 7.

245 *to be used:* Paul Montgomery, "CORE to Continue its Direct Action," *New York Times,* August 10, 1964, p. 15.

246 *affront to us all:* Martin Luther King, Jr., "Of Riots and Wrongs Against the Jews," *SCLC Newsletter* (July–August, 1964), p. 11.

246 *millions of dollars:* Ibid., pp. 2–3.

247 *drive off fear:* Sally Belfrage, *Freedom Summer* (London: André Deutsch, 1966), p. 4.

247 *those places anyway:* Ibid., p. 9.

248 *interracial comity:* Cf. William B. Huie, *Three Lives for Mississippi,* in Grant, *op. cit.,* pp. 336–39. See also Nicholas von Hoffman, *Mississippi Notebook* (New York: David White Co., 1964).

248 *several young militants:* "Cross-Section of Views," *Atlanta Enquirer,* April 4, 1964, p. 5.

249 *keep on keeping on:* Belfrage, *op. cit.,* p. 166.

249 *poll conducted:* Cf. "Negro Leaders Ban Demonstrations," *Christian Century* (August 12, 1964), p. 1005.

249 *moratorium:* Ibid.

250 *had Kennedy lived: Why We Can't Wait,* p. 147.

250 *Hosea Williams:* "SCLC Puts Might of Its Organization Against 'Gold-waterism,'" *SCLC Newsletter* (October–November, 1964), pp. 1–2.

250 *charisma alone:* James Laue, "The Changing Character of Negro Protest," *Annals of the American Academy of Political and Social Science* (January, 1965), p. 121.

251 *"I think he knows it":* Quoted by Robert Penn Warren in *Who Speaks for the Negro?* (New York: Random House, 1964), p. 228.

252 *white man to me:* Ibid., pp. 219–21.

252 *violence and riots:* New York Times, August 10, 1964, p. 15.

252 *Negro Movement:* Warren, *op. cit.*, p. 224.

253 *best possible:* Ibid., p. 203. "Even the most poverty-stricken among us can purchase a 10-cent bar of soap; even the most uneducated among us can have high morals": Benjamin Muse, *op. cit.*, p. 109.

254 *God had given him:* Miller, *op. cit.*, p. 99.

254–55 *affairs of the movement:* Coretta King, *My Life*, p. 171.

255 *blessings upon him:* Ibid., p. 3.

256 *about that subject:* "J. Edgar Hoover and the FBI," *Newsweek* (December 7, 1964), p. 22.

256 *debate with him:* "Off Hoover's Chest," *Newsweek* (November 30, 1964), p. 30.

257 *get him to vote:* Drew Pearson, "Meeting with Hoover," *Washington Post*, December 5, 1964, p. E15. From Walter Fauntroy's account to the author.

257 *Communists:* See Victor Lasky, *Robert F. Kennedy: The Myth and the Man* (New York: Trident Press, 1968), p. 15.

258 *he assured Britons:* "Dr. King, Preaching in London, Calls on Negroes for Restraint," *New York Times*, December 7, 1964, p. 6.

259 *economic sanctions:* "Dr. King Bids West Act on South Africa," *New York Times*, December 8, 1964, p. 53.

259 *Jericho Improvement Association:* "Dr. King, Preaching in London, Calls on Negroes for Restraint," *New York Times*, December 7, 1964, p. 6.

260 *all over the world:* "How Martin Luther King Won the Nobel Peace Prize," *U.S. News and World Report* (February 8, 1964), p. 76.

260 *foreign elements are withdrawn:* "Dr. King Proposes a Rights Alliance," *New York Times*, December 10, 1964, p. 58.

261 *such a ridiculous thing:* Coretta King, *My Life*, p. 11.

261 *King is a Nobel Prize winner:* Quoted in David Halberstam, "The Second Coming of Martin Luther King," *Harper's* (August, 1967), p. 44.

CHAPTER 9   CRISIS AND COMPROMISE—THE WALK TO SELMA BRIDGE

264 *protruding heels, for instance:* Paul Good, "Beyond the Bridge," *Reporter* (April 8, 1965), p. 24.

267 *unlawful assembly:* John Herbers, "Two Alabama Officials Clash over Arrests," *New York Times*, January 21, 1965, p. 22.

268 *in the Negro community:* John Herbers, "Negro Teachers Protest," *New York Times,* January 23, 1965, p. 18.

268 *by the thousands:* John Herbers, "Plea to Nation," *New York Times,* January 22, 1965, p. 16.

268 *her husband's cause:* Cited in *Jet* (March 11, 1965), pp. 28–30.

268–69 *willing to hear Dr. King:* Coretta King, *My Life,* p. 256.

269 *Andy Young called it:* Ron Gibon and Larry Corcoran, "Dallas Voter Board to Comply," *Birmingham News,* February 5, 1965, p. 6.

270 *honestly miss him:* John Herbers, "Negroes Offer Prayers for Sheriff Clark," *New York Times,* February 13, 1965, p. 1.

270 *James Free wrote:* "King's 'Master Plan' for Selma May Be Fizzling," *Birmingham News,* February 11, 1965, p. 1.

272 *tour of Africa:* See George Breitman, *The Last Year of Malcolm X: The Evolution of a Revolutionary* (New York: Schocken, 1968), pp. 44–51.

273 *Katzenbach . . . had pleaded:* Good, *op. cit.,* p. 26.

274 *I went down:* Warren Hinckle and David Welsh, "Five Battles of Selma," *Ramparts* (June, 1965), p. 27.

275 *would take place:* Roy Reed, "Alabama Police Use Gas and Clubs," *New York Times,* March 8, 1965, p. 20.

270 *Judge Johnson customarily enjoined:* John Herbers, "U.S. Mediated Peaceful Confrontation," *New York Times,* March 10, 1965, p. 22.

276 *season of suffering:* Reported in Roy Reed, "New Selma March Today," *New York Times,* March 9, 1965, p. 23.

279 *as we move on:* Roy Reed, "Dr. King Leads March," *New York Times,* March 10, 1965, p. 22. See also "Civil Rights, the Central Point," *Time* (March 19, 1965), pp. 23–30.

281 *things aren't that bad:* Ibid., p. 26.

281 *taken Sunday:* Martin Luther King, Jr., "Behind the Selma March," *Saturday Review* (April 3, 1965), p. 57.

282 *militant white South:* Eldridge Cleaver, *Soul on Ice* (New York: McGraw-Hill, 1968), p. 74.

283 *Wallace joked:* Eric F. Goldman, *The Tragedy of Lyndon Johnson* (New York: Knopf, 1968), p. 315.

285 *the President's action:* Anthony Lewis, *Portait of a Decade* (New York: Bantam, 1965), p. xii.

285 *disarmingly sincere:* Martin Luther King, Jr., "Next Stop the North," *Saturday Review* (April 3, 1965), p. 16.

287 *SNCC agreed:* Renata Adler, "Letter from Selma," *New Yorker* (April 10, 1965), p. 141.

290–91 *only a handful of people:* Coretta King, *My Life,* p. 268.

293 *SCLC boycott:* Junius Griffin, "SCLC Continues Economic Withdrawal in Alabama," *SCLC Newsletter* (April–May, 1965), pp. 1 and 2.

294 *class struggle:* "King Introduces Class War Theme," *Birmingham News,* May 11, 1965.

295 *buses and lunch counters:* Martin Luther King, Jr., *Where Do We Go from Here: Chaos or Community?* (New York: Bantam, 1968), p. 6. Referred to henceforth as *Where Do We Go.*

CHAPTER 10   THE FIRE NEXT TIME

299   *work we began here:* SCLC Newsletter (April–May, 1965), p. 15.
300   *"Conservative Militant":* August Meier, "On the Role of Martin Luther King," *New Politics* (Winter, 1965), reprinted in Melvin Drimmer (ed.), *Black History: A Reappraisal* (New York: Doubleday, 1968), p. 444.
301   *presented an advance copy:* Lee Rainwater and William Yancey, *The Moynihan Report and the Politics of Controversy* (Cambridge: MIT Press, 1967), p. 188.
302   *typically rousing speech:* SCLC Newsletter (June–July, 1965), p. 4.
302   *even between nations:* King to Dr. Joseph Tusiana, August 8, 1959, BUColl, I, 40B.
302   *Viet Cong:* Martin Luther King, Jr., "Quote and Unquote," *SCLC Newsletter* (June–July, 1965), p. 4.
303   *Politicking by James Farmer:* Benjamin Muse, *The American Negro Revolution: From Nonviolence to Black Power, 1963–1967* (Bloomington: Indiana University Press, 1968), p. 231.
303   *Bill Berry:* SCLC Newsletter, (June–July, 1965), p. 2.
304   *"this ego thing":* David Halberstam, "Notes from the Bottom of the Mountain," *Harper's* (June, 1968), p. 42.
304   *organization's endorsement:* William Robert Miller, *Martin Luther King, Jr.: His Life, Martyrdom, and Meaning for the World* (New York: Weybright & Talley, 1968), p. 228.
304   *message was clear:* "A Rebuke to Dr. King," *U.S. News and World Report* (August 30, 1965), p. 16.
304   *demeaning counsels:* David Halberstam, "The Second Coming of Martin Luther King," *Harper's* (August, 1967), p. 50.
305   *win spurs:* Ibid., p. 40.
305   *Robert Conot:* Rivers of Blood, Years of Darkness (New York: Bantam, 1967), p. ix.
306   *that interpretation:* Where Do We Go, p. 133.
306   *these youngsters:* Rainwater and Yancey, *op. cit.,* p. 193.
306   *Northern-derivative progress:* Martin Luther King, Jr., "Next Stop the North," *Saturday Review* (November 30, 1965), pp. 33 and 105.
307   *who causes the darkness:* Ibid.
307   *settlement was imminent:* Halberstam, "The Second Coming of Martin Luther King," pp. 49–50.
309   *begged the question:* Rainwater and Yancey, *op. cit.,* p. 200.
309   *rationalize oppression:* Ibid., p. 202.
311   *white man's business alone:* Martin Luther King, Jr., "Peace: God's Man's Business," *Chicago Defender,* January 1–7, 1966, p. 1.
311   *editorials proclaimed:* Atlanta Enquirer, January 13, 1966, p. 4.

CHAPTER 11   THE PIED PIPER OF HAMLIN AVENUE—
               CHICAGO AND MISSISSIPPI

313   *want to be freed:* In Arnold Schuchter, *White Power, Black Freedom* (Boston: Beacon Press, 1968), p. 64.

314 *assault on Daley's machine:* Ibid., p. 65.

315 *tend to flounder:* Louis Lomax, *The Negro Revolt* (New York: New American Library, 1963), p. 98.

315 *Chicago Tribune reporter:* Arthur Jackman, "Dr. King's Flat, Although Painted, Is Very Dismal," *Chicago Tribune*, January 26, 1966, p. 8.

316 *brotherhood and justice:* "King Briefs Police," *Chicago Tribune*, January 27, 1966, p. 3.

316 *housing-code violations:* "Plan New Drive on Slumlord," *Chicago Tribune*, February 10, 1966, p. 1.

317 *Martin conferred with Elijah Muhammed:* "King, Muslims, Join Forces," *Chicago Defender*, February 26–March 4, 1966, p. 1.

317 *Martin scholasticized:* James Sullivan, "Dr. King Takes over Slum Building," *Chicago Tribune*, February 24, 1966, p. 3.

318 *Napolitano:* "Legal and Illegal Slum Campaigns," *Chicago Tribune*, March 8, 1966, p. 12.

320 *summer of peaceful nonviolence:* "King Discloses Plan for Rally," *Chicago Tribune*, May 27, 1966.

322 *by many militants:* O. Wehrwein, "Dr. King Disputes Negro Separatist," *Chicago Tribune*, May 28, 1966, p. 26.

322 *throw her into the Mississippi:* Gene Roberts, "Troopers Shove Group Resuming Meredith March," *New York Times*, June 8, 1966, p. 26.

322 *techniques to win: Where Do We Go*, p. 31.

323 *holding the bag:* Gene Roberts, "Mississippi March Criticized," *New York Times*, June 11, 1966, p. 1.

323 *get Negroes registered:* Ibid.

324 *"We shall overrun":* Paul Good, "The Meredith March," *New South* (Summer, 1966), p. 9.

325 *"They know what he means":* Ibid.

325 *at any cost: Where Do We Go*, p. 35.

326 *despair and disappointment:* Ibid., p. 51.

326 *deliver on our promises:* Ibid., p. 52.

328 *Take it easy:* "Gas King, 2000, in March," *Chicago Tribune*, June 25, 1966, p. 1.

328 *"black and white together":* Paul Good, "A White Look at Black Power," *Nation* (August 8, 1966), pp. 112–17.

328 *Great Society:* James Baldwin, "A Report From Occupied Territory," *Nation* (July 4, 1966), p. 43.

329 *undermined Dr. King: Nation* (August 5, 1966), p. 116.

329 *killed your own brother:* David Halberstam, "The Second Coming of Martin Luther King," *Harper's* (August, 1967), p. 51.

329 *close my eyes:* José Yglesias, "Dr. King's March on Washington, Part II," *New York Times Magazine*, March 31, 1968, p. 70. Cf. "The March-in Step and Out," *Newsweek* (July 4, 1966), p. 15.

330 *Andy Young protested: Nation* (August 8, 1966), p. 115.

330 *not happen in the United States: Where Do We Go*, pp. 67–68.

330 *quickly as possible:* Ibid., p. 67.

331 *nonviolent movement:* "Crisis in Color," *Newsweek* (August 22, 1966), p. 58. Cf. "Too Many Cooks, Too Much Spice," *Christian Century* (July 6, 1966), pp. 880–81.

332 *violent campaign:* "King Tells Goals," *Chicago Tribune*, July 11, 1966, p. 2.

332 *demanded by the oppressed:* Ibid.

332 *eight demands:* "King's Chicago Demands," *New York Times*, July 10, 1966, p. 1.

333 *small talent:* Paul Good, "Bossism, Racism, and Dr. King," *Nation* (September 19, 1966), p. 240.

334 *Daley was not a bigot:* "Daley, King, Aides, Meet on Rights," *Chicago Tribune*, July 12, 1966, p. 2.

335 *not for violence:* Ibid.

336 *motives of the rioters:* Malcolm Boyd, "Violence in Los Angeles," *Christian Century* (August 8, 1965), p. 1093.

337 *ideally suited:* "Freedom Movement a Riot Remedy: King," *Chicago Tribune*, July 22, 1966, p. 5.

337 *forms of recreation: Where Do We Go*, p. 135.

339 *so hostile and so hateful:* "Dr. King Felled by Rock," *Chicago Tribune*, August 6, 1966, p. 1.

339 *attacks on policemen:* "600 Police Halt Hecklers," *Chicago Tribune*, August 8, 1966, p. 1.

341 *Cody . . . McDermott:* "Demonstrations Should End, Cody Says," *Chicago Tribune*, August 11, 1966, p. 1.

342 *defy the injunction:* "Daley Makes Plea to Cody," *Chicago Tribune*, August 20, 1966, p. 1.

342 *"What more do they want?":* C. Vann Woodward, "What Happened to the Civil Rights Movement?" *Harper's* (January, 1967), p. 33.

342 *his demonstrations:* "The Touchiest Target," *Newsweek* (August 15, 1966), p. 29.

346 *far-reaching move had been made:* David Halvorsen, "Cancel Rights Marches," *Chicago Tribune*, August 27, 1966, p. 2.

346 *city in the nation: Where Do We Go*, p. 67.

348 *Monroe Sharp stated:* "Defer Plan for March into Cicero," *Chicago Tribune*, August 28, 1966, p. 1.

348 *white neighborhoods: Chicago Tribune*, August 27, 1966, p. 5.

348 *his morality: New York Review of Books* (August 24, 1967), p. 3.

349 *boost Martin:* "Still King," *Christian Century* (September 7, 1966), pp. 1071–72.

349 *roaches out of my house: Nation* (September 19, 1966), p. 240.

350 *congenial accommodations:* "Cicero March Called Off," *Chicago Defender*, August 27–September 2, 1966, p. 1.

350 *have to live with: Nation* (September 19, 1966), p. 240.

352 *one way or the other:* "Cicero Holds Up Permit," *Chicago Tribune*, September 1, 1966, p. 5.

CHAPTER 12   KILLERS OF THE DREAM

354 *revolution of values:* David Halberstam, "The Second Coming of Martin Luther King," *Harper's*, (August, 1967), p. 48.

355 *Sharp's attack:* "Martin Luther King: Mercy Killer," *Chicago Defender*, September 10–16, 1966, p. 1.

356   *would not predict:* Andrew Kopkind, Review of *Where Do We Go
      From Here: Chaos or Community?* in *New York Review of Books*
      (August 24, 1967), p. 3.
356   *ready for the world: Ibid.*
357   *Senator Paul Douglas: Chicago Defender,* November 12–18, 1966, p. 1.
358   *peace march:* "Signs of Erosion," *Newsweek* (April 10, 1967), p. 32.
358   *Young angrily dismissed: Harper's* (August, 1967), p. 49.
358   *70 per cent:* "Negro View of King vs. Jackson," *Chicago Defender,*
      October 15–21, 1966, pp. 1–2.
359   *foreign policy:* Martin Luther King, Jr., *The Trumpet of Conscience*
      (New York: Harper & Row, 1968), p. 21.
359   *manipulation of the poor: Ibid.,* p. 23.
360   *'Thou shalt not kill':* Bill Adler (ed.), *The Wisdom of Martin Luther
      King* (New York: Lancer Books, 1968), p. 45.
360   *The man was right:* Coretta King, *My Life,* p. 294.
361   *Geneva agreement:* Douglas Robinson, "Dr. King Proposes a Boycott
      of War," *New York Times,* April 5, 1967, p. 1.
361   *Violated by the United States:* "100,000 Rally at U.N.," *New York
      Times,* April 16, 1967, p. 2.
362   *inflicted injury: Ibid.*
362   *anyone get to him:* David Halberstam, *op. cit.,* pp. 50–51.
363   *"It's us and the NAACP": Newsweek* (May 15, 1967), p. 33.
363   *hate, and violence:* In Leroi Jones and Larry Neal (eds.), *Black Fire:
      An Anthology of Afro-American Writing* (New York: William Morrow,
      1968), pp. 90–91.
363   *"self-flagellating" policy:* Eldridge Cleaver, *Soul on Ice* (New York:
      McGraw-Hill, 1968), p. 108.
364   *burdens the conscience: Where Do We Go,* p. 81.
365   *greater today than ever: Ibid.,* p. 107.
365   *violence paid off:* Louis Lomax, *To Kill a Black Man* (Los Angeles:
      Holloway House, 1968), p. 190.
366   *"transforming role":* Martin Luther King, Jr., "Showdown for Non-
      violence," *Look* (April 16, 1968), p. 24.
366   *grocery corporations: Where Do We Go,* p. 171.
366   *Dominican Republic:* Martin Luther King, Jr., "A Testament of Hope,"
      Playboy (January, 1969), p. 231. It is possible that this article does not
      represent his final views. The circumstances of its composition remain
      to be clarified.
367   *foreign policy statements:* "Dr. King Now a Peace Hawk," *Detroit
      News,* April 6, 1967, p. B12.
367   *vaunted consensus:* "Dr. King's Disservice to His Cause," *Life* (April
      21, 1967), p. 4; author's italics. *Newsweek* (April 10, 1967), p. 32.
367   *political assassination:* Carl Rowan, "Martin Luther King's Tragic De-
      cision," *Reader's Digest* (September, 1967), pp. 37–42.
368   *propaganda has brought us:* "Johnson, King, and Ho Chi Minh,"
      Christianity Today (April 26, 1968), p. 25.
369   *massive nonviolence, or riots:* Martin Luther King, Jr., "Showdown for
      Nonviolence," *Look* (April 16, 1968), p. 25.
369   *black-nationalist ideologies:* in Bill Adler, *op. cit.,* p. 137.

370 *mass civil disobedience:* Martin Luther King, Jr., *The Trumpet of Conscience* (New York: Harper & Row, 1963), p. 15.

370 *world perspective: Ibid.,* p. 68.

371 *sensitive young people: Ibid.,* p. 41.

371 *connection with Vietnam:* "A Testament of Hope," p. 234.

371 *President Johnson: Ibid.,* p. 232.

371 *Russian roulette:* "Showdown for Nonviolence," p. 23.

371 *close at hand: Ibid.,* p. 24.

372 *Commission's report: Report of the National Advisory Commission on Civil Disorders* (New York: Bantam, 1968).

372 *declined to endorse: Los Angeles Herald-Examiner,* March 17, 1968, p. 1.

373 *SCLC in the Poor People's Campaign:* George Goodman, "He Lives, Man!" *Look* (April 15, 1969), p. 30.

373 *to its citizens:* "Showdown for Nonviolence," p. 25.

373 *legislative feints:* See José Yglesias, "Dr. King's March on Washington, Part II." *New York Times Magazine,* March 31, 1968, p. 60.

374 *pressure on congressmen:* "Showdown for Nonviolence," p. 25.

375 *teachings of Jesus:* Yglesias, *op. cit.,* p. 57.

375 *lost their support: Ibid.,* p. 59.

375 *Negro himself: The Trumpet of Conscience,* p. 16.

377 *more redemptive:* Adler, *op. cit.,* p. 142.

377 *he was failing:* Goodman, *op. cit.,* p. 29.

377 *peace, and righteousness:* Adler, *op. cit.,* pp. 189–91.

378 *union dues:* "These Are the Issues," *Memphis Commercial Appeal,* February 20, 1968, p. 1.

380 *disease is rampant:* "King Urges Work Stoppage," *Memphis Commercial Appeal,* March 19, 1968, p. 1.

381 *break some windows:* Lomax, *op. cit.,* p. 193.

381 *"full-scale riot":* "Guardsmen Back Riot Curfew," *Memphis Commercial Appeal,* March 29, 1968, p. 1.

382 *his own hands:* Goodman, *op. cit.,* p. 29.

383 *"written Memphis off":* Lomax, *op. cit.,* p. 191.

384 *such a state:* Lerone Bennett, Jr., *What Manner of Man,* 3rd rev. ed. (Chicago: Johnson Publishing, 1968), p. 238.

384 *shared it quietly:* Coretta King, *My Life,* p. 312.

385 *Abernathy has admitted:* Goodman, *op. cit.,* p. 29. Cf. Mrs. Coretta King's denial of this allegation in "Mrs. King Says Look Story Untrue," *Jet* (April 17, 1969).

385 *mace or injunctions:* "King Challenges Court Restraint," *Memphis Commercial Appeal,* April 4, 1968, p. 1.

385 *want that to happen": Ibid.*

Selected Bibliography

In addition to the materials listed here, thorough use was made of the materials in the Martin Luther King, Jr., Collection, Mugar Library, Boston University.

BOOKS

ADLER, BILL, ed. *The Wisdom of Martin Luther King, in His Own Words*, New York: Lancer Books, 1968.

AHMANN, MATHEW H., ed. *The New Negro*. Notre Dame, Ind. Fides Publishers, 1961.

———, ed. *Race: Challenge to Religion*. Chicago: Henry Regnery, 1963.

BALDWIN, JAMES. *The Fire Next Time*. New York: Dial Press, 1963.

BANFIELD, EDWARD C. *Big City Politics*. New York: Random House, 1965.

———. *City Politics*. Cambridge: Harvard University Press, 1963.

BELFRAGE, SALLY. *Freedom Summer*. New York: Viking, 1965.

BENNETT, LERONE. *Before the Mayflower: A History of the Negro in America*, 1619–1968. Rev. ed. Chicago: Johnson, 1969.

———. *What Manner of Man*. 3rd rev. ed. Chicago: Johnson Publishing, 1968.

BLAUSTEIN, ALBERT P., and ZANGRANDO, ROBERT L. *Civil Rights and the American Negro*. New York: Washington Square Press, 1968.

BONDURANT, JOAN V. *Conquest of Violence: The Gandhian Philosophy of Conflict*. Berkeley: University of California Press, 1965.

BREITMAN, GEORGE. *The Last Year of Malcolm X: The Evolution of a Revolutionary*. New York: Schocken, 1968.

———, ed. *Malcolm X Speaks: Selected Speeches and Statements*. New York: Grove Press, 1966.

BRIGHTMAN, EDGAR SHEFFIELD, ed. *Personalism in Theology: A Symposium in Honor of Albert Cornelius Knudson*. Boston: Boston University Press, 1943.

———. *Persons and Values*. Boston: Boston University Press, 1952.

CARMICHAEL, STOKELY, and HAMILTON, CHARLES V. *Black Power: The Politics of Liberation in America*. New York: Random House, Vintage, 1967.

CASH, WILBUR J. *The Mind of the South*. New York: Alfred A. Knopf, 1941.

417

CHAMBERS, BRADFORD. *Chronicles of Black Protest*. New York: New American Library, 1968.

CHAPMAN, ABRAHAM, ed. *Black Voices: An Anthology of Afro-American Literature*. New York: New American Library, 1968.

CLARK, KENNETH B. *Dark Ghetto*. New York: Harper & Row, 1965.

———, ed. *The Negro Protest*. Boston: Beacon Press, 1963.

———, and PARSONS, TALCOTT, eds. *The Negro American*. Boston: Beacon Press, 1967.

CLAYTON, EWARD TAYLOR. *Martin Luther King: The Peaceful Warrior*. Englewood Cliffs, N.J.: Prentice-Hall, 1954.

CLEAVER, ELDRIDGE. *Soul on Ice*. New York: McGraw-Hill, 1968.

CONOT, ROBERT. *Rivers of Blood, Years of Darkness*. New York: Bantam, 1967.

CRUSE, HAROLD. *The Crises of the Negro Intellectual*. New York: William Morrow, 1967.

DAVIS, HARRY R., and GOOD, ROBERT C., eds. *Reinhold Niebuhr on Politics: His Political Philosophy and Its Application to Our Age as Expressed in His Writings*. New York: Scribner's, 1960.

DORMAN, MICHAEL. *We Shall Overcome*. New York: Dell, 1965.

DOYLE, WILBUR BERTRAM. *The Etiquette of Race Relations in the South*. Chicago: University of Chicago Press, 1937.

DRIMMER, MELVIN, ed. *Black History: A Reappraisal*. Garden City, N.Y.: Doubleday, 1968.

DUBOIS, W. E. B. *Dusk of Dawn*. New York: Schocken, 1968.

———. *The Souls of Black Folk*. New York: Fawcett, 1961.

ECKMAN, FERN MARJA. *The Furious Passage of James Baldwin*. New York: Popular Library, 1967.

ESSIEN–UDOM, E. U. *Black Nationalism*. Chicago: University of Chicago Press, 1962.

FANON, FRANTZ. *Black Skin, White Masks*. New York: Grove Press, 1968.

———. *Wretched of the Earth*. New York: Grove Press, 1965.

FARMER, JAMES. *Freedom—When?* New York: Random House, 1965.

FISCHER, LOUIS. *Gandhi: His Life and Message for the World*. New York: New American Library, 1954.

FRANKLIN, JOHN HOPE. *From Slavery to Freedom*. Rev. ed. New York: Alfred A. Knopf, 1967.

———, and STARR, ISIDORE. *The Negro in Twentieth-Century America*. New York: Random House, Vintage, 1967.

FRAZIER, E. FRANKLIN. *Black Bourgeoisie*. New York: Macmillan, 1956.

———. *Negro Church in America*. New York: Schocken, 1964.

GALLAGHER, BUELL. *American Caste and the Negro College*. Staten Island, N.Y.: Gordian Press, 1938.

GANDHI, M. *Non-Violent Resistance*. New York: Schocken, 1961.

GARVEY, AMY-JACQUES, ed. *Philosophy and Opinions of Marcus Garvey.* New York: Atheneum, 1969.

GILBERT, BEN W., ed. *Ten Blocks from the White House.* New York: Praeger Publishers, 1968.

GOLDMAN, ERIC F. *The Tragedy of Lyndon Johnson.* New York: Alfred A. Knopf, 1968.

GRANT, JOANNE, ed. *Black Protest: History, Documents, and Analysis from 1619 to the Present.* New York: Fawcett, 1968.

GREGG, RICHARD BARTLETT. *The Power of Nonviolence.* New York: Fellowship of Reconciliation Publications, 1959.

GREGORY, DICK. *Nigger.* New York: Dutton, 1964.

HALBERSTAM, DAVID. *The Unfinished Odyssey of Robert Kennedy.* New York: Random House, 1968.

HAMILTON, MICHAEL P., ed. *The Vietnam War: Christian Perspectives.* Grand Rapids, Mich.: Eerdmans, 1967.

HARRINGTON, MICHAEL. *The Other America.* New York: Macmillan, 1962.

HARRIS, ABRAM. *The Negro as Capitalist.* Philadelphia: American Academy of Political and Social Science, 1936.

HAYDEN, TOM. *Rebellion in Newark.* New York: Random House, 1967.

HENTOFF, NAT. *Peace Agitator: The Story of A. J. Muste.* New York: Macmillan, 1963.

HERSEY, JOHN. *The Algiers Motel Incident.* New York: Alfred A. Knopf, 1968.

HERSKOVITS, MELVILLE. *The Myth of the Negro Past.* Boston: Beacon Press, 1958.

HOPKINS, CHARLES H. *The Rise of the Social Gospel in American Protestantism, 1865–1915.* New Haven: Yale University Press, 1940.

JACOBSON, JULIUS, ed. *The Negro and the American Labor Movement.* Garden City, N.Y.: Doubleday, 1968.

JOHNSON, CHARLES S. *Growing up in the Black Belt.* Washington, D.C.: American Council on Education, 1941.

JOHNSON, JAMES WELDON. *The Autobiography of an Ex-Colored Man.* New York: Alfred A. Knopf, 1927.

JONES, LEROI, and NEAL, LARRY, eds. *Black Fire: An Anthology of Afro-American Writing.* New York: William Morrow, 1968.

JORDON, WINTHROP. *White over Black.* Chapel Hill: University of North Carolina Press, 1968.

KAHN, TOM. *The Economics of Equality.* New York: League for Industrial Democracy, 1964.

KIERKEGAARD, SOREN. *Purity of Heart.* New York: Harper & Row, 1956.

KILLEN, JOHN OLIVER. *Black Man's Burden.* New York: Trident Press, 1965.

420 *King*

KING, CORETTA SCOTT. *My Life with Martin Luther King, Jr.* New York: Holt, Rinehart & Winston, 1969.

KING, MARTIN LUTHER, JR. *The Measure of a Man.* Philadelphia: United Church Press, 1968.

———. *Strength to Love.* New York: Harper & Row, 1963.

———. *Stride Toward Freedom: The Montgomery Story.* New York: Harper & Row, 1958.

———. *Trumpet of Conscience.* New York: Harper & Row, 1968.

———. *Where Do We Go from Here: Chaos or Community?* New York: Harper & Row, 1967.

———. *Why We Can't Wait.* New York: Harper & Row, 1964.

LANDIS, BENSON Y. *A Rauschenbusch Reader: The Kingdom of God and the Social Gospel.* New York: Harper & Row, 1957.

LASKY, VICTOR. *Robert F. Kennedy: The Myth and the Man.* New York: Trident Press, 1968.

LE BON, GUSTAVE. *The Crowd.* New York: Viking, 1960.

LESTER, JULIUS. *Look Out Whitey, Black Power's Gon' Get Your Mama.* New York: Dial Press, 1968.

LEVY-BRUHL, LUCIEN. *How Natives Think.* New York: Washington Square Press, 1966.

LEWIS, ANTHONY. *Portrait of a Decade: The Second American Revolution.* New York: Random House, 1964.

LIEBOW, ELLIOT. *Tally's Corner.* Boston: Little, Brown, 1967.

LINCOLN, C. ERIC. *The Black Muslims in America.* Boston: Beacon Press, 1961.

LOGAN, RAYFORD W. *The Betrayal of the Negro.* New York: Macmillan, 1965.

LOKOS, LIONEL. *House Divided.* New Rochelle, N.Y.: Arlington House, 1968.

LOMAX, LOUIS. *The Negro Revolt.* New York: New American Library, 1963.

———. *To Kill a Black Man.* Los Angeles: Holloway House, 1968.

MALCOLM X. *The Autobiography of Malcolm X.* New York: Grove Press, 1964.

MARSHALL, BURKE. *Federalism and Civil Rights.* New York: Columbia University Press, 1964.

MAYS, BENJAMIN. *The Negro's God as Reflected in His Literature.* New York: Atheneum, 1968.

MEIER, AUGUST, and RUDWICK, ELLIOTT M. *From Plantation to Ghetto.* New York: Hill & Wang, 1966.

———. *Negro Thought in America, 1880–1915.* Ann Arbor: University of Michigan Press, 1963.

MELTZER, MILTON. *A History of the American Negro.* Vol. 3. New York: Thomas Y. Crowell, 1967.

MILLER, WILLIAM ROBERT. *Martin Luther King, Jr.: His Life, Mar-

tyrdom, and Meaning for the World. New York: Weybright & Talley, 1968.

————. *Nonviolence: A Christian Interpretation.* New York: Association Press, 1964.

MUSE, BENJAMIN. *The American Negro Revolution: From Non-violence to Black Power, 1963–1967.* Bloomington: Indiana University Press, 1968.

MYRDAL, GUNNAR. *An American Dilemma.* Rev. ed. New York: Harper & Row, 1962.

NIEBUHR, REINHOLD. *Christian Realism and Political Problems.* New York: Scribner's, 1953.

————. *Christianity and Power Politics.* New York: Scribner's, 1940.

————. *Moral Man and Immoral Society.* New York: Scribner's, 1932.

OSOFSKY, GILBERT. *Harlem: The Making of a Ghetto.* New York: Harper & Row, 1964.

PADMORE, GEORGE. *Pan-Africanism.* London: Dennis Dobson, 1956.

PECK, JAMES. *Freedom Ride.* New York: Simon and Schuster, 1962.

PETTIGREW, THOMAS. *A Profile of the Negro American.* Princeton: Van Nostrand, 1964.

PUCKETT, NEWBELL. *Folk Beliefs of the Southern Negro.* Chapel Hill: University of North Carolina Press, 1926.

QUARLES, BENJAMIN. *Black Abolitionists.* New York: Oxford University Press, 1969.

RAINWATER, LEE, and YANCEY, WILLIAM. *The Moynihan Report and Politics of Controversy.* Cambridge: MIT Press, 1967.

RAUSCHENBUSCH, WALTER. *Christianity and the Social Crisis.* Edited by Robert D. Cross. New York: Harper & Row, 1964.

————. *Realism and Political Problems.* New York: Scribner's, 1953.

————. *A Theology for the Social Gospel.* New York: Macmillan, 1917.

REDDICK, LAWRENCE. *Crusader Without Violence.* New York: Harper & Row, 1959.

Report of the National Advisory Commission on Civil Disorders. New York: Bantam, 1968.

ROWAN, CARL T., *Go South to Sorrow.* New York: Random House, 1957.

SAUNDERS, DORIS, ed. *The Kennedy Years and the Negro: A Photographic Record.* Chicago: Johnson Publishing, 1964.

SCHLESINGER, ARTHUR M., JR. *A Thousand Days: John F. Kennedy in the White House.* Boston: Houghton Mifflin, 1965.

SCHUCHTER, ARNOLD. *White Power/Black Freedom.* Boston: Beacon Press, 1968.

SHRIDHARANI, KRISHNALAL. *War Without Violence.* Bombay: Bharatuya Vidya, 1962.

SILBERMAN, CHARLES. *Crisis in Black and White.* New York: Random House, 1964.

STONE, CHUCK. *Black Political Power in America*. Indianapolis: Bobbs-Merrill, 1968.

SUTHERLAND, ELIZABETH, ed. *Letters from Mississippi*. New York: New American Library, 1966.

VON HOFFMAN, NICHOLAS. *Mississippi Notebook*. New York: David White, 1964.

WALKER, JACK L. *Sit-ins in Atlanta*. New York: McGraw-Hill, 1964.

WALLBANK, R. W. *A Short History of India*. Rev. ed. New York: New American Library, 1958.

WARREN, ROBERT PENN. *Who Speaks for the Negro?* New York: Random House, 1964.

WASHINGTON, BOOKER T. *Up from Slavery*. New York: Bantam, 1959.

WHITE, THEODORE H. *The Making of the President 1960*. New York: New American Library, 1967.

———. *The Making of the President 1964*. New York: Atheneum, 1965.

WITCOVER, JULES. *Eighty-five Days: The Last Campaign of Robert Kennedy*. New York: Putnam, 1969.

WOODWARD, C. VANN. *The Burden of Southern History*. Baton Rouge: Louisiana State University Press, 1960.

———. *The Strange Career of Jim Crow*. Rev. ed. London: Oxford University Press, 1958.

YOUNG, WHITNEY. *To Be Equal*. New York: McGraw-Hill, 1964.

ZINN, HOWARD. *SNCC: The New Abolitionists*. Boston: Beacon Press, 1964.

———. *The Southern Mystique*. New York: Alfred A. Knopf, 1964.

MAGAZINE ARTICLES

ADLER, RENATA. "Letter from Selma." *New Yorker*, April 10, 1965, pp. 121–57.

ALEXANDER, ROBERT. "Negro Business in Atlanta." *Southern Economic Journal* 17: 451–64.

BALDWIN, JAMES. "The Dangerous Road Before Martin Luther King." *Harper's*, February, 1961.

———. "A Report from Occupied Territory." Nation, July 4, 1966, pp. 37–43.

BLAYTON, JESSE. "The Negro in Banking." *Banker's Magazine*, December, 1936.

BOSMAJIAN, HUG A. "Rhetoric of Martin Luther King's 'Letter from Birmingham Jail.'" *The Midwest Quarterly* 8: 66–67.

BOYD, MALCOLM. "Violence in Los Angeles." *Christian Century* 82: 1093.

Christian Century
"Conversation in Ghana," April 10, 1957.

Selected Bibliography

"No False Moves for King," July 17, 1963.
"King Wants White Demonstrator," June 3, 1964.
"Negro Leaders Ban Demonstrators," August 12, 1964.
"Why We Went," August 26, 1964.
"Peace Prize Causes Controversy," January 13, 1965.
"Too Many Cooks, Too Much Spice," July 6, 1966.
"Black Power for Whom?" July 20, 1966.
"Still King," September 7, 1966.
"Johnson, King, and Ho Chi Minh," April 26, 1968.
"Copyright Case Involves 'New' Use of Material." *Publisher's Weekly*, April 6, 1964, p. 6.
CRUSE, HAROLD. "Rebellion or Revolution." *Liberator*, January, 1964, pp. 14–16.
"Dr. King's Disservice to His Cause." *Life*, April 21, 1967, p. 4.
DUNBAR, E. "A Visit with Martin Luther King." *Look*, February 12, 1963.
Ebony
    "The Woman Behind Martin Luther King," January, 1959.
    "Martin Luther King's Tropic Interlude," June, 1967, pp. 112–19.
GALPHIN, BRUCE M. "Political Future of Dr. King." *Nation*, September 23, 1961, pp. 177–80.
GOOD, PAUL. "Beyond the Bridge." *Reporter*, April 8, 1965.
———. "Bossism, Racism, and Dr. King." *Nation*, September 19, 1966.
———. "The Meredith March." *New South*, Summer, 1966.
———. "A White Look at Black Power." *Nation*, August 8, 1966.
GOODMAN, GEORGE. "He Lives, Man!" *Look*, April 15, 1969.
HALBERSTAM, DAVID. "Notes from the Bottom of the Mountain." *Harper's*, June, 1968, pp. 40–42.
———. "The Second Coming of Martin Luther King." *Harper's*, August, 1967, pp. 39–51.
HARDWICK, ELIZABETH. "The Apotheosis of Martin Luther King." *New York Review of Books*, May 9, 1968, pp. 3–4.
HENTOFF, NAT. "A Peaceful Army." *Commonweal*, June 10, 1960.
HERBERG, WILL. "The Religious 'Right' to Violate the Law." *National Review*, July 14, 1964.
"It Ain't No Vaudeville." *New Republic*, April 2, 1956, p. 2.
Jet, March 11, 1965, pp. 28–30.
KEATING, EDWARD M. "The Yellow Rose of Texas." *Ramparts*, June, 1965, p. 17.
KING, MARTIN LUTHER, JR. "Advice for Living." *Ebony*, December, 1958.
———. "Behind the Selma March." *Saturday Review*, April 3, 1965.
———. "Bold Design for a New South." *Nation*, March 30, 1963.

————. "The Danger of a Little Progress." *SCLC Newsletter*, February, 1964, pp. 7–8.

————. "Fumbling on the New Frontier." *Nation*, March 3, 1962.

————. "It's a Difficult Thing to Teach a President," *Look*, November 17, 1964, p. 61.

————. "Let Justice Roll Down." *Nation*, March 15, 1965.

————. "My Trip to the Land of Gandhi." *Ebony*, July, 1959.

————. "A Need for Soul Searching." *SCLC Newsletter*, October–November, 1964, p. 7.

————. "The Negro Revolt in 1964." *SCLC Newsletter*, January, 1964, p. 7.

————. "Next Stop, the North." *Saturday Review*, April 3, 1965.

————. "The President Has the Power: 'Equality Now.' " *Nation*, February 4, 1961.

————. "Quote and Unquote." *SCLC Newsletter*, June–July, 1965, p. 4.

————. "Showdown for Nonviolence." *Look*, April 16, 1968, pp. 23–25.

————. "The Terrible Cost of the Ballot." *SCLC Newsletter*, September, 1962, pp. 1–2.

————. "A Testament of Hope." *Playboy*, January, 1969, p. 174.

KING, SLATER. "Albany, Georgia." *Freedomways*, 4: 93–101.

————. "Our Main Battle in Albany." *Freedomways*, 4: 417–23.

KOPKIND, ANDREW. Review of *Where Do We Go from Here: Chaos or Community.* *New York Review of Books*, August 24, 1967.

LEONARD, GEORGE B. "Midnight Plane to Alabama." *Nation*, May 10, 1965.

LOMAX, LOUIS E. "The Negro Revolt Against 'the Negro Leaders.' " *Harper's*, June, 1960.

MAHONEY, WILLIAM. "In Pursuit of Freedom." *Liberator*, September, 1961.

"Martin Luther King, Jr., and Mahatma Gandhi." *Negro Historical Bulletin*, May, 1968.

MAYFIELD, JULIEN. "Challenge to Negro Leadership." *Commentary*, April, 1961.

MORGAN, THOMAS. "Requiem or Revival." *Look*, June 14, 1966, pp. 73–75.

Newsweek

   "Nobelman King," October 26, 1964.

   "Off Hoover's Chest," November 30, 1964.

   "J. Edgar Hoover and the FBI," December 7, 1964.

   "The Hoover-King Meeting," December 14, 1964.

   "Up from Montgomery," December 21, 1964.

   "What to Do Next," November 29, 1965.

   "Gamble in the Ghetto," January 31, 1966.

"The March—in Step and Out," July 4, 1966.

"Black Power: Politics of Frustration," July 11, 1966.

"Line in the Dust," July 18, 1966.

"Grenada Revisited," July 25, 1966.

"Crisis in Color, '66," August 22, 1966.

"Watts Today," December 13, 1966.

PECK, JAMES. "The Freedom Ride and the Truman Walk." *Liberation*, Summer, 1961.

PRICE, RICHARD, and STEWART, BOB. "Watts, L.A.: A First-Hand Report, Rebellion Without Ideology." *Liberator*, September, 1965.

"Profiles in Courage." *Liberator*, June, 1963, p. 2.

QUARLES, BENJAMIN. "Martin Luther King in History." *Negro History Bulletin*, May, 1968.

ROMERO, PATRICIA. "Martin Luther King and His Challenge to White America." *Negro History Bulletin*, May, 1968, pp. 6–8.

ROWAN, CARL T. "Martin Luther King's Tragic Decision." *Reader's Digest*, September, 1967, pp. 37–42.

RUSTIN, BAYARD. "From Protest to Politics." *Commentary*, February, 1965.

―――. "The Meaning of Birmingham." *Liberation*, June, 1963.

―――, and KAHN, TOM. "Civil Rights." *Commentary*, June, 1965.

SCLC Newsletter. May, 1961, through June-July, 1964, especially: May, August, and September, 1961; February, March, April, and December, 1962; August and September, 1963; and June, 1964.

SHUTTLESWORTH, FRED. "Birmingham Shall Be Free Some Day." *Freedomways*, Winter, 1964.

Time

"Poorly Timed Protest," April 19, 1963.

"Man of the Year," January 3, 1964.

"Youngest Ever," October 23, 1964, p. 27.

"Letter from the Publishers," March 19, 1965, p. 21.

"Civil Rights," March 26, 1965, p. 19.

"King Moves North," April 30, 1965, p. 33.

"The New Racism," July 1, 1966, pp. 11–13.

"Civil Rights," July 15, 1966, pp. 15 and 16.

"The South," September 23, 1966, p. 26.

U.S. News & World Report

"How Martin Luther King Won the Nobel Peace Prize," February 8, 1961.

"The FBI and Civil Rights, J. Edgar Hoover Speaks Out," November 30, 1964, pp. 56–58.

"A Rebuke to Dr. King," August 30, 1965.

WALKER, WYATT T. "Achievement in Albany." *New South*, June, 1963.

―――. "The Congo, U.S.A.: Albany, Georgia." *SCLC Newsletter*, September, 1962.

————: "If Not Now—When?" *SCLC Newsletter*, July–August, 1964.

WELSH, DAVID, and HINCKLE, WARREN. "Five Battles of Selma." *Ramparts*, June, 1965.

WILLIAMS, HOSEA. "SCLC Puts Might of Its Organization Against 'Goldwaterism' to Aid Us Win." *SCLC Newsletter*, April–May, 1965.

NEWSPAPER ARTICLES

Afro-American
    "Boycotters Refute Fund Charges," June 23, 1956. p. 1.
    "Rev. King to Get Lovejoy Award," June 23, 1956, p. 6.
    Louis Lautier, "Leaders Impressed," July 5, 1958, p. 5.

Albany Herald
    "Albany Negro Students March, Protest Trials," November 27, 1961, p. 1.
    "A Foolish, Dangerous March," November 28, 1961, p. 1.
    Vic Smith, "Charges Brought Against Agitators by Albany State," November 29, 1961, p. 1.
    "Huge Urban Renewal Set for City," December 6, 1961, p. 1.
    "Our Revolution and Africa," December 10, 1961.
    "Freedom Riders Face Trials Here," December 11, 1961, p. 1.
    Vic Smith, "Jail Negro Demonstrators as Trials of 11 Open Here," "December 12, 1961, p. 1.
    "New Negro Demonstrators Cited for Court Contempt," December 13, 1961, p. 1.
    Vic Smith, "Albany Guard Alerted," December 14, 1961, p. 1.
    "The Passing Storm," December 14, 1961, p. 1.
    "Albanians for Albany," December 14, 1961, p. 3.
    "Negro Committee Demands All Violators Be Released," December 15, 1961, p. 1.
    Vic Smith, "City Officials Reject Negro Group's Demands," December 16, 1961, p. 1.
    "Peace Prevails as Police Jail More Demonstrators, Including Martin Luther King," December 17, 1961, p. 1.
    Vic Smith, "Standing for Law and Justice," December 17, 1961, p. 1.
    "Trials Delayed, City Confers with Negroes," December 18, 1961, p. 1.
    "Demonstrations, Boycott Called Off by Negroes Here," December 19, 1961, p. 1.

Atlanta Daily World
    "Let Albany Have Its Chance," December 19, 1961, p. 6.
    "Let Us Stick to Issues and Methods, Please Mr. Walker," December 21, 1961, p. 6.

"Let's Keep the Record Straight," December 26, 1961, p. 6.

"Leadership Conference Assembly at Hurt Park Today, 10,000 Expected," December 15, 1963, p. 1.

"Hurt Park Assembly Draws Many Despite Bitter Cold," December 17, 1963, p. 1.

Atlanta Enquirer

" 'Riders' Experience Favors Continuation," July 29, 1961, p. 1.

Bill Strong, "Time to Take a (Firm) Stand," August 5, 1961, p. 2.

Ruby Doris Smith, "Non-Violence Can Work in United States, Rider Says," August 5, 1961, p. 10.

Wallace Westfeldt, "Settling a Sit-in," August 5, 1961, p. 14.

"Who Should Be Supported for Mayor?" August 26, 1961, p. 2.

"Rev. M. L. King's Group Denies 'Meddling' and 'Defeat' in Albany," December 23, 1961, p. 1.

"Deny Students Have Lost Faith in King," January 6, 1962, p. 1.

"King Aide Takes Editor to Task," January 25, 1964, p. 1.

"Cross-Section of Views," April 4, 1964, p. 5.

"Georgia Council Answers Hoover's Attack on Dr. King," November 28, 1964, p. 2.

"Bond, SNCC, Viet Nam," January 15, 1966.

Birmingham News

"10 More Negroes Arrested in Sit-ins," April 5, 1963, p. 2

"32 Negroes Jailed After March Try," April 6, 1963, p. 2.

"65 Negroes Held After Sit-ins, March," April 7, 1963, p. A2.

"More Racial Moves Set," April 11, 1963, p. 8.

"Current of Compromise Flows Through Tension Here," April 14, 1963, p. A2.

"Mrs. King's Phone Call Story Is Said to Be 'Just a Bit Phony,' " April 18, 1963, p. 4.

"Fire Hoses, Police Dogs Used to Halt Downtown Negro Demonstrations," May 3, 1963, p. 2.

"City Firemen Again Hose Down Rock-throwing Demonstrators," May 4, 1963.

"Police, Firemen, Disperse Demonstrators with Fire Hoses, Nearly 250 Go to Jail," May 5, 1963, p. A8.

"Demonstrations Said Suspended," May 8, 1963, p. 2.

"White House Studying Birmingham," May 8, 1963, p. 2.

"Demonstrations off Pending More Talks," May 9, 1963, p. 2.

"Blasts Rock Home of King's Brother and Gaston Motel, at Least Three Reported Hurt," May 12, 1963, p. 1.

Ron Gibson, "King, 250, Jailed for Selma March," February 1, 1965, p. 1.

Ron Gibson, "Students Arrested in Selma," February 2, 1965, p. 1.

Al Stanton, "Probe Selma, Congress Urged," February 3, 1965, p. 1.

Ron Gibson, "Negroes to March Despite Court Defeat," February 4, 1965, p. 1.

Ron Gibson, "Dallas Voter Board to Comply," February 5, 1965, p. 1.

Ron Gibson, "Negroes to Shift Drive to Capital," February 6, 1965, p. 1.

"King Leads Uneventful Capital March," February 9, 1965.

James Free, "King's 'Master Plan' for Selma May be Fizzling," February 11, 1965, p. 1.

"NAACP to Direct Voter Drive with State," May 1, 1965, p. 2.

"King Boycott Backfires in Business Circles," May 2, 1965, p. 1.

"Selma Whites, Negroes Talking but Problems Not Yet Solved," May 3, 1965, p. 7.

"Negotiate, or Agitate?" May 6, 1965, p. 15.

"King Introduces Class War Theme," May 11, 1965, p. 6.

Chicago Defender (Weekly)

"My Dream—Peace: 'God's Man's Business,' " January 1–7, 1966, p. 10.*

Betty Washington, "Dr. King Will Occupy Chicago Slum Flat in New Rights Drive," January 8–14, 1966, p. 1.

"My Dream: The Violence of Poverty," January 8–14, 1966, p. 10.

"My Dream: Message for My People," January 15–21, 1966, p. 10.

"My Dream: Is Non-Violence Doomed?" January 22–28, 1966.

Betty Washington, "Dr. King Meets with Top Cops, Map Plan to Prevent Violence," January 29–February 4, 1966, p. 1.

"My Dream: Bond and the Constitution," January 29–February 4, 1966, p. 10.

"My Dream," February 12–18, 1966.

"My Dream," February 19–25, 1966.

"King, Muslims, Join Forces in War on Slums," February 26–March 4, 1966, p. 1.

"My Dream: Our Jewish Brother," March 5–11, 1966, p. 10.

"My Dream: Never Negative Normalcy," March 12–18, 1966, p. 10.

"Dr. King Misses Big Daley Slum Parley," March 19–25, 1966, p. 1.

"My Dream: Creative Non-Conformist," April 2–9, 1966.

"My Dream: A Prayer for Chicago," April 16–22, 1966.

"Dr. King, SCLC, Join Fight on Alabama Voting Results: 'Seriously Suspicious' of Wallace Win," May 7–14, 1966, p. 1.

"Cicero Teens Bludgeon Youth with Baseball Bats," May 28–June 3, 1966, p. 1.

Glenn Douglas, "Sweden Gives King $100,000 for His Work," July 16–22, 1966.

"Politicians Meet King, Raby, Agree to Civil Rights Demands," August 6–12, 1966, p. 1.

---

* "My Dream" is the title of the weekly column of Martin Luther King, Jr.

"The W.G.N.—and Justice," August 13–19, 1966, p. 1.

"Cicero March Called off, King, Realty Forces, Reach Agreement," August 27–September 2, 1966, p. 1.

Adolph J. Slaughter, "Martin Luther King—Mercy Killer," September 10–16, 1966.

"Dr. King Makes Plea for 'Striped Power,'" September 24–30, 1966, p. 1.

"Negro View of King vs. Jackson: Carmichael and Mohammad Also Measured," October 15–21, 1966, p. 1.

Gordon Hancock, "A Critique: Dr. Martin Luther King and Southern Jim-Crowism," November 12–18, 1966, p. 11.

Chicago Tribune

"Daley, U.S. Government Clash on Control over Poverty War," January 2, 1966, p. 1.

"Dissent Rally Ends in Impasse," January 16, 1966, p. 5.

Arthur Jackman, "Dr. King's Flat, Although Painted, Is Very Dismal," January 26, 1966, p. 8.

"Dr. King, Mate, Live in Flat—for One Day," January 27, 1966, p. 5.

"Plan New Drive on Slum Lords," February 10, 1966, p. 1.

"Lincoln, in 1838, Hit Disregard for Law," February 12, 1966, p. 2.

"Dr. King Tells Plan for Negro Boycott," February 12, 1966, p. 5.

"Dr. King Takes over Slum Building," February 24, 1966, p. 3.

"City Stays Clear of Slum Grab," February 26, 1966, p. 3.

"Owner Acts in Building Grab," March 5, 1966, p. 3.

"Dr. King Assailed by Committee of 100," March 8, 1966, p. 8.

"Legal and Illegal Slum Campaigns," March 8, 1966, p. 12.

"Daley Calls Parley of Clergy on Slums," March 15, 1966, p. 1.

"Daley, Clergy, Talk on Race," March 19, 1966, p. 3.

"Daley, Clergy, Meet Again on Race Problem," April 1, 1966, p. 22.

"South Side Rights Group Seizes Flats," April 8, 1966, p. 1.

"King Discloses Plan for Rally, March on City Hall on June 26," May 27, 1966, p. 1.

"Negro Beaten by Gang with Ball Bat, Dies," May 30, 1966, p. 1.

"Meredith Ambushed, Shot," June 7, 1966, p. 1.

"King Takes Up Vote March," June 8, 1966, p. 1.

"7 Shot in New Disorders," June 14, 1966, p. 1.

"Hard Campaign Waged for Passage," June 14, 1966, p. 1.

"Gas King, 2000, in March," June 24, 1966, p. 1.

"Civil Rights Militants Rapped," July 4, 1966, p. 3.

"King and Daley to Talk in City Hall Monday," July 9, 1966, p. 7.

"King Tells Goals, March on City Hall," July 11, 1966, p. 1.

"Daley, King, Aide, Meet on Rights," July 12, 1966, p. 1.

"Links Riots and King Aides," July 16, 1966, p. 1.

"Daley Appoints 23," July 26, 1966, p. 6.

"Three Arrested During March on Daley House," August 5, 1966, p. 10.

"King to March Today," August 5, 1966, p. 16.

"Dr. King is Felled by a Rock," August 6, 1966, p. 1.

"600 Police Halt Hecklers," August 8, 1966, p. 1.

"Cicero Officials Ask for Alert of Troops," August 10, 1966, p. 1.

"Housing Protest March in Loop," August 11, 1966, p. 1.

"Tell City's Renewal Plan," August 12, 1966, p. 1.

"Police Keep Bogan March Peace," August 13, 1966, p. 1.

"Dr. King, Realtors, Agree to Meeting," August 14, 1966, p. 1.

"5 Cops Hurt in Race Disorders," August 15, 1966, p. 1.

"King Rejects No March Appeal," August 18, 1966, p. 1.

"King Plans Rights Test Today," August 19, 1966, p. 1.

"More Effrontery," August 19, 1966, p. 18.

"Daley Makes Plea to City," August 20, 1966, p. 1.

"King Orders New March Held Today," August 21, 1966, p. 1.

"Arrest 20 During South Side March," August 22, 1966, p. 1.

"King Asked to Stop March," August 23, 1966, p. 1.

"Tell Cicero March Plans," August 26, 1966, p. 1.

David Halvorsen, "Cancel Rights Marches," August 27, 1966, p. 1.

"Defer Plan for March into Cicero," August 28, 1966, p. 1.

"Cicero to Permit March, Asks for Troops," August 31, 1966, p. 1.

"Cicero Holds Up Permit on Rights March," September 1, 1966, p. 1.

"March Ends in a Rock Fight," September 5, 1966, p. 1.

Commercial Appeal (Memphis, Tennessee)

Joseph Thompson, "Garbage Truck Kills 2 Crewmen," February 2, 1968, p. 1.

Joseph Sweat, "Garbage Dispute Drones On," February 14, 1968, p. 1.

Joseph Sweat, "Loeb Ultimatum Hurled in Strike," February 15, 1968, p. 1.

"These Are the Issues," February 20, 1968, p. 1.

"Committee Gives In to Sit-in of Strikers," February 23, 1968, p. 1.

"Angry Sanitation Workers Clash Briefly with Police," February 24, 1968, p. 1.

Dorothy Butt, "Strikers, Backers to March Today," February 26, 1968, p. 1.

Joseph Sweat, "Striking Union Seeks Transfer into U.S. Court," March 1, 1968, p. 1.

"Mayor, Pastors, Meet," March 2, 1968, p. 1.

Thomas Fox, "Marchers Draw Little Attention," March 3, 1968, p. 1.

Larry Scroggs, "117 Strike Backers Take Stroll to Jail," March 6, 1968, p. 1.

Joseph Sweat, "Roy Wilkins, Bayard Rustin, Due Here to Support Strike," March 13, 1968, p. 1.

"King to Lend Vocal Support in Strike Rally," March 17, 1968, p. 1.

K. W. Cook, "King Urges Work Stoppage by Negroes to Back Strike," March 19, 1968, p. 1.

"Guardsmen Back Riot Curfew," March 29, 1968, p. 1.

Thomas Beviar, "King Disappointed in March—He'll Try Again Next Week," March 30, 1968, p. 1.

"King Challenges Court Restraint, Vows to March," April 4, 1968, p. 1.

John Means, "Dr. King Is Slain by Sniper," April 5, 1968, p. 1.

Danville (Virginia) *Register*

"Freedom Is for the Law-abiding Only," June 6, 1963, p. A4.

"Fire Hoses, Billy Sticks, Rout Night Demonstrators," June 11, 1963, p. 1.

"An Uneasy Calm Prevails as Racial Troubles Mount," June 12, 1963, p. 1.

"After King Talks and Negroes Walk," July 12, 1963, p. A1.

"White Agitator Now Heads Danville Demonstrations," July 18, 1963, p. 1.

Detroit News

"Dr. King Now a 'Peace Hawk,'" April 6, 1967, p. B12.

Montgomery (Alabama) *Advertiser*

"Police Reports," December 2, 1955.

"Negro Groups Ready Boycott of City Lines," December 4, 1955, p. 1.

Joe Azbell, "5000 at Meeting Outline Boycott," December 6, 1955, p. 1.

"Bus Boycott Conference Fails to Find Solution," December 9, 1955.

"Tell It to Old Grandma," December 12, 1955, p. A4.

"Tell It to Old Grandma," December 15, 1955, p. A4.

Tom Johnson, "Truce Sessions Set Today in Effort to End Tiff," December 17, 1955, p. 1.

"Committee Fails to Reach Settlement in Bus Boycott," December 18, 1955, p. 1.

"Bus Officials Press Demand for Fare Hike," January 4, 1956, p. 1.

"Bus Officials Win Approval on Fare Boost," January 5, 1956, p. 1.

"New Bus Pact by City Lines Likely Today," January 17, 1956.

"City Commission States Position on Bus Services," January 22, 1956, p. 1.

Joe Azbell, "Mayor Stops Boycott Talk," January 24, 1956, p. 1.

"Boycott Boss Gets $4 Fine in Speed Case," January 29, 1956.

Joe Azbell, "Blast Rocks Residence of Bus Boycott Leader," January 31, 1956, p. 1.

Joe Azbell, "5 Negroes Attack Segregation Laws in Federal Courts," February 2, 1956, p. 1.

"Negro Woman Withdraws Action," February 3, 1956, p. 1.

Steven Lesher, "Five Lawyers Ready Defense of Boycotters," March 18, 1956, p. 1.

Tom Johnson, "Defense Uses 28 Witnesses in King Trial," March 22, 1956, p. 1.

"Court Fines King $500 on Boycott Law Charge," March 23, 1956, p. 1.

New York Herald Tribune

David Miller, "Inside the Jail," December 18, 1961, p. 1.

David Miller, "A Loss for Dr. King," December 19, 1961, p. 1.

New York Times

"Dr. King Is Jailed for Georgia Protest," July 11, 1962, p. 1.

C. Phillips, "Kennedy Requests Reports on Dr. King," July 12, 1962, p. 1.

"Dr. King Threatens New Drive for Negro Rights in Albany, Georgia," July 16, 1962, p. 1.

Claude Sitton, "Negroes Defy Ban, March in Georgia," July 22, 1962, p. 1.

Claude Sitton, "Dr. King Denounces U.S. Judge for Ban on Georgia Protests," July 23, 1962, p. 1.

Claude Sitton, "Albany, Georgia, Police Break Up Protest by 2000 Negroes," July 25, 1962, p. 1.

"Dr. King Sets a Day of Penance After Violence in Albany, Georgia," July 26, 1962, p. 1.

"Dr. King Is Jailed Again at Prayer Rally in Georgia," July 28, 1962, p. 1.

"Negro Lawyer Is Beaten, 37 Arrested in Albany, Georgia," July 29, 1962, p. 1.

H. Smith, "Dr. King Set Back in U.S. Court Test," July 31, 1962, p. 1.

Martin Luther King, Jr. "The Case Against 'Tokenism,'" *Magazine*, August 5, 1962, p. 11.

"Dr. King Set Free After Conviction," August 11, 1962, p. 1.

Claude Sitton, "Robert Kennedy Unable to Budge Alabama Governor on Race Issue," April 26, 1963, p. 17.

"Dr. King Convicted: Gets Mild Sentence," April 27, 1963, p. 9.

"Alabama Sets Murder Charge in Killing of Postman in March," April 28, 1963, p. 84.

Foster Haley, "500 Are Arrested in Negro Protest at Birmingham," May 3, 1963, p. 1.

Foster Haley, "Dogs and Hoses Repulse Negroes at Birmingham," May 4, 1963, p. 1.

Foster Haley, "U.S. Seeking a Truce in Birmingham: Hoses Again Drive off Demonstrators," May 5, 1963, p. 1.

Foster Haley, "Birmingham Talks Pushed," May 6, 1963, p. 1.

Claude Sitton, "Birmingham Jails One Thousand More Negroes," May 7, 1963, p. 1.

Claude Sitton, "Rioting Negroes Routed by Police at Birmingham," May 8, 1963, p. 1.

Claude Sitton, "Peace Talks Gain at Birmingham in a Day of Truce," May 9, 1963, p. 1.

Claude Sitton, "Birmingham Pact Sets Time Table for Integration," May 10, 1963, p. 1.

H. Smith, "Bombs Touch Off Wide-Spread Riot at Birmingham," May 11, 1963, p. 1.

Claude Sitton, "U.S. Sends Troops to Alabama," May 13, 1963, p. 1.

Tom Wicker, "Troops Won't Go into Birmingham if Peace Prevails," May 14, 1963, p. 1.

Claude Sitton, "Whites Cautious on Alabama Pact," May 15, 1963, p. 1.

Claude Sitton, "Birmingham Pact Picks Up Support," May 16, 1963, p. 1.

Anthony Lewis, "Supreme Court Legalizes Sit-ins in Cities Enforcing Segregation," May 21, 1963, p. 1.

Claude Sitton, "Negro Students Ousted for Birmingham Protest," May 21, 1963, p. 1.

Claude Sitton, "Alabama University Told to Admit Negroes," May 22, 1963, p. 1.

Foster Haley, "The Birmingham Story: Segregation Is Teetering Under Fire," May 26, 1963, p. 58.

"Joint Negro Council Allocates $565,000 to Rights Groups," July 18, 1963, p. 10.

M. S. Handler, "Marchers Widen Rights Demands," August 21, 1963, p. 24.

Peter Grose, "Americans Abroad Give Support to Rights March," August 22, 1963.

"Capitol Is Ready," August 28, 1963, p. 1.

"200 Thousand March for Civil Rights," August 29, 1963, p. 1.

"Dr. King Says He Needs 'A Long Period of Rest,'" December 5, 1964, p. 19.

"Dr. King Arrives in London: Speaks at St. Paul's Today," December 6, 1964, p. 2.

"Dr. King, Preaching in London, Calls on Negroes for Restraint," December 7, 1964, p. 1.

"Dr. King and Family Reach Oslo," December 9, 1964, p. 3.

"Dr. King Proposes a Rights Alliance," December 10, 1964, p. 58.

James Feron, "Dr. King Accepts Nobel Prize as 'Trustee,'" December 11, 1964, p. 1.

James Feron, "Dr. King Stresses Nonviolence Role," December 12, 1964, p. 1.

"Dr. King Explains Tactics of a Mississippi Boycott," December 13, 1964, p. 56.

John Herbers, "Dr. King Punched and Kicked in Alabama Hotel," January 19, 1965, p. 1.

Peter Kihss, "Rights Units Feel a Financial Pinch," January 19, 1965, p. 21.

John Herbers, "67 Negroes Jailed in Alabama Drive," January 20, 1965, p. 1.

John Herbers, "Two Alabama Officials Clash over Arrests in Negro Vote Drive," January 21, 1965, p. 1.

John Herbers, "Selma Campaign: Plea to Nation," January 22, 1965.

John Herbers, "Negro Teachers Protest in Selma," January 23, 1965, p. 18.

"Woman Punches Alabama Sheriff," January 26, 1965, p. 1.

Fred Powledge, "Atlanta Praises Dr. King at Fete," January 28, 1965, p. 15.

John Herbers, "Dr. King and 770 Others Seized in Alabama Protest," February 2, 1965, p. 1.

"520 More Seized in Alabama Drive," February 3, 1965, p. 1.

John Herbers, "Negroes Step Up Drive in Alabama," February 4, 1965, p. 1.

John Herbers, "Speed Negro Vote, Alabama Is Told," February 5, 1965, p. 1.

Roy Reed, "Dr. King to Seek New Voting Law," February 6, 1965, p. 1.

John D. Pomfret, "President Promises Dr. King Vote Move," February 10, 1965, p. 1.

Roy Reed, "165 Selma Negro Youths Taken on Forced March," February 11, 1965, p. 1.

John Herbers, "Negroes in Selma Offer Their Prayers for Stricken Sheriff Clark," February 13, 1965, p. 1.

John Herbers, "Dr. King Leads 2300 in 3 Alabama Vote Marches," February 16, 1965, p. 18.

John Herbers, "Negroes Beaten in Alabama Riot," February 19, 1965, p. 1.

Roy Reed, "A Twilight March Stopped in Selma," February 24, 1965, p. 1.

Roy Reed, "Selma Reported to Seek Harmony," February 26, 1965, p. 1.

"266 Apply to Vote as Selma Speeds Negro Registration," March 2, 1965, p. 1.

Roy Reed, "White Alabamians Stage Selma March to Support Negroes," March 7, 1965, p. 1.

Roy Reed, "Alabama Police Use Gas and Clubs to Rout Negroes," March 8, 1965, p. 1.

Roy Reed, "New Selma March Today," March 9, 1965, p. 1.

Roy Reed, "Dr. King Leads March at Selma," March 10, 1965, p. 1.

John Herbers, "Mayor and Police Block Three New Marches in Selma," March 11, 1965, p. 1.

"Selma Marchers in Street Third Day," March 12, 1965, p. 1.

"Johnson Pledges Vote for All," March 14, 1965, p. 1.

Roy Reed, "Selma March Held After U.S. Court Arranges Accord," March 16, 1965, p. 1.

Gay Talese, "Burly Sheriff Clark Is Selma Symbol of Racism," March 16, 1965, p. 32.

Roy Reed, "Police Rout 600 in Montgomery," March 17, 1965, p. 1.

Fendall W. Yerxa, "Johnson Calls Up Troops," March 21, 1965, p. 1.

Roy Reed, "Freedom March Begins at Selma," March 22, 1965, p. 1.

Roy Reed, "25,000 Go to Alabama's Capitol," March 26, 1965, p. 1.

Roy Reed, "Meredith Is Shot in Back on Walk into Mississippi," June 7, 1966, p. 1.

Gene Roberts, "Troopers Shove Group Resuming Meredith March," June 8, 1966, p. 1.

Gene Roberts, "March's Leaders Demand Action by U.S. on Rights," June 9, 1966, p. 1.

Gene Roberts, "Mississippi March Gains Momentum," June 10, 1966, p. 1.

Gene Roberts, "Mississippi March Criticized by Evers," June 11, 1966, p. 1.

Gene Roberts, "Mississippi Reduces Police Protection for Marchers," June 17, 1966, p. 1.

Walter Rugaber, "A Negro Is Killed in Memphis March," March 29, 1968.

Walter Ruagber, "Dr. King to March in Memphis Again," March 30, 1968.

José Yglesias, "Dr. King's March on Washington, Part II," *Magazine*, March 31, 1968.

Earl Caldwell, "Court Bars March in Memphis," April 4, 1968.

Earl Caldwell, "Martin Luther King Is Slain in Memphis," April 5, 1968.

"King Cited Threat Day Before Death," April 5, 1968, p. 24.
Homer Bigart, "Dr. Martin Luther King Buried in Atlanta," April 10, 1968.

Pittsburgh Courier
Trezvant W. Anderson, "How Has Dramatic Bus Boycott Affected Montgomery Negroes?" *Magazine,* December 21, 1957, p. 6.
Trezvant W. Anderson, "How Has Dramatic Bus Boycott Affected Montgomery Negroes?" *Magazine,* December 28, 1957, p. 3.
"Dr. King Awaits Appeal as Brother Also Is Jailed," February 18, 1961, p. 8.
"Jackson Ousts Martin L. King," September 16, 1961, p. 2.
Trezvant W. Anderson, "King Won't Fight Firing by Jackson," September 23, 1961, p. 2.
Trezvant W. Anderson, "What's Martin Luther King's Role in Bank Dealing?" June 30, 1962, p. 1.

Washington (D.C.) *Evening Star*
"Giant Appeal Is Made Under Lincoln's Eyes," August 28, 1963, p. 1.
"Leaders Go to Capitol," August 28, 1963, p. 1.
"Throng Gets Quick Start," August 28, 1963, p. 1.
David Broder, "Successful March Pleases Leaders of Civil Rights Drive," August 29, 1963, p. 1.

Washington (D.C.) *Post*
"Crowd Chants for the Ballot at Pilgrimage, President, Congress, Called upon to Lead Struggle for Equality," May 18, 1957, p. 1.
Alvin Spivak, "Negro Leaders Here to See Ike," June 23, 1958, p. A3.
"Negro Leaders Ask Ike to Act," June 24, 1958, p. A12.
Drew Pearson, "Meeting with Hoover Angers King," December 5, 1964, p. E15.

UNPUBLISHED SOURCES

DAVID, WILLIAM EDWARD. "A Comparative Study of the Social Ethics of Walter Rauschenbusch and Reinhold Niebuhr." Ph.D. dissertation, Vanderbilt University, 1958.
KING, MARTIN LUTHER, JR. "A Comparison of the Conceptions of God in the Thinking of Paul Tillich and Henry Nelson Wieman." Ph.D. dissertation, Boston University, 1955.
SMITH, KENNETH LEE. "The Social Gospel Movement," manuscript, March 11, 1962.

INTERVIEWS AND CORRESPONDENCE

AMOS, MRS. INDIA. August, 1968.
BARBOUR, J. PIUS. Minister. September, 1968.

BENNETT, LERONE, JR. Author. September, 1968.

BERRY, WILLIAM. Director, Chicago Urban League. September, 1968.

BRAZIER, ARTHUR. Director, Woodlawn Organization. September, 1968.

BUFORD, K. L. Director, NAACP (Montgomery). August, 1968.

CARMICHAEL, STOKELY. Former Director, SNCC. August, 1968.

CARTER, HAL. Minister. January, 1969.

CHALMERS, ALLAN K. (correspondence). Theologian, January 13, 1969.

CLAYTON, MRS. EDWARD T. Community Affairs Coordinator. August, 1968.

DEWOLF, L. HAROLD. Theologian. September, 1968.

FARMER, JAMES. Former Director, CORE. December, 1968.

FAUNTROY, WALTER. Director, SCLC (Washington, D.C.). September, 1968.

FRANKLIN, JOHN HOPE. Historian. September, 1968.

GOLLIN, ALBERT E. Research associate, Bureau of Social Science Research. March, 1969.

GRAY, FRED. Attorney. August, 1968.

HAIRSTON, MRS. BEATRICE. Retired schoolteacher. August, 1968.

HAMILTON, MRS. GRACE T. Member, Georgia House of Representatives. August, 1968.

HARPER, MRS. C. L. August, 1968.

HOOVER, J. EDGAR (correspondence). Director, FBI. September 9, 1968.

KELLER, ANDREW Z. Epidemiologist. August and October, 1968.

KING, CHEVENE. Attorney. August, 1968.

KING, SLATER. Businessman. August, 1968.

LAUE, JAMES H. Community Relations Service. February, 1969.

LEVISON, STANLEY. Attorney. November, 1968.

LEWIS, JOHN (correspondence). Former Director, SNCC. December, 1968.

LEWIS, MILTON. Community Relations Service. October, 1968, and April, 1969.

LEWIS, MRS. S. M. August, 1968.

MACDONALD, DORA (correspondence). Private Secretary to Martin Luther King, Jr. May 22, 1969.

MAYS, BENJAMIN. President Emeritus, Morehouse College. August, 1968.

MEEK, RUSS. Chicago militant. September, 1968.

MEIER, AUGUST. Historian. January, 1969.

MILLER, WILLIAM F. Community Relations Service. August, 1968.

MOORE, MRS. JANE BOND. August, 1968.

MUSE, MRS. MAXINE. Attorney, August. 1968.

NIXON, E. D. Retired pullman porter, August, 1968.

POPPER, MRS. ROBERT L. (correspondence). September 12, 1968, and November 3, 1968.

QUARLES, BENJAMIN. Historian. January, 1969.

REDDICK, LAWRENCE. Historian. December, 1968.

ROBINSON, MRS. JOANN (correspondence). Schoolteacher. November 14, 1968.

SHERROD, CHARLES. Former field secretary, SNCC. August, 1968.

SMITH, KENNETH L. Theologian. September, 1968.

THORNELL, RICHARD P. Formerly of Community Relations Service. March, 1969.

WALKER, MRS. ROSLYN POPE. August, 1968.

WILKINS, ROY. Director, NAACP. November, 1968.

WILLIAMS, SAMUEL. Philosopher. August, 1968.

YATES, CLAYTON R. Businessman. August, 1968.

Index

A. Philip Randolph Institute, 357
Abernathy, Mrs. Ralph D., 82
Abernathy, Ralph David, 51–52, 66,
  75, 79, 80, 88, 96, 108, 132, 147,
  149, 153, 159, 161, 164, 174, 175,
  182, 183, 184, 191, 192, 233, 244,
  260, 268, 273, 277, 290, 329, 368,
  375, 384, 386, 387, 388, 389, 391;
  conceives MIA, 56; presents Montgomery boycott demands, 58; as
  MIA committee chairman, 61;
  posts King's bond, 69; in jail, 74;
  and California vacation, 76; boards
  desegregated bus, 81; in Atlanta,
  82; and bombing of church and
  home, 82; as treasurer of SNLC,
  89; meets with Vice-President
  Nixon, 94–95; Albany appeal of,
  152; on trial in Albany, 167; Birmingham arrest of, 199; in Danville, 212; St. Augustine imprisonment of, 241; and European trip,
  254; and Hoover meeting, 256–57;
  jailed, 367; in Memphis, 380; on
  Poor People's Campaign, 385
Abrams, Creighton W., 203
Abrams, Morris, 128
Abyssinian Baptist Church (New
  York City), 256
Adams, Julius, 212
Adams, Sherman, 88–89
AFL-CIO, 169, 250, 286, 331, 351,
  357; Memphis Central Labor
  Council, 379
Africa, 272
African Methodist Episcopal de-
  nomination, 73, 392
African Methodist Episcopal Zion,
  54, 56
Afro-American, 94
Agape, 44, 103
Agenda Committee, 319, 351
Ahimsa, 72

Ahmann, Mathew, 215, 221
Ahmedabad, India, 102, 103, 104
Aiken Construction Corporation, 10
Alabama, 135; Marion, 40, 42, 271;
  Perry County, 41, 271; Alabama
  State College, 48, 49, 53, 147–48;
  Marengo County, 51; Alabama
  Negro Baptist Center, 60–61, 66;
  Anniston, 71, 132, 175; Univer-
  sity of Alabama, 71, 85, 215; and
  King tax case, 121; Gadsden, 175;
  Talledega, 175; Alabama Christian
  Movement for Human Rights,
  177; Alabama Council on Human
  Relations, 191; state supreme court
  ousts Hanes, 200; Dallas County,
  269, 270; Camden, 270, 293; Wil-
  cox County, 270; Mobile, 272;
  Highway 80, 273, 280, 288;
  Lowndes County, 288; St. Jude,
  289; Demopolis, 294; Greensboro,
  294; Eutaw, 294
Alabama Christian Movement for
  Human Rights (ACMHR), 172,
  173, 175, 179, 182, 199; peace demands of, 195; and settlement,
  200
Alabama Human Relations Council,
  59, 61, 62
Albany, Ga., 94, 103, 112, 140–70;
  158, 168, 185, 192, 207, 212, 239,
  243, 250, 267, 383; Albany State
  College, 142–43; Criterion Club,
  142, 145; NAACP Youth Council,
  142, 143, 145; Ministerial Alliance, 145; Federation of Women's
  Clubs, 145; Negro Voters League,
  145; Freedom Train, 146
Albany Herald, 140, 143, 146, 148,
  149–50, 153, 155
Albany Movement, 145, 146, 147–
  70; injunction against, 161, 175,
  177

439

Aldrich, Alexander, 286
Alexander, T. M., Sr., 73
Allen, Ivan, Jr., 233, 255, 266
Alliance For Progress, 166
American Federation of State, County, and Municipal Employees, 378, 379; Local 1733, 378, 379
American Friends Society, 99; Service Committee, 319
American Jewish Council, 215, 222
American Jewish Theological Seminary, 286
American Nazi Party, 342
American Negro Labor Council, 214, 221
Amos, Mrs. India, 16
Amsterdam (Netherlands), 254
"An Appeal for Law and Order and Common Sense," 186, 187
Anderson, William G., 143, 147, 148, 149, 164, 167; as president of Albany Movement, 145
Angola (Africa), 186
Antioch College, 40, 41
Antipoverty program, 251, 309
Appalachia, 373
Aquinas, Saint Thomas, 51
Archer, Samuel H., 19
Armstrong, Mrs. Louis, 90
Arnold, Benedict, 77
Aryanayakam, Ashadevi, 101
Ashby Street (Atlanta), 16
Assistant Corporation Counsel, 317
Associated Press, 67; and nullification of bus segregation, 79
Atlanta, Ga., 46, 73, 112, 114, 133, 136, 142, 156–57, 185, 201, 203, 204, 206, 231, 232, 244, 245, 270, 273, 299, 300, 319, 351, 384; race riot of 1905, 5; Voters' League, 5; SNCC meeting in, 120–21; march on, 233; Summit Leadership Conference in, 233, 234; Hurt Park, 233; Heart of Atlanta Motel, 234; Magnolia Ballroom, 248; St. Joseph's Infirmary, 255; Nobel reception in, 266–67; Dinkler Plaza Hotel, 266; SCLC meeting in, 368; Southview Cemetery, 392

Atlanta Constitution: student manifesto in, 114, 266
Atlanta Daily World, 10, 73, 157
Atlanta Enquirer, 299, 311
Atlanta Journal, 14
Atlanta Life Insurance Company, 9, 22, 157
Atlanta Mutual Building Loan and Savings Association, 9
Atlanta University, 10, 18, 24, 73, 120, 391; laboratory high school of, 15; Student Dormitory Council of, 114
Auburn Avenue (Atlanta), 9–10, 15, 245, 319
Azbell, Joe, 53, 55, 62

Baez, Joan, 224, 225, 289
Bagley, J. E., 62, 65
Baker, Ella, 108, 113, 115, 120, 136, 137, 213
Baker, Josephine, 225
Baker, Wilson, 265, 267, 275, 277, 281, 283
Baldwin, David, 217
Baldwin, James, 131, 204, 220–21, 224, 225, 239, 251, 289, 299, 376; *Harper's* article by, 131; and meeting with Robert Kennedy, 217–18; on Mississippi, 328
Ballou, Maude, 66, 113
Bankhead, Tallulah, 76
Baptist Ministers Conference, 173
Barbour, J. Pius, 26, 27–28, 30, 31, 32, 33, 36, 57, 213, 260, 354
Baton Rouge, La., 63
Beamon Cafe, 319
Beard, Charles, 177
Belafonte, Harry, 91, 156, 182, 217, 224, 225, 289, 299, 318, 361; SCLC meeting at apartment of, 176
Belfrage, Sally, 248
Bender, John, 317, 318
Benedict, Don, 319
Bennett, L. Roy, 53, 54, 56, 57, 58
Bennett, Lerone, 13, 94, 116, 206; on Albany, 169; and Chicago criticism of King, 334

Bennett, Marion, 114
Bennett, Tony, 289
Berkeley, George, 39
Bernstein, Leonard, 289
Berry, Marion, 113, 120, 125, 136
Berry, William, 217, 303, 304, 315, 319; on *The Today Show*, 337
Beulah Baptist Church (Montgomery), 77
Bevel, James, 137, 179, 192, 194, 195, 251, 270, 276, 280, 286, 287, 314, 339, 340, 352, 358; in Memphis, 380, 387
Bhave, Vinoba, 101, 102, 104
Bibb, Leon, 289
Big Bethel Church (Atlanta), 10
Bill of Rights for the Disadvantaged, 368
Billingsley, Orzell, 74, 185
Billups, Charles, 173, 194, 231
Bimini (Bahamas), 256
Birmingham, Ala., 104, 132, 137, 156, 169, 170, 171–209, 186, 210, 211, 224, 231, 232, 235, 244, 293, 352, 383; Senior Citizens Committee in, 173; and Project C, 174, 176, 177, 178, 181, 191, 192, 197; and B Day, 176, 209; and D Day, 192, 193; Chamber of Commerce, 197; Trust National Bank, 198; settlement, 200; riot in, 202; Federal Building, 203; church bombing in, 205–6; Federal Savings and Loan Association, 295; Municipal Auditorium, 304
Birmingham Manifesto, 177
Birmingham News, 175, 202, 270
"Black Billy," 13
Black Muslims, 108, 125
Black Power, 253
Blackstone Rangers, 331
Blackwell, Randolph T., 244
Blair, Ezell, Jr., 113
Blake, Eugene Carson, 215, 221
Blake, J. F., 47, 50
Blanton, Sankey L., 29
Blaustein, Albert P., 95
Blough, Roger, 198
Bond, Julian, 114, 231, 233, 311, 353
Bondurant, Joan V., 85

Booker T. Washington High School (Atlanta), 4, 12, 15, 16, 17
Borders, H. L., 91
Boston, Mass., 43; and Roxbury, 295, 298, 373; King visit to, 298; Common, 299
Boston University, 28, 29, 31, 38, 45, 47; School of Theology, 39; King collection, 254; Mugar Library, 254
Boutwell, Albert, 175, 177, 184, 195, 204, 209, 293
Bowles, Chester, 123; and letter to King, 97–98
Bowne, Borden P., 39, 40
Boyle, Sarah Patton, 190
Boynton, Amelia, 267
Boyte, Harry, 241
Branch, Benjamin, 388
Brando, Marlon, 224, 225
Brandt, Willy, 254
Brazier, Arthur, 319, 320
Brethren Church, 215
Bricklayers Union (Montgomery), 66
Brightman, Edgar S., 29, 38, 39, 43
Bristol, James, 101
Bronfenbrenner, Urie, 308, 311
Brooke, Edward, 367, 370, 396–97
Brooks, Sadie, 75
Brooks, Stella, 74
Brotherhood of Sleeping Car Porters, 53
Brothers for Afro-American Equality, 352
Browder, Aurelia, 48
Brown, H. Rap, 356
Brown, John, 305
Brown Chapel A.M.E. Church (Selma), 268, 269, 270, 272, 273, 275, 276, 279, 283, 287
Brown v. Board of Education of Topeka (1954), 117
Brownell, Herbert, appeal of, to SCLC, 88–89
Browning, Joan, 146
Bryan, William Jennings, 3, 23
Buckley, William, Jr., 188
Buddhism, 108
Bunche, Ralph, 90, 121, 225, 255, 286, 290; telegram to King, 72; on Vietnam, 357, 358, 361

Burgess, Mrs. John, 240
Burks, Mary Fair, 52
Burns, Haydon, 241

California, 120, 210; University of California, Berkeley, 362; California Democratic Council, 372
Campbell, Lawrence, 212
Camus, Albert, 44
Canadian Broadcasting Corporation, 370
Canipe Amusement Company, 389
Caplan, Kivie, 118
Carmichael, Stokely, 248, 299, 322, 356, 358, 361; MFDP position of, 253; and Mississippi freedom march, 321, 324, 325, 327, 328
Carnegie, Andrew, 30
Carnegie Hall, 376
Carpenter, C. C. J., 187
Carter, Eugene, 74, 75, 79
Carter, Hal, 29, 46
Carter, Robert, 74
Carver, George Washington, 266
Cash, Real "Rooster," 14, 15
Cathedral of St. John the Divine (New York), 76
Catholic Interracial Council, 319, 341
Cavanaugh, Jerome, 277
Cellar, Emmanuel, 106
Centenary Methodist Church (Memphis), 322
Central High School (Little Rock), 85
Chad Mitchell Trio, 289
Chalmers, Allan Knight, 39, 118
Chandler, Edgar H. S., 319
Chandler, Gladstone L., 18–19
Chandler, Len, 289
Chaney, James, 247, 250, 327
Chapman, Oscar L., 124
Chase, L. C., 212
Chew, Charles, Jr., 341
Chicago, Ill., 120, 121, 158, 210, 249, 297, 300, 303, 307, 313–55, 352, 366, 393, 396; University of Chicago Theological Seminary, 93; State Street, 303; Lawndale, 315, 322, 337, 349, 373; South Hamlin Avenue, 315; North Kenmore Avenue, 317; Chicago Renewal Society, 319; Cicero, 321, 340, 343, 344, 345, 348, 350, 352; riot in, 325, 335; Soldiers Field CCCO rally, 331, 333, 334, 337; Belmont-Cragin, 338, 339; Marquette Park, 338; Hanson Park, 339; Fullerton Avenue, 339; Linder Avenue, 339; Loop demonstration, 340; Bogan Park, 340; Gage Park, 340; Jefferson Park, 340; Federation of Labor, 341; Real Estate Board, 341; Cook County, 343; Palmer House, 346, 351; antiwar march in, 357
Chicago and Northwestern Railroad, 312
Chicago Defender, 309–11, 358, 359
Chicago Movement, 319, 334, 338, 341, 344; demands of, 332-33; modified demands of, 341; in Palmer House, 346; and "Summit Agreement," 346–47, 348, 349
Chicago Sun Times, 177
Chicago Tribune, 315, 316, 318, 333, 341, 346
Children's Crusade, 192
Chivers, Walter, 19, 21
Christian Century, 349, 351
Christianity Today, 368
Chuckut, Mildred, 340
Cicero, Ill., 321, 340, 343, 344, 345, 348, 350, 352
Citizens Trust Company, 8–9, 22, 73, 112
Civil Rights Acts, Title II, 119; Title VII, 230
Claflin College, 112
Clark, James, 264, 265, 266, 267, 268, 269, 270, 272, 274, 275, 285, 286; enjoined, 294
Clark, Mrs. James, 269–70
Clark, Joseph, 159
Clark, Kenneth, 217, 245, 308
Clark College, 10, 114; Student Government Association, 114
Clarke, Don, 114
Clayborn Temple (Memphis), 381
Clayton, Edward T., 227
Cleaver, Eldridge, 363; attacks King, 87; on Pettus Bridge, 282

Clement, Rufus, 73, 114
Clergy and Laymen Concerned About Vietnam, 320
Cloud, John, 274, 280
Cobras, 336
Cody, John P., 332, 341, 346
Coffin, William Sloane, 320, 359
Coles, Robert, 308
Collins, John, 258
Collins, Leroy, 278, 281, 288
Collins, Norma, 145–46
Columbia Broadcasting System (CBS), 128
Colvin, Claudette, 48, 60
Commentary: Rustin article in, 295
Committee for Independent Political Action, 314
Committee of One Hundred, 318, 336
Commodore Hotel (New York), 215
Commonweal, 123
Community Relations Service (CRS), 278, 281, 283, 287, 314, 328
"Confederate Air Force," 288
Conference of Concerned Democrats, 372
Congo (Africa), 260
Congress of Racial Equality (CORE), 35, 72, 108, 131, 134, 137, 177, 214, 219, 221, 246, 303, 308, 309, 314, 322, 334, 344, 352, 379; as sponsor of Freedom Rides, 132; rejects moratorium, 250; and World's Fair plan, 253; and Selma, 266, 279, 281; and Black Power compromise, 326; Baltimore convention of, 331; and Cicero march, 345
Connor, Eugene ("Bull"), 171, 172, 173, 175, 177, 181, 182, 184, 185, 186, 193, 194, 195, 196, 197, 199, 203, 256, 380; and dismissal of, 200
Conot, Robert, 305
Conyers, John, 303
Coordinating Council of Community Organizations (CCCO), 303, 314, 317, 344, 351; and Chicago Movement demands, 332–33, 341; and Cicero march, 345

Coronet, 118
Cotton, Dorothy, 179, 240, 244
Council for United Civil Rights Leadership (CUCRL), 219, 222, 236
Council of Federated Organizations (COFO), 246, 247
Cousins, Norman, 106
Covell, Howard V., 225
Cox, William Harold, 130
Coxey, Jacob, 214
Crenshaw, Jack, 62, 65
Crowell, T. L., 293
Crozer Theological Seminary, 20, 26, 27–37, 41, 45
Crusade for Citizenship, 93
Cruse, Harold, 204
Currier, Stephen, 218, 220; and CUCRL cochairmanship, 219
Curry, Izola, 98, 211

Dabbs, James McBride, 190
Daley, Richard, 313–14, 318, 319, 331, 334, 338, 340, 341, 343; and meeting with King, 334–35; and "Summit Agreement," 346, 351
Daniels, Fred, 55
Dansky, Claude ("Pop"), 18
Darin, Bobby, 289
Daumier, Honoré, 391
David T. Howard Elementary School, 12, 13
Davis, George W., 29, 34
Davis, Jeff, 288
Davis, L. O., 241, 242
Davis, Ossie, 204, 376
Davis, Sammy, Jr., 76, 91, 225, 289
Dawson, William, 314, 320
Day, Officer, 47
Deacons For Defense, 322
Declaration of Independence, 227
Dee, Ruby, 91, 289
Delany, Hubert, 122
Delany, Martin, 86, 87
Delhi (India), 104; Delhi School of Economics, 101; Delhi University, 101
Delhi Times, 100
Democratic Party: National Convention of (1956), 89; National Com-

Democratic Party (*cont.*)
mittee of, 123; National Convention of (1960), 124; National Convention of (1964), 245 252; platform committee of, 251; in New Hampshire primary, 372

Detroit, Mich., 120, 210, 227, 277; Woodward Avenue, 210; Cobo Hall, 210; riot in, 365

Detroit News, 366

DeWolf, L. Harold, 28, 39, 42, 43, 304, 305, 397; and King collection, 254

Dexter Avenue Baptist Church (Montgomery), 46, 47, 51, 52, 109

Diggs, Charles C., 74; and prayer pilgrimage, 91; lectures King, 107; at Selma, 269

Dillon, Douglas, 198

Dirksen, Everett, 244

Disciples of Christ, 305

Ditto, Frank, 338, 344, 352

Diwakar, Ranganath, 96, 102, 103, 104

Doar, John, 275, 278, 327

Dobbs, Mattawilda, 22

Dolan, Joseph F., 194, 199

Dombrowski, James, 110

Dominican Republic, 366

Dorchester Academy, 138, 174

Dos Passos, John, 45

Dostoevski, 270

Douglas, Mrs. Paul, 276

Douglas, Paul, 106, 231, 357

Douglass, Frederick, 87, 266

Drew, John, 172, 175

Drury, Allen, 160

DuBois, W. E. B., 10, 87, 88, 376; and *Souls of Black Folk*, 140

Duke University, 29, 113

Dungee, Mrs. Erna A., 57

Dunlap, A. I., 212

Durick, Joseph A., 187

Dye, Bradford, 324

Dylan, Bob, 225

Eastland, James O., 70, 71, 110, 248, 257

Ebenezer Baptist Church, 4, 10, 11, 15, 24, 25, 88, 133, 157, 319, 370, 375, 376, 377, 386, 390

Eddy, Norman, 168

Edwards, J. L., 311

Edwards Street (Chester), 27, 32

Eisenhower, Dwight D., 89, 128; appeal to SCLC, 88; meets with King, 100; and second civil rights bill, 119; and statement on King imprisonment, 127

Eliot, J. Robert, 130, 161, 167, 182

Ellington, Buford, 145, 146

Ellis, Talbott, 208

Ellwanger, Joseph, 270

Emancipation Proclamation, 227

Emery University, 121

Engelhardt, Sam, 81

Enslin, Morton Scott, 29

Equal Employment Opportunity Bill, 230

Erickson, Eric, 308

Eros, 44

Everett, Howard ("Mole"), 14, 15

Evers, Charles, 247, 323, 328, 329

Evers, Mrs. Medgar, 224

Evers, Medgar, 215, 218, 225; assassination of, 211

Executive Order 8802, 92

F. W. Woolworth Company, 113

Fair Employment Practices Act, 226

Farmer, James, 35, 72, 132, 213, 220, 221, 239, 276, 280; on Malcolm X, 217; at Kennedy meeting, 219; rejects moratorium, 250; sees Johnson, 303

Faulkner, William, 45

Fauntroy, Walter, 223, 312, 314; at Hoover meeting, 256–57

Federal Bureau of Investigation, 186, 249, 256, 286, 328

Federal Fair Labor Standards Act, 226

Felder, James, 114

Fellowship House (Philadelphia), 34

Fellowship of Reconciliation, 35, 72, 80–81, 108, 109, 110, 113

Field Foundation, 136, 138, 271

Fields, U. J., 77, 121

First Amendment, 182, 385

First Baptist Church (Montgomery), 51, 66, 133; bombing of, 82
First Congregational Church (Atlanta), 10
Fisk University, 17, 73, 113, 120
Fitzgerald, Ella, 289
Fletcher Farm (Vermont), 43
Florida, 135; Jacksonville, 139, 241; Palm Beach, 186; St. Augustine, 231, 240–44, 299, 352; Orlando, 240; Miami, 320, 369; Tallahassee, 367
Ford Foundation, 17
Ford Motor Corporation, 198
Forman, James, 134, 144, 145, 222, 233, 253, 276, 279, 280, 286, 287, 299
Fortune, 371
Fountain, H. Stanley, 280
Fourteenth Amendment, 130, 159
Franklin, C. L., 210
Franklin, John Hope, 286, 300
Freedom Budget, 323
Freedom Ride Coordinating Committee, 132
Freedom Rides, 132, 135, 138, 142; Freedom Riders, 132, 133, 145
Freedom songs: "We Shall Overcome," 148, 159, 183, 197, 201, 224, 280, 288, 324, 328, 350, 379, 392; "Aint Gonna Let Nobody Turn Me 'Round," 161, 179, 380, 381; "Woke Up This Mornin' with My Mind Stayed on Freedom," 179; "It Isn't Nice," 207–8; "I Been 'Buked and I Been Scorned," 225; "If You Miss Me at the Back of the Bus," 247; "Ain't Gonna Let Jim Clark Turn Me 'Round," 268; "I Love Jim Clark in My Heart," 268, "Blowin' in the Wind," 289; "We Shall Overrun," 324
Freedom Walk, 210
Freedomways, 257, 376; Slater King article in, 169–70; Shuttleworth article in, 206
French, E. N., 56, 57
Friendship Baptist Church, 11
Frye, Marquette, 305

Fukuah, Carl, 344
Fulbright, J. William, 360
Fulton County Prison (Georgia), 126

G.I. Bill of Rights, 207
Galbraith, John Kenneth, 367
Gallup Poll, 358
Gandhi, Mohandas K., 29, 34, 36, 96, 98, 99, 101, 102, 103, 134, 162–63, 210, 232, 270, 330, 334; impact of, on Montgomery bus boycott, 64
Gans, Herbert, 311
Gardner, Edward, 173
Garvey, Marcus, 86, 87
Garveyism, 86
Gaston, A. G., 172, 175, 178, 288, 295; and bail money, 199
Gaston Motel, 174; Room 30, 183, 192; bombing of, 201, 213
Gayle, W. A. ("Tackie"), 62, 65; 70, 71, 74, 79, 82; denounces boycott, 68
Georgia, 132, 135; Fulton County, 121; DeKalb County, 121, 126, 128; Talnall County, 126; Savannah, 138, 174, 240, 245; Baker County, 141, 150; Terrell County, 141, 150; Oglethorpe, 141; Americus, 141; Ellaville, 141; Cordele, 141; Kinchafoonee Creek, 141; Colquit County, 150; Camilla, 162; Dougherty County, 165; Rome, 211
Georgian, The, 5
Geneva (Switzerland), 307
Germany: East Berlin, 254; West Berlin, 254
Ghana: Achimota Village, 90; Accra, 90
Gianotti, Frank, 385
Gibson, E. R., 201
Gilmore, Mrs. Georgia, 75
Gingras, George L., 276
Gladden, Washington, 30
Glasco, R. J., 61
Glazer, Nathan, 311
Gober, Bertha, 145, 146
Gold Coast, 90

Goldberg, Arthur, 305; at civil rights meeting, 307
Golden, Harry, 190, 254
Goldman, Eric, 238, 311
Goldstein, Israel, 76
Goldwater, Barry, 250
Good, Paul, 333
Goodman, Andrew, 247, 250, 327
Goodman, George, 382
Goodman, Paul, 370
Goss, Helen R., 64
Grace Episcopal Cathedral (Los Angeles), 292
Graetz, Robert, 61; and bombing of home, 71, 82
Grafman, Hilton L., 187
Granger, Lester, 94; at Eisenhower meeting, 100, 118
Gray, Fred, 49, 50, 56, 69, 71, 74, 77, 122
Gray, James, 140, 141, 149
Greek Orthodox Church, North American, 285
Greeley, Dana McNeal, 285
Green, S. L., 73
Greensboro, N. C., 113
Gregg, Richard, 36, 72, 108
Gregory, Dick, 195, 234, 289, 314, 331; receives Rosa Parks Award, 231
Greyhound Bus Company, 132
Grove Lutheran Church (Chicago), 339
Guardian, 220

Haile Selassie (emperor), 238
Hairston, Beatrice, 212, 213
Halberstam, David, 305, 337, 362
Haley, W. J., 202
Hall, Blanton, 145
Hall, David, 288
Hall, Peter, 74
Hallinan, Paul, 255
Halvorsen Real Estate Agency, 339
Hamer, Fanny Lou, 247
Hammermill Paper Company, 293
Handel, George Frederick, 227
Hanes, Arthur, 184, 185, 203, 204, 379, 380
Hansberry, Lorraine, 217

Harald (crown prince), 261
Hare, James, 264
Harijan, 102
Harnack, Adolf von, 30
Harper, C. L., 12, 15
Harper, Carrie, 12
Harper's, 131, 337, 368
Harriman, Averell, 98
Harrington, Cornelius J., 341
Harrington, Michael, 311, 373
Harris, Louis, 371
Harris, Walter, 159
Harrold, Frank, 242
Hartal, 72, 103
Hartsfield, William, 125
Harvard University, 38, 44, 247
Hayden, Tom, 146
Hayes, Charlie, 319
Hayling, R. N., 240; secures federal injunction, 244
Hegel, Georg W. F., 20, 39; Philosophy of Right, 39, 51
Heidegger, Martin, 39
Heineman, Ben, 312
Hemingsford, Lord, 91
Hemingway, Ernest, 45
Henry, Aaron, 246, 253; receives Rosa Parks Award, 254
Herald Dispatch (Los Angeles), 107
Herndon, Alonzo F., 9, 10
Herndon, Calvin, 216, 363
Herron, George D., 30
Herzog, Elizabeth, 308
Heschel, Abraham, 286
Heston, Charlton, 224
Hi-Low Corporation (Chicago), 366
Hibbler, Al, 179, 183, 184, 192
Highlander Folk School, 136, 137
Hinduism, 108
Hirsh, Richard G., 276
Hitler, Adolf, 36
Holiday Inn, Rivermont (Memphis), 382
Holloman, Frank, 379–80
Hollowell, Donald, 126, 127, 128, 151
Holt Street Baptist Church, 57, 58, 60
Honey Fitz, 308
Hoover, J. Edgar, 256–58

Horne, Lena, 217, 225, 231
Hotel Carlyle, 218
House Un-American Activities Committee (HUAC), 131
Howard University, 34, 248, 308, 312, 322; award to King, 93; Johnson's speech at, 301
Hubbard, Fred D., 320
Hubbard, H. G., 52
Huey, Jerome, 321, 343
Hughes, Langston, 297
Hugo, Victor, 307
Hulsey, William H., 198
Humphrey, Hubert, 124, 229, 265, 269, 307, 309, 372, 384
Hunter, David K., 276
Hunter Street (Atlanta), 10–11, 235
Hurley, Ruby, 148, 161, 169, 286

"I Have A Dream" speech, 187, 227–29
Iakovos, Archbishop, 285
Ickes, Mrs. Harold, 276
India, 34, 36, 108, 120, 183; King's visit to, 99–105; Bombay, 101, 102; Calcutta, 101; Patna, 101, 102; Madras, 101, 102; Gandhi village, 102; Kerala, 102; Ahmedabad, 102, 103, 104; Sabarnati, 102; Kishangarh, 104
Ingalls, Luther, 65
Intercollegiate Council, 24
Interdenominational Theological Center, 114
International Garment Workers Union, 76
Interstate Commerce Commission, 138, 143, 144, 150, 168, 184; first ruling of, 60
Invaders, 381, 383, 387
Invictus, 19
Iowa State University, 287
Israel, Richard, 169

Jackson, Jesse, 339, 366, 388
Jackson, Jimmie Lee, 271, 272, 286
Jackson, Joseph H., 157, 333, 336, 358; attacks King, 158

Jackson, Mahalia, 91, 225, 227, 289, 331, 338, 392
Jackson, Ralph, 378
Jackson, Sullivan, 278
Jahn, Gunnar, 261
Jainism, 108
Javits, Jacob, 106, 231
Jemison, Theodore, 63
Jenkins, P. C. ("Lummy"), 271
Jenkins, Tim, 136
Jenkins, W. A., 182
Jet, 94
Joe Louis Gymnasium (Morris Brown College), 302
Johns, Vernon, 46, 47, 48, 51, 75, 79
Johnson, Frank M., Jr., 78, 275, 276, 278, 280, 281, 283, 285, 286; issues injunction, 277
Johnson, James Weldon, 10, 46, 202
Johnson, Leroy, 231
Johnson, Lyndon B., 124, 219, 238, 242, 244, 276, 289, 300, 304, 305, 307, 309, 323, 327, 328, 371, 372, 396–97; and letter to King, 129; and civil rights meeting, 230; assumes Presidency, 237; King's electoral support of, 250; and antipoverty program, 251; opposes Selma-Montgomery march, 277, 283; and meeting with Wallace, 283; press conference of, 284–85; "To Fulfill These Rights" address of, 301–2; see civil rights leaders, 303; and White House civil rights conference, 311; and alienation from King, 312; press statement of, 330; declines renomination, 384
Johnson, Mordecai, 34, 35, 91
Johnson, Paul, 321, 327
Johnston, Robert, 341
Jones, Charles, 136, 137, 144, 146, 155, 159, 161, 163
Jones, Clarence, 186, 217, 218
Jones, Oliver ("Sack"), 14, 15
Jones, Solomon, Jr., 388
Jordan, Dupree, 33
Joyce, James, 45
Jubilee Temple Christian Methodist Church (Chicago), 317

Kafka, Franz, 45

Kahn, Tom, 222

Kaplan, Kivie, 125

Katzenbach, Nicholas de B., 269, 273, 327, 328

Keating, Kenneth, 106

Kelley, Asa, 145, 146, 147, 149, 155, 160, 168

Kelsey, George D., 18, 23, 25, 26

Kenilworth Knights (Washington, D.C.), 224

Kennedy, John F., 124, 129, 130, 133, 161, 165, 171, 187, 237, 244, 250, 258, 371; telephones Coretta, 128, 186; meets with King, 174; Birmingham position of, 194, 196; intervenes in Birmingham, 198; sends troops to Birmingham, 203; deplores Birmingham violence, 205; and speech on civil rights, 209; and civil rights bill, 215; and March on Washington, 216, 218, 219, 220, 222; and civil rights meeting, 230; assassination of, 235

Kennedy, Robert F., 128, 129, 133, 135, 151, 167, 191, 384, 392; and "cooling-off" period, 136; on Albany, 149; telephones Coretta, 186; on Birmingham, 194, 196, 197, 198; contacts Shuttlesworth, 199; and meeting with Baldwin, 217–18, 219, 221, 223; and civil rights meeting, 230; and King wiretapping, 257; and New Hampshire primary, 372

Kenny, Tom, 287

Kerner, Otto, 344

Kierkegaard, Sören, 39, 382

Killens, John, 91

Killian, Lewis, 311

King, Alan, 289

King, Alberta (Mrs. Martin Luther King, Sr.), 73

King, Alfred Daniel, 12, 13, 15, 16, 191; and bombing of home, 201; in Selma, 280

King, Bernice Albertine, 177

King, Chevene B., 143, 144, 154, 161, 163, 165

King, Clennon W., 142, 143

King, Coretta Scott, 40–43, 57, 67, 69, 73, 74, 96, 98, 122, 128, 150, 159, 167, 177, 236, 254–55, 259, 261, 305, 315, 317, 319, 364, 376, 386; and bombing of parsonage, 70; and California vacation, 76; predicts MIA triumph, 78; visits Ghana, 90–91; visits India, 99–105; visits Albany, 165–66; phones President Kennedy, 186; talks with Malcolm X, 268–69, 272; on Selma-Montgomery march, 288, 290, 291

King, Dexter, 186

King, Edwin, 253

King, James Albert, 6

King, Lonnie, 114

King, Martin Luther, Jr.: date of birth of, 3; and nickname "Mike," 4; as "M. L.," 7; and white playmates, 11; suicide attempts of, 13–14; and nickname "Tweed," 15, 32; and Elks oratorical prize, 16; in Hartford, 17; at Morehouse, 18–25; summer jobs of, 21; and Webb Oratorical Contest, 24; as "ambivert," 25; at Crozier Theological Seminary, 27; as president of Crozier student body, 32; and Pearl M. Plafker citation, 38; and J. Louis Crozier fellowship, 38; enters Boston University, 38; and Philosophical Club, 38; and Ph.D. dissertation, 43–44; and "Three Dimensions of a Complete Life," 46, 227, 259; and MIA presidency, 56; first Montgomery boycott speech of, 58; on citizens' committee, 60; as vice-president of Alabama Human Relations Council, 61; and bombing of home, 66, 70; in Montgomery jail, 74; found guilty, 75; and California vacation, 76; boards desegregated bus, 81; foresees death, 82–83; as "L. L. J.," 83; and development of nonviolent philosophy, 88; visits Ghana, 90–91; and Prayer Pilgrimage (Washington, D.C.), 91, 93; receives Spingarn Medal,

93; confers with Vice-President Nixon, 94–95; elects jail, 96–97; and letter to Bowles, 98; and New York stabbing, 98; visits India, 99–105; and Eisenhower meeting, 100; and Ebenezer co-pastorship, 108–9, 113; and SCEF, 110; and Atlanta University student leaders, 114; addresses Shaw University meeting, 115; and views on NAACP, 119; on *Meet the Press*, 120, 293; and Alabama tax case, 121–22; letter of, to Rosa Parks, 122–23; and Committee to Defend Martin Luther King, 123; seven major national demands of, 123–24; on Black Muslems, 125; addresses SNCC conference, 125; sent to Reidsville State Prison, 126–27; *Nation* articles by, 130, 197; and Highlander Folk School, 136–37; in Albany, 147–70; leaves Albany jail, 150–51; explains leaving Albany jail, 154–55; and J. H. Jackson dispute, 158; and Albany injunction, 161; and Birmingham struggle, 171–209; and meetings with President Kennedy, 174, 219, 230; and Belafonte apartment meeting, 176; and *Birmingham Manifesto*, 177–78; and Birmingham arrests, 185, 199; and "Letter from Birmingham Jail," 187–91; and Birmingham negotiations, 195; Birmingham press statement of, 201; on Birmingham pact, 202–3; deplores Birmingham violence, 205–6; Detroit speech by, 210–11; in Danville, 212–14; confession of, to Barbour, 213; "I Have a Dream" speech by, 227–29; *Look*, response by, to Kennedy assassination, 235–36; on Lyndon B. Johnson, 237–38, 371; meets with Johnson, 237, 303; *Time* article on, 238–39; demands by, in *Nation*, 239; in St. Augustine, 240–44; St. Augustine imprisonment of, 241; and Harlem riots, 245–46; on anti-semitism,

246; "Bill of Rights to Disadvantaged," 248, 251; Jackson, Miss., speech by, 249; and moratorium on demonstrations, 249–50; talks to Robert Penn Warren, 252; and MFDP position, 253; and European trip, 254; Vatican audience of, 254; and confrontation with Hoover, 256–58; in London, 258–59; and Nobel Prize trip, 259–62; Nobel acceptance speech by, 262; Atlanta Nobel reception for, 266–67; Washington conference of, 269; in Selma, 264–92; and Pettus Bridge compromise, 278–82; *Saturday Review* articles by, 285, 295, 306; Selma-Montgomery march address by, 291–92; Vietnam position of, 296, 357, 359; on Watts, 306; and meeting with Goldberg, 307; *Church Defender* article by, 309–11; in Chicago, 315–55; Chicago strategy of, 316; and Mississippi freedom march, 321–29; on Black Power, 326–27, 330; and telegram to Johnson, 328; Soldiers Field speech of, 332; and Chicago Movement demands, 332–33; and meeting with Daley, 334–35; on *The Today Show*, 337; contests Chicago injunction, 341; and announcement of Cicero march, 343; and "Summit Agreement," 346, 348, 349; and Chicago antiwar march, 357; and argument with Whitney Young, 358; Riverside Church speech by, 359–60; and U.N. antiwar rally, 361–62; at Berkeley, 362; visits Jamaica, 364, 376; on Dubois, 376; in Memphis, 380–89; and *Playboy* article, 385; "Mountaintop" speech by, 386; assassination of, 389

King, Martin (Michael) Luther, Sr., 13, 18, 23, 26, 42, 74, 234, 360; birthplace of, 6–7; against Martin's return to Montgomery, 73; and Kennedy phone calls, 129; in Scandinavia, 261

King, Slater, 143, 154, 163, 250,

King, Slater (*cont.*)
  384; wife assaulted, 162; *Freedom-ways* article of, 169–70
King, Tom, 175
King, Yolanda Denise (Yokie), 51, 166
Kirby, George, 289
Knudson, Albert C., 39
Kopkind, Andrew, 356
Ku Klux Klan: in Montgomery, 80; in Albany, 162, 168; in St. Augustine, 240, 241, 242; in Selma, 280
Kyles, Samuel, 387, 388

Lancaster, Burt, 224
Langford, Charles, 74
Laue, James, 278, 386, 388, 389
Laursen, Per, 146
Lawson, James, 108, 114, 115, 116, 120, 137, 179, 321, 322, 376, 378, 379, 387
Le Bon, Gustave, 229
League of Labor and Education, 352
Lee, Bernard, 137, 146, 179, 244, 314, 315, 341, 364; and meeting with Goldberg, 307
Lee, Cager, 286
Lee, William, 341
Lehman, Herbert, 118
Lenud, Philip, 24, 38
Leo XIII (pope), 29
Lester, Julius, 216, 313
Letherer, James, 289
"Letter From a Birmingham Jail," 187–91
Levison, Stanley, 131, 219, 382; on Vietnam, 357
Lewis, Hylan, 308
Lewis, John, 114, 133, 220, 221, 226, 239, 265, 286, 290; March on Washington speech of, 222–24; rejects moratorium, 250; in Selma, 267, 274, 275; leads Selma-Montgomery march, 273
Lewis, Rufus, 48, 66; nominates Martin to MIA, 56; as MIA committee chairman, 61
Liberator, 204–5

Liberty Babtist Church (Chicago), 355
Life, 367
Lincoln, Abraham, 285, 316; *Gettysburg Address*, 187
Lincoln Memorial, 91, 153, 223, 224, 225, 291
Lincoln Missionary School (Marion, Ala.), 41
Lingo, Al, 197, 271, 277, 286
Little Rock, Ark., 133, 142, 172
Liuzzo, Viola, 292
Lloyds of London, 78
Lock, Henry, 378, 379
Logan, Marion, 261
Logical positivism, 45
Lomax, Louis, 118, 315, 365; *Harper's* article by, 119; *The Negro Revolt*, 160; *San Francisco Chronicle* article by, 215–16
London: King's arrival in, 258; City Temple Hall, 258; St. Paul's Cathedral, 258, 259
Look, 235, 371, 382
Lord, John Wesley, 276, 280
Lorraine Motel, 386, 389; Room 306, 387, 388; Room 308, 388
Los Angeles, Cal., 210; King's visit to, 107; Shrine Auditorium, 124; SCLC rally in, 156, 176; Watts, 281, 295, 307, 309, 330, 335, 337, 349; riot in, 306
Lotze, Hermann, 39
Louisiana, 135; New Orleans, 132; Placquemine County, 211
Louisville, Ky., 136
Lowenstein, Allard K., 372
Lowery, Joseph E., 293
Lucas, Robert, 344, 352
Lucy, Autherine, 71
Luther, Martin, 188
Lutheran Trinity Church (Montgomery), 61
Luthuli, Albert, 255, 259

McCall, Walter, 24, 32, 33, 34
McCarthy, Eugene, 360, 372, 384
McCollum, Salynn, 144
McDermott, John, 319, 341
McDonald, Dora, 364

McGill, Ralph, 190, 266, 355
McKissick, Floyd, 221, 308, 309, 312, 356, 361; and Mississippi freedom march, 321, 322, 325, 327, 328
McNamara, Robert, 198
McNeill, Joseph, 113
Maddox, Lester, 391
Madison Square Garden (New York), 76
Madrid (Spain), 254
Malcolm X, 107–8, 125, 211, 220, 239; on Birmingham, 206; on March on Washington, 216; in London, 258; in Selma, 268; killing of, 271
Manly, Norman, 90
Manucy, Holsted ("Hoss"), 242, 244
March on Washington, 215, 220–31, 232, 244, 290; and Guardian, 220
Marienkirche, 254
Marshall, Burke, 136, 194, 195, 197, 198; telephones Coretta, 159
Marshall, Thurgood, 93, 128, 312
Martin, Rose, 22
Martin Luther King and the Montgomery Story, 113
Marx, Karl, 20, 35, 37, 354, 395
Marx, Robert, 341
Marxism, 31, 35
Maryland: Cambridge, 211; Baltimore, 294–95
Mason Temple Church (Memphis), 379, 386, 387
Massachusetts, 298, 299
Massey lectures, 370
Mauldin, Charles, 274
Maxey, Charles E., 10
May, Elaine, 289
Mays, Benjamin, 7, 17, 18, 19, 23, 25, 26, 73, 93, 222, 234, 266, 392
Mays, Willie, 114
Meany, George, 215, 357
Meek, Russ, 333, 334, 344, 345
Meet the Press, 120, 167, 293
Mellon, Andrew, 218
Memphis, Tenn., 355, 376, 378, 393, 397; Main Street, 378; Memphis Central Labor Council, 379; and King visit, 380–89; Invaders in,

381, 383, 387; Beale Street, 381; Handy Park, 381; Lorraine Motel, 386, 387, 388, 389; South Main Street, 387, 389
Memphis Commercial Appeal, 381
Meredith, James, 190, 321, 322, 324, 327, 329, 331, 332
Metropolitan Baptist Church (Washington, D.C.), 91
Metropolitan Opera, 172
Meulder, Walter, 39
Michigan: Saginaw, 289; Grosse Pointe, 376, 380
Miles College, 172–73
Millard, Richard, 286
Miller, Fred, 278, 279
Miller, William R., 72, 226, 254
Mills, Robert, 217
Milton, Betty, 22
Ming, William R., 122
Minneapolis Tribune, 67
Mississippi, 135, 215, 228, 246, 322, 373, 393; Emmett Till murder in, 59; Poplarville, 105; Jackson, 133, 211, 248, 249, 321, 322; Philadelphia, 171, 250, 327, 329; NAACP, 247; Tougaloo College, 247; Chaney, Schwerner, Goodman murders in, 247–48; Vicksburg, 248; Meridian, 248; Greenwood, 248–49, 324, 325, 328; University of Mississippi, 321; Highway 51, 321; Penola, 323; Grenada, 323, 324; Yazoo, 325, 326; Canton, 327, 328
Mississippi Freedom Democratic Party, 246–47, 248, 252–53
Mississippi Freedom Summer, 243, 248
Mitchell, Clarence, 124, 308
Mitchell, Oscar, 121, 126, 127, 128
Mixon, Officer, 47
Monrovia (Liberia), 90
Monson Motor Court (St. Augustine), 240, 241, 243
Montgomery, Ala., 44–83, 85, 96, 105, 113, 132, 133, 142, 149, 156, 172, 175, 185, 206, 208, 273, 275, 276, 286, 289, 290, 292, 295, 352, 393; city bus lines in, 47, 62, 67,

Montgomery, Ala. (*cont.*)
83; Court Square, 47; Women's
Political Council, 49, 50, 52, 54;
League of Women Voters, 49;
Parks and Recreation Board, 49;
Baptist Ministerial Alliance, 52;
Interdenominational Ministerial
Alliance, 53–54; city conditions in,
58–59; White Citizens Council,
63, 65, 70; Citizens Club, 66; Men
of Montgomery, 67; City Commission, 68; opposition to bus desegregation in, 81–82; King's return to,
91; Dexter Avenue, 290; Decatur
Street, 290

Montgomery, James, 175

Montgomery Advertiser, 48, 55, 65,
67; and Robinson leaflet, 53; and
Joe Azbell reporting, 53, 55, 62;
letters published in, 64; and false
boycott settlement report, 68;
presses for peace, 83

Montgomery bus boycott, 35, 88, 89,
103, 274; announcement of, 52;
and King's first speech, 58; and
Abernathy's presentation of demands, 58; MIA committees organized in, 61; car pool created in,
63; and Citizens Committee, 65;
and trial of leaders, 74–75; car pool
enjoined in, 78; and restraint-of-
trade verdict, 79; and share-a-ride
plan, 80; ends, 81; and resumption
of city bus lines service, 83

Montgomery Improvement Association (MIA), 56, 62, 63, 65, 66, 67,
68, 69, 73, 80, 97, 106, 112; officers of, 57; contributors to, 71–72;
and trial of leaders, 74–75; charges
of financial irregularities against,
76–77; and enjoinment of car pool,
78–79; charged guilty of trade restraint, 79; and share-a-ride plan,
80; and circular on bus conduct,
81; and organization of SCLC, 88;
Ghana trip donation of, 90;
NAACP donation of, 93

Moore, Richard, 204

Moore, William L., 215

Morehouse College, 5, 8, 10, 17–25,
32, 38, 44, 73, 132, 391, 392;
Maroon Tiger, 25; awards King
degree, 93

Moreland, John Y., 19

Morgan, Charles, 391

Morgan, Juliette, 64, 65, 72

Morgenthau, Henry, 217

Morris Brown College, 10, 302; Student Government Association, 114

Morse, Wayne, 186

Morsell, John, 358

Morton, Charles Evans, 24

Morton, Thruston, 124

Moses, Robert, 247, 253

Motley, Constance Baker, 286

Moynihan, Daniel P., 301, 308, 309

Muhammed, Elijah, 271, 317

Murphy, William, 12, 14

Muse, Maxine, 212

Muste, A. J., 35, 36, 72, 106, 305,
359

Mutual Federal Savings and Loan
Association (Atlanta), 10

Myer, Agnes, 124

Nabrit, James, Jr., 312

Nabrit, James III, 342

Napolitano, Richard A., 318

Nash, Diane, 114, 136, 137, 179

Nation, 130, 239, 329, 333; King
blasts Kennedy Administration in,
197

National Advisory Commission on
Civil Disorders, 368, 371–72, 384

National Association for the Advancement of Colored People (NAACP),
5, 24, 89, 93, 94, 119, 128, 139,
177, 198, 200, 204, 207, 214, 222,
223, 246, 252, 290, 304, 308, 323,
324, 344, 358, 378; Camden, N.J.,
branch, 34; Montgomery, Ala.,
chapter, 48, 51; MIA contributions
to, 71; and Roy Wilkins, 76;
awards Spingarn Medal, 93; and
Robert Williams, 107; basic philosophy of, 117–18; and Albany
Youth Council, 142, 143, 145; in
Albany, Ga., 142, 145; and Ruby
Hurley, 148; Legal Defense and
Educational Fund, 219; in Atlanta,

234; in St. Augustine, 240; in Mississippi, 247, 249; and *New York Times* poll, 249; in Selma, Ala., 266, 276; in Chicago, 314; on Vietnam, 357

National Baptist Convention, 26, 157, 333

National Broadcasting Corporation (NBC), 128

National Catholic Conference, 215, 221

National City Lines, Inc., 64

National Council of Churches, 215, 221

National Council of Negro Women, 219

National Maritime Union, 200

National Review, 188

National Student Association, 136

National Tea Company (Chicago), 366

Negro Heritage Library, 244

Nehru, Jawaharlal, 98, 99, 100

Nelson, William Stuart, 108

New Deal, 140

New Delhi (India), 99

New England Conservatory of Music, 40

New Frontier, 166

New Jersey: Jersey City, 249; Atlantic City, 252; Newark riot in, 365

New Liberty Baptist Church (Chicago), 344

New Pilgrim Baptist Church (Birmingham), 194

New South, W. T. Walker article in, 169

New York City, 120, 210, 245, 289, 359, 381; King reception in, 265; Harlem, 211, 245, 252, 271, 295, 395; Central Park, 361; garbage strike in, 378

New York Herald Tribune, 151

New York Review of Books, 348, 356

New York State: Albany, 120, 289; Rochester, 245; and New York City Council, 286; and New York Bar Association, 298; Westchester County, 309; Great Neck, 358

New York Times, The, 138, 159, 160, 166, 192, 219, 224, 249, 270, 276, 322

Newsweek, 231, 342, 349, 367

Ngo Dinh Diem, 370

Nichols, Mike, 289

Niebuhr, Reinhold, 29, 30, 31, 35, 36, 37, 43, 395

Nietzsche, Friedrich Wilhelm, 35, 37

Nigeria, 264

Nixon, E. D., 48, 49, 50, 51, 52, 53, 56, 58, 76; selects King, 57; as MIA officer, 61; and bombing of home, 71; as MIA treasurer, 77

Nixon, Richard M., 105–6, 128, 129, 385: SCLC appeal to, 88; in Ghana, 90–91; agrees to meet King, 94, 95

Nkrumah, Kwame, 96; invitation to King, 90

Nobel Peace Prize, 153, 255–63, 357

North Carolina: Raleigh, 115, 116, 120; Raleigh conference, 121; Durham, 300, 303

North Carolina Agricultural and Technical College, 113

North Carolina College, 113

Norton, Edward, 198

Norway: Oslo, 258, 260; Gardernoen Airport, 259; Norwegian Broadcasting Orchestra, 262

Nuclear Test Ban Treaty, 298

Oakland Committee for Community Improvement (Chicago), 338

O'Boyle, Patrick, 221, 223

O'Dell, James, 212, 257, 376

Odetta, 224, 225, 289

Ogilvie, Richard B., 343

Ohio: Western College for Women, 247; Oxford, 247; Cleveland, 289, 307, 336, 337

Olaf V (king), 216

Olsen, Clark, 282

"Operation Breadbasket," 233, 317, 355, 366

Overseas Press Club, 360

Packing House Workers (Chicago), 319

Page, Marion, 143, 147, 152, 161

Palmer House (Chicago), 346, 351, 355
Parham, Grosbeck Preer, 208, 209
Paris (France), 220, 265
Parker, Mack, 105
Parks, Frank A., 62
Parks, Rosa, 47, 48, 49, 50, 51, 54, 55, 56, 58, 60, 76, 109, 122, 291, 303
Parson, James B., 318
Parsons, Talcott, 308, 311
Patterson, Floyd, 289
Patterson, John, 133
Paul VI (pope), 254
Pauling, Linus, 106
Peabody, Mrs. Malcolm, 240
Pearson, Drew, 256
Peck, James, 132
Penn, Lemuel, 250
Penn, William, 27
Pennsylvania: Chester, 26, 27, 28, 32; University of, 34; Philadelphia, 249; Erie, 293
People-to-People tours, 175, 246, 297, 303
Perkins, Anthony, 289
Perkins, Della, 75
Perry, Hemon E., 9, 11
Personalism, 39, 40
Peter, Paul, and Mary, 224, 225, 289
Petition Campaign and Youth for Integrated Schools, 106
Pettus Bridge (Selma), 274, 276, 280, 281, 299, 327
Philia, 44
Pickett, Clarence, 106
Pierce, James, 49
Pike, James A., 118
Pitts, Lucius, 172
Pitts, Mrs. C. S., 11
Pittsburgh Courier, 151
Playboy, King article in, 385
Plummer, Frank, 198
Poitier, Sidney, 91, 224
Poland, 36
Pollack, Louis, 198
Poor People's Campaign, 368, 369, 373, 374, 376, 380, 382, 383, 384
Pope, Roslyn, 114
Pope, Verle, 242

Popper, Hermine, 364
Powell, Adam Clayton, Jr., 76, 90, 124, 131, 217, 252, 256, 322, 382; and Prayer Pilgrimage, 91; on SCLC board, 118; and March on Washington, 216; criticizes King, 245
Powell, Mary, 40, 42
Powell, Tom, 379
Powell, W. J., 54
Prasad, Rangendra, 101
Prayer Pilgrimage (Washington, D.C.), 91–93, 94, 214; King's address at, 93
Prinz, Joachim, 215, 222
Pritchett, Laurie, 140, 145, 146, 149, 150, 151, 159, 160, 162, 165, 168, 181, 265
Proctor, Emmett, 12
Proctor, Samuel, 231
Progressive, 299
Progressive Baptist Alliance, 158
Proust, Marcel, 45
Pucinski, Roman, 343
Puttaway, Monroe, 271

Quaker Center (Delhi), 101

Raby, Al, 303, 314, 317, 319, 336, 338, 339, 340, 341
Radhakrishnan, Sarvepalli, 99
Rainey, Lawrence, 327, 329
Rajagopalachari, C., 102
Raleigh conference, 121
Ramachandran, G., 101, 104
Ramage, Edward, 187
Randolph, A. Philip, 53, 76, 90, 91, 108, 124, 131, 214, 216, 218–19, 221, 222, 224, 227, 286, 290, 310, 312; and Prayer Pilgrimage, 91–92; proposes March on Washington, 214; and moratorium on demonstrations, 250
Rather, Ernest E., 336
Rauschenbusch, Walter, 27, 29, 30, 31, 35, 37, 44
Reader's Digest, 367
Reagan, Cordell, 143, 144, 147, 159, 163

Realty Mortgage Company (Birmingham), 198
Reconstruction, 119
Reddick, Lawrence D., 53, 108, 231; visits India, 99–105
Reeb, James, 282–83, 284
Reese, Jeanette, 71
Reeves, Jeremiah, 48, 60
Reidsville State Prison (Georgia), 126, 128
Renouvier, Charles, 39
Republican Party: National Committee of, 123, 124; platform committee of, 124
Rerum Novarum, 29
Reston, James, 171, 205
Reuther, Walter, 215, 221, 226, 230, 285, 286, 379
Reynolds, I. P., 9
Reynolds, Mrs. Elmer H., 66
Richards, Robert, 311
Rich's Department Store (Atlanta), 125
Riessman, Frank, 311
Ritschl, Albrecht, 30
Ritter, Norman, 133
Riverside Church (New York City), 252, 359
Robinson, Chester, 344, 348
Robinson, Jackie, 91, 118, 225, 358
Robinson, James, 108
Robinson, Jo Ann, 49, 50, 51, 52, 54, 58; as MIA officer, 61
Robinson, Thomas, 385
Robinson, William, 341
Rockefeller, Nelson, 120, 159, 176, 265
Rockefeller family, 18
Rockwell, George Lincoln, 342
Rogers, William P., 106
Roman Saints, 336
Romney, George, 277
Roosevelt, Eleanor, 76, 123, 124
Roosevelt, Franklin D., 92, 187, 214, 218
Rostow, Eugene V., 198
Rothschild, Jacob, 266
Rowan, Carl T., 67, 68, 367
Roy, Ralph Lord, 167, 168
Royal Crown Cola Company, 198

Russell, Henry E., 65
Russell, Nipsey, 289
Rustin, Bayard, 35, 41, 80, 81, 108, 123, 131, 132, 222, 223, 224, 232, 254, 257, 261, 290, 302, 304, 305, 306, 308, 309, 369, 373, 385, 387; and MIA contribution, 72; six-point program of, 94–95; Indian document of, 101; seven major national demands of, 123–24; and "Journey of Reconciliation," 132; as march organizer, 221; and moratorium on demonstrations, 249–50; and MFDP compromise, 252–53; *Commentary* article by, 295; and meeting with Goldberg, 307; on Vietnam, 357; in Memphis, 379
Ryan, Robert, 224

St. Jude, 289
St. Louis, Mo., 283
St. Matthew's Cathedral (Washington, D.C.), 236
Saint Paul, 188
Salinger, Pierre, 186
San Francisco Chronicle, 216
San Juan, P.R., 305
SANE, 304
Sartre, Jean Paul, 39
Saturday Review, 285; King articles in, 295, 306
Satyagraha, 34, 72, 85, 101, 103; elements of, 103–4
Savoy Ballroom (Boston), 38
Sayre, Francis, 384
Scandinavia, 265
Schwerner, Michael, 247–48, 250, 327, 329
SCOPE, 302
Scott, C. A., 73, 157
Scott, Michael, 90, 91
Scott, Obadiah, 41
Scott, William A., Jr., 10
Screvane, Paul, 286
Secrest, Max, 278
Sellers, Cleveland, 321
Sellers, Clyde, 62, 63, 97, 160
Sellers, Juanita, 22
Selma, Ala., 103, 175, 243, 251, 264–92, 293, 294, 297, 299, 300, 315,

Selma, Ala. (*cont.*)
352, 353, 384, 385, 393; "Progressives" in, 265, 272; Hotel Albert, 265; and Selma-Montgomery marches, 273–75, 285, 287–93, 394; Broad Street, 273, 280, 288; Pettus Bridge, 274, 276, 280, 281, 299, 327; Sylvan Street, 279, 288; Alabama Avenue, 285

Selma-Montgomery march, 294; first march, 273–75, 285; second march, 287–93; and address by King, 291–92

Shanti Sena, 101

Sharp, Monroe, 344, 348, 352, 355

Shaw University, 115

Sherman, William T., 223

Sherrod, Charles, 142, 143, 144, 147, 152, 154, 163, 164, 213, 260, 314

Shiloh Baptist Church (Albany), 148, 153, 161, 164

Shores, Arthur, 74, 172, 175, 185

Shriver, Sargent, 128

Shuttlesworth, Fred, 108, 137, 156, 173, 175, 178, 179, 182, 183, 196, 198, 199, 201; and Prayer Pilgrimage, 91; as ACMHR president, 172; at Belafonte apartment meeting, 176; *Freedomways* article by, 206; in Danville, 212; in Selma, 280, 286; jailed, 367

Siegenthaler, John, 133

Silberman, Charles, 311

Simone, Nina, 289

Sixteenth Street (Chester), 27

Sixth Avenue Baptist Church (Birmingham), 184, 192, 193, 205

Smarak Nidhi, 99, 101, 104

Smiley, Glenn E., 72, 80, 81; boards desegregated bus, 81

Smith, C. Miles, 234

Smith, Jerome, 217

Smith, Kenneth Lee, 28, 29, 30, 35, 57

Smith, Lillian, 121; and letter to King, 97, 190

Smith, Mary Ann, 114

Smith, Maury, 281

Smith, Ruby Doris, 135

Smitherman, Joseph T., 265, 277, 280, 284

Smyer, Sidney, 198

Sobornost, 72

Social Gospel, 29–30, 31, 35, 36, 37, 354, 394

Socrates, 51

Sophienkirche, 254

Souls of Black Folk, 140

South Africa, 186, 255, 259

South Carolina, 132; South Carolina State College, 112

South Jackson Street parsonage (Montgomery), 57, 70

Southeast Asia, 303, 308

Southern Christian Leadership Conference (SCLC), 82, 94, 113, 114, 116, 118, 123, 126, 127, 128, 131, 133, 136, 137, 144, 146, 148, 149, 153, 154, 157, 163, 169, 170, 173, 174, 179, 182, 191, 192, 194, 196, 197, 202, 203, 214, 219, 232, 233, 246, 248, 249, 251, 253, 297, 299, 329, 331, 343, 346, 351, 352, 357, 366, 367, 373, 376, 382, 385, 390, 396; and Southern Leadership Conference on Transportation and Non-Violent Integration, 88; New Orleans meeting of, 89; as Southern Negro Leaders Conference, 89; moves to Atlanta, 108; Auburn Avenue headquarters of, 109; and donation to SNCC, 115; Advisory Committee of, 118; Rockefeller contribution to, 120; and Field Foundation, 138, 139; annual budgets of, 156; Chattanooga conference of, 173; Birmingham peace demands of, 195; and Birmingham settlement, 200; and Danville, 212; *Newsletter*, 225–26, 227, 232, 233, 238, 242–43, 246, 250, 293, 297; Richmond convention of, 231; Orlando rally of, 240; in St. Augustine, 241, 242, 243; Savannah conference of, 245, 253; and *New York Times* poll, 249; FBI surveillance of, 257; and Scandinavian trip, 260; in Selma, 266, 272, 276,

280; and Selma-Montgomery march proposal, 273; as "Slick," 286; and Alabama boycott, 293; Baltimore meeting of, 294–95; position on Vietnam, 296; and SCOPE, 302; Petersburg, Va., rally of, 302; Durham conference of, 303; annual convention of, 304; in Chicago, 314, 315, 316, 321; Miami convention of, 320; and Black Power compromise, 326; Chicago Movement demands of, 332–33; and Chicago riot, 335; and modified CCCO demands, 341; and Cicero march, 345; Atlanta meeting of, 368

Southern Conference Educational Fund (SCEF), 109, 110, 257
Southern Regional Council, 177
Southview Cemetery (Atlanta), 392
Southwestern Fidelity and Fire Insurance Company (Atlanta), 10
Spelman College, 8, 10, 18, 24, 108, 112, 120, 135; Student Government Association, 114
Spencer, Herbert, 30
Spike, Robert, 280
Spingarn Medal, 93
Spock, Benjamin, 359, 361, 362
Spring Mobilization Campaign, 310, 358–59, 362
Stallings, Earl, 187
Standard Life Insurance Company, 9
Steele, C. K., 88; and Prayer Pilgrimage, 91
Steele, Rosa, 288
Stevenson, Adlai, 124
Steward, Francis, 33
Stewart, E. A., 267
Stone Temple Baptist Church (Chicago), 348
Stride Toward Freedom, 34, 98, 160, 259, 302
Strong, Bill, 119–20
Students for a Democratic Society (SDS), 146
Student Nonviolent Coordinating Committee (SNCC), 115, 142, 143, 144, 145, 146, 163, 177, 196, 214, 219, 221, 223, 233, 234, 243, 246, 248, 251, 264, 265, 299, 304, 314, 321, 322, 344, 352, 355, 379; as temporary SNCC, 120; Atlanta meeting of, 120–21; Atlanta conference of, 125; Direct Action Projects Division of, 137; Voter Registration Division of, 137; and Albany opposition, 152; in Danville, 212; rejects moratorium, 250; in Selma, 266, 276, 279, 286; and Selma-Montgomery march proposal, 273; threatens Selma-Montgomery boycott, 287; Anti-Vietnam platform of, 311; and Black Power compromise, 326; Cicero march, 345

Student Voice, 119
Sumner, Willam Graham, 30, 133
"Summit Agreement" (Chicago), 346–47, 348, 349, 351, 352, 354, 355, 363; Palmer House, 346
Symington, Stuart, 124

Taconic Foundation, 136, 218, 271
Tait, Lenore, 146
Talmadge, Eugene, 25
Talmadge, Herman, 149
Tennessee, 113, 136, 321; Nashville, 114, 132; Chattanooga, 173, 311; Memphis, 290
Tennessee Coal and Iron Company (Birmingham), 198
Texas, Houston, 300
Thales of Miletus, 44
Thomas, Daniel, 272
Thomas, Norman, 225
Thoreau, Henry David, 103, 108; *On Civil Disobedience*, 20, 57; and impact on Montgomery bus boycott, 64
Till, Emmett, 59, 85
Tillich, Paul, 29, 31, 43, 44
Time, 16, 239, 245, 298, 299; on King, 91, 134; and King as Man of the Year, 238
Time-Life, 133
"To Fulfill These Rights" speech, 301–2

Tobey, Mrs. Charles, 277
Tolstoi, Leo, 108
Tonkin Gulf, 258
Torn, Rip, 217
Toronto (Canada), 277
Totem Pole nightclub (Boston), 38
Totten, C. K., 65
Trailways bus system, 132, 144; and Albany bus station, 145
Travis, Jimmy, 247
Tufts University, 38
Turner, Jesse, 378
Turner, Nat, 86, 87, 88
Tuttle, Elbert P., 162

Union of American Hebrew Congregations, 276
Union Theological Seminary, 143–44
United Auto Workers, 200, 215, 221, 331, 337, 341, 348; and MIA contributions, 71
United Presbyterian Church, 215
United States Civil Rights Commission, 95–96
United States Department of Housing and Urban Development, 320–21, 373
United States Department of Justice, 95–96, 119, 144, 149, 160, 165, 167, 178, 199, 206, 257, 277–78; King appeal to, 89
United States Information Agency, 367
United States Steel, 198
United States Supreme Court, 214, 367; and nullification of separate equality doctrine, 48, 59; and nullification of bus segregation, 79, 80; and nullification of school segregation, 91, 100; and legalization of sit-ins, 200, 204
University of Chicago Theological Seminary, 93
University of Pennsylvania, 34
University of Wisconsin, 133
Unnithan, R. K., 101, 104, 105
Urban League, 89, 100, 117, 214, 219, 221, 303, 304, 324, 369, 396; basic philosophy of, 117–18; in Chicago, 314; on Vietnam, 357

Valdosta, Ga., 16
Vanderbilt University, 114, 203
Vandiver, Ernest, 147, 149, 162
Varloga, Joseph, 344
Vesey, Denmark, 86, 87, 88
Vice lords, 336
Viet Cong, 302, 304
Vietnam, 238, 302, 307, 308, 309, 310, 312, 320, 328, 343, 355, 361, 363, 370, 375, 396; Saigon, 307; and Chicago march, 357; Riverside Church speech on, 359–60; National Liberation Front (NLF) in, 361, 370; and United Nations antiwar rally, 361–62; and Diem, 370; King position on, 296
Vietnam Summer, 362
Virginia: Prince Edward County, 105; Petersburg, 137, 232, 302; Danville, 211–14, 223, 224; Harpers Ferry, 305
Vishwananda, Swami, 101
Vivian, C. T., 137, 231, 240, 244
Voice of India, 104
Volpe, John A., 298

Wagner, Robert, 176, 245, 246, 265
Waldbühne amphitheater, 254
Walden, Col. A. T., 73, 234
Walk To Freedom, 81
Walker, Martha, 74–75
Walker, Wyatt Tee, 108, 132, 137, 138, 144, 148, 152, 153, 156, 157, 161, 163, 170, 173–74, 175, 234, 251, 300; *New South* article by, 169; in Birmingham, 176, 186; SCLC convention speech by, 232; leaves SCLC, 243–44; and Magnolia Ballroom, 248; talks to Robert Penn Warren, 252; jailed, 368
Wallace, George, 191, 197, 203, 268, 272, 277, 284, 286, 289, 293, 294; meeting with Johnson, 283
Ware, J. L., 173, 175, 178
Warren, Earl, 367
Warren, Robert Penn, 252
Washington, Booker T., 87, 88, 162, 208, 266, 356
Washington, D.C., 132, 227, 250,

271, 276, 287, 308, 312, 320; March on Washington 220–31; Union Station, 221; Louisiana Avenue, 221; Constitution Avenue, 221; Ellipse, 221; Washington Monument, 221, 224; Pennsylvania Avenue, 221; National Airport, 224; Military Air Transportation Terminal, 224; White House sit-in, 283; clergymen to White House, 283; Lutheran Church of the Reformation, 283; Potomac River, 307

Washington, George, 187

Washington Cathedral (Washington, D.C.), 384

Weaver, George, 304

Weaver, Robert, 320

Webster-Haynes debates, 187

Wells, Samuel B., 153, 161, 164

Weltansicht, 86

WERD radio station, 10

Wesley, Cynthia, 205

West, E. Gordon, 130

West, Mrs. A. A., 53; as MIA officer, 61

West Side Federation, 314, 317

West Side Organization, 334, 344

West Virginia, 373

Western Christian Leadership Conference, 176

Western Lunch Box (Boston), 38, 40

Wheat Street Baptist Church (Atlanta), 11

Where Do We Go From Here?, 295, 325, 356, 364, 365

White, Byron, 367

White, Theodore H., 129

White, Walter, 10, 239, 266, 356

White House Conference on Civil Rights, 308, 311, 322

Whittaker, John P., 9

Why We Can't Wait, 207, 238, 245, 295

Wieman, Nelson, 29, 31, 43, 44

Wilkes, William, 392

Wilkins, Roy, 76, 89, 91, 94, 118, 124, 231, 236, 237, 290, 293, 301, 322, 323, 358; and Prayer Pilgrimage, 91; and meeting with Eisenhower, 100; and Kennedy meeting, 219, 221–22, 223; March on Washington speech by, 226; and moratorium on demonstrations, 249–50; sees Johnson, 303; in Memphis, 379

Willard, John, 388

Williams, Alfred Daniel, 4–5, 41

Williams, Camilla, 225

Williams, Hale, 319

Williams, Hosea, 240, 294, 302, 313, 325; and support of Johnson, 250; in Selma, 267, 274, 275, 287; leads Selma-Montgomery march, 273

Williams, Mrs. Alfred Daniel, 13

Williams, Orloff B., 282

Williams, Robert, 24, 107, 117, 134, 211

Williams, Samuel, 18, 20, 114, 234

Willis, Benjamin C., 235, 303, 340

Wilson, James, 308

Wilson, O. W., 316

Winston, Henry, 109, 110

Winters, Shelley, 289

Wirtz, Willard, 230

Wofford, Harris, 128, 129, 136

Wolf, H. E., 242

Woodlawn Organization, 314

Woodward, C. Vann, 342, 368

Women Strike for Peace, 305

Wright, Irene, 143

Wright, Richard, 266

Wurf, Jerry, 378

Yale University, 242, 320; Hillel Foundation, 168; law school, 198

Yates, C. R., 73

Yonge Street Elementary School (Atlanta), 12

Young, Andrew, 137, 164, 179, 244, 251, 306, 308, 330, 336, 343, 345, 375, 376, 377, 386, 387, 388, 389, 396; and Hoover meeting, 256–57; in Selma, 268, 269, 278, 279, 286, 287; and Goldberg meeting, 307; in Chicago, 314, 331; in Memphis, 380

Young, Whitney, 94, 221, 222, 230, 237, 239, 290, 293, 301, 308, 312, 322, 323, 370; and Kennedy meeting, 219; and CUCRL cochairmanship, 219; and moratorium on demonstrations, 249–50; sees Johnson, 303; and argument with King, 358

Zangrando, Robert, 95
Zellner, Robert, 146, 212
Zetterberg, Abe, 259, 260
Zimmerman, Charles, 76
Zinn, Howard, 112
Zion Hill Church (Birmingham), 183
Zola, Emile, 74
Zwerg, James, 133